Communication Skills for Information Systems

Tony Warner

The Business School
Norwich City College

FINANCIAL TIMES
PRENTICE HALL

Pearson Education Limited
Edinburgh Gate
Harlow
Essex CM20 2JE

and Associated Companies around the world

Visit us on the World Wide Web at:
www.Pearsoned-ema.com

First published in Great Britain 1996

© Tony Warner 1996

ISBN 0 273 60910 6

British Library Cataloguing in Publication Data
A CIP catalogue record for this book can be obtained from the British Library.

10 9 8 7 6 5 4

Typeset by PanTek Arts, Maidstone, Kent.
Printed and bound in Great Britain by Redwood Books, Trowbridge, Wiltshire

The Publishers' policy is to use paper manufactured from sustainable forests.

CONTENTS

1   COMMUNICATIONS
1.1   Introduction *1*
1.2   Using language *2*
1.3   Working with others *5*
1.4   Communications models *5*
1.5   Codes and jargon *14*
1.6   Organising data *18*
   1.6.1   Finding data *18*
   1.6.2   Storing data *20*
1.7   Non-verbal communication *24*
   1.7.1   Dress *24*
   1.7.2   Non-speech utterances *25*
   1.7.3   Proxemics *27*
   1.7.4   Gesture *28*
   1.7.5   Position *28*
   1.7.6   Posture *29*
   1.7.7   Gaze *30*
   1.7.8   Facial expression *30*
   1.7.9   Touch *30*
   1.7.10   Reading the code *31*
1.8   Oral communication *33*
   1.8.1   Egocentric *33*
   1.8.2   Orders and instructions *34*
   1.8.3   Asking questions *34*
   1.8.4   Information giving *34*
   1.8.5   Social routines *34*
   1.8.6   Informal contact *34*
   1.8.7   Expressing emotions and attitudes *35*
   1.8.8   Performative *35*
   1.8.9   Latent messages *36*
1.9   The efficient student *36*
1.10   Real world applications *40*

2   GROUPS AND THEIR EFFECTIVENESS
2.1   Why work in groups? *43*
2.2   The purpose of groups *43*
2.3   Work-based groups *45*
2.4   Personal performance *47*
2.5   Formal meetings *49*
   2.5.1   What goes wrong? *51*
2.6   Formal structures *53*
   2.6.1   Procedure *53*
   2.6.2   Large meetings *56*
   2.6.3   Roles *57*
2.7   Running a meeting *60*
   2.7.1   Problem people *61*
   2.7.2   Information giving and decision making *63*
   2.7.3   Discussion groups *66*
   2.7.4   Team briefings and project groups *66*
2.8   Individuals in meetings *68*
   2.8.1   Task roles *69*
   2.8.2   Maintenance roles *71*
2.9   Student group assignments *73*
2.10   Conclusion *75*

3   ASSERTION AND NEGOTIATION
3.1   Negotiation *76*
   3.1.1   Defining negotiation *76*
   3.1.2   Beginning negotiation *79*
   3.1.3   Structuring objectives *81*
   3.1.4   Alternatives to agreement *82*
   3.1.5   The other party *83*
   3.1.6   Preparing your position *84*
   3.1.7   The two teams *86*
3.2   Personal negotiating skills *88*
3.3   Formal negotiating processes *92*
3.4   Working together *94*
3.5   Moving towards an agreement *95*
3.6   Final solutions *97*
3.7   Closing the deal *99*
3.8   Other negotiating media *101*
   3.8.1   Everyday negotiation *102*
3.9   Being assertive *103*
   3.9.1   The passive response *104*
   3.9.2   The aggressive response *104*
   3.9.3   The assertive person *105*
   3.9.4   Assertive communication *108*
   3.9.5   Conclusion *110*

4   ORAL PRESENTATIONS
4.1   The purposes of presentations *111*
4.2   Content *112*
4.3   The audience *113*

4.4   Planning the delivery *113*
      4.4.1 The script *114*
      4.4.2 The voice *115*
      4.4.3 Language *118*
      4.4.4 Timing *118*
      4.4.5 The delivery *121*
      4.4.6 Group presentations *123*
4.5   Using visual aids *124*
      4.5.1 Choosing visual aids *124*
4.6   Conclusion *132*

5   WRITING REPORTS
5.1   The audience *134*
5.2   Word processing *139*
      5.2.1 Page layout *139*
      5.2.2 Spacing *142*
      5.2.3 Identifying text *142*
      5.2.4 Typefaces and fonts *143*
      5.2.5 Widows and orphans *144*
      5.2.6 Text offsets *144*
      5.2.7 Headings and numbering *145*
      5.2.8 Spelling, grammar and style
            checkers *146*
      5.2.9 Printing *148*
      5.2.10 Conclusion *149*
5.3   An example report format *149*
5.4   Mind your language *159*
      5.4.1 Sentences *160*
      5.4.2 Paragraphs *162*
      5.4.3 Active or passive? *162*
      5.4.4 Tone and style *163*
      5.4.5 Slang and clichés *164*
      5.4.6 Grammar *165*
5.5   Charts and diagrams *165*
      5.5.1 Tables *166*
      5.5.2 Graphs *168*
5.6   Smaller reports *170*
      5.6.1 Memoranda *170*
      5.6.2 Minutes *174*
5.7   An example report *174*

6   INTERVIEWING
6.1   Perceiving others *182*
6.2   Preparing the interview *185*
      6.2.1 Key personnel *186*
      6.2.2 Setting aims and objectives *188*
6.3   Setting up the interview *189*
      6.3.1 The time, the place *190*

6.3.2 The context *190*
      6.3.3 Recording and transcription *191*
      6.3.4 Listening triads *194*
6.4   What questions? *194*
6.5   Listening *198*
6.6   Interview procedures *200*
      6.6.1 Effective behaviour *200*
      6.6.2 Taking control *202*
      6.6.3 Bad interviews *204*
      6.6.4 Triangulation *206*
      6.6.5 Participant observation *207*
      6.6.6 Using graphical representations *207*
6.7   Management interviews *209*
      6.7.1 Employment interviews *209*
      6.7.2 Assessment and development
            interviews *211*
6.8   Conclusion *213*

7   USER DOCUMENTATION
7.1   Defining the problem *214*
7.2   The users *216*
      7.2.1 The beginner *217*
      7.2.2 The novice *218*
      7.2.3 The learner *218*
      7.2.4 The expert *218*
      7.2.5 The accidental user *218*
      7.2.6 Fitting documentation to users *219*
7.3   Structure *222*
      7.3.1 Analysis and planning *222*
      7.3.2 Determining the content *223*
      7.3.3 Speaking to the user *224*
      7.3.4 Improving reference *227*
7.4   Layout *229*
      7.4.1 The printed page *229*
      7.4.2 Graphics *230*
7.5   Binding *232*
      7.5.1 Choosing paper size *232*
      7.5.2 Binding permanent documents *233*
      7.5.3 Binding changing documents *235*
      7.5.4 Packaging *237*
7.6   On-line manuals *238*
7.7   Prototyping and testing *242*
      7.7.1 Prototyping *242*
      7.7.2 Field testing *244*
      7.7.3 Editing *245*
      7.7.4 Reviewing *246*
      7.7.5 Warning messages *247*
7.8   A simple application *249*
7.9   Conclusion *252*

8 TRAINING USERS

8.1 The training context *253*

8.2 Motivation *254*

8.3 Memory *260*

8.4 What is to be learned? *263*

  8.4.1 Company level *263*

  8.4.2 Training room level *266*

8.5 Learning methods *272*

  8.5.1 Lectures *272*

  8.5.2 Reading *274*

  8.5.3 Audio-visual *274*

  8.5.4 Demonstrations *275*

  8.5.5 Discussion group *275*

  8.5.6 Practice by doing *276*

  8.5.7 Immediate application and
      teaching others *277*

  8.5.8 Computer-based training *279*

8.6 Presenting the training *283*

  8.6.1 Establishing objectives *283*

  8.6.2 Content of training *284*

  8.6.3 Timing *285*

  8.6.4 Stage management *287*

  8.6.5 Assessment *290*

  8.6.6 Feedback *294*

8.7 Applications: training in progress *295*

  8.7.1 Some naive users *295*

  8.7.2 Abandoning the typewriter *297*

  8.7.3 Introducing databases *297*

8.8 Conclusion *301*

Bibliography 304

Index 305

ACKNOWLEDGEMENTS

This book was only made possible by the unstinting help and support of friends, colleagues, commercial companies and organisations and many others, including students past and present. More specifically I would like to thank the following for permission to incorporate their own professional efforts as examples in this book: Mike Taylor, Trevor Jones, Neil Scarlet, Andrew Fisher, Daniel Howden, Anita Sutton, Paul Sparkes, Andrew Watson and Emma Pearce. Midwich Thame, Gaze and Son, Mid Suffolk Health Trust and Amber deserve thanks for providing materials used to illustrate specific applications of communication skills in the IS area.

Thanks are particularly due to Norwich City College for help and support over the last year, opening up gaps of time and space and providing important facilities. Special thanks are due to Ian Dormer and to Steve Phillips and his staff as well as to my other colleagues in information systems for their advice and encouragement. John Cushion, my editor, managed to calm my worst excesses; those that are left are the result purely of the author's stubbornness.

Avoiding clichés when thanking one's own family is particularly difficult. They did a lot more than just provide cups of tea; without them doing many of my domestic chores, running errands and providing sanctuary from the telephone, this book would never have been written.

CHAPTER 1
Communications

1.1   INTRODUCTION

Discussions about communications in the information systems world usually revolve around technical questions such as networks, modems or bulletin boards. Companies have established their competitive advantage by being able to acquire, manipulate and transmit data faster and more efficiently than their competitors. They are examples of the 'information society', where information has a value like any other commodity and can be shipped around the globe to its consumer.

This book is not so much concerned with the technicalities of that information but with its content and ordering. Someone, somewhere has to generate raw data and put it into a transmittable form. This transmittable form may be words, pictures or program code. At some point the data will need to be interpreted or manipulated by someone so that it can be used for a specific purpose. Data has become information. The information in its turn is transmitted to others who will make use of it in some way. What concerns us is how that data is generated in the first place and how it is ordered, transmitted and negotiated by the human agent.

However sophisticated our information systems might be they still depend on human beings for their existence. We use information systems because they provide the goods and services that we want. The ordering and point of sale system in the supermarket ensures that goods are on the shelf whenever we want them, that the bills are totalled accurately and that we do not spend large amounts of time waiting at the checkout. A travel agent's booking systems tells us instantly whether the holiday we want is available; the accounts package speeds up the production of returns, even for non-accountants; the word-processor produces better quality documents to a higher level of correctness and faster than typewriters ever could.

All of these exist because of consumer demand; companies exist in order to make, sell and service such products. Once demand ceases then the companies will either have to change or go out of business, whether they are a multi-national conglomerate or an individual consultant. It is human beings who buy and sell computers and computer systems; it is human beings who spot applications for IS products and gaps in the market; it is human beings who have to be persuaded to make resources available for the production or purchase of new systems. Although the speed of communication with them may be a factor when time is pressing, it is the content of that communication that will persuade them to take action, to purchase goods or services, to make resources available or to alter company policy.

How and when you do this is the subject of this book. We will be looking both at the IS professional as an individual, dealing with colleagues, clients and purchasers, and as a part of an organisation, involved in operating within groups and making collective decisions. In particular we will be concentrating on how you order your data and how it is transmitted. At this level we will consider the standard process of oral communication, particularly when presenting information to clients, and the production of business reports. On a more personal level we will consider how IS professionals gather information and the communications skills that they need to develop to increase their efficiency in the process.

Finally, we will be looking at what we might call the 'after-sales service' that involve the consumers. These include both the negotiations which take place with clients to convince them to purchase the system and the training which may be provided once installation has taken place. Alongside the technical parts of the system stands the documentation which supports the user and we will be considering how this can best be structured to give the maximum benefit to a whole range of consumers.

Throughout these chapters we need to bear in mind that old computer adage 'Garbage in – garbage out'. Whatever our means of communications we have to have something to say and be able to say it well. To help you achieve those two objectives is the aim of this book.

1.2 USING LANGUAGE

'In the beginning was the word' states the Gospel of St. John and it is the word which has enabled we human beings to reach our present state of social and technological sophistication. Although animals and insects such as bees can operate socially and pass limited amounts of information to one another, none of them have the range and subtlety of human language. We can pass complicated information across huge distances in both space and time, investigate people's motives and emotions, detail how to fly aeroplanes or to sail boats, how to build, service and program computers.

Through the centuries human beings have been able to write down their knowledge and their discoveries so that future generations can build upon them and make new discoveries of their own. In the social field we use language to pass on important information about how one is expected to behave in the social group and to convey what penalties will be imposed if one does not. As our societies have become larger and more complex so have systems of law and political economy developed to deal with that complexity. Given that most of us in the western world no longer grow our own food we have to communicate even to eat.

Anybody who has ever updated from a simple computer to a more advanced one is aware of the difficulties of sophistication. My ageing Amstrad 8256 works perfectly adequately as a word processor and will even handle simple databases. It is easy to handle, never breaks down and I can teach anyone to word process on it in about an hour. The advanced 486 laptop on which I am writing these words will do huge numbers of things, including running style writing programs, spreadsheets and advanced databases. I can import graphics from other programs, run a mail merge and produce documents ready for direct printing.

Yet it has its problems. Learning to do all the different things on the machine takes time; there are large numbers of commands which do not seem to be at all obvious like the ones on my old Amstrad. Doing anything, especially complicated functions, seems to take ages and demands the help of the nearest computer wizard. From time to time the whole thing will lock solid, only to be freed by Control-Alt-Delete. The more the machine can do the less I seem to be able to do with it.

The same is true of communications in general. The more varied and sophisticated our means of personal communication become the more difficult they are to deal with. On the level of 'Give eats' there is very little problem (although wait until you have to decide whether a baby is crying because it wants food, wants a cuddle or has colic). Once we progress to trying to instruct someone in how to program using C++ or to normalise data the choices with which we are faced seem so many and confusing as to be over-whelming. Concepts such as 'using your common sense' no longer apply when it comes to problems of learning, teaching and disseminating complex technical instructions.

Let us return to the word for a moment, that basic unit which underpins our whole civilisation. Children pick up words by a process of familiarisation and a certain amount of trial and error. Parents talk to their children, even 'baby talk' is no longer dismissed by child psychologists. Within this continuing chatter the child learns to pick out recurring patterns which are repeated with varying degrees of success. At a certain point words are joined up into sentences and sentences into whole conceptual and grammatical structures.

Most school systems insist on pupils spending large amounts of time studying their native language. This is because language is the basic teaching medium. Pupils learn because they are told about things, because things are explained to them, because they are discussed and polished using language. Despite this there remain pupils who stay at a basic level and find it hard to progress. Others seem to feel that moving beyond a certain standard is not necessary, that technical expertise is sufficient for everyday needs. Even students who reach the level of degree courses and beyond may find that their use of language has not kept pace with the demands of their course and the pro-fession to which it leads.

It is this problem which has convinced many employers and examining bodies such as the Business and Technology Education Council to demand that communication skills are taught and examined throughout college courses. The British Computer Society goes as far as to say that '*The ability to express oneself clearly, concisely and correctly in writ-ing is inherent in the notion of professional competence*' (Examination regulations, 1994). An article in *The Times* of 6th September 1991 declared: '*Industrial employers looking for staff complained about shortages in certain areas [and] were anxious that not enough graduates [had] general leadership and communications skills. In the* non-industrial *sector communications skills were thought to be the **most** important attribute for a graduate.*' Another writer complained that '*Systems people with a combination of business consul-tancy and personal communication skills are already chronically scarce*' (Gunton).

Despite all the insistence on the importance of communication skills we still leave it as much to chance as the child learning to speak its native language. Some develop fully because they are fortunate enough to be in a nurturing environment, perhaps at home, at school or in a company which puts a strong emphasis on communication skills. Most of us develop adequately in some areas but not in others, or find ourselves in situations where our needs in the communications area have outstripped our abilities.

Within information systems changes in the industry are demanding multi-skilled professionals capable of handling a range of situations. Twenty years ago colleges of higher education, including universities, turned out computing students who were expected to spend their working lives writing and maintaining programs for mainframe computers. The users of the mainframes were most probably programmers themselves who handled data for the accounting or personnel departments.

In those early days it was quite possible for a programmer to go through life without meeting anyone who used his program, except in the works canteen. Some students in this era could program anything you wished but could not do anything else: work in tandem with other students or explain the program that they had written. But the world had a place for their talents, so why bother?

Even today major programs still have to be written, mainframes are still in use. What has changed, though, is the revolutionary explosion of the personal computer industry. In the early seventies a computer was beyond the wildest dreams of all except the largest company. Now students at college have a computer on their desk in the hall of residence which is ten times more powerful than the mainframe computer some colleges were using in the seventies. It has a greater variety of software, much of which comes packaged in with the price of the machine, and runs a simple user-friendly interface which demands virtually no technological expertise. Since programs are bought 'off the shelf' users do not need to be able to program or even to deal with operating systems such as DOS.

Programming skills are still in demand for larger systems, for customising standard packages or for writing macros but they are no longer the sole criteria for selection for employment, as we saw from the quotations above. Gunton goes as far as to claim: '*From the point of view of managers who organise information systems, skills in dealing with people are assuming greater weight compared with skills in dealing with technology.*' Work within information systems has steadily shifted from dealing with the computer itself towards dealing with its users.

As prices have plummeted analysts have been employed to decide on the benefits of installing a computer system and to decide which of the available systems suits the user's needs. To do this the analyst needs to employ a whole new range of skills. The existing system has to be investigated, processes described and existing computer skills assessed. Such detailed work demands a high level of interviewing and interactive skills together with the ability to explain to the client exactly what it is that has been discovered and how this knowledge can be utilised for the good of the business. Once a system has been installed it may also be the task of the analyst to explain how it is to be operated, both verbally and in writing, and perhaps to train users in its use.

To do all this demands that ability identified by the BCS to '*express oneself clearly, concisely and correctly*'. It also demands that one records information in a like manner, identifying gaps in knowledge and taking appropriate steps to fill them. Such a description could also be described as the correct approach to being a student.

Certainly the skills of the analyst and the skills of the successful student overlap and transfer into the whole work environment.

1.3   WORKING WITH OTHERS

It is still the case that most employees work in a co-operative environment. The company works as a team to produce the best product possible, on time and at the lowest possible price. Very rarely do the workers find themselves in direct contact with the opposing organisations, even assuming that such a concept operates in that particular industry. Who is 'the opposition' for a hospital data processing department, for example, or for a local council?

The best analogy for co-operation within a competitive environment is teams games such as football, hockey or rugby. A team's success is often built on internal organisation, where the talents of the players are welded together to produce a unity which is greater than the mere sum of its parts. Gifted individuals may even be unwelcome as disrupting the smooth running of the team. We can all produce examples from our personal experience of sport and business where a collection of glorious individualists has been outplayed by a well-organised team of average ability.

Few of the people who read this book will ever find themselves face-to-face with the competition. They will be cogs in a well-oiled machine, doing their best towards the particular job in hand. Co-operation and the ability to work with others will be their most important assets as far as their employers are concerned.

Information systems professionals sometimes work alone producing analysis, codes or reports whilst at other times working with a team of people to produce larger and more complex products. We all need to be able to work with colleagues, superiors and clients in order to ensure that the job is done efficiently and well. Sometimes this is formulated into complex project management methodologies such as PRINCE, with its project management teams, often with changing personnel depending on the stage that the project has reached. At other times the day-to-day running of the company may depend on regular meetings being held within sections or by the complete personnel of the company. Because of the amount of time, effort and expectation invested in these meetings it is vital that they should operate with maximum efficiency.

In Chapter 2 we will be looking in detail at how this might best be done. For the moment let us take a closer look at the communications process itself and examine what structures can be identified within communications in general and communications within the informations systems area in particular.

1.4   COMMUNICATIONS MODELS

From the late 1940s onwards communications theorists have been developing models in order to explain how the communications process works. Many of these were based on electrical and electronic transmission of data and their principles underlie much of informations systems thinking today. They emphasised the importance of transmitters and receivers (in a technological sense) and the problems of system overload brought about by the failure to weed out redundant data.

Another important concept was that of 'noise'. This is an idea taken from radio transmission, where all sorts of atmospheric and equipment malfunctions could cause interference on the line which would lead to difficulties in receiving the message. A low battery, for example, might cause the signal to become weaker, whilst an electrical storm would blot out communication totally. Such problems could be represented graphically as a flow diagram, with 'noise' operating as an outside agency on the process.

Obviously the modes or channels of communication must be compatible; both transmitter and receiver, if computers, must be using the same operating system. Shannon and Weaver provide a useful model for explaining the transmission of data along telephone lines using a modem, emphasising the compatibility of all equipment used.

For people the channel of communication might be words (we are both speaking English), diagrams (a formal structured design system which we both understand) or symbols (such as mathematics). The whole process can be disrupted by internal faults in the equipment or by outside agencies. Thus one of the speakers may have an imperfect command of English; one party may never have seen systems analysis before, or the symbols used may have changed with mathematical fashion.

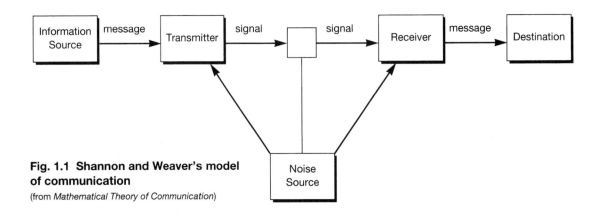

Fig. 1.1 Shannon and Weaver's model of communication
(from *Mathematical Theory of Communication*)

Shannon and Weaver's model is a good introduction to the process of one-way communication. What it lacks is any concept of a conversation, including conversations between machines. When we talk to people we do not operate in chunks of information that float about in some sort of void. The whole idea of a conversation is what the behavioural psychologist B.F. Skinner calls 'verbal ping-pong'. You deliver a statement to me; I consider it and return a statement to you. You examine your thinking in the light of my statement, reformulate your ideas and return them to me. Thus:

Writer: *When we communicate we do more than just throw ideas in to the void.*

Reader: *I don't understand; surely Shannon and Weaver's diagram implies just that, the ideas flow along the communication channels and are picked up. (1)*

Writer: *Yes, but there is more to them than just being picked up. The receiver takes them in and examines them in some way before making some sort of response. (2)*

Reader: *That would be the sort of response where he might show that he did or did not understand the idea? (3)*

Writer: *Yes; or understood it imperfectly in some way. There are a whole range of possible responses. (4)*

Reader: *Such as anger, agreement, joy or sadness, depending on how he felt about the message. (5)*

Writer: *Exactly. I am delighted to know that you now understand what I am trying to say to you. (6)*

(1) The Reader receives service and asks for clarification.

(2) The Writer offers clarification and presents more information.

(3) The Reader takes this into account and offers a formulation in his own words.

(4) The Writer encourages by hinting that there might be further considerations.

(5) The Reader suggests what those considerations might be and implicitly asks *'have I got it right now?'*

(6) Agreement is reached that they are both operating on the same lines and the Reader is encouraged for his percipience!

What we have now come up with is a circular model where each player in the game gives feedback to the other and the conversation may continue almost forever. With a circular model we also have to reconsider the concept of 'noise', factors which may interfere with the communications process. De Fleur's model of communication (Fig. 1.2) emphasises that there can be interference at any point in the process.

So far we have dealt with transmission models of communication, of how data flows from A to B. These assume that there is no difficulty with the production of the message or with its reception. The content is in no way problematic. In the real world, rather than the electronics laboratory, this is clearly not so. People misunderstand one another all the time for all sorts of reasons, many of which we will examine later, during the construction, transmission and reception of the communication. Human beings are superior to computers in their ability to deal in what is now termed 'fuzzy logic'. This is reasoning where all the variables and their values are not known and the thinker needs to deal in approximations and 'best guess' solutions. When we are dealing with such imperfect and imprecise ideas our problem is often how they can be encoded and transmitted in such a way that they can be comprehensible to others.

A simple diagrammatic version of this is found in Stanton's *What do you mean, Communicate?* She presents us with human beings who have ideas. These then have to be formulated in some transmissible form. Here she does not just mean putting the idea into words, say, or diagrams, but into the right words or diagrams. As we will see later, psychologists who have studied the way we use words have concluded that there are a whole range of sub-languages that are spoken even by native speakers of a lan-

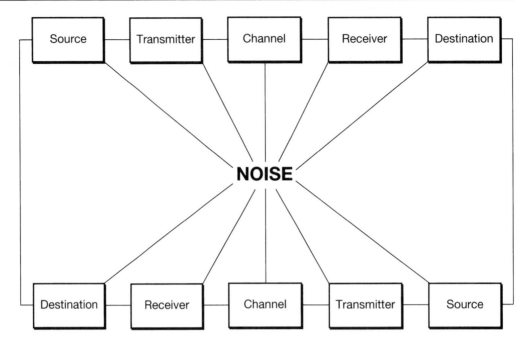

Fig. 1.2. De Fleur's model of communication
(from *Theory of Mass Communication* (1966))

guage. One of the charges made against workers in the information systems area is that they have evolved an impenetrable sub-language deliberately in order to maintain the mystique of their profession and to give it added status. So difficult is it that it has become a code, a hidden language designed to keep out the uninitiated.

Such an accusation is increasingly unfair, but it does help to explain a central concept, that of 'encoding'. An idea needs to be ordered in such a way that it will be understood by the intended recipients. Computers which are programmed in the language C++ can only be 'talked' to in that language. People who have what Bernstein calls 'a restricted language code' can only be talked to within the restraints of that restricted language. You may have found yourself that half of the problem of learning about information systems is learning the language, what different words and phrases mean.

As you can see from Fig. 1.3, Stanton has encoded her message and sent it off through the usual channels. The message is received and then has to be decoded. A good communicator has picked the code well, it fits the capabilities of the recipient who has no problems about decoding the message, analysing the resultant data and processing it so that Stanton's message is understood. Reception is then confirmed by some form of feedback which goes through the same process.

There are more problems inherent in this model than at first appears. Noise only seems to appear during the transmission process, whereas we know that it can occur anywhere in the model. Here we are in a noisy office, trying to work out why our PC is not behaving itself. There has to be an answer, but the phone keeps ringing and colleagues keep asking for advice, we just cannot concentrate. That is, noise at the 'Idea occurs' stage.

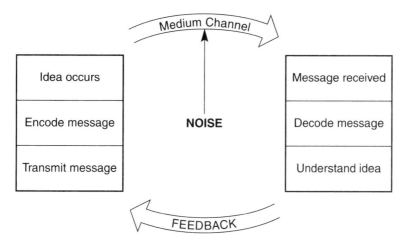

Fig. 1.3 Stanton's communication model (1982)

Once we have our ideas we may have difficulty in encoding them, either encoding them at all or encoding them in an appropriate manner. How often have you wanted to say something reasonably intelligent but found that you just do not have the words for the subtlety of the thought that you wish to express? On the other hand you may be in the position where you have to explain the arcane procedures of systems analysis to a client who has never heard of it before. You need to put all those complex ideas into simple and meaningful words that your client will understand. This is a problem at the 'Encode message' stage. Similar problems occur with decoding the message and understanding the idea.

Still, as long as we bear those problems in mind Stanton's version does move us a little further along the line of understanding human communications processes. What is left out of the model is the human perceptual process itself. Our perceptions are wonderful instruments for ingesting raw data from the world around us. They are usually accurate and as we get older we come to rely on them implicitly. Without reliable perceptions we could not drive a motor vehicle or cross a busy road in safety.

Our perceptions are intimately tied up with our experience. We know something is a tree because we have seen trees before. Even a part of a tree glimpsed through a window can be correctly identified, as can a swift line drawing done by a child. Our interpretative facilities are intimately bound up with what we see, hear, feel, touch and taste.

Because we rely so heavily on our perceptions we can also be misled by them, although this is most frequent in extreme circumstances. Imagine that you have been working late and are walking home in the rain down the wide main street. Suddenly a figure on the other side of the road jumps out of an alley, throws a brick through a shop window, scoops up the goods in the window and makes off with them back down the shadowy alley. As a good citizen you report what you have seen to the police. Let us use another communications model to help us through your experience (Fig. 1.4).

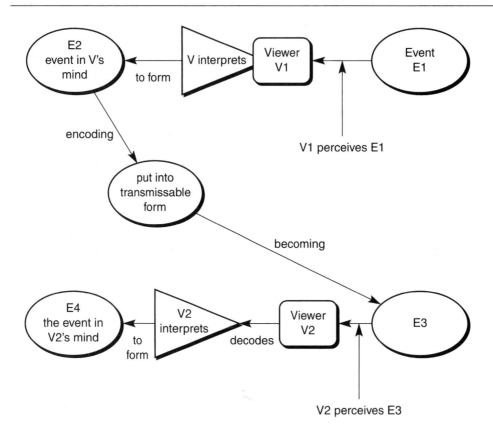

Fig.1.4 Amended version of Gerbner's model of communication (1956)

E1 is what actually happened to you and V1 is the viewer, you yourself. Your brain takes in all the data and tries to make sense of it. This is a problem. It was dark and raining, you were not paying proper attention, you were tired, it all happened very quickly, you have never experienced such a thing before. Still, you do the best you can and mull it all over on your way to the police station. By the time you get there you have sorted out what happened to the best of your satisfaction (E2).

At this point you need to give a statement to the police that reflects in the best manner you can your memory and understanding of what happened (E2). You talk to the police, encoding your message in a manner that you feel they will understand. This is a public event (E3) which the police (V2) listen to and decode. It is raw data which they examine in the light of their own background and experience, trying to make sense of it. Eventually they clarify in their mind what actually happened (E4).

We now have two viewers (at least), four events, two interpretations, one encoding and decoding and two sets of perceptions. And your statement hasn't even been written down yet! You may feel that such a model and such an example unduly complicates matters. For the majority of cases this is perhaps so, and for ordinary human intercourse where precision and clarity are not primary features and where extensive opportunities for feedback are present such a complex model is of little use.

Where it does help us is in cases where data has to be gathered clearly and precisely, interpreted in a logical manner and the resulting information used as the basis for action. Such a case occurs with the gathering of data for systems analysis, where the perceptions of actors within the company and the analyst's own perceptions become part of the system. How the analyst communicates with the other actors on the scene becomes of primary importance; the encoding and decoding of all the messages, including verbal communication, body language, diagrams, manuals and general company documentation, intimately affect the progress and success of the work.

So far we have assumed total goodwill on the part of both sender and receiver. The sender has a clear message which is to be sent accurately to the receiver with no subtext attached to it. The receiver is eager and willing to receive the message and is neutral in intent regarding all other factors. A moment's reflection reveals that this is rarely so. All senders are affected by the milieu in which they find themselves, by the image they have of themselves, by certain fears and expectations that they may have, by the experiences which have happened to them in similar situations in the past and by changing political and economic circumstances. Similarly all receivers have similar responses, compounded by the position they hold in the receiving audience, by their response and hierarchical position vis-à-vis the sender and so on. This can be expressed in the model shown in Fig. 1.5.

Although Maletzke's model was derived in order to explain mass communication it also helps to make clearer some aspects of everyday business communication. During 1994 Emma, a student, was on placement with a computer hardware supply company. The company had a computer system which was ten years old and was replacing it with another developed by its holding company. Emma's job was to investigate all the existing processes that the company used, compare them to the processes demanded on the new system and evolve a transition document for staff to illustrate how their working practices would change prior to the new system being implemented.

Imagine that she now has to present her findings to the fifty staff as a group. Along the left hand side of Maletzke's model you will see a range of factors which affect her performance. As a student she is at the bottom of the hierarchy; some people in the audience have given her information which they regard as confidential; many people at the presentation are those she works with every day; the management team are also there, and so on. Looking at the second column on the model, we can see that Emma has huge amounts of data, from which she needs to select the most relevant. Because she is using an overhead projector rather than a projected VDU screen she is slightly limited in what she can present and how.

On the receiver's side there are a range of similar and related forces, including personality, position in the organisations and previous perceptions. There may be some who are fearful for their jobs with the introduction of the new system, or some who just hate technology anyway. Others may not believe that the change is ever going to happen. Not surprisingly the amount that the various members of the audience take in, their attitude to it and their understanding of its implications can vary tremendously. Emma will be doing an excellent job if she can get her message over to seventy-five per cent of her audience.

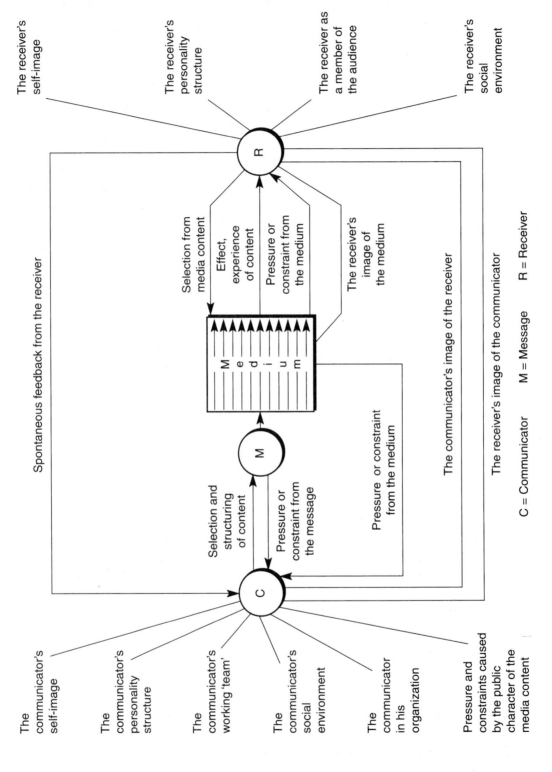

Fig.1.5 Maletzke's model of communication

A similar point is made in Fig. 1.6. This is an attempt to apply Maletzke's model to a company sending a fax message to Taiwan to order goods.

Finally, there are times when messages are just sent off into the public domain with little or no control by the sender over their method of reception. In the past theorists have conceived of this as being peculiar to the mass media such as television, newspapers or radio. Nowadays information technology systems have evolved which emulate these but on a smaller scale. A fax message, for example, might operate in a similar way to radio in that the message is sent off to a receiver who may be thousands of miles away and who may not respond.

Schramm's model might help us here (Fig. 1.7). He shows us the human agent gathering data from a range of sources and decoding them. They are then put together as a unique message which is encoded and sent off into the communications channel. Eventually the transmission is picked up by an audience who decode it, interpret it and perhaps discuss it with others. At other times the receiver will perhaps pass on the message to others who have not received it themselves: '*I picked up some very interesting information on the bulletin board last night.*'

Not that you will be making television programmes, but there are some practical information systems applications of Schramm's model. A simple poster, for example, is an attempt at mass communication; you are trying to reach a large amount of people who will not necessarily engage with you in any sort of feedback. On a more complicated level, an interpretation of what happens when posting messages on a computerised bulletin board is shown in Fig. 1.8.

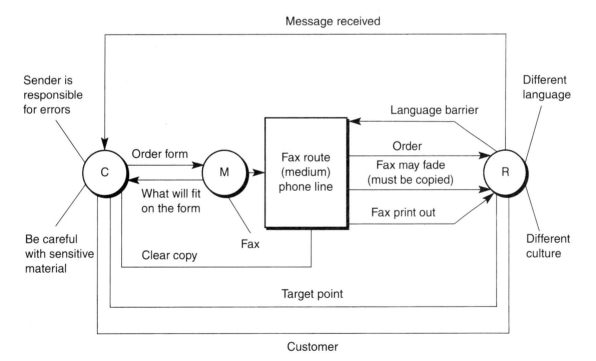

Fig.1.6 Ordering goods from Taiwan, using Maletzke's model

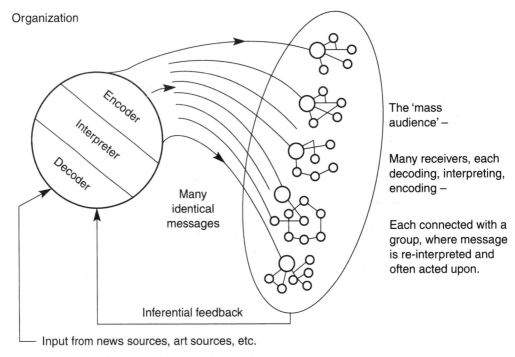

Organization

The 'mass audience' –

Many receivers, each decoding, interpreting, encoding –

Each connected with a group, where message is re-interpreted and often acted upon.

Many identical messages

Inferential feedback

Input from news sources, art sources, etc.

Fig.1.7 Schramm's model of mass communications

Communications models operate in the same way that systems analysis diagrams do. That is, they help us to understand the processes that are occurring and to recognise where breakdowns may happen. They are not something that we use all the time, but are aids to understanding systems in general and the one in which we are currently operating in particular. If we have a diagrammatic model in reserve we can use it to refer to when something goes wrong, in the same way that an electrician would refer to a wiring diagram if the electrics on your car were to malfunction.

Like a simple model of business they illustrate that communications involves production, distribution and consumption of the message and that each of these processes have their own associated skills and problems. If we are to become efficient communicators we need to be efficient ourselves in each of these three areas whilst aware of the possible limitations of others. At its best, informations systems is about fast, accurate and efficient communications; at its worst it is only as good as its practitioners.

1.5   CODES AND JARGON

The normal medium for expression in science, business and ordinary social life is language. We speak, write, label diagrams and so on using a recognisable national language, which allows us free rein to our expression and gives us the ability to say many complicated and subtle things. A moment's thought, though, reminds us how

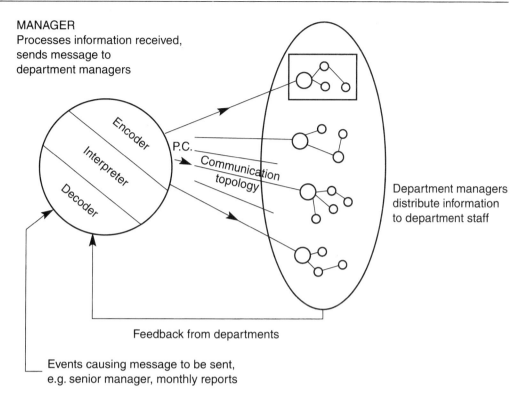

MANAGER
Processes information received,
sends message to
department managers

Department managers
distribute information
to department staff

Feedback from departments

Events causing message to be sent,
e.g. senior manager, monthly reports

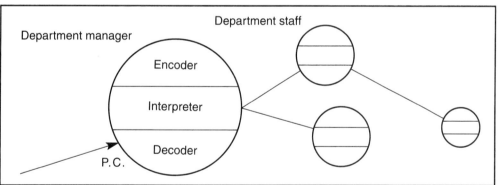

Department manager

Department staff

Encoder

Interpreter

Decoder

P.C.

Fig.1.8 Posting a message to a computerised bulletin board, using Schramm's model

often we have been misunderstood and how often we have misunderstood others. When students are told that their assignments should be *no more than* two thousand words some of them will write up to twenty thousand while others will spend valuable time trying to pad out their work up to two thousand. This is not a criticism of language but an illustration of how many meanings it can carry, especially when the feedback loop is not operated effectively.

Imagine that each word is a little burr, like those that attach themselves to the fur of animals in the summer. Each burr has hundreds of tiny hooks which cling to the animal and to one another. Words are like these burrs, they have not one meaning but several, depending on the context in which they are used rather than on any dictionary definition. This is known as their **connotation** and it is these which create the subtlety and vivacity of language. A simple word like 'cat', for example, can refer to a soft friendly feline or to a large, fierce African beast. You might also use it of the woman next door, or of a whip or of a two-hulled sailing craft. By the time this book has been published there might even be a completely new usage which has crept into the language in the same way that gay (homosexual) has overtaken gay (happy and joyful in disposition).

Because language is so slippery at times many attempts have been made to reduce its ambiguity either by producing artificial languages or by developing restricted versions of existing ones. Some international companies now use 'International English', a pidgin version of business English with a restricted vocabulary of around 1500 words. The objective is to achieve a direct one-to-one correlation between the word and the object or concept that it denotes in the same way that school children use substitution codes. Thus A is 1, B is 2 and so on. You can see how simple this makes communication. All we have to do is to work out the code, transmit the data and ensure an efficient channel. Data received then corresponds exactly with data sent, with no problems of interpretation or misunderstanding.

The computing world, as a new linguistic area, has to some extent been able to invent its own artificial language which is supposedly free of ambiguity. Words like program, byte, bus, ring, RAM and so on all have their specific and defined meaning. Use of these and other words and phrases allow systems personnel to converse about technical areas quickly and effectively, in the same way that International English allows users in Hong Kong, Chile and Frankfurt to conduct business on the same level. In effect, information systems has become a code which anyone has to learn before engaging in the activity, in the same way that children have to learn their native language before entering into formal education.

As long as systems personnel are conversing with one another the existence of this code is an advantage. Once they try to communicate to the outside world it becomes quite the opposite. What is a potential customer and technophobe to make of the salesman who insists that what is needed is a 486 SX 33MHz with 8 megs of RAM running a range of 4GLs? Or try this beautiful example of computer speak from the IT Services section of a college:

> 'There is insufficient DOS memory available for a station to be able to access Rigel and run large DOS applications such as Excelerator during the same session. Rigel access requires a TCP stack loaded at boot time. Three machines will be configured to support large DOS applications by default and one configured for UNIX access. A boot-time dialogue will be implemented so that the TCP stack can be optionally loaded or skipped on all stations.'

Now that may make sense to you as an information systems professional, but what does it mean to the ordinary user? Your problem here is to make yourself bi-lingual. You need to be able to use the language common in your profession whilst being able to express the same ideas clearly and simply to those who do not possess the same codes and jargon as yourself. If we return for a moment to communications models such as

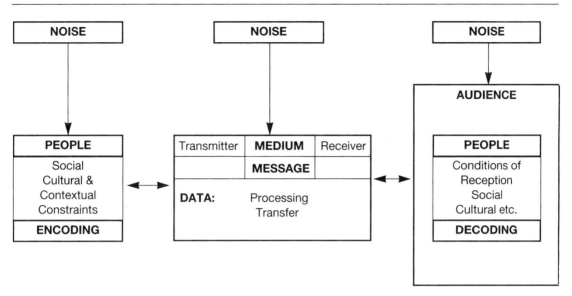

Fig.1.9 Generalised view of communications

Schramm's we can see what this means in practice (Fig. 1.9). Input comes from IT sources, which is then decoded. You then interpret it and encode for a general audience before transmitting it. Receivers than decode and interpret the message themselves.

Even within artificial codes mistakes can be made. Those of you who have played games or sports where there are set calls will have had experience of this. Rugby players use codes for the throw in to the lineout, bridge players have a whole complex of bidding systems, American football could hardly function without codes for a variety of set plays. The players practise these limited ranges of signals for hours at a time, and still get it wrong! In normal human intercourse we leave most things to chance, hoping that the other person will take the same meaning from what we write or say as we thought we put in it. As the psychologist J.Parry expresses it: '*In human communication a great deal of failure comes about not because information has been lost in transmission but because the sender is unable to express what he has to say, or because the receiver is unable to interpret the message in the way intended.*'

We learn to use language almost from the day we are born. Very soon we forget all about it, it becomes a natural part of the way we function, beyond the range of conscious thought. As you read this you are not having to consider the rules of grammar, the structure of the English language or the meaning of every word that is used. Language has become transparent. Because of this transparency we fail to be reflective about its use in various situations, we fail to recognise that our language codes are not necessarily those of others and our full message may not be getting through.

Since we are such complex and elegant communicators the opportunity for malfunction is vast and will never be eliminated. The good communicator is the one who is aware of the pitfalls and problems and constantly tries to eliminate them or reduce their effects. Hopefully this book will go some way to enabling you to become a good communicator.

1.6 ORGANISING DATA

Communication is about putting data and information into the public domain. Good communicators organise their data in such a way that it has a predictable effect on other people. While there are times when a communication event is empty, '*a thing of sound and fury, signifying nothing*' as Shakespeare put it, most often the intention is to convey information, thoughts, decisions and judgements. This demands the gathering, organising and judging of data by the communicator.

Gathering data is easier now than at any other time in the past. Books, journals, directories and indexes are available in public libraries free of charge. Informational databases, bulletin boards and CD ROM systems can be accessed for a fee. If we have a problem with information it is that we have so much of it that we sink beneath its weight, we spend so much time gathering it that we have no time to make sense of it.

But one stage at a time. Let us first set out to gather our information, then we can concern ourselves with how it can be organised and stored.

First stop is the library. With luck it has an on-line catalogue system.

1.6.1 Finding data

In the past libraries were spaces for the storage and accessing of books. Now they are the centres for inter-connecting with a wide variety of information systems, so much so that many colleges now have 'learning centres' rather than libraries. However, it is still books that predominate and it is with them that we will begin.

First find your book. This is done quickly through the **cataloguing system**. With paper-based systems you are limited to the author catalogue and the subject catalogue, boxes of file cards or bound folders through which you have to plough to obtain your information. More modern on-line systems have all the advantages of a database, allowing you to interrogate the system by author, title, subject or key words. This should give you a list of at least some of the books that you will find useful as well as telling you whether or not they are currently on loan to other borrowers.

There is often a temptation to stop at this point, to take the books that you have identified from the catalogue and cease your search. Instead, go and **search the shelves** among those numbers that have been indicated to you as the area for which you are seeking. You may not be able to judge a book by its cover, but you cannot rely purely on its title either. Have a look at those books which catch your eye, whether they seem up to date or particularly well produced and presented. Somehow books like 'The Joy of Programming' which seemed so dull and inconsequential on the catalogue screen suddenly turn out to be exactly what you wanted once you have them in your hands!

In a good library even esoteric subjects like data compression and encryption or knowledge-based systems may have many books for you to choose from. Life is very short, the demand for information may be very pressing. How do we sort out what book is for us?

The answer is to use the **navigation aids** with which we are provided. These take the form of the *contents pages*, the *index* and the *chapter summaries* or *introductions*. In our first browse through the shelves we turn to the contents pages of books looking for references to whole sections which document the subject we are seeking. This provides us with a range of books which have sizeable chunks that we can really get our teeth in to.

Unfortunately, contents pages are not alphabetical, nor are they exhaustive and there may be subjects which are dealt with by the book which do not appear in them. We therefore need to double check by turning to the alphabetical index at the back of the book and noting the extent of the references to our subject. In particularly difficult cases the index references may be all that we can find. These must be noted down and those references quickly read through, making notes as we go. Quite often this supplies us with all the information that we need.

At the other end of the scale we may have found several books, all of which promise to give us vast amounts of information. They need to be sifted by means of the use of chapter summaries or introductions. These short passages indicate the ground that is covered by the chapter and the ideas that are presented. Thus Alan Clements introduces his section on the Central Processing Unit (CPU):

> *'Although most of this text is based on a modern complex instruction set computer, the 68000, we have introduced some of the principles governing the reduced instruction set computers that have done so much to increase the performance of microprocessors.... RISC architectures have taken a step backwards and returned to the fundamental principles governing the von Neumann computer.'*

Clements has told us that he has dealt mainly with the 68000 computer but also has referenced this to modern PCs and to RISC architectures. If we are looking for any of that, then it is worth reading this chapter. Should we have a different slant on the CPU we can safely ignore his book and look elsewhere.

One other tactic remains open to us, especially when confronted with several books which seem to demand to be read in their entirety. This is to flip through the pages, trying to spot by the complexity of diagrams or the headings of sections whether the book is too simple or too complicated for us to use. The section headings also suggest whether there is a large amount of overlap between books, making it less important which ones we choose. By using the navigational aids in the books themselves and by judicious sampling of their contents we can be reasonably sure that we have maximised our information flow with the minimum expenditure of time, achieving high benefits with low costs.

Magazines, periodicals and newspapers are prime sources of information. They may contain an analysis of current business trends, such as the sales of a variety of computer packages, comparisons of hardware and software, or carefully considered accounts of 'cutting edge' applications and developments. The periodicals themselves are usually referenced within libraries on standard catalogues held on paper, on microfiche or on-line in a computerised system. Specialist indexes detail specific articles each quarter according to their subject matter, often with a brief summary, and are an important source of information about current publications and research. However, all you are told is where to find the article, leaving you to track down the publication itself or to obtain a copy through the inter-library loan system.

CD ROM systems go further by loading the articles themselves on to a video disk, allowing the reader first to scan the database for appropriate articles and then to call them up on the screen. Many libraries have facilities for downloading onto paper or disk. Although there may be a fee for this it compares favourably with the cost of photo-copying. Because of the simplicity of the system there is a temptation to load disks full of information 'just in case', to fill up your disk case in the same way that your book shelves are full of videos recorded off-air which you never watch.

1.6.2 Storing data

Squirreling away every piece of information that we acquire leads to overload of the filing system. We need to be constantly analysing our information for quality of content, reducing it to the smallest form commensurate with use and understanding and then storing it in a system that has optimum retrievability.

Paper storage is meant to be one of the problems that computerisation will over-come. Whole rooms of filing cabinets have been replaced by networked PCs and lockable disk cases. Despite this, paper is still a popular medium, even in the informa-tion systems industries themselves, particularly for low volume data flows, such as personal notes and diaries. Consider its advantages for a moment:

- low technology
- demands minimum maintenance
- easy to use
- cheap
- widely portable
- does not depend on a power source

Putting down ideas on paper is something anyone can do virtually anywhere, at any time, from taking down notes in a lecture or from an article displayed on CD ROM to scribbling down ideas whilst in the bath. The problem with information on paper is that it is bulky and difficult to order. Given that at least some of our data will be stored in this way we need to minimise the effect that these disadvantages have on our efficiency.

The easiest way to reduce bulk in any information storage system is to reduce the actual amount we store. Given that the number of ideas will remain constant we need to reduce the number of characters that we use to record them. Shorthand systems were devised for just this eventuality. The shorthand writer was provided with a system which allowed sounds rather than words or letters to be recorded, thus reducing the amount that was written down and allowing the writer to record what was said verbatim.

However, we need to go further than this, we need to cut through what was actually said or written and arrive at the core of the ideas. To do this we cut down our text to the main ideas, the key words or phrases that contain the central feature of what is being said.

Think of any message as being like a medicine. There is a key idea, an active ingre-dient that the sender wishes you to take. This has to be dressed up in words, in grammatical structures, so that you can understand it better. Dressing it up in this way is what communications theorists refer to as 'coding', a concept which we have already examined. For the medicine this dressing up takes the form of mixing it with inactive ingredients or ones which mask its taste so that we can swallow it easily. Once we have swallowed it the inactive ingredients melt away harmlessly, leaving the active one to do its job.

Similarly, once we have read or heard the message and understood it we no longer need the inactive ingredients, the grammar and the enabling words, when we re-examine it. For our notes, therefore, all we need to do is to write down the central ideas, the headings and pointers in the message. Where we have a retainable source, such as a photocopied article, a company report or a text printout from the computer, the key ideas can be identified on first reading using a marker pen. On future readings these sections would be all that we would need to read.

Marker pens lead us on to the idea of **colour coding** our information. Where you gather information in clearly identifiable conceptual areas you can use different colour markers. Articles on data compression may be marked in red, data encryption could be in green, expert systems in yellow, and so on. Where you have made your own notes you might simply mark them with an appropriate colour code in the top right hand corner.

Once individual sheets have been produced and identified they need to be stored. Where order is significant they are best kept in a **clip file**, where they cannot move about. Either individual subjects can be kept in different files or coloured tabbed dividers utilised to keep sections apart. This would be the standard way of keeping student notes, for example. For notes where order is not significant or for 'work in progress' which is not yet ready to be ordered in to a file, then coloured **envelope files** can be used. These fit easily into a briefcase or filing cabinet, keep the contents in a reasonable condition and are easy to use. Again, use different colours for different sections or subjects.

Card indexes are a useful way of recording information on books and articles. The main information is written across the top of the card, with perhaps a synopsis of the book and comments on its contents or usefulness on the rest of the card. Subject areas or alphanumeric cataloguing can be signalled by sectional tabbed cards. Like most paper systems index cards retain their popularity because of their ease of use. They can be spread out easily on the desk, giving the user instant access to a whole range of ideas and information at the same time.

Whatever paper system is used it still needs to be fitted into some sort of storage system. For clip files an ordinary shelf, perhaps with stuck-on labels, would be sufficient. Card indexes can be stored in their own box. Bulkier material may need a filing cabinet, perhaps of the small box type which are now so popular. Whatever system is chosen it needs to be easy to access and to maintain. Throwing your envelope files into the nearest large drawer is not a solution!

Computer storage is supposed to be a central function of information systems. Once in the system the data can be moved or manipulated at will and vast amounts of it can be stored in a small space. This is undeniable and the best computer systems will run rings round paper-based systems in terms of time, space and ease of use. However, there are some pitfalls connected to a reliance on computer-based systems which means that they are not always the best ones to use in all circumstances.

We have already noted the ease with which data can be downloaded from one system on to another and that this can cause overload on the human part of the system in particular. If we do load data on to our system we need to sieve it first, to get rid of those 'inactive ingredients' and reduce it to a manageable entity. Data has to be compressed, not by increasing the holding capacity of our disks, but by ensuring that only key words and ideas are retained. Alongside this, PC users in particular must keep to a strict housekeeping schedule, updating data which has become stale and removing files which are no longer current, either by full deletion or by downloading to a holding disk. Like any other business you need to decide on archiving procedures and to determine the length of time for which archived material is held.

Once data is held on file it will need to be accessed. We therefore need to sort out some kind of identification system both for the disks themselves and for individual files. Most disks currently on sale have wrap-around sticky paper labels of different colours. Where you are holding information on different subjects you can keep it on specific disks, in the same way that you use envelope files, and use a different colour wrapper for each. This makes picking out disks which are standing on edge in disk holders even simpler. Of course you will label the contents of each one on the wrapper, probably in pencil, since the contents are bound to change over time. Thus your disk on computer architecture might be red, systems analysis yellow, business systems green and your personal accounts blue.

Within a disk individual files need to be labelled for greatest efficiency. This means being as descriptive as possible within the limits of the number of characters that the system allows you to use. Labelling by date is not effective, nor is simple numbering: 'bisstruc7', for example. Utilise the existence of sub-directories, in the same way that you would use different drawers of your filing cabinet, to break down your subject by topics. This gives you greater opportunities to use real language in your filing. Thus the sub-directory may be Business Structures, with individual files being labelled 'horzint.doc' and 'vertint.doc' (for horizontal integration and vertical integration) respectively.

Using hierarchical filing systems allows you to access documents much faster and more efficiently than paper-based system. If, however, you allow your disks and directories to descend into chaos most of the advantages of electronic systems are lost since you may end up with gross duplication of data and slow retrieval speeds. All you are left with is a pile of disks which need to be ploughed through before you can find the information that you want.

We have already noted that electronic systems may only have marginal advantages over paper-based systems if they are merely used as media for information storage. Electronic information systems come into their own when the data itself is to be manipulated rather than merely stored. A filing cabinet will keep your household bills quite effectively, what it will not do is to order them according to significant criteria and cross-reference them with your regular and irregular income. As soon as you begin to manipulate data on a database, spreadsheet or desk top publishing package you are adding to its value, moving out of data processing and into information systems.

If data comes to you in any but electronic form it needs to be entered on to your system in some way. Should you not have a scanner this means keying it in by hand, a time-consuming process. Viewed from a cost-benefit point of view this may not be effective. The more key strokes you enter the more time is being wasted. That time can only be justified by the 'added value' that accrues to the information by entering it onto your system. So, for example, to type in a whole article of several thousand words is not cost effective if you are not subsequently intending to manipulate the information. It is quicker and simpler to photocopy the article and save it in an envelope file.

On the other hand, you may key in a range of values onto a spreadsheet, which are subsequently re-arranged, re-interpreted and automatically turned into a range of graphs. The increased understanding resulting from the 'what if' calculations you have performed and the graphs that you have produced have added value to the data and made the time you spent keying it in worthwhile.

As a general rule, therefore, we can state that data should be retained in the form in which it comes unless there is a pressing reason for changing that form. From a perspective of cost-effectiveness, data should only be keyed into a computer if it is to be manipulated in some way to increase its value. Thus, it would be a waste of time for a student to type up lecture notes rather than simply going through them with a marker pen to identify the key ideas. On the other hand, the student might enter a range of experimental data on the down-time of various network systems and save hours or even days in calculation time.

Disk storage in particular is prone to loss and corruption. Because they are so easily portable they are equally easily forgotten in a disk drive or shopping bag. Individual files or whole disks are liable to damage from a range of sources, from cups of coffee and electrical fields down to the gremlins which inhabit every system. Being sensible, you naturally back up every disk on a regular basis as well as saving current data periodically to your machine's hard disk. Experience suggests that even IS professionals only learn to do this following a great disaster, when vast amounts of data have suddenly gone missing!

Once the data has been backed up, keep it in a safe place. For larger companies this should mean a fireproof safe; smaller ones make do with the managing director taking the back-up files home every evening. Individuals perhaps keep a second set of disks in another room or in the filing cabinet. Remember that it is not only your systems disks that need backing up but data disks as well. If the data is valuable enough to keep then it must be valuable enough to save in a second copy.

There are still good reasons for using paper storage systems, not least of all legal requirements for the retention of certain documents. In some instances paper may be the most appropriate medium to use, especially if the data is not to be manipulated in any way. Electronic storage cuts down on the space used and allows cross-referencing and sophisticated manipulation techniques. Whichever you use, probably both, its efficiency will be enhanced by:

- using colour coding
- keeping like information with like

- introducing strict cataloguing systems
- working with directories and sub-directories
- storing data in a safe place
- backing up data.

1.7 NON-VERBAL COMMUNICATION

Communications is a word which is very loosely used. Most writers and commentators use it to indicate any action, event or state pertaining to a human being from which we can gain information about that human being. This tells us more about the reasoning power of the observer than it does about the skills of the sender and for that reason we need to be more precise than this. It is important to differentiate between states and actions over which we have control and those over which we do not. We need to further differentiate between managed and unmanaged messages and to take account of context and feedback. Our working definition of Communication is therefore:

> *Any action, event or state pertaining to a human being which is intentionally used by that human being to convey information to others.*

The important word in this definition is *intention*. This states that we are passing this information on deliberately and that we wish it to be received. Thus a student who always dresses in black, with gold earrings and ornate snakes painted on the back of her leather jacket, is making a deliberate statement about how she wishes to be viewed and the sub-culture to which she belongs. An intentional act is one that we choose to make, in the same way that we choose which words to utter. In fact, words themselves also fall under the category of 'actions'.

Naturally, we can also intend to deceive. We can tell people lies, control how much information we allow them to have or suppress information completely. Our bodies can act in a similar way by manipulating the signals that we send to others. Many courses on non-verbal communications specialise in teaching sales personnel and mangers how to use this manipulation in order to persuade workers or clients to perform as they wish. Let us first look at the factors over which we might have some form of deliberate control.

1.7.1 Dress

Dress has already been used once above as an example of how we can transmit signals. In the workplace we often have to wear uniforms in order to conform with the standards of the organisation. IBM is still known as 'Big Blue' after the alleged habit of its sales personnel in wearing blue suits. City bankers traditionally wear grey pinstripes, students wear jeans, teachers wear corduroy trousers, and so on. At weekends these people may dress completely differently depending on the message they wish to send. City bankers may be weekend punks, teachers may wear smart suits for formal dinners, students may find themselves in a waiter's formal black outfit.

Dress, when used in this way, flies the flag for the sub-group that we wish to be part of *at that time*. Like chameleons we can take off or put on this colouring at will. In this sense we are all actors, playing many roles.

Much of the time, of course, we do not have total choice. The company we work for almost invariably has some sort of dress code in which certain garments or modes of dressing are not acceptable. There are also other situations in which we deliberately take on the colouring of the world which we are entering in order that we may be taken seriously. A freelance systems analyst may wear jeans and tee-shirt most of the time whilst working on reports at home, but changes into suit and tie when interviewing on a company's premises. To fail to do so may mean that the analyst is not taken seriously by his clients or by the organisation's employees. It is said that Richard Branson's problems with Lord King of British Airways were partly fuelled by King's inability to take seriously a businessman who did not wear a suit and who sported a beard.

Whether or not this is true, clothes are certainly seen in our society as a badge of respectability and a reflection of the wearer's competence. Students on placements or carrying out projects with companies must conform to their code of dress. Freelance workers can dress any way they like, as long as they are prepared to accept that non-conformity may lead to a loss of custom. In general, it is better to dress overly smartly when first entering a new situation and then 'dress down' on subsequent occasions once you have sorted out the local dress code. Only incredible bravery, or incredible stupidity, would lead an interviewee to turn up for a job interview in anything other than the traditional 'interview suit'.

1.7.2   Non-speech utterances

Adolescents often have rows with their parents over quite trivial matters. Statements which they regard as bland or inoffensive will spark off terrific rows, the result of apparent over-reaction on behalf of the parents. If we were to write down what was originally said we would probably be unable to comprehend how anyone could ever take offence, since the verbal content of the message is quite unexceptional.

The verbal content of anything we say, that is the words that we use, are only a half of the message. The other half is made up of tone and context. '*You are very clever*' said in an admiring tone of voice means precisely what it says. Said in a tone of sarcasm it can mean precisely the opposite: you think you are being smart but we will catch you out no matter how careful you might be. '*Are you going out tonight?*' can be a perfectly straightforward query. On the other hand, said in a tone of astonishment it can be shorthand for '*you have exams ahead and work to finish, are you seriously suggesting that you might be allowed to go off socialising?*'

The mutual incomprehension of parents and children is frequently a failure to recognise the importance of tone of voice. Although the use of tone in speech is an everyday event it is not one for which we are trained, we pick it up like a tourist in a foreign country learning the language. And, like language learners, some of us are quicker and more subtle in its use than others, some just have a better 'ear' for the music of the language. Both parents and teachers have a role in pointing out when the child or student is using the wrong tone. Speakers also need to listen attentively to themselves and others in order to get a clearer idea of the full message that is being sent.

Let us look at a simple example. An analyst has been employed to investigate the information handling problems of a chain of estate agents. Sarah is the assistant in a small branch which is headed by Norman, a chartered surveyor. The analyst is trying to find how the office actually operates.

Analyst: *What exactly are your working hours?*
Sarah: *Nine till five thirty, every day.*
Analyst: *Is that Monday to Friday?*
Sarah: *NO (heavy emphasis), that's Saturday as well.*
Analyst: *But Norman is around the office most of that time.*
Sarah: *(Pause) Some of the time. He spends a lot of time out of the office visiting clients and doing valuations. We are supposed (light but obvious emphasis) to arrange lunch hours between ourselves so that the office is always manned. That is not always possible to arrange.*
Analyst: *What happens then? Do you close down the office?*
Sarah: *No. I work straight through. It is company policy that the office should never be closed, whatever the circumstances. I just have to snatch a bite when I can (said rather wearily).*

This is a simple and common sort of exchange, where the analyst has come across someone who wants to complain about her boss. How is this conclusion reached? Certainly not from the words that were uttered, which are merely a factual account of working practices. It is from the tone of voice and emphasis on certain words that it is deduced that Sarah is not happy with a six day week (she probably feels exploited). The pause before confirming that Norman is supposed to be in the office much of the time implies that Sarah wishes to say more but feels she cannot. Similarly, the emphasis on 'supposed' in the answer '*we are supposed to arrange lunch hours*' implies that this does not happen, as does the weary tone in which Sarah tells of having to grab a bite of lunch whilst running the office on her own.

All this seems simple and straightforward on paper but is much more difficult to pick up and deal with in a live interview. It is also important to note that Sarah is attempting to manipulate the analyst. By hiding her statements in her non-verbal utterances she is subtly sliding opinions in to the interview under cover of a factual account and attempting to manipulate the impression she gives.

As well as using words in our speech we also use 'fillers' such as 'um' or 'err' or whole words or phrases such as 'like' or 'you know'. Generally these are used to cover the space where we are seeking the exact word to use in that context. While we rapidly scan the mind's thesaurus we say to others '*wait, I haven't finished yet, don't break in on what I am saying too quickly.*' In normal conversation this is perfectly acceptable as long as it is kept below the level of a mannerism. To be like addressed in sort of meaningless like fillers all the time like is, er, you know, like kind of boring, like!

Even in formal presentations fillers can be present, although the acceptable level is much lower because the presenter no longer has the excuse that one of the listeners is likely to interrupt. Too many such pauses implies that the speaker has not rehearsed the presentation or is not in control of its basic details. Once the audience begins to distrust the expertise of the messenger it will seriously question the validity of the message.

This leads us on to the problem of accent. For historical reasons to do with geography and history Great Britain has a range of regional accents. Indeed, many towns have an accent which is recognisably different from the countryside which surrounds them. There is also a form of received pronunciation or 'Oxford English' which is spoken by a small minority of the population but which is not limited by geographical residence. Research indicates that the British still stereotype speakers according to their accent. Yorkshiremen are blunt and straightforward; Midlanders know about commerce; Devonians are slow and steady; people from Norfolk are rather dim and so forth. An Oxford English accent is still taken as a voice of authority, with the speaker being recognised as being educated and intelligent. Giles and Powesland report experiments to support this conclusion

Such stereotypes are not helpful in dealing with others at whatever level. The blunt Yorkshireman may in fact be pulling the wool over our eyes, the slow Devonian might be one of the country's leading programmers and used car dealers in Norfolk are just as sharp as anywhere else, though far more disarming. Even if our first response to somebody's voice may be instinctive liking or distrust we need to fight against our prejudices.

We also need to be aware of the response others have to us. Do you have a strong accent? What effect does that produce in other people? It is useful to know the answer to these questions before you can do anything about it. In general, your strong regional accent will mean that you are perceived by others as being less intelligent than those with no discernible accent and much less intelligent, and certainly less of an authority in your field, than those with an 'Oxford English' accent. What you do about it is up to you. Like Mrs. Thatcher you could employ a voice coach to improve your image (very successfully as it turned out) or just learn to live with it as part of your personal identity.

1.7.3 Proxemics

In simple language, how close are people to one another? Generally we stand or sit closer to people we know well and like. In pre-sexual encounters the progress of the putative affair can be monitored from afar by watching the distance between the protagonists. The closer they come to one another the better progress is being made towards a more intimate relationship. Apart from intimate contacts we all of us carry with us an invisible aura defining our personal space. When others come within this aura we become defensive and shrink away, perhaps even making a verbal comment about the other's proximity, such as the crude American 'get out of my face'. Over-proximity can, in extreme situations, be seen as an invitation to a fight.

The more polite world of information systems still has its unwritten laws about distance. Coming too close to a colleague at work or to an interviewee can seriously unsettle that person and can, for example, be construed as sexual harassment, however unreasonable that may seem to you. The point is that some aspects of non-verbal behaviour are so deeply ingrained in us that reactions may be instinctual rather than logical.

Open plan offices and crowded workspaces are prime sites for arguments over proxemics. Some psychologists claim that we are still territorial animals and resent any invasion of our privacy by others. Do you get angry when the other person's papers creep across onto your work station? Then why do you sit on the edge of the other person's desk when you talk to him? Invading the private space of others is a sure way to begin a business relationship on the wrong foot.

1.7.4 Gesture

Everyone is aware of certain commonly used gestures, especially the ones from such places as football stadia. Apart from these the British do not use gesture very much, nowhere near the amount of the Italians, for example. Desmond Morris's book *Manwatching* contains an entertaining discussion of this topic When we become excited we tend to gesture more and to use our bodily movements to emphasise what we are saying. Within the limits of our culture it is possible to build upon this and to deliberately utilise gesture to reinforce verbal messages. ('*It was this big!*')

Keeping an audience of whatever size involved and interested with words alone for any length of time is extremely difficult; gestures add a visual impact. At a personal level grandiloquent gestures can easily seem false and overdone but when involved in any kind of public speaking they are a potent weapon in the armoury. Compare, for example, those lecturers who read drily from a prepared set of notes with those who stride about the stage, gesturing wildly as they go. The content may not be as good but at least they keep you awake!

Our most commonly used gestures in everyday conversation are to nod our head for 'yes' and to shake it for 'no'. (Be careful when travelling in Bulgaria and Greece, since the convention is exactly the reverse.) Nodding the head is also used when listening to others to encourage them to continue: '*Yes, I am listening, please go on speaking*'. Interviewers in particular use this as a deliberate device.

1.7.5 Position

It is still true in many places that when one is called to see the head teacher or the boss of the organisation that person will be found seated at the end of the room behind a desk. The polite visitor will stand by the door until invited to advance. While you stay on one side of the desk, itself a symbol of authority, the head teacher remains on the other, dominating the encounter. For the whole of its duration the desk remains as a barrier between you, emphasising your inferior position and the refusal of the person in authority to descend to your level. There is little or no discussion, you are told what is to be done.

For an analyst this is a situation to be approached with care. Interviewing someone across a desk or a table has about it an air of authority and confrontation. You may have noticed that, for this very reason, family doctors have changed the position of their desk and chair in the consulting room. Sitting next to someone whilst they are being interviewed is also a problem. This implies a co-operative task where the two of you are united against the world. It also allows the interviewee to avoid eye contact.

Eye contact is important in our society as it is taken as a guarantee of honesty. People who avoid eye contact are thought to be shifty and dishonest. High pressure salesmen are taught to achieve and keep full eye contact at key moments of their 'pitch' and to place their clients in such a position that they cannot achieve eye contact with one another. Analysts are not in the position of salesmen but it is important to utilise it nonetheless.

Interviewees should be placed at ninety degrees to the interviewer in order to keep the right balance between formality and informality. You are, after all, in charge of the situation. This also enables you to judge times when the interviewee is avoiding your gaze or gives way to involuntary movements, those gestures which exhibit stress or discomfort. Do not assume that these mean that the interviewee is telling untruths; it may be that you have touched on a particularly painful topic, such as the cash flow of the business or the efficiency of the new business information system. Your job is to probe these areas, rather than to cast doubt on the veracity of others.

1.7.6 Posture

There is a famous drawing by van Gogh of a prostitute, entitled 'Sorrow'. The woman is seated but bent over so far that she is almost doubled up into a foetal position. Her head is buried in her arms and even her scrawny flesh seems to hang downwards like the boughs of a weeping willow. We are in no doubt at all about her mental state, even without the title underneath.

You might try an experiment at the next lecture you attend. Sit where you can see most of the other listeners and analyse what message you can glean from their posture. Several will be leaning forward on their arms, probably yawning ostentatiously. Others will be stretching backwards, head pointed at the ceiling. A few might be gazing abstractedly into space. With luck there may even be some who are sitting up attentively with quizzical expressions on their faces, taking notes from time to time. When the marks for that subject are published try correlating them against the postures you have noted. The results are guaranteed to be statistically significant!

The experiment above demonstrates that it is possible to deduce the student's interest and application at any given time from the posture exhibited. Posture also works the other way round, in that we can use our posture to put ourselves into different 'mind sets', to go from being a lounging student to a sharp, attentive trainee analyst. Our posture also affects the view that others have of us. No doubt you will often have been told to sit straight at interviews and slightly forward in order to say to the interviewer '*you are an interesting person. I am clever and eager to learn; I hang on your every word.*' It works! Not only at interview but also in general business, especially in situations where you are trying to impress others.

During formal presentations it is important to maintain this air of confidence at all times. Students have a tendency to slouch across projector screens or to lounge in seats looking as if they are home on the sofa. Business people are not impressed by this and may even find it offensive. If the person is as casual as this in presentation, how can we rely on the accuracy of the coding or analysis?

1.7.7 Gaze

When we talk to people we look at them in order to show that we are paying attention to what they are saying and to pick up extra clues to their meaning from their facial expression. Because these factors are so important we look at the speaker for about three quarters of the time. The speaker, on the other hand, looks at us only about forty per cent of the time. This is because the speaker is not so worried about completing the meaning of the communication from your facial expression but is concerned that the message is getting across. Thus the speaker tends to look at the listener more towards the end of a sentence or when a point is being made. During the conversation speaker and listener will gaze at the other for around three seconds at a time.

One of the reasons many people find giving formal presentations so disconcerting is because they are being stared at *all* of the time. Under normal circumstances to stare at someone we are not having a conversation with is regarded as rude, if not threatening. Feminist writers over the last decade have pointed out that the male gaze in public is a symbol of male power and aggression. As a result, staring at others outside of specific contexts is no longer seen as acceptable. In situations when we are forced to invade one another's private space, as in crowded trains or lifts, we go to great lengths to avoid making eye contact.

1.7.8 Facial expression

Because we spend so much time looking at faces, we have developed great sensitivity to facial expression. Joy, sadness, terror and delight can all be conveyed by one's face alone. Behavioural psychologists have gone to great length to chart precisely what movements of mouth or eyebrows are involved in any particular motion. Without trying to detail them here, suffice it to say that we all have a range of expressions which we use deliberately to reinforce our verbal expressions or to substitute for them. A quizzical raising of an eyebrow, for example, might be enough to signal disbelief. The tutors of the philosopher Ludwig Wittgenstein decided early that he must be the most intelligent student of his year '*because he is the only one who ever looks puzzled*'.

Some of our expressions are purely involuntary, such as a grimace of pain or a pleasurable laugh. Others can be produced at will, such as a wink or the dismissive downturn of the mouth. It is at precisely this point that we need to take care. Is what the other person is 'saying' with their face an involuntary expression, what we might call a leakage of information, or is it with the intention of deliberately conveying an attitude or opinion?

1.7.9 Touch

The amount that we touch one another outside of a sexual relationship varies greatly from culture to culture. Many British men in particular would draw the line at anything beyond a formal handshake and even then might feel discomforted if it were prolonged beyond a few seconds. My Mediterranean brother-in-law, on the other hand, greets me with a full embrace and a kiss on each cheek. I confess that even after twenty years I still feel uneasy.

Yet touch is something which is basic to our growing up. The contact between mother and child involves almost continuous touching and we automatically pick up a crying child in order to comfort it. In some societies the young infant is carried on its mother's back until old enough to walk on its own, a practice which has gained some adherents in the western world. When a friend or relative is frightened or upset we automatically hold them, perhaps stroking their head as we do so. Not only does the act of stroking calm the recipient it also calms the stroker, so much so that dogs and cats have now begun to be admitted into hospital wards, such is their calming effect on their owners.

Other circumstances also allow of systematic touching. Football players wrap themselves round one another after scoring a goal. Even macho rugby players may tap a player on the bottom as a sign of congratulation. In the north of England girls used to come out of the factories at clocking out time with their arms around one another's waists, whilst male drunks can be seen some hours later with their arms round one another's shoulders.

Touch, then, seems to answer to a natural human need whilst at the same time infringing on social taboos, perhaps because of its intimate connection with human sexuality. While a light touch, almost imperceptible by the recipient, enhances the persuasive power of the message by as much as a factor of ten, other forms of touching can be seen as aggressive. A person who is innocently enthusiastic in his use of touch may be described by others as 'mauling' them. Similarly, figures higher in the hierarchy use touch in a controlling manner, aping the actions of an authoritarian parent in the physical control they exercise over others.

For everyday life the message seems to be to avoid touching Anglo-Saxons unless you do it so lightly that they almost do not notice. Should you be successful in this you will be more likely to get your own way than others who do not use touch. You may feel that this is unduly manipulative, but then the whole use of words themselves to persuade people to agree with you is similarly manipulative. We seem to have different moral codes when dealing with non-verbal communication.

1.7.10 Reading the code

Some writers in the past have implied that non-verbal communication (NVC) is a language in its own right and that all we need to do is to learn it in order to find out what others are thinking or what they feel. This is a partial and inaccurate view of the way that we use our bodies to communicate; it also fails to distinguish changing patterns of social behaviour.

Only in rare situations do we dispense with words entirely. In noisy factories, in television studios where instructions should not reach the microphone or in signalling to friends across distances where the voice will not carry, special forms of sign language are developed. Even here they are directed at replacing the speech that has somehow become impossible or undesirable. Non-verbal communication is normally used to **complement** speech, to help out in loading or reinforcing the message that we are trying to convey. A deliberate stabbing motion with the forefinger, for example, drives home the point that the speaker wishes to make. The girl rejects the man's advances whilst at the same times folding her arms, placing a physical barrier between them. The head teacher who stands on the stage is symbolically placed above the rest of the school, perhaps even using a lectern to further emphasise this separation.

In all these examples speech is primary, actions are used to reinforce it. Context is another complicating factor. '**Postural echo**' is the phenomenon where people who find themselves in accord naturally drop into the same posture. What are we to make of a group of students in a lecture, all with their heads on their arms. Are they suddenly discovering some group solidarity? More likely, it is a very boring lecture! Another problem for protagonists of NVC is that social interaction is fluid, the conversation moves on, actions move on. We do not keep the same posture for long, our extremities tend to become weary if we do. Obviously this constant movement cannot convey a constantly changing attitude to the company with which we find ourselves.

So there are objections to seeing NVC as an easily read language of its own. Despite this, it does have a power which speech on its own does not have. This can be illustrated by doing things which are contrary to certain conventions, such as talking to people in lifts, sitting next to other students in an almost empty coffee bar, overusing touch or standing too close to people during normal conversations. Anybody taking part in such an experiment or in organising one has to be very careful to be ready to explain the purpose of the exercise should unwitting participants start to become aggressive. It is indicative of the power of NVC that this often happens. Despite changing fashions the wearing of makeup by males seems singularly provoking to other males.

Such strong reactions indicate both the power of NVC and our fear that others are using it to manipulate us. At times of stress we often find ourselves unable to control ourselves physically, sending uncontrollable messages through our body language. A female student was carrying out some systems analysis on a seaside hotel as part of her final project. Things were not going well. The system seemed too small to make a reasonable project and it was too late to embark on another. She sat talking to her supervisors twisting her house keys in her dress so tightly that she seemed likely to ruin the fabric completely. For twenty minutes she mistreated her keys and her dress while negotiating an alternative approach to her project. Finally she was sent away with the words '*We seem to have your project all sorted out. Perhaps you will be less nervous next time you come to see us.*' '*How did you know I was nervous?*' she replied. She had not even noticed what she had been doing!

This is the concept of '**leakage**' mentioned earlier. Although we do not intend to send messages others can make inferences from our behaviour and draw conclusions from them. Thus we know that someone is embarrassed because they blush, someone is nervous because they cannot keep control over their facial muscles. Some people change their tone of voice when they tell a lie (most of us learn to control this!). Salespeople are taught to look out for such signals, as are nurses, though for different reasons. Obviously alert systems analysts can also gain extra information from leakages whilst at the same time withholding information by controlling their own bodily responses.

Non-verbal signals are often a significant indicator when they conflict with the verbal message. An operator who talks about hating computers yet uses them every single second, including for jobs that are more easily done without, obviously has some sort of problem. A programmer who tells you that coding is exciting and enjoyable yet always leaves it to subordinates might be trying to indicate the need to deal with an uncomfortable hierarchy by identifying with those in a subordinate position.

Whatever the complications and limitations that non-verbal communication might have, anybody working in the information industry ignores its messages and potential at their peril.

1.8 ORAL COMMUNICATION

We have already noted the variable and ambiguous role of language. To be more accurate, language itself is neutral in this respect, the ambiguity lies in the use that human beings make of it. It is the application of the tool rather than the tool itself that is problematic.

Because we are now a word-based society language has come to occupy many social functions and to satisfy many personal needs. Whether we recognise it at the time or not, every verbal utterance falls into its own social space and has its own effect on the hearers. Interviewers are often brought up short by a chance remark by the candidate, often in the more social part of the process, who has 'given the game away' by revealing part of past background or character which had best remain hidden.

Michael Argyle and others have proposed a certain number of functions of language. For our purposes these have been reduced to the nine which are the most relevant to the informations systems area.

1.8.1 Egocentric

Scholars maintain that at one time all readers read aloud, there was no such thing as silent reading. Nowadays merely moving one's lips whilst reading is taken as a sign of low intelligence, even editors of tabloid newspapers dismissively describe their readership as *'people who move their lips whilst reading.'* Talking to oneself is similarly viewed askance, although it is something we all do. Most of us do it by ourselves for fear of being thought mad or senile, but on occasions it still slips out. The American tennis player John McEnroe was famous for his inability to hold in his imprecations to himself whilst on court, however impolite they might be.

Most of the time we talk to ourselves 'in our heads', a process which we call thinking. Many people find that verbalisation improves their thinking process, that to actually speak out loud improves their internal logic. This causes confusion when it occurs in conversation, where your interlocutor is merely rehearsing his thoughts on you before coming to some sort of conclusion. No response is required and the person may seem quite disorientated if one is forthcoming.

Writing notes from books or lectures is another example of egocentric communication, as is working out one's personal finances on paper or keeping a diary. The important factor here is to recognise these sorts of utterances in others and to keep quiet, as well as recognising them in oneself and consciously integrating them into your intellectual processes.

1.8.2 Orders and instructions

In any hierarchical situation, even informal ones, the issuing of orders and instructions is part of the functioning of the social group. The leader needs to organise the group, assign tasks and to issue any instructions about how those tasks are to be fulfilled. This is usually associated with ...

1.8.3 Asking questions

Asking questions is a task-oriented activity aimed at producing enough data for a procedure to be carried out. Naturally the skill here is in the formulation of the question in such a way as to elicit the required response. '*Is there a word limit on this assignment*' could produce the sarcastic response '*Yes*' (with no further comment) or an incomplete answer such as '*Up to four thousand words*'. The real question was '*How little can I get away with?*' Questions, then, need to be precise if they are to be effective. In an honest exchange asking questions leads in to information giving.

1.8.4 Information giving

This could be formalised, as in '*The train now standing at platform 4 is the 1330 for Birmingham*', or social, as in '*I'm just going to the shops, I'll be back in an hour*'. Complicated information giving usually appears in a written form so that it can be retained and referred to at leisure. A good example of this is a computer manual or a college text book.

1.8.5 Social routines

These are probably the commonest forms of communication. Things like greetings '*Good morning, how are you?*' come under this category. They are meant to elicit a formalised response ('*Fine, thank you, how are you?*') rather than to form part of any conversation. Somebody once defined a bore as someone who responded to '*How are you?*' with a detailed description of his state of health. Some theorists also term this 'phatic communication', exchanges which are redundant in the grammatical sense that the words themselves convey no information. Social routines often shade off into a form of informal contact.

1.8.6 Informal contact

Informal contact is the sort of conversation that we indulge in with our friends, although it also spills over into our working lives. We talk in order to maintain relationships, often with no ulterior aim or purpose. Sports haters will talk football with friends who are football fanatics in order to demonstrate closeness, for example. Silence in social situations worries our society so much that we take steps to eliminate it.

Conversation is rarely neutral, however, so that other things may be going on in simple social contact. Eric Berne gives the example of a colleague who has been away on holiday. Normally your early morning conversation would go as follows:

You: *Good morning, how are you?*
Him: *Fine thank you, and yourself?*
You: *Great.*

At this point you both go your separate ways, having performed your social routine and, in Dr. Berne's words, given one another a couple of 'social strokes'. But then you don't see your colleague for some days, which produces the following conversation:

You: *Good morning, how are you? I haven't seen you around for some time.*
Him: *No, I've been on holiday.*
You: *Go anywhere interesting?*
Him: *We went to Ibiza, but it was terribly crowded.*
You: *You didn't enjoy it, then?*
Him: *Oh, it was all right, especially when we managed to get back up into the interior for a couple of days.*
You: *That sounds fun. Suppose I'd better be getting on with some work at last. See you around*
Him: *Bye.*

A lot more 'social strokes' in this encounter, because we are trying to catch up on the ones we missed over the holiday period. Berne goes on to point out that the number of 'strokes' declines until they reach their previous level.

We can use this in a practical manner in two ways. First, we need to make sure that we are maintaining relationships efficiently by giving friends and colleagues the correct number of 'strokes'. Anyone who neglects to do so tends to be shunned by others or regarded as manipulative. ('*She only ever speaks to me when she wants something*'.) The other is to observe others' behaviour. Are they giving an unusual number of 'strokes' for no apparent reason? This usually means that some sort of manipulation is in train, so watch out!

1.8.7 Expressing emotions and attitudes

Again this is one of the commonest functions of language. '*I love you*', '*Spinach makes me sick*', '*Students are just parasites and layabouts*' are simple examples of this kind of utterance. Theorists who claim that business is purely about reaching economic objectives would claim that such utterances are out of place in the business world. Realists have heard the phrase '*I am frightened of computers*' often enough to know that emotions and attitudes provide most of the motivation for the behaviour of human beings and are important factors to be identified and dealt with. Interviews are vitally important in this respect.

1.8.8 Performative

Performative utterances are of two kinds: illocutions and perlocutions. Illocutions are where the speech act *is* the action, as in verbal voting or saying '*I do*' at the appropriate time in the wedding service. Perlocutions are more important to us in an information systems context in that they are utterances which are aimed at achieving a goal of some sort. Thus they may try to persuade you to buy a new system, to intimidate you so that you do not make a formal complaint to a higher authority, to cajole you into taking an action and so on. If all the other functions of speech provide the groundwork for social and business communication it is performative utterances which are the cutting edge, where manipulation and goal achievement are at their most blatant.

1.8.9 Latent messages

Latent messages involve the sending of messages which are not part of the grammatical structure of the sentence. Someone who says to you *'I was telling the Queen last night how important foreign aid is to the people of Africa'* is saying little about attitudes to foreign aid but an awful lot about what an important person the speaker is to be chatting to Her Majesty. Colleagues may tell you that they have an important meeting to go to (they must themselves be important) or that the boss is interested in the progress of the program you are writing (which is already late...).

As we will see later, it is one of the great skills of the interviewer to be able to pick up latent messages and to analyse correctly whether they are conscious or are the result of 'leakage' in the interviewee's expression.

1.9 THE EFFICIENT STUDENT

In this section we will look in greater detail at how you as a student can improve your performance at college by improving your communication skills, particularly in the areas of acquiring, recording and using information which were mentioned earlier. The important word here is 'improve'. No amount of well intentioned advice will do anything for you if you do not attend lectures, fail to hand in assignments and have no clue where the college library is.

Most courses at western universities are based on the lecture and seminar system. Lectures are a cost effective way of conveying large amounts of information to a large amount of people at the same time. Alternatively, one wag described them as *'a means of passing information from the notes of the lecturer to the notes of the student without passing through the brain of either.'* Certainly there are horror stories of lecturers whose notes are headed 'June 1955', with no evidence of more recent updating, or of lecturers who seem to have read the set course text the night before. In general, though, lecturers will have read the main authorities on the subject, they may even be one themselves, and will have synthesised these into a comprehensive overview for their students. At other times the lecturer may well be drawing on a wealth of experience in the area, perhaps gained through personal research or by employment or consultancy work.

Given this expertise in practical and theoretical perspectives and the width of knowledge covered by the lecturer's analysis of secondary information sources it does seem a waste of a valuable resource not to make the best use of the lecture as a learning aid. You will notice the use of the expression 'learning aid' rather than 'teaching aid'. That is because teaching is, in itself, a useless occupation. The only important activity that takes place in a lecture hall or classroom is learning; if you are not learning then no real purpose is being served. A class of bored, sleepy inattentive students will negate any attempts by the lecturer to teach them. Exam results at the end of the session will reflect this. A good teacher is one who sets up the ideal conditions in which students learn.

This is not a universally held view among either teachers or students. In Chapter 7 we will look at what it means for you as trainers of computer users; for now we will deal with what it means for you as a student. One of the reasons why it is an unpopular view among students is that it gives them nobody to blame. Whether the lecturer is no good, the exam too hard, the assignments unclear or the course content too woolly is immaterial. The fact is that you did not learn your material or write the assignment. As a student you have a responsibility to learn, you have to make the best of the situation on offer. The lecturer cannot do your learning for you. All that can be done is to present the relevant material and learning experiences in the best way possible and expect you to do the learning.

All of this is encapsulated in the trendy educational phrases 'the student should take charge of his or her own learning' and 'student-centred learning'. If you reflect a moment you will see that this is an essential step towards employment . *'There is a new piece of software on the market, obtain a demonstration disc and let me have a report on whether or not the company should purchase it.'* 'We have been approached by a government in Eastern Europe to supply equipment and expertise for their civil service. Do some quick research into the political and economic situation of the country to establish whether this is likely to be a safe and rewarding contract.'* One student, for example, was asked by a company trading with a country which had no convertible currency to research the possibility of arranging a three-way barter arrangement. This involved much research in libraries and writing to the trade departments of embassies and to overseas Chambers of Commerce. In business there is rarely any expert to check back with, you are responsible for acquiring and using the information and checking its validity yourself.

College, then, is a transition stage from what we might term a dependency learning culture towards the outside world and an autonomous learning culture. There are many pitfalls along the way, not least the failure to realise that no-one is standing behind you forcing you to work. Should you fail to do so the institution will part quite happily with your presence and lecturers will heave a hearty sigh of relief at having one less assignment to mark.

How do we avoid this unhappy situation and get the best out of the learning environment? First, by accepting that we are in control of our own destiny. Only your own skills as a student will see you through to that degree or diploma at the end. Second, by using every facility that is on offer; and third, by involving yourself in the full range of learning opportunities.

Let us look first at that basic unit of higher education teaching, the **lecture**. Lectures are intrinsically boring. In an age of fast-moving images where American children average ninety seconds on any one television channel, to stand a person before a large audience for an hour or more is hardly an exciting prospect. That that person is likely to talk in depth on a particularly difficult subject, often without the use of visual aids and reading from a prepared text, presents the listener with extra problems.

There are many excellent books on study skills, of which *Use Your Head* by Tony Buzan is deservedly the most popular. These deal with topics such as note taking and essay writing, so we are not going into them here. Instead, let us look at a neglected topic which is an essential skill for everyone in the information systems area, **listening**. By 'listening' we mean more than mere 'hearing'. When you study in the evening you probably have the radio or music on in the background as a kind of 'aural wallpaper'. You know when you have been studying well because you cannot remember what was on the radio during that time; you heard the sounds but you were not listening to them. Listening involves attention and concentration, it is an active process not just a passive state, as hearing is.

Listening to a lecture requires concentration, the blocking out of external distractions. You need to forget the whispered conversation behind you, thoughts of what you are going to do this evening or the distraction of the lecturer's loud tie. The whole point of the exercise is what the lecturer is trying to put across. If you are not concentrating on that you might as well have stayed in bed. Similarly, if the conversation behind you is too loud or distracting, you will need to eliminate the interference by asking them to shut up. This will gain you the thanks of other students in the room and the lecturer.

Concentrating for an hour or more is not easy. **Taking notes** is an aid to concentration as well as being a method of recording what has been said. On the other hand, you must remember that you are not a journalist looking for quotes or a shorthand recorder for 'Hansard'. What you are listening for are main ideas, the 'meat' of what the lecturer has to say, the meaning of the overall message rather than the detail. A good lecturer will use plenty of examples to reinforce the main argument. Obviously you do not need to make detailed note of these, but you do need to listen carefully in order to observe how broad principles have been applied. Once you have done this you can then write down **in your own words** the drift of the lecturer's point or argument. This is a way of making the information your own, of ensuring that it passes through your brain and not just through your notes.

A similar situation arises when assignment work is being set or returned. By their nature the written directions to assignments cannot cover every eventuality. Nor can they set out in vast detail the precise areas which you will be required to cover or in how much depth. These are the sorts of question you will need to ask. Again the answers should be attended to and noted down since they contain essential guidance which affect your future performance. Not quite so pressing is feedback on assignments which have been marked. Assessors are under great pressure to provide full information to students on the reasons for the mark assigned. This is valuable information for the future which you need to read and discuss with the assessor concerned.

Thus you know what you have done wrong and how you might improve your performance in the future.

Earlier, standard higher education was characterised as being a mixture of lectures and seminars. So what of **seminars**? Seminars are sessions which contain a smaller number of students, sometimes as small as one or two, often organised around work presented by the students themselves and based on a discussion format. Discussion methods are valuable in that they allow learners to examine topics thoroughly, to run 'what if' statements, if you like, and to test out their own ideas on others. They allow you to test out your understanding of the topic and to fill in any gaps. In a good seminar, where all the students take a responsible part, students learn as much from one another as they do from the lecturer, who only operates as an academic 'referee' and information source.

A good seminar depends as much on the students to play by the rules as it does on the expertise of the lecturer. No student participation means that it deteriorates into a kind of extempore lecture without notes or visual aids, often a miserable and depressing time for everybody. On the other hand, well prepared students who are willing to take part on an equal basis without trying to impose their egos on one another or just to score points find that their understanding increases by leaps and bounds.

Not that all seminars are on a formal basis. Students sometimes set up their own informal seminar in the pub or coffee bar on the basis of '*I didn't understand old so-and-so's lecture, can anybody help me?*' This is an excellent practice and a sign that students are taking control of their learning, again on the model of the business environment noted earlier. Alongside other students there are a whole range of useful people who can be engaged by the enthusiastic student. Tutors and lecturers themselves are usually willing to give extra time and to help elucidate knotty problems, even for students they do not teach themselves. Do not feel shy about approaching lecturers in this way, unless it is for information that was given in a lecture which you did not bother to attend!

Many colleges now have tutor librarians, that is librarians who may have special expertise in the subject matter of one particular department or set of courses. These and other librarians should be utilised to the full both as sources of information and as experts in how to find other information sources. They may know of specialist databases or be keepers of CD ROM discs, for example, or know which software directory is the most valuable.

Finally, an excellent source of help and information is people 'in the trade', that is information systems people themselves. At various times in your course or in your social life you will make contact with **IS professionals**, who are always ready to 'talk shop'. They are also very approachable when it comes to getting information for assignments. '*How would a company go about issuing an invitation to tender for a new IT system?*' Yes, you should have something on that in your notes but it would also be interesting to find out how a company *actually* went about it. Contacting someone in the industry could shed an extra light on the procedure. Perhaps they have a standard procedure they have produced themselves, or have deviated from the methodology which your lecturer has suggested for reasons of their own. You will be extending your own knowledge as well as, hopefully, improving your marks.

To sum up, you can improve your performance as a student by:

- improving your listening skills
- taking notes efficiently
- asking for guidance
- testing your own understanding
- taking control of your learning
- making use of a range of learning aids
- consulting experts

1.10 REAL WORLD APPLICATIONS

Using communications skills is something that we all do every day, for better or worse. In succeeding chapters we will illustrate particular aspects using specific activities within the world of information systems. To conclude this first chapter let us take a look at the work of a computer consultant in order to illustrate the range of communications skills employed.

Frank works for himself supplying PCs to accountancy firms. When he first started he had to decide which niche in the market he should aim for. Since his background before he went into IT was accountancy he decided to specialise in packages for accountants. Of late he has begun to get repeat business from companies which have bought one of his machines with the associated accounting software and wish to increase their capability by networking this with other terminals.

Having made his choice of specialism and being new to the area he had to publicise himself and his services. This he did by putting together a letter about himself and what he could offer and sending it to all the accountancy firms listed in the local 'Yellow Pages'. This letter needed to be easy to read and free from any computer jargon, whilst at the same time laying out what the new company could do for prospective clients. It also needed to show that the writer could use the same accountancy language as the clients and would be able to talk to them in a way that they could understand.

Frank followed up his mailshot with telephone enquiries to selected prospects. These were people he had heard of through the 'grapevine' and medium-sized companies that might be in the market for their first computerised system. He needed a firm and confident telephone manner and an assertive approach to allow him to get past 'gatekeepers' in the company, to arrive at those who held the power and the finance.

Once firm enquiries started to come in Frank was ready to go out and see his potential customers. He based all of his approaches on strict systems analysis principles, using structured and unstructured interviews in order to ascertain his clients' wants and needs. Because of the small size of the companies he was able to interview all of the participants, recording the answers carefully and cross-checking for accuracy. Once this had been done he was able to discuss with the client the areas of the business that were to be covered by the new system and the financial parameters within which he would be working. This often made large demands on Frank's political skills since the client's expectations of performance from an IT system were not always matched by the depth of the client's pocket.

Having established these parameters Frank spent some time with the users of this system, questioning them about their everyday work and asking questions about things he did not understand. He drew up data flow diagrams and logical data structures which he discussed with the users and altered in the light of their comments before finally presenting the client with a choice of possible systems that would meet requirements.

Sometimes he would find that he needed to present all this work in writing for consideration by the various partners in the business, some of whom were dubious about spending money on computer systems which they regarded as impenetrable and unreliable. Once or twice he also had to give a full oral presentation and demonstration to the partners and senior staff in order to point out the benefits of the system that he was trying to sell them.

Because of the rise in the number of companies producing and selling hardware and software there is not a great deal of profit in that area for intermediaries like Frank. Costing out his time he found that his payment per hour was relatively low, especially when he was reduced to 'cold calling' on customers. Luckily he also found that, despite the increase in IT awareness in recent years, most of his clients and their staff either could not use a computer system at all or had difficulty in transferring their existing knowledge to the new system.

He therefore began to offer training and backup packages to add to his portfolio. Clients were keen to take up these options because they could get the most out of their new system in the quickest possible time. They were able to use their own data and to set up parallel procedures to those they had been used to. Moreover, they did not have to rely on manuals, which all seemed to have been written in a foreign language. Frank was able to help here as well. As part of the training fee he would supply the company with copies of the simple manual that he had written for new users.

At the same time he was also negotiating with suppliers. Frank needed the biggest discounts from them that he could get, since this represented most of his profit in the hardware/software area. He also needed guaranteed and reliable delivery times and firm warranties in order to keep his customers happy. As the number of his customers grew and his work tended more towards systems analysis rather than supply and installation he also began to put together documents calling on manufacturers to tender for supplying larger systems as well as writing tender documents himself for wider-ranging consultancy work. Since the larger work was too much for him to handle on his own he co-operated with other consultants that he knew. This led to a series of regular meetings both in the planning and in the operational stages of the project.

Apart from this he was in constant touch with his bank manager, inland revenue and his own accountant. He visited computer exhibitions where he closely questioned exhibitors on the efficacy of their products and studied new developments in the computing press. From time to time he undertook training himself when he took on representation for a product that was new on the market.

If we take a brief look at the areas that Frank has operated in we have a list that is something like this:

Public relations
Marketing
Sales
Purchasing
Systems analysis
Systems installation
Writing manuals
Negotiation
Tendering

That is a sizeable list. The important thing about it from our point of view is that nearly all of them are primarily about dealing directly with people; that is, using communications skills. Without his ability to write clear and accurate letters and reports Frank would have had difficulty contacting clients or convincing partners of the efficiency of his analysis. Nor could he have attracted extra custom through his 'starter' manuals. He needed good interviewing and recording skills to gather data and to make sense of it. Negotiating with clients and suppliers increased and improved his cash flow, whilst his collaborators demanded consultation and negotiation. Finally, he found that an ability to train the users so that they could use their systems quickly was both good public relations in the long term and remunerative in the short term.

None of this is to deny that Frank must have a high level of informations systems expertise before he starts. Without it he would be unconvincing to his clients and incompetent in his operations. His expertise is necessary, but it is not sufficient. It is his communications skills which gain him the clients, enable him to do his job and enable him to maximise his income by offering a range of 'added value' services to his clients.

CHAPTER 2
Groups and their effectiveness

2.1 WHY WORK IN GROUPS?

Dr. Charles B. Handy in his seminal works on organisations claims that:

> *'On average, managers spend 50 per cent of their working day in one sort of group or another. Senior managers can spend 80 per cent.'*

A collection of programmers sharing a room and brought together almost at random may begin to perceive themselves as a group; the employees of a small software house may regard themselves as a coherent unit, IT trainers who meet only for an hour or so each day may still feel themselves united by a common purpose.

As a student in a college you will often find that a large amount of your learning and assessment happens in groups. When the groups operate effectively and everything goes well this can be an invigorating and rewarding experience. When things go badly there is much back-biting and recriminations, together with the complaint that groupwork does not allow individuals to shine. This section looks at the rationale for using the team approach both at college and at work.

2.2 THE PURPOSE OF GROUPS

Why do we work in teams at all? In the past great discoveries have been made by individuals apparently working alone. We also know from our own experience that there are some tasks which can be done most efficiently by one person working unaided. There is no inconsequential chatter, more time for reflection and thought, no-one to get in the way. No great battle was ever won by a committee of generals sitting down to discuss the next move.

All this may be true, but it only tells part of the story. Scientific discoveries of the past grew out of a scientific community which shared its knowledge through reading one another's writings, either in a published form or as letters. As technology has become increasingly complex scientists have taken advantage of communications technology to exchange information more rapidly. Companies and governments have discovered the advantages of putting experts together in one place in order that they can work together more efficiently to produce new ideas and new products. Bill Gates did not write MS BASIC from scratch, he had other examples to work from and colleagues at MIT to consult.

Generally bold and decisive action during an emergency needs the will and drive of one person. We tend, though, to remember when that person got it right rather than when they got it wrong. Bill Gates's declaration that pen-operated computers would sweep the world is generally forgotten besides all the successes of Microsoft. Napoleon is remembered more for his decisive victories against the odds than for his defeats in Spain, Russia and at sea. Although the stock market may be shaken when the founder and driving force of a company is forced out by a boardroom coup, the business generally lives on and grows bigger and stronger under collective management.

A more pointed argument in favour of team working is based on simple mathematics. An individual has a limited number of ideas. If one person has two ideas there can only be one connection between them. Two people, each with two ideas, gives us four ideas and increases the number of simple connections to six. Although in theory this means that the larger the number of people working together the better, experience tells us that the more complex a system becomes the more difficult it is to handle and disfunctionalities begin to creep in. About six people has been suggested as the maximum size for an efficient group, large enough to contain a range of expertise, small enough to be manageable.

Finally, consider the old saw 'a camel is a horse designed by a committee'. This is taken as being an attack on committees but is actually no such thing. What horse can you find that will cross terrain ranging from hard rock to shifting sands, carrying heavy loads and going for days without water? Indeed some historians ascribe the fall of the Roman empire to the ability of the Arab invaders to cross the Sahara desert and take control of the Roman grain lands in North Africa, denying the empire its primary source of food. Whichever committee designed the camel did an excellent job!

The basic purpose of a group may therefore seem to be the pooling of ideas, but there is much more to them than that, especially as far as individuals are concerned. Human beings are social animals who need one another for both physical and psychological support. When early hominids descended from the trees of the Great Rift Valley they did not hunt alone. They were too weak and puny so, like hyenas, they hunted their prey in packs, using their social organisation and superior reasoning powers to trap their stronger prey.

The social unit also supplied support in times of grief, illness, death and childbirth, as it does today. Historically, where units have broken down as a result of natural or man-made disaster we have made great efforts to replace them with others, be they political, religious or purely based on the needs of the moment. Although our individual needs vary we still retain this desire to belong to some sort of 'club', often one which regards outsiders as being different or inferior.

Organisations can take advantage of this need by constructing a group identity, producing an effective team whose desire for group solidarity is based on the work place and whose antipathy is aimed at the competition. That the formation of such groups is purely arbitrary is unimportant. Handy quotes formal research to demonstrate that this occurs, but anyone who cares to consider school or college life can confirm that groups of disparate students put together for no other reason than by alphabetical sorting of their surnames can quickly form an identity. Moving students across groups can produce antagonism at first, but the student soon takes on the identity and values of the new group. Similar attitude changes occur in business where a programmer, say, is moved to the sales team, abandoning the views of the first group and taking on those of the other.

To a large extent we also identify ourselves by our group membership, particularly by our membership of work groups. What do you say at parties when asked '*What do you do?*' The majority of the time you reply '*I am a systems analyst*' or '*I work as a software maintenance technician*' rather than '*I listen to Bach and Iron Maiden*' or '*I spend my time building racing cars*'. The latter activities are not as group-oriented as the work activities, we feel that they do not define us as completely within the social continuum.

For individuals, then, it is important to belong to groups:

- so that we can perform tasks that are important to us
- to achieve some sort of social identity
- to create a social support mechanism
- to satisfy our inbuilt need to 'belong'.

2.3 WORK-BASED GROUPS

It is very unusual for anyone in employment not to be a member of a group or team. Even writers of software nowadays find themselves in meetings to discuss the need for the product, its potential market and the financial advantages of different design methodologies and programming languages. Information systems professionals may find themselves part of a data processing department, as part of a user support network or integrated within the wider departmental structure of the business. Ideally, decisions are made by bringing together the expertise of all the members of the group and arriving at an optimum solution. In practise the business world is a much more complex place than this.

Work-based groups are like families: we are stuck with them whether we like them or not. You do not have to like someone to do business with them or to work with them, although it is obviously pleasanter if you do. From the point of view of the business all that matters is that the group achieves its business objectives in the most efficient manner possible.

A lot has been written on hierarchical structures and leadership in traditional industries, such as car manufacture and aeroplane plant. These emphasise the flow and dissemination from a central point outwards and the difficulties of conveying instructions to a tightly structured workforce. The information industries tend to take their personnel from highly skilled professionals, much in the way that legal practices and hospitals have done in the past. Even the most junior workers can be operating autonomously for much of the time, with little or no supervision from their notional line manager. One student spent a year working on placement for a government agency, virtually the lowest post in the whole establishment. After an initial training period he spent the rest of the year sorting out users' problems, logging faults and issuing id's with very little reference to anyone else. He was virtually autonomous in his actions.

Such a position is not unusual nowadays, where skills and knowledge have become more specialised and more volatile. Students fresh from college may find that they know more than anyone else in the whole DP department when it comes to the application of new developments, such as virtual reality or knowledge-based systems, especially if the company has been locked into one supplier's hardware or software for some time. Companies therefore need to get the best out of everyone's expertise, unlike the old manufacturing industries with their mundane and repetitive tasks. Thus information-based companies tend to have a very flat hierarchy in their supervisory structure. Indeed, there may be times when the hierarchy is inverted for a short time in favour of the 'expert'.

Such a way of working is difficult to manage and difficult to maintain. However, it is also very effective, especially in areas with indeterminate outcomes, that is ones that cannot be accurately predicted beforehand. Tasks are assigned according to competence rather than seniority and outcomes are often the result of the efficiency of the group's teamwork rather than a coefficient of the time spent on the task. To work to that model the company needs to be very clear what its objectives are in establishing groups.

Within early industrialised models the first function of groups was to distribute tasks across the workforce, to ensure that everyone had their job and that the processes proceeded smoothly. As organisations grew larger, work units were established on a hierarchical model. Departments and sections were established under their own leader and work was organised with these smaller sections. For most companies this is still the formal organisational model.

Once the larger group has been sectionalised communication problems arise between the various groups. Working parties from the various groups are set up to establish and maintain an information flow and to prevent them from divorcing themselves from the common purpose. Meetings of departmental heads or managers from different sites are prime examples of this sort of hierarchy grouping. Because of the strong tendency of individuals to identify with their group some companies deliberately physically remove managers from the site on which their departments operate and put them together as a management group. The objective is to have a management whose primary loyalty is to the company as a whole, as epitomised by management tasks, rather than allowing them to 'go native' on the shop floor and identify too strongly with their subordinates.

The problem of communication within larger organisations has already been mentioned. As well as establishing management groups to deal with this (a '*horizontal team*') companies may also establish groups from all levels of the organisation ('*vertical teams*') such as works committees, management-union liaison groups or departmental meetings. As well as dealing with information flows they may at various times be involved in general negotiations, discussions about objectives, problem solving and co-ordinating activities within the company. Depending on the size of the company there may be formal or informal groupings which carry out such functions, taking in the whole of the workforce or only their representatives.

2.4 PERSONAL PERFORMANCE

What we have been discussing here is what is known as 'formal groups'. That is, they have been brought together for a specific task. They may be durable groups, such as a DP department in a large company, or temporary groups, such as a project team brought together from different parts of the company to solve a pressing problem. Formal groups are chosen by others, they do not choose themselves as informal friendship groups do. Their group dynamic is therefore different, calling for extra commitment by the members.

As well as being constructed from outside, formal groups are also task-oriented. There is a job to do and they must do it, everything else is secondary. Some informal groups, such as families, seem to have no set tasks at all. Even within sports groups, which would seem aimed at winning games, the task may seem fuzzy. Many players may be turning out just for fun, to stay reasonably fit or for the beer afterwards. Winning is not always their key objective.

The same is true in formal groups as well. We all bring to them our own personal agendas. Some wish to boost their egos, others are aiming for promotion in whichever way they can, one or two may be just hanging on desperately for retirement. In counselling groups these personal agendas become the focus of the whole team effort. In work groups they need to be acknowledged as having an effect on the proceedings without being allowed to dominate them.

Any newly-formed group will start with a period of circling round one another, analogous to the way that dogs sniff each other on first acquaintance. Larger groups or committees often expect members to introduce themselves formally to the others. Small and less formal groups have a period of jocularity and 'in-jokes' prior to the beginning of formal proceedings. Even at the start of the proceedings themselves there is usually a certain amount of non-functional behaviour, where one or more members express nervousness by intense verbosity or where members wish to develop their self-expression to the exclusion of the task in hand. Think of that person at work who insists on telling you how the present government has got it all wrong and should do this instead, how a particularly knotty programming problem was overcome or how clever he has been in getting equipment from a software supplier.

We should not dismiss this sort of behaviour totally. As well as providing self-expression, something which is important for all humans, it is also a form of social cement. Because the work group has been thrown together, cohesiveness needs to be engendered within it. Informal and seemingly inconsequential chatter is often the manner in which this is done. For more durable groups, such as the DP department, after-work drinks on somebody's birthday or the Christmas dinner are more tangible examples of bonding.

Within any group there will be people that you will like and others you will like less. Sadly, there may be some that you cannot stand. This is completely normal and causes few problems as long as you keep it to yourself and do not allow your feelings to cloud your judgement. Student groups frequently find a scapegoat in their midst, a student who is different in some way, and put off all their animosity on to the unfortunate victim. Whatever the scapegoat says in class is scoffed at and disregarded, however sensible it might be. Other groups do this to a lesser extent, 'freezing out' individuals they feel do not belong. Thus a valuable intellectual resource is lost and the group becomes less efficient in its operations.

At the other end of the spectrum is the group which has become too cosy. They look forward to going to work every day to meet their friends, have a chat, arrange social events. The objectives of the organisation are forgotten in an amiable fog. Examples of this include the student who spends all day in the college coffee bar and never attends lectures and the programmers who vie with one another in writing games in company time. These are extreme examples, but productivity in any organisation will drop off as soon as no-one is prepared to move the group as a whole back on-task.

Groups which last for any length of time are said to go through standard stages which relate to the situations discussed above. First they go through a **formation stage**, during which the members of the group feel out the situation concerning the group's dynamics and establish the task which is to be carried out. Information should be laid out and shared among the group members and the manner in which the group will approach the task is clarified. It is at this stage that the group decides whether or not it wishes to operate formally, with full procedural rules and minuting of meetings, or informally.

The next stage, which in tight organisations may not occur at all, is referred to as the '**storming**' stage. Members who are perceived as operating on their own agendas are brought back to the control of the group or ejected from it. The group itself may also use this opportunity to gain independence from management and other outside influences. For example, management may want to obtain software from one particular supplier for cost reasons, whilst the computer users group may demand that suitability for the task is the only criterion that it is prepared to accept.

Once the interior conflict is over, the group can get down to establishing its own working practices. Conventions such as whether everything should be said through the Chair are laid down, as is the amount of personal and commercial openness that might be expected. Much of this is not verbalised but comes about through the group's acceptance of some behaviour and rejection of others. If a group member makes a comment about a proposal directly to another group member a colleague may raise a counter objection in such a way as to include the question of violations of norms at the same time: '*I am not sure, **Madam Chairman**, that such a proposal is one that this company can entertain....*' The heavy emphasis on the title is meant as an obvious rebuke. This stage is usually referred to as '**norming**'.

Conflicts over and a working relationship established, the group should smoothly begin to **perform** its stated task. Everyone knows what roles and responsibilities they have and subordinate their own egos to achieving the task in hand. This is the best time for all involved. Conflicts between individuals are subordinated to the maintenance of the group, whilst achieving something acts as an exciting motivator to those involved.

As we have noticed before, this can degenerate over time into a group-maintenance culture rather than a task-achievement culture. The group may avoid taking on new tasks, becoming devoid of ambition or sense of purpose. At this stage an alert management takes steps to break up the group in order to replace it with one that will be more task-oriented. Knowing at what stage to do this is a very delicate skill. Do it too late and the company has wasted months, or even years, of productive time from highly paid professionals. Too early, and the group rightly feels resentful that it has not been allowed to reach its full potential due to yet another meddling piece of interference by an ignorant management. Reorganisation, whether for good reasons or bad, is rarely popular among those who feel they have little to gain by it!

2.5 FORMAL MEETINGS

So far we have dealt with work groups which have a reasonably continuous being and are limited by aim or function. Some sort of records might be kept, for costing purposes for example, but generally work groups commit little to paper and organise themselves with the minimum of formality.

Formal meetings are necessary when disparate individuals come together at intervals in order to arrive at policies or decisions which affect all of the participants. Some organisations, particularly those in the public sector which are directly accountable to the public, demand periodic meetings which are fully documented. In the private sector project teams which operate under formal project methodologies such as PRINCE hold regular meetings in order to ensure that projects are on task.

You might have seen in offices one of those joke notices which workers use to let off steam headed '*Meetings, the alternative to work.*' That this is a common attitude is an indictment of organisations which have not clarified what they want from their meetings and have failed to convince the participants of their necessity. Certainly some meetings are held out of sheer inertia, they are held because they always have been held whether there is anything to be discussed or not. This is expensive and inefficient. Consider the costs: participants' salaries, secretarial support, travelling expenses, the use of facilities, refreshments and so on. A quick chat over a cup of coffee would be much more cost effective.

Let us look at the alternatives for a moment. Depending upon what you wish to achieve and who needs to be involved you have several alternatives. A one-to-one conversation is obviously the quickest and most effective, a few minutes and agreement may be reached. Even if the person is not present a telephone call or exchange of fax messages may be sufficient. Where both of you need to spend some time researching information before you reply, fax, letter or e-mail is the solution. If all you need to do is to distribute information then newsletters, circular mail shots and posters would be appropriate.

Gaining information is more problematic. Questionnaires have their drawbacks, as does making requests for solutions. One solution is the Delphi technique, where experts are requested for their views on a topic and the results collated by the organiser. The experts may be exterior to the organisation, such as governments asking for comments on their policies from economic experts, or internal, where heads of sections are asked for written comments.

From this quick discussion we can see that meetings are *not* appropriate when:

- we wish only to give information
- decisions can legitimately be made by one or two people acting together
- we wish to garner information from a limited number of individuals
- the need for extra information forces large time gaps between 'moves' in the process.

One other alternative we have is to do nothing, not to communicate information at all. This has the same effect as building a dam across a stream. For a while it is effective, but slowly a head of water builds up behind the dam. Water finds its own way and gradually seeps around the dam and along channels that the builders had not considered, finding faults in the surrounding rocks and forgotten conduits. Information is like water, it finds its own level. People need information to explain their lives and if it is not available they will invent it. A potent mixture of invention plus the bits of information that have seeped round or through the blockage comes together to nourish what is generally referred to as the **grapevine**.

Where information is plentiful and accurate the grapevine is a fragile plant, finding it difficult to take root and being easily disregarded. Allowed to grow on its own with no competition from official information sources it can be strong and vigorous and command attention and respect. No organisation can afford to leave its communication structure in the shade of the grapevine because of its possible detrimental effects on morale, attitudes and loyalty of the staff. Clearly focused meetings may well be the alternative.

Where agreements are fixed informally it is often necessary to confirm them in writing, using the company meeting structure as a base. As Mayer, the film magnate, once famously declared: 'an oral contract isn't worth the paper it is written on'. And this might in itself be a good reason for holding a formal meeting. Minutes from meetings flow into the system, they become official documents, and sometimes even legal evidence.

Consider a project team which is developing a system for Redwood Hospital Trust. Although the system is due to go live shortly no back-up or reversion procedures have so far been developed. The team is concerned about this. It wishes to delay implementation until procedures have been developed and the operating staff thoroughly trained in their use. The team leader insists that this is unnecessary, being anxious that the system be delivered on schedule. You and the rest of the team bring up the matter at a regular meeting and insist that your concerns are minuted for the consideration of upper management.

At best, the minutes will be read and your superiors will realise that the need for proper back-up procedures overrides the desire to deliver the system on time. At worst, you have put your feelings on record. If data is lost, particularly data about patients, as a result of non-existent procedures you can stand before your superiors or board of enquiry and point to the fact that your team's strong recommendations were overruled. The 'Pontius Pilate scenario' is well tried and trusted in a range of organisations, especially those with a steep management hierarchy.

Meetings therefore can be used to:

- give information, particularly when it leads to –
  gaining information through feedback
- make decisions
- consult with a range of others
- insert information and opinions into the information network
- brief and support teams.

2.5.1 What goes wrong?

If meetings are so good for doing all these things why do they not deliver the product? Any particular meeting may fail to produce the goods for a whole host of reasons, many of them beyond the control of the participants. However, when they consistently fail to operate effectively, when people fail to take them seriously or try to avoid attending, it is usually because:

- the objectives of the meeting are unclear
- it is badly run
- it is attended by the wrong people
- it lasts too long
- it is unclear what action will be taken as a result of the meeting.

Objectives are vital to any business operation. If we do not know where we are going we do not know how to get there or whether we have arrived. For smaller organisations or sub-sections in particular the problem is compounded by the fact that meetings may have a variety of purposes subsumed within the whole. Rarely would a project team meeting be given over purely to an information function. Rather some parts of the team may be giving information to other parts, individuals may request feedback on what they have done so far and decisions may need to be made on the basis of current knowledge and progress.

In theory the solution is to have separate meetings; in practise this is rarely possible. Instead, each item has to be clearly identified in the minutes or by the chairperson in order to identify it by type. The participants therefore know what is expected of them and what sort of conclusion they may be expected to reach. For example, they will not be frustrated by trying to reach a solution to a problem presented by the team leader as an item of information since it will have been made clear that the decision will be made by higher levels of management. They may, however, expect their team leader to convey upwards their concerns and recommendations about the matter.

Running the meeting is a complex and serious task which will be considered in detail later in this chapter. A good leader will need to be aware of the full range of verbal and non-verbal behaviour as well as the mechanics of procedure and structure. Participants need to be made to feel that there are opportunities for all within a helpful and supportive atmosphere which is free from threat by others. The meeting must be orderly and run to time. One that gets out of hand leaves the participants angry and frustrated; one that fails to progress leaves them bored and irritated.

The **wrong people** at a meeting increases costs and decreases effectiveness. Is the managing director's presence necessary, or is it merely a question of tradition? How is it that we need to have thirty people round a table to decide on the matters in hand? Do those present have the expertise to enter the discussion and make informed decisions? Every extra person is an extra cost in terms of salary and of lack of efficiency in the meeting itself.

Leslie Rae suggests that there are only three reasons for people to be present:

- to give information
- to represent others
- to contribute effectively.

Thus the DP manager may represent the department at a higher-level meeting in order to subsequently brief the data processing team. An analyst may be called in to help the sales team with expertise on how the team might improve its information flow into the rest of the organisation. All participants should know why they are there and be confident that their expertise will be useful, at least in part, to the others. Using Rae's criteria we should be able to reduce our meeting of thirty people to a bare dozen, if not less.

Lasting too long is a common fault of meetings. Lack of focus is a common cause, no-one being clear about the objectives of the meeting or how they are to be achieved. Even with the variety of tasks that are to be found in most meetings, it is difficult to maintain functional concentration for longer than an hour. Any longer that this and productivity declines. Longer meetings could well be split into smaller ones with clearly defined functions and pared-down membership to reflect those functions. Naturally huge formal events, such as shareholders' meetings, are subject to their own limitations based on the amount of material to be considered and the transport difficulties of the participants.

A **plan of action** is essential if a meeting is to have an outcome. The plan reflects our objectives and states how they are to be carried out, by whom, to what time scale and using what resources. It is important that participants know from the outset what the outcomes of their discussions are to be. If it is to be action they must know whether they or others are expected to take the action and whether or not they will be in control of it. To spend valuable time discussing a vital matter only to find that your results are purely advisory is most disheartening. Similarly, to make proposals that are not implemented because no-one was delegated to be responsible for them is frustrating.

Having set out the characteristics of an effective meeting, we are now in a position to set out briefly what an organisation might expect to gain from work-based meetings:

- **Saves time.** If we get the people concerned together all at once we can cut down the length of our communication structures, in terms of space and time, and quickly arrive at quality conclusions. Even the alternatives of e-mail or fax messages are not as rapid or as effective as holding a meeting.
- **A variety of views are expressed.** As we noted earlier, the larger the number of inputs the greater the number of possible connections of ideas. By pooling expertise the meeting allows a range of ideas to be examined, some of which would not have been developed by individuals working on their own.

- **Involvement.** A meeting allows a larger representation of the people affected by decisions to take part in producing or discussing those decisions. Being part of the decision-making process increases commitment to the subsequent actions and a greater will to make them effective. Workers who have been consulted about changes in their operations show a marked increase in output.
- **Assess support for ideas.** Some change can only be brought about with the active support and agreement of those involved. The depth of this support is best gauged by passing on the idea, checking that it is understood and then dealing with any objections, a process ideally suited to a meeting.
- **Pooling knowledge.** As well as expertise individuals have knowledge about markets, systems and individuals which they have developed by experience and which has never been committed to paper. Bringing them together in a task-oriented environment provides an opportunity for this knowledge to be shared and evaluated.
- **Building work relationships.** Bringing work groups together at fixed periods helps to establish the individuals as a group, however disparate their work patterns or geographical location might be. Besides social bonding, a respect for each other's expertise can be nurtured, based on the contributions made to topics under discussion, leading to a feeling of mutual trust and respect within the work group.
- **Establishing collective responsibility.** In some circumstances it is important to establish that an identifiable group of people have agreed on a plan of action. In politics this might be the cabinet; for a company it could be the board of directors; at a lower level it might be a project team. There is an implicit statement that this is the best solution available and we all stand by it and agree to accept any consequences. Given the seriousness of such an undertaking the participants need physical reassurance of the full involvement of the other parties and the opportunity for an airing of all the arguments in favour of their position.

2.6 FORMAL STRUCTURES

Most of the meetings you will come across will be hybrids. That is, they will appear to be informal in structure, and may operate completely informally for the majority of the time, whilst having a formal substructure. For this reason the following section sets out how formal meetings operate, leaving you to transpose this underlying form to the hybrid meetings that you actually attend.

2.6.1 Procedure

A formal meeting will always have an agenda, which is published well in advance. This allows the participants to do their homework, to prepare presentations to the group or to look up relevant information. You may be approached by your supervisor, for example, who wants a status report on various projects you are involved in for a forthcoming meeting. Papers and reports may also be attached to the agenda for perusal and comment. The agenda sets out the order in which matters are to be taken and, in some cases, the timing of the meeting itself. Some organisations may have strict rules on how long certain portions of the meeting may last or on the duration of the meeting itself and this timetable will be clearly laid out in the agenda.

The length of the agenda should be determined by the length of the meeting, rather than the other way round. Meetings that drag on beyond their allotted time are expensive and ineffective. Whoever is preparing the agenda (usually the chairperson or secretary) should consult members first about what items need to be included and their relative importance. From this items can be assigned to the three categories of

- must be included
- should be included
- could be included.

Those in the third category need to be closely examined to see whether they could not be dealt with in another way, by inclusion in a newsletter, for example, or by discussion between a couple of people outside the general meeting. Remaining items should be assigned to the agenda in descending order of importance, so that it is the least important that are squeezed by time pressure rather than the most important.

Good agendas supply the maximum amount of information to the participants in advance. Each item should have a full description, the objectives of the item and the group's discussion of it, who is responsible for it and reference to any related papers. One such item might look like this:

Item: *Marlingford Hospital patient details.*

Description: *Marlingford Hospital wish to install a full network linked across all three sites, initially for the recording of patient details. An invitation to tender has been received from them.*

Objectives: *To decide: 1) Whether the company should tender for the contract.*
2) Who should be the team leader if we do tender.
3) The level of resources that we can assign to this project.
4) Reporting procedures and time scales for the project.

Leader: *Mrs. Jane Goode, Head of Sales and Marketing.*
References: *Invitation to tender from Marlingford Hospital (enclosed).*
Report on Redwood Hospital Project (see minutes of 24/4/95)

In the past meetings have always included an item for 'any other business' on the agenda. Modern thinking is to dispense with this for reasons of efficiency. There is a temptation for team members to be lazy and not to notify their items in advance. This means that group members cannot prepare themselves either by thinking about the topic or by reading the relevant papers, and enables unscrupulous operators to sneak topics in through the back door. The chairperson should only accept 'any other business' if it is the result of a genuine emergency or a problem that has only just arisen. Otherwise it can go through the pre-meeting process for the next meeting like any other item.

Attached to the agenda should be the minutes of the last meeting. These vary in layout and depth between organisations. A social services case conference will record a digest of almost all that is said by all the participants, followed by a series of recommendations. The Royal Air Force is much more terse in its recording. Their standard minutes tend to record what was agreed and who is to take action, with little indication of discussion. Between these two extremes we can identify sub-headings for recording minutes as:

- What is the topic?
- What main points are made?
- Any significant dissension?
- Motions passed; resolutions made; agreements reached
- Who will implement those?
- In what time span?

Modern thinking is moving towards the idea of dispensing with formal minutes in situations where they are not a legal requirement or demanded by the organisation's distribution and control of data. After all, they tie up expensive secretarial resources, take up a certain amount of the chairperson's time and are a very slow way of disseminating information. Leslie Rae suggests they wherever possible they should be replaced by the 'action note'. This is close to the R.A.F. minimal minute, where the objective is to establish the nature of the problem and who will be called upon to deal with it.

An action note will deal purely with the outcomes of the meeting and will detail:

- what is the topic or decision
- who is dealing with it
- how it is to be dealt with
- over what time scale
- to what standard
- how implementation will be achieved
- the nature and frequency of reporting back to the meeting.

At each meeting the minutes from the previous meeting will be taken first, perhaps with a small report from those identified as taking action. Any mistakes in the minutes should also be identified at this point, although in many cases draft minutes may have been circulated for correction ahead of the meeting in order to save time. Ongoing projects may have their own standing agenda items for reporting which may take the place of lengthy reports in the minutes. Like any other feature of a meeting the minutes need to be tailored to the needs of the participants, concentrating on their information requirements and their ease of use.

TEAM MEETING ACTION MINUTES					
Date of meeting	Apologies		In attendance		
Absences					
Agenda	Action		By whom	When	Done
Agenda					
Agenda					

Fig. 2.1 A pro-forma for a set of action minutes

2.6.2   Large meetings

In large meetings, such as a general meeting of the students' union, formal motions may be set down for debate. Usually they have to be notified in advance and have a proposer and at least one seconder, in order to reduce their number. They are taken in the order laid down on the agenda or in the space allowed for general motions if the agenda is published early. Amendments can be proposed to motions under the same rules as proposing motions themselves. Amendments are voted on first and, if successful, are added to, or take the place of, the original motion, being known as the **'substantive motion'**.

In a smaller meeting there may be no such things as motions in themselves but instead suggestions as to future courses of action. A good chairperson will identify these clearly and will take the feel of the meeting as to whether they are approved, probably with the words '*are we all agreed that...*' Again, the resolution needs to be carefully recorded along with attendant responsibilities.

Large meetings have complex regulations about how they are to proceed. Listen to parliamentary debates on the radio to get an idea of how convoluted these can become when they develop over hundreds of years. More straightforward rules in general meetings set out who can speak and in what circumstances. The proposer and seconder of a motion usually have a right to begin the debate on that motion, although only the proposer may sum up. Often a speaker is only allowed to speak once on any motion. Where these rules have been broken any member of the meeting may call attention to the deviation by raising a **'point of order'**.

Procedural motions such as '*that the question be now put*' or that '*the meeting has no confidence in the Chair*' take precedence over any other motion and should be debated at once before business may proceed. Points of Order and Points of Information can be decided by the chairperson without further debate. As you can imagine, the combination of a 'barrack room lawyer' and a weak chairperson can reduce a large meeting to chaos!

2.6.3 Roles

Formal committees and meetings have a steering group with clearly defined roles. The smaller the meeting the smaller the group and the less clearly defined the roles, but one would usually expect to have a chairperson, a vice-chairperson and a secretary.

Chairperson

The chairperson is the boss whose job is to open and close the meeting and to ensure order within it. Our paradigm in this case is the chairperson of the board of directors, a 'first among equals' to which the others defer because of the position in the company. The chairperson's word is law. Only a vote by the meeting can remove a chairperson from the post and allow the possibility of the replacement overturning a ruling.

Removing the chairperson by a vote of 'no confidence' is quite rare, as is the strict application of the convention that the chairperson does not speak on contentious issues. Where that convention is in force, the chairperson must relinquish the chair for the duration of the debate on that issue. An example of this might be the chairperson of a council housing committee where the motion proposed is to pull down the street of houses where the chairperson lives. There would be a natural desire to speak on the motion. In such a case a financial interest in the matter might also be declared, which could debar the chairperson from the chamber altogether. Additionally, some meetings, such as full county council meetings, do not allow the chairperson to vote except in the event of a tie.

Below the board of directors level the application of strict rules governing the chairperson are unusual. The smaller the meeting the more likely it is that the chairperson will merely have a control function, though this may be validated by the place in the hierarchy. Whatever the size of the meeting the chairperson has clearly defined functions:

- declare the meeting open; at this point minutes begin to be taken
- check that there is a quorum of members present
- ask for any apologies for absence, which are noted
- announce the first item on the agenda, probably the agreeing of the minutes of the previous meeting
- establish the agenda
- take agenda items in order
- close the meeting at the appropriate time.

It is also the chairperson's task to determine that the meeting is quorate. Most organisations have rules which demand that a certain number or a fixed proportion of members are present before a meeting has legal status. This is to prevent abuses from a small clique failing to inform others of the meeting and then taking decisions themselves which can have important consequences for others. Student unions, trade unions and shareholders' meetings are examples of organisations which demand a fixed quorum.

As you know from your own experience or from listening to parliament on the radio there is a tendency for debates to get out of hand. The chairperson therefore needs to define clearly who it is who is speaking now and who will be speaking next. The number of interruptions has to be kept down and participants prevented from talking at the same time. Paradoxically this is often easier in large meetings with their formal rules than in smaller, more relaxed formats. Within debate the chairperson also has to control the language used to what is acceptable and to prevent debate spilling over into verbal aggression rather than reasoned argument.

At the end of each topic the chairperson declares it closed, making it clear for the record what has been decided. A good chairperson will allow free expression of viewpoint whilst still observing any time restraints there might be. At the end of the meeting the chairperson will fix the time and place of the next meeting if appropriate.

Where meetings are decision-making bodies, such as the board of directors, urgent problems may arise between meetings. In this case the chairperson has to consult as widely and rapidly as time allows and then make a personal decision based on the information available. This is known as 'taking chairperson's action' and is quite common where meetings are held at monthly or quarterly intervals.

Within the meeting itself votes may be taken. Although a few organisations have now moved on to electronic voting, with each participant pressing a button to cast the vote which is then automatically recorded and tallied by the computer, most still operate through a show of hands. In smaller meetings the chairperson merely counts the votes for and against, plus the abstentions, and arrives at a result. For larger meetings this is not practicable and a proper series of *tellers* are employed. The tellers will count the votes individually, compare their results and then relate their figures to the chairperson who will announce them to the meeting. Some meetings demand four tellers, two to count the aye votes and two for the nay votes. Tellers are permitted to vote themselves.

There may be times when the chairperson is called upon to interpret the vote of the meeting rather than merely to record it. In the case where voting is close and the abstentions, those who voted neither for nor against the motion, are large there may be a case for leaving the matter open for later consideration. For example, our information systems company holds regular meetings of the workers, the majority of whom are also shareholders. The motion to the meeting was:

'In the light of the losses incurred at Redwood Hospital this company will not tender for the Marlingford Hospital Trust contract, or for any other hospital contract.'

Votes in favour	*12*
Votes against	*10*
Abstentions	*9*

Technically the vote has been carried and in many meetings this will be deemed to have been so. Our chairperson in this case, however, realises the grave disquiet expressed by the large number of abstentions. This may be the result of having a poor motion which conflates two issues: the Marlingford contract itself and the general issue of hospital contracts, or a feeling that there is a lack of information about the new tender. Are the workers merely being over-cautious or are there real issues that need to be dealt with? If there is sufficient time the chairperson will postpone taking action pending consultation with proponents of both sides of the argument as well as the abstainers in order to uncover the issues that they feel have not been resolved. In a company such as this, which depends on the support and morale of its worker-shareholders, it is particularly difficult to proceed with a course of action that does not command a majority of the participants voting in favour.

Vice-chairperson

The vice-chairperson is a reserve chairperson who steps in when the chairperson is unable to attend a meeting for some reason, when the chairperson vacates the chair to speak in the debate or has been removed by a motion of 'no confidence'. Within the steering group the vice-chair also takes on a variety of tasks in order to even out the workload.

Secretary

There is a difference between a 'secretary' and a 'minutes secretary'. The latter is responsible only for taking, writing up and disseminating the minutes. In a company this usually means using the chairperson's personal assistant or somebody from the typing pool. A secretary, on the other hand, is a senior member of the steering group who deals with all correspondence, both internal and external, prepares the agenda and its attendant paperwork and publishes the minutes, working with the minutes secretary if such a post exists. When problems arise the secretary may also be called upon to advise the chairperson.

Because of the control of the group's recording and communications the secretary is in a powerful position, being in a position to write history, so to speak. As the keeper of the agenda the secretary may also decide what is to be debated and in what order. Secretaries have been known to move motions of which they do not approve to the end of the meeting where they may be dropped for lack of time. To be fair to secretaries, they do huge amounts of unseen work and keep many voluntary organisations afloat. Not all secretaries are Josef Stalins in the making!

Efficient meetings are often the result of close liaison between all three officers, before, during and after the meeting. They work together to produce a clear agenda and supply all participants with a full set of documents well ahead of time. At least one of them will keep notes (possibly in addition to the minutes secretary) so that decisions can be referred to quickly later and to reconcile any disagreements or misunderstandings with the minutes secretary. Much of the post-meeting action also devolves to the officers, even if it is only ensuring that others are carrying out the tasks that they were assigned. The secretary in particular will be expected to keep a full record of any correspondence or other communication flows into and out of the group.

2.7 RUNNING A MEETING

At some point in your career you will find yourself leading or running a meeting. Perhaps you will be in a position where your standing in the company means that you have become a section leader or the head of a project team. Alternatively, you may be called upon to lead discussion within a larger meeting of a project or topic with which you have been concerned. As we have noted earlier, the flat organisational structure of the communications industries means that topic leadership can devolve to even the most junior of employees.

In the case of large formal meetings the role of the chairperson may be controlled by strict rules and reinforced by the expectations of its members. Smaller formal meetings, especially those that we have categorised as 'hybrids', which fall on the formal/informal boundary, can be more problematical when it comes to leadership. The chair of such a meeting has fewer conventional structures to fall back on and may meet added resistance from the membership. In these situations the effectiveness of the meeting depends heavily on the communications skills of its leader.

The chairperson of any meeting has three functions:

- control
- management
- facilitation

Control is the bread and butter work of organising and running the meeting. Agendas are organised, rules are followed, votes are called for and counted. In smaller meetings this role may form only a minimal part of the leader's function.

Management of the meeting involves the leader in enforcing performance by the participants. The group is encouraged to stay on task, not to degenerate into a general moan session or to wander off into interesting but irrelevant byways. The chairperson in this case is not an autocrat cracking the whip, making sure that everything is done 'by the book'. However, the role does involve ensuring that objectives are achieved within the limits of time and function; if that is not achieved then the meeting has been a waste of time and it is the chairperson who must bear the responsibility for it.

Facilitating the meeting is the activity of getting the best out of the participants. Over-active participants need to be controlled, the quiet and retiring encouraged to contribute, contributions valued and recognised. Where the chairperson is also the team leader alternatives for action may be introduced for consideration and may indeed form the main purpose of the meeting itself. In this case it is essential that the chairperson encourages the widest contribution from the meeting as a whole and does not fall into the defensive behaviour of dominating others in order to defend favoured proposals.

Another aspect of the facilitator role is ensuring that all participants understand the stage that the meeting as a whole and the constituent topics within it have reached. Thus the chairperson declares the meeting open at the beginning and closed at the end. Topics are introduced and 'signed off' when they have been dealt with. On opening the topic the chairperson may need to summarise its main points and to indicate what the purpose is of including it in this meeting. Is it for information, a problem to be solved or the question of setting up a project team?

During discussion the chairperson might summarise contributions that have been made in order to clarify them for all, or summarise the stage that the discussion has reached. On concluding the topic it is again the chairperson's job to summarise what has been agreed or what stage has been arrived at, stating who is to take what subsequent action and over what time scale. The exact nature of the final summary will depend on the type of meeting and its original objectives.

Although the three functions of control, management and facilitation have been treated separately they do, of course, interweave and the chairperson will move from one to the other as the situation dictates. Within this balancing of roles the chairperson also needs to identify when decisions have been made. More formal meetings will move to a straight vote with conclusions determined according to the rules of the meeting, usually demanding a **majority** vote in favour. Smaller groups often have less structured ways of making their decisions. Some demand that their decisions are **unanimous**, that everyone agrees. This is naturally difficult to achieve.

More often the meeting may arrive at a general **consensus** of opinion, perhaps with only a small number of dissenting voices. An alert chairperson needs to identify the moment at which such a consensus has been arrived at, whilst allowing dissenters the opportunity to air their views. Careful attention to the body language of the participants should indicate that minds have been made up despite counter-arguments and the time has arrived to indicate what the consensus is felt to be and to put it to the meeting.

Where conflict is more severe or interests more entrenched the meeting may make decisions by **compromise**. Members will trade off parts of their position against concessions by opposing parties. How this operates is covered in a more detailed form in the section on Negotiation. For now it is sufficient to note that it is the chairperson's job to referee this process and to avoid positions becoming entrenched and immobile, thus becoming referee, recorder, manager and facilitator all at once.

2.7.1 Problem people

People are not perfect, nor do their goals always coincide exactly with those of the organisation. The chairperson needs to be able to recognise dysfunctional behaviour and either deal with it or channel it into productive paths. When discussing individual behaviour in meetings we have already identified the main areas of difficulty with personal behaviour; what actions can the chairperson take to minimise the impact of negative behaviour?

Aggressive and **dominant** behaviour are not exactly the same but they may have similar effects. Aggressive behaviour manifests itself in a biting and confrontational tone of voice, often allied with an attack upon the person rather than upon the idea put forward. A dominant person makes lengthy speeches, often in a loud and positive voice, ignoring and 'over speaking' others in the meeting. Their effects are similar in that they prevent others making their points, either out of fear of attack or from the sheer impossibility of getting a contribution heard.

Where the chairperson is in a position of hierarchical authority part of the problem can be dealt with outside the meeting by privately pointing out the behaviour to the individual concerned and asking for amendment. Where this is not possible and during the meeting itself the chairperson needs to take firm action. Long speeches can be broken up by asking the speaker to move quickly to the point. 'Overtalking' or breaking in on others should be firmly prevented: *'I'm sorry, Jack, but Janet has not finished making her point. You will have chance to voice your objections later.'*

Dealing with aggressive behaviour is more difficult but also more pressing, since we do not wish that sort of interchange to become the norm in the group. With short exchanges the chairperson can utilise the summarising function as a weapon, divesting what was said of its personalised and aggressive coating in order to get to the objective part of the statement: *'What I think you are saying is that the pricing structure of the Redwood Hospital contract was poorly done. Leaving aside any attribution of blame, is that your position?'*

Where speeches are longer, which often indicates an increase in aggression, the chairperson may need to interrupt them, repeatedly if appropriate: *'Could we please move away from the question of personalities and towards a firm proposal as to what we are to do in this case?'* If the culprit carries on the chairperson has no alternative but to cut speeches short; *'We quite understand that you blame the accounts director for the problems we have had, but these constant attacks are getting us nowhere. If you have a new point to make, please make it succinctly. Otherwise I think we should get on with the business in hand.'*

Less of a problem are the **digressor** and the **recognition seeker**. These two may be looking to be noticed or perhaps are talking out of sheer nervousness. The chairperson's job is simply to cut short the digressions and to point out to the offenders that others wish to speak or that time is getting short. *'I'm sorry, you have had your turn to speak. Frank and Janet have been waiting some time for the opportunity to put their views.'*

Another person who needs to be kept quiet on occasions is the **comedian**. Useful at the beginning of the meeting for breaking the ice and setting people at ease, the comedian becomes a liability when insisting on the comic possibilities of every topic or comment. Not only does this become wearing it also has the danger of becoming offensive when badly handled. Mostly it can be dealt with by the suggestion that humour is no longer appropriate and that there is a serious task in hand: *'Can we handle this in a more businesslike manner, please. There is a lot of money involved in this contract, besides being important for many people's jobs.'*

So far we have dealt with people who contribute too much or in inappropriate ways. There are also those who cause problems by contributing too little. Among these is the **blocker**, whose terse comments of '*it just won't work*' add little to the discussion apart from an air of negativity. The chairperson's response is to insist on rigorous arguments and supporting evidence to back up such contributions: '*Why not? Please spell out your objections clearly so that we can see if they can be overcome.*' The blocker's other tactic is to keep coming back to a topic that has already been dealt with or to prevent the meeting from moving on to the next one. A firm ruling from the chair is usually quite sufficient to restore order in this case.

Further down the continuum are those who under-contribute, including those who say nothing at all. Where this happens on a given topic it may be that the person does not feel qualified to comment, a sensible enough position. Where the behaviour is persistent the chairperson needs to take action to bring the person into the discussion by pointed questions: '*John, this concerns your section as well. What are your thoughts on the matter?*' John may be delighted to be asked, allowing him to overcome his shyness or feeling that, as a junior in the company, his opinion does not count. Where repeated questions reveal that he is truly out of his depth we have a perfect opportunity of increasing efficiency by reducing the meeting by one member and returning John to more productive activities.

Lastly, there are the back-row chatterers. These sit around having private conversations and disrupting those around them. '*I'm sorry, do you have a point to make?*' usually suffices, although a repetition can sometimes need to be made. Where there are several persistent offenders the chairperson needs carefully to examine the meeting itself to determine whether it has the right people engaged in the right task in the right manner, since this is an obvious case of feedback indicating that communication is not taking place.

The chairperson's detailed actions are dominated by the objectives of the meeting. Although most meetings are an amalgam of different topics with contrasting objectives it is still helpful to categorise their various purposes and the activities that go with them.

2.7.2 Information giving and decision making

We have already noted that the giving of information on its own is not a cost-effective objective for a meeting since there are so many cheaper ways of achieving this. However, the giving of information when followed by attempts to make decisions based on that information is perhaps the most common reason for calling groups of people together.

The information giving itself is frequently the province of the chairperson, although it may be devolved to a topic leader. Whoever gives the information needs to check that it has been received and that it has been understood by asking confirmatory questions and welcoming feedback. Group members have their part to play in this process. If the meeting is conducted in an unthreatening atmosphere they will feel relaxed about asking questions and being open about the areas that they do not understand. Some group members will take it upon themselves to summarise and rephrase the information, allowing the information giver the opportunity to clarify grey areas and to correct any misunderstandings.

At this point the topic leader needs to sum up the position in order to establish the ground for the problem-solving exercise which is to follow. This will involve the group in generating and exploring all of the possible options, perhaps by using brainstorming techniques or buzz groups, which can then be explored in depth. Once all of the options are on the table it is the topic leader's job to ensure that each one is given due weight without spending inordinate amounts of time on the process. Some options can be rejected quickly, if they are not technically feasible, for example, or if they demand capital beyond the company's powers.

Active topic leaders are alert to similarities and connections between proposals which allow them to be amalgamated in whole or in part. Thus options can be further reduced to a reasonable number which can be handled in the available time. Unless there are pressing external reasons for reaching a decision immediately, the topic leader has also to be aware of the possibility that the group may not be in a position to have all the data needed to make an informed decision. In this case discussion will need to be adjourned, either temporarily or until a subsequent meeting.

Hopefully our group can arrive at a solution quite quickly. Before the topic is signed off it needs to be clear how it will be implemented, by whom and within what time scale, otherwise there is the danger that no action at all will be taken. Finally, the chairperson or topic leader will conclude the item with a short summary of what has been decided so that everyone can be clear that progress has been made and implementation strategies decided upon.

The stages in a decision making meeting are:

1. Give information
2. Check on its reception and understanding
3. Seek feedback and confirmation
4. Produce interim summary
5. Seek all possible options
6. Decide on a solution
7. Confirm implementation strategies
8. Final summary.

In the discussion above we made reference to ways of producing alternative options, particularly by using brainstorming techniques and buzz groups. Let us look at how these operate in slightly more detail.

Brainstorming is a technique for producing a large number of ideas on a subject free from self-imposed constraints of 'common sense' or *'what the company will allow'*. Once the topic has been introduced and summarised a time limit is set for the generation of ideas. Members of the group are then encouraged to throw in any suggestions that they have, which are carefully recorded. No discussion is allowed at this point, it being the leader's function to maintain the momentum of the flow of ideas. Depending on the time available, the complexity of the situation and the sophistication and knowledge of the participants this part of the exercise can be set anywhere between two and ten minutes.

Once the time limit has been reached, or when ideas have dried up if this happens early, then the sifting of the ideas can begin. It is usual to examine the total idiocies first as these can often be quickly rejected. Beware, though, of being too cavalier with your rejections; objections such as '*it just wouldn't work*' need to be unpacked to ensure that they are based on fact rather than prejudice. After all, who would consider a crazy idea such as etching a computer's memory on to a small piece of silicon!

The next set of ideas are those which have merit in part, where changes can be made which will make them workable. Often these display similarities, as much in the changes they require as in their implementation. We are beginning to see where organisational structures, hardware restrictions or availability of capital are limiting our freedom of manoeuvre. Our meeting may conclude that steps are taken to remove the constraints in order to make the company more flexible and profitable.

The third group of ideas are those that have been proposed or tried in the past but have been rejected. Why were they rejected? Have material conditions altered since then, allowing these solutions to become viable options? Technology may have moved on, we may have more money to spend, there may be a wider client base who will purchase the new product.

Finally, there are those ideas which are obviously viable immediately with little or no change. Our group needs to examine them to determine not only their viability but their cost effectiveness in the current situation. If we are hard pressed then a solution which is quick and easy to implement may be the correct one. With fewer constraints it may be rejected in favour of one from the 'usable with change' category which gives us much higher returns.

Although the theory of brainstorming is that it produces a wider range of ideas, Handy reports that they in fact produce fewer ideas than individuals operating on their own. However, because of the pooling of solutions and the sum of critical attention which is devoted to them, the quality of ideas produced by brainstorming is far higher and more beneficial to the organisation.

Buzz groups are formed by the breaking down of larger groups into sub-sections of four or five. This is usually done where the parent group is too large to allow of productive discussion or where it is dysfunctional in some way. For example, the parent group may be dominated by a few loud contributors and the chairperson has difficulty in keeping them under control and enabling contributions by other people. Similarly, the group may be totally unforthcoming, steadfastly refusing to make either comments or suggestions. In these cases the small groups are given individual tasks or topics, which they discuss and report back to the main meeting. Of course the loud and dominant people are carefully allocated to the same group.

Once in the buzz groups it is up to the participants to decide how they will proceed. Some operate as brainstorming sessions, others draw up a formal list of questions that they will seek to answer. Once all groups have gone as far as they can the main meeting is reconvened and their conclusions and deliberations fed back to the other participants. These become the basis of further discussion. With unforthcoming groups the ownership of the new material which they have produced has been shown to sharply increase the amount and level of individual contributions.

2.7.3 Discussion groups

Once all are clear on the content of the information it is the job of the topic leader to define the purpose of the ensuing discussion and to describe its parameters. For example, the discussion may be purely about whether we tender for the Marlingford Hospital contract at all in the light of our experience with Redwood Hospital. Any wider consideration of tendering is outside the scope of our discussion. The purpose may be to make decisions in our own right or to pass on recommendations to higher management.

Once underway the discussion needs to be kept on track, with all contributions limited by the original objectives. It is the chairperson's role to maintain this orientation within the group, indicating that '*we seem to be getting away from the main point*' or that '*Janet's suggestion is a valuable one which we need to consider in the context of the policy review, but we are not yet at that stage.*' This needs to be tempered by a feeling of the group dynamics. For example, after a rather tense exchange or the resolution of a particularly difficult matter most groups indulge in a short period of banter and unrelated comments in order to let off steam and dissolve the tension. A good chairperson allows them to do this but brings them back to the matters in hand as rapidly as possible.

We have already examined the role of individuals within meetings insofar as they concern increasing efficiency and reducing dysfunctional behaviour. The chairperson's job during discussions is to encourage behaviour which increases efficiency and to discourage behaviour which decreases it. Participants who do not join in are encouraged to do so, perhaps with direct questions ('*How do you think that this change would affect your section?*'), whilst pointing out to more vocal or insistent members that other people might wish to be heard ('*Yes, we understand your reservations on this matter, Jack. Now I think that Frank has got a point that he wishes to make*').

Some contributions may just go astray, either because they have not been heard or because they have been deliberately ignored for some reason. If the points are not picked up by other members of the group it is the chairperson's job to do so ('*I'm not sure that we have picked up on Janet's point about the possibility of repeat business as a result of this contract*'). However, where discussion is going well and all are contributing to the best of their ability towards the agreed objectives the chairperson's task is merely to stay above the fray and to let the group operate as a unit.

As in all group situations the chairperson's final task is to sum up the conclusions and to indicate further action. Some words of congratulation and encouragement on how well the group performed its task are always helpful in building and maintaining optimum performance.

2.7.4 Team briefings and project groups

The larger an organisation the more difficult its information flow becomes. Despite news letters, posters and works councils the rumour machine can take over, spreading misinformation and causing disquiet in all parts of the company. As a consequence many companies have decentralised their internal communications, 'cascading' information down the hierarchy in a series of meetings at various levels of the structure.

Where information systems professionals are part of a wider structure, as a specialist DP department for example, they may well be regarded by management as an appropriate production section to handle its own information meetings. In smaller organisations, typical of communications industries, the whole workforce may be small enough to form an effective communications unit. Within formal project methodologies regular meetings of the project group, sometimes with changing personnel, are expected as part of the procedures.

As well as having an information function the team briefing can have the sort of team-building function that we noted earlier in this chapter. We may need to weld together a bunch of individuals so that they are aware of what others are doing and how they each contribute to the common aim. Where people are geographically cut off from one another, by working in different offices or in different buildings, this can be particularly important. Some workers may be cut off from others by the nature of their work. Sales staff, for example, may spend much of their time out of the company giving demonstrations or contacting prospects. The team meeting helps to build up a dialogue between sales and production staff where problems can be aired and suspicions and resentments dissipated.

A good team meeting is therefore as much about attitudes and participation as it is about information flow. The overall objective is to instil loyalty to the team and to the company among all of the participants. How is this to be achieved?

Certainly not by the managing director haranguing the troops or by statements of grand intentions. The ideal meeting is concerned with matters which directly affect the group members and the progress that the group as a whole is making. Programmers will be interested to know about the installation of their new program in the personnel department and any problems that have been encountered by the users as well as the progress being made in tendering for future contracts. Above all, the content of the meeting must be directly relevant to the group.

Team meetings should be an integral part of the team's working life and as such must be held at regular intervals. Depending on the difficulties of bringing the participants together, they should be at no greater than monthly intervals, more often if possible, and integrated into the working day. Project teams and sub-teams may meet more frequently, often devoting Monday mornings to a review of the previous week and mapping out the tasks and timetable for the week ahead. When pressure of work decreases for the team so does the frequency of their meetings.

As frequency is related to need and content, so is the length of the meeting. For a small closely-knit team thirty minutes might be sufficient; for a more diverse group an hour (no longer) would be needed. At all times we must ensure that the participants do not feel that their time is being wasted and they could well be getting on with more important matters.

In any good meeting, information should flow in all directions. As well as information cascading down the organisation the team meeting should operate as a mechanism by which information and opinions are pumped back up the hierarchy. Where participants are merely told what will happen they become dissatisfied and 'switch off'. Participation and the invitation for feedback increases their motivation towards the task, whilst obvious action from others as the result of their feedback confirms the opinion that the meetings are constructive and worthwhile. This calls for honesty on behalf of all parties. Management cannot expect informed comment if they hold back parts of the data which others need to inform their opinions. Conversely, objections and problems which are not articulated cannot be dealt with or eliminated.

To sum up, our team meetings should

- increase information flow up, down and across the organisation
- reduce misunderstanding and rumour
- increase understanding
- provide an opportunity for feedback
- build acceptable attitudes
- increase loyalty
- build an effective team.

In order to do this the team meeting will be:

- as short as possible
- held at regular intervals
- part of the normal work contract
- held in an atmosphere of honesty on all sides
- relevant to the needs of the participants
- seen to be an effective part of the decision making process.

2.8   INDIVIDUALS IN MEETINGS

Larger organisations in particular operate within a system of formal and informal meetings. Information systems professionals also spend much of their working lives in a variety of meetings and team discussions. Information systems users and providers may meet regularly to discuss the quality of the service, maintenance performance and the provision or updating of services. Analysts will spend time in discussion with clients, attempting to discover their wants and needs and discovering what systems might suit them best. Others may be in negotiation with suppliers, determining the price, specification and installation of equipment. Even the freelance computer consultant may be doing all of these things in addition to discussions with the bank manager, accountant and Inland Revenue.

Since it is such an important aspect of working life one might expect some form of training to take place. Sadly this takes the form of 'learning by doing' or 'sitting by Nelly'. It works in the end, but is not terribly efficient in terms of time taken or the number of mistakes made along the way. Let us look at what is happening in meetings and what kind of behaviours you can employ to maximise the benefit you derive from the meetings you attend.

2.8.1   Task roles

Any meeting is a collection of tasks that have to be fulfilled. Given that the joint salaries of those present may run into thousands of pounds per hour the tasks need to be carried out rapidly and effectively. Even if you are carrying out an analysis for a company which has two directors and one secretary, to hold a meeting with the two directors is effectively to engage the main resources of that company for that time. Through your intervention the company has virtually ceased to function.

Read the papers

Your first task is to do your homework. If there are papers attached to the agenda they must be read in advance, annotated if necessary and added to with further information. When meeting with the two directors mentioned above it would be helpful to have researched the sort of market they are operating in well in advance. For example, if they are a printing company some research into specific hardware and software would be helpful so that time is not wasted as they explain what system they currently run or are thinking of purchasing.

Proposing

All participants need to be clear about their tasks and goals. If they are not explicit, then you should make them so. An analyst might begin a meeting with a company with an introduction such as: '*I am here today because you have requested help with your stock handling system. Can you please tell me how your system operates at present?*' We now know the direction we expect the discussion to take. During the course of the meeting further subsidiary goals might be proposed or courses of action laid out.

Within a problem-solving meeting you may find yourself putting forward suggestions which come either from your work or project group or from yourself alone. Where possible you will have prepared a report which will have been circulated to the members of the meeting in advance so that they can read through it and do any extra research they feel is needed or discuss the matter with the people that they represent. As an addition to this information giving and feedback procedure there is nothing to stop you lobbying other members in advance of the meeting. From this you can gauge the amount of support that your proposal has as well as the likely range of objections that it is likely to encounter. If as a result you can eradicate some of the unpopular features or muster better arguments in their defence so much the better.

Lobbying also helps to bolster your performance at the meeting itself. Perhaps as a result of your discussions the chief accountant has decided that your proposal has merit. There will be time for the accounts department to do their own research and to speak in your support when the matter is raised. Catching people by surprise may sometimes stifle overt disagreement but it does not necessarily lead to approval.

Even if you have submitted a detailed written report the chairperson is likely to ask you to introduce your item. You do this as briefly as possible, setting out the main points that you wish to make and leaving out the subsidiary ones. Since you have to be brief it is essential to keep to the point whilst including the benefits of your scheme.

Remember that the 'telling' has been done in the main document: now is your opportunity for 'selling' the scheme. When you have finished, shut up. Let the other members have their say and make their points. A good chairperson will bring these together in a summary and offer them to you for your comments and response. This sort of procedure prevents you becoming too defensive and attempting to dominate the discussion.

Giving and obtaining information

It is unlikely that all participants have equal amounts of data about the subject in hand. If decision making is to be genuine then all information should be freely available. Consequently, it is your duty to make all your data freely available without the need for questioning on behalf of others. Others may not be so forthcoming, so it is also your duty to seek information from them or at least to provide them with the space into which they might interject their contribution. Only as a last resort should you need to demand information, since one would expect other professionals to behave in a sensible and open manner. Withholding data is an attempt at a power-play on behalf of the individual concerned and should not be tolerated by the group as a whole.

Once the data is 'on the table' discussion can begin in earnest. Suggestions can be put forward as to the interpretation of the data and its significance, thus turning it into 'information'. New ideas are put forward and clarified and suggestions made. Without these behaviours the discussion cannot move forward. You may not be particularly good at this, or feel that your level of knowledge or lack of seniority precludes you from making a contribution. On the other hand, you would not have been invited to take part unless it was felt that you had something to offer. In student groups in particular it is common for outward-going students to dominate at the expense of the more introvert.

A good chairperson realises that quiet people also have something to say and will ask them directly for a contribution. In an informal group it may be up to you to force your way gently in to the discussion to put forward your point. As a group member you need to be aware that some of your colleagues have not had their say and ask for silence so that they can be brought forward. Where a quieter colleague has made a point with which you agree, or which you feel deserves greater discussion, you must be prepared to be ready to put yourself forward in defence of its status on the agenda. Comments like '*I don't feel we have properly dealt with Henry's objection to the use of parallel implementation*' helps to re-focus the group onto aspects which seem likely to be ignored.

This is the activity usually referred to as **'bringing in'**. It is an important skill of the chairperson in particular but is also valuable in all participants. The opposite is **'shutting out'**, ignoring or disregarding the contribution of one or more individuals. This is a form of 'scapegoating', of making the assumption that contributions from certain individuals are worthless. If that is true, then the individual should not be in the meeting. On the other hand, it seems hardly credible that someone's every utterance should have absolutely no value at all.

Shutting out does not have to be completely consistent or all-embracing. Individuals with unpopular views can be shut out from discussion on particular topics; personal animosity or jealousy may lead to attempts on behalf of one individual to shut out another. It is the job of the meeting as a whole to prevent this happening. Where the meeting does not do this the chairperson needs to take the matter in hand. Remember that because a view is unpopular does not mean that it is necessarily wrong.

All good listeners try to draft what others say in their own words. In meetings it is important that someone tries to clarify what is being said or proposed into as simple language as possible. Where there is no chairperson this may fall to whoever is taking notes or to the leader of the current discussion. Even if no conclusion is reached it is valuable to **summarise** the points made so that the current state of the discussion may be defined. At this point it should be possible for the group to arrive at a consensus or to agree what data is missing from its deliberations.

2.8.2 Maintenance roles

So far we have dealt with technical aspects of a meeting, those things which have to happen for there to be any meaningful meeting at all. How do the participants inter-react with others?

Encouraging others

We have already noted that some people may not be particularly forthcoming. Drawing information out of others when then may be too reticent to volunteer it themselves is an important skill which the analyst in particular needs to develop. This is best done in an encouraging a way as possible; the subject will be frightened off if it is felt that contributions will be ridiculed or disregarded. The whole mood of the meeting is important here, especially where an analyst is attempting to win the trust of a client.

In such a situation the first move is up to the analyst. How can trust be established in the clients? Animals do this naturally by dropping their guard and making themselves vulnerable; your dog when it rolls over for you to scratch its tummy is also telling you that it has full trust and confidence in you. As part of our complex culture we have developed formal symbolic actions to convey the same thing. Shaking hands, for example, derives from demonstrating that neither party is carrying a weapon.

These are what are known as **'open behaviours'**, which expose the individual who makes them to a certain amount of risk. They are discussed at greater length in the section on assertiveness. An analyst when meeting our two managing directors might begin by admitting to little knowledge of the business in hand and admit to relying on them to provide an insight into its complexities. Besides involving a certain amount of flattery this removes the analyst from the pedestal of outside consultant by admitting to areas of ignorance. (Naturally the analyst would always retain the impression of total competence in the area of information systems!) Such an admission allows room for the directors to feel happy about their own lack of expertise within the systems area and not to become defensive and reserved about it.

A similar open behaviour may be appropriate at internal company meetings. There will be times when you have got it wrong. Objections you have made within the meeting may have been ill-founded or, more importantly, you failed to perform an assigned task adequately. Open behaviour in this case would be to admit your fault, but without being too defensive about it. To pursue such a course facilitates the business in hand by allowing free discourse and in a rational world would be natural at all times.

A related activity which we have already mentioned is that of **'building'**. A builder listens to the propositions that are made and carefully and dispassionately weighs their value. Where necessary the proposals are improved, wherever possible they are supported. The builder is constantly on the lookout for positive features wherever they may be found

The opposite to open behaviour is 'blocking'. **Blocking** is as blunt and solid as it sounds. '*It will never work.*' '*I can't accept that*' '*We don't want any of them computers in here*', are all examples of blocks to discussion, offered with no argument or reasons to support them. They are meant to end discussion, but they rarely do so. The correct response is along the lines of '*Can you tell me why/why not*', repeated in various formulations until a set of reasons or prejudices begin to appear. Blocking proposals are never helpful and only exceptionally do they achieve the blocker's objective.

Blocking is not to be confused with simply **disagreeing**. If all participants started from exactly the same position of knowledge and agreement there would be little point in having a meeting. Your colleagues may feel that, in view of the total fiasco involved in the Redwood Hospital contract, the Marlingford tender should be avoided at all costs. On the other hand, you feel that the experience gained from the mistakes made at Redwood will enable the company to carry through a trouble-free and lucrative contract. Your point of view is put forward politely, carefully dealing with objections from your colleagues. As in any negotiation you take care to deal with policies and not personalities.

Once your comments begin to be directed at personalities your activity becomes one of **attacking**. This is an assault on any front and in its worst form can bring the meeting to a complete standstill, since it is also an attack on the very basis of co-operation and tolerance that allows it to proceed. The other end of this behaviour is being **defensive**, taking any disagreement with your ideas as being an attack on yourself. Such a view makes it impossible to deal rationally with the other person's arguments, often leaving your ideas undefended.

Those on the periphery of the discussion may wish or be asked to **volunteer views and feelings** on the subject. These are in effect feedback to the main participants on how convincing their arguments have been. Although mere feelings may not be thought to have a place in objective decision making they are in fact vitally important. If antipathy and nervousness, for example, are not countered in some way the individual may not take a full and decisive part in implementing any decisions. End users, for example, may have an understandable reaction against having their manual procedures and inter-personal contacts replaced by a machine. Once these feelings have been expressed they can be dealt with and overcome, improving both speed and quality of system implementation.

Behaviour in meetings can be summed up in the following table:

Positive behaviour	Negative behaviour
Proposing	Blocking
Supporting	Dismissing all ideas
Summarising	Failing to bring ideas together
Seeking information	Withdrawing
Giving information	Withholding information
Bringing in	Shutting out
Building	Being defensive
Disagreeing	Attacking
Testing understanding	Assuming perfect understanding
Giving views and feelings	Withholding views

2.9   STUDENT GROUP ASSIGNMENTS

Tutors may set a variety of group assignments, varying in their length and complexity. The one that follows is typical of the sort of assignment that higher-level students may be asked to undertake:

The task. The Head of Department has decreed that the department needs a new information system, linked to the college management information system whilst not being part of it. This will supply the Head of Department, administrative staff and course leaders with the information they need on student applications, take-up of places, existing students, student grades, final grades and an archiving system to help course tutors write references for students who have finished their course and left. The Head of Department would like a feasibility study which will investigate whether this is a practical idea for all or part of his intended system. You will be working in groups of four and the task is to be completed by the end of next week.

Your first task is to get your group together in a suitable setting where the integrity of the group will not be invaded by others. It is possible to do this in pubs or the college canteen but only if you can be sure that all of you can ignore the many distractions and temptations inherent in those places. A quiet room in the hall of residence is more amenable to a working atmosphere. Whether or not you elect a chairperson is up to you. What you must have is a secretary. The secretary records decisions made and notes who is to do what jobs as well as recording the date and place of the next meeting. These all become an appendix to your final report.

For efficient groups such an appendix records how well the process went, how they organised themselves and what alternative plans of action were considered. Sometimes emergencies will occur, such as the Head of Department being called away to an urgent meeting at the time booked by the group for the main interview, and these will need to be carefully recorded for the assessor's benefit. For less efficient groups the secretary's record becomes an insurance policy in case important work does not get done. In any class there will be someone who is ill, who cannot get in to college for some reason that week or who is a total skiver and is relying on the others in the group to do the work. Lecturers take a dim view of the latter in particular. They want those who worked hard at the task to be rewarded for their efforts and those who are 'swinging the lead' to be treated accordingly. If it is clear who was assigned which tasks it becomes much easier for your lecturer to do this.

You will find that your group needs to meet more frequently at the beginning and end of the assignment than in the middle. To start with, you need to be very clear about where you are going, who does which tasks and how quickly. In the early days these will tend to be preparing ideas for discussion, such as setting out an interview schedule, preparing lists of individuals to be interviewed, drawing up a timetable to which the group should adhere. Once these have been agreed upon the group might then break up into sub-sections to gather the relevant data. Experience suggests that even at this stage the group should meet as a whole at least once each day, the earlier the better, in order to discuss progress. Take no notice of the member who 'can't come in because...' That person is contracted to get the college work done and if this involves driving twenty miles just for a half hour meeting, then so be it.

If you have allocated roles and responsibilities in a fair and efficient manner and you have worked solidly and consistently you should arrive at Thursday afternoon with all the information you need. What if you haven't? Do not panic. Ask yourselves some simple questions. What information do we need to find? Is it indispensable? Can we find it in time? Whose job was it to come up with this? Is this a failure of effort or 'just one of those things'?

If the information is indispensable you must go and find it, at first hand if possible but at second hand if necessary. As a last resort confess all to your lecturer and ask for assistance. Where a group member has not produced the appropriate work it is not the job of the rest of the group to do the work themselves. A lecturer may be handed an assignment by a five-person group which contains five carefully labelled sections and a conclusion. Each section is labelled by author; one section is completely blank, giving the information that is needed for assessment purposes.

As far as typing up is concerned it is simpler and fairer to spread the job around rather than to allocate it all to one particular scribe. Each person should complete a section and then they can be file-merged into the completed document. Again the conclusion, the most important part of the document, could be written up in draft form and presented for group discussion at the last meeting. Final printing is always a problem because of pressure on college resources. Remember that everyone else will be trying to get their work printed in time for that four o'clock Friday deadline as well as you. If you can get your printing (or some of it) done in advance or at home that is a great advantage. However you do it, it should all be on the same printer and in the same style and layout in order to ensure consistency.

2.10 CONCLUSION

Whether at work, in your social life or as a student, you will frequently be called upon to work in a group or team. Little is gained from trying to avoid this form of social contact, however uncongenial you may find it. Group work is part of your social and professional world and it is important for you to make yourself as efficient at it as possible. Train yourself to use positive behaviour and to spot and overcome negative behaviour in others. Not only will this improve your efficiency it will also make life a lot pleasanter.

CHAPTER 3
Assertion and negotiation

INTRODUCTION

One of the day-to-day skills that we all need in both our private lives and at work is that of negotiation. In our personal contacts, at meetings, with our closest friends we are constantly trying to improve our lives by arranging the world so that we can derive the greatest benefit from it. At the same time, we are in the company of others with their own attitudes and objectives which may conflict with our own. As well as knowing how to negotiate with those around us we also need to know how to assert our own values and objectives and to claim our own rights as individuals within the limits of the social context in which we find ourselves.

3.1 NEGOTIATION

The highest-profile form of business negotiation is the Advisory Conciliation and Arbitration Service (ACAS). Mass media foster the view of shirtsleeved men in smoke-filled rooms, hunched around a table covered with the remnants of the night's beer and sandwiches. What has that got to do with a small business or a smoothly running data processing department?

ACAS is the tip of a very large iceberg, some would say the tip of the whole of business itself. Unless you have been locked away in your sick bed for the last week, it is likely that you will have negotiated something with someone at least once every day of that week. Did you and your partner organise where you would go for Saturday night out? If you had different ideas you probably discussed the alternatives and came to a decision. Did you have an urgent job on at work that cut across your regular tasks? Then you had to negotiate priorities with your boss to decide which should be done first and to what time scale. You may even have discussed overtime pay if the job spread over in to your own time. Perhaps you bought some goods from a shop and haggled over the price, the delivery date or the length of the warranty.

3.1.1 Defining negotiation

All of these are everyday examples of negotiation. Within business, managers spend around half of their time negotiating with other managers, a smaller but still substantial amount of time negotiating with subordinates and a variable amount, depending on their responsibilities, negotiating with outside buyers, suppliers and consultants. Whenever you want an article or a service that someone else is able to provide you are likely to enter into some form of formal or informal negotiation. Fowler defines negotiation as:

'A process of interaction by which two or more parties who need to be jointly involved in an outcome, but who initially have different objectives, seek by the use of argument and persuasion, to resolve their differences in order to achieve a mutually acceptable solution.'

This is a rather complicated definition, but the issues will become clear if we break it down into its constituent parts.

Two or more parties. Like ballroom dancing, negotiation needs at least two participants but can have any number larger than that. Again like dancing, the larger the number the more difficult it is to achieve a satisfactory outcome, since each party will have its own agenda. One of the problems of British industrial relations in the sixties and seventies was the large number of trades unions that were involved in wage negotiations with company management. Fords at Dagenham, for example, had to deal with eighteen different unions and spent long hours trying to satisfy all of them. German companies, by contrast, only had six national unions to deal with instead of Britain's five hundred, making agreement far easier. When Japanese companies established themselves in Britain they insisted on having single union agreements in their factories, so that they could deal with one single workers' representative.

The larger the number of participants, then, the more complex the process and the less likely that all will achieve their minimum objectives. Always try to keep the number of parties in a negotiation down to two, even if this means splitting your processes into several sub-negotiations with different parties. Only when agreement has been reached separately do you bring everyone together, and not even then if you can avoid it. For example, you may be negotiating with different suppliers for the purchase of mutually compatible hardware. There is no reason why the makers of the keyboards need to know what deal you have struck with the printer suppliers.

Who need to be jointly involved in an outcome. If you can do something on your own you do not need to negotiate. The price of a new laser printer may fall within the area covered by your department's contingency fund over which you have complete control. Since you do not need to consult anybody else you can go ahead and buy it. If, on the other hand, there is a central company fund for such things then you will need to negotiate with others who control that fund or who have some interest in its spending. Your aims can only be achieved through their agreement.

Once you have that agreement you may phone around suppliers to obtain the right equipment at the right price. You need the suppliers to supply the goods, they need your custom to stay in business. Suppliers and buyers need one another to achieve their desired outcomes.

Initially have different objectives. Your objectives are to buy the best quality laser printer for the lowest price. The supplier's objectives are to sell their equipment at the highest price. If the supplier completely meets your requirements everyone is happy and a deal can be struck. More likely this is not so and one or both parties have to modify their aims, perhaps the buyer ending up with the Rolls Royce of all printers but at a price to match. How this comes about we shall consider later.

Seek to resolve differences. In our example of the laser printer it is probably the supplier who is trying hardest to resolve the differences in price and quality. After all, there are plenty of suppliers and the buyer can easily go elsewhere. For the supplier it is important to keep the channels of communication open, since the consequences of failing to do so are that the buyer will go elsewhere and a sale will be lost. The consequences of a breakdown of negotiation are less beneficial than continuing to negotiate so that at least one of the parties is trying very hard to resolve existing differences.

Achieve a mutually acceptable solution. As we shall see later the solution that is arrived at may have little reference to either party's original objectives. What it must do is to fulfil both party's needs. Thus the buyer may buy the top of the range laser printer, despite its price, having been convinced that it will last three times as long as any other whilst giving appreciably better quality reproduction. The supplier may have had to reduce the price a little in order to effect a sale but has a still retained enough of a margin to show a profit. Both parties are happy.

As well as these considerations arising from Fowler's definition of the negotiation process there are others criteria that the partners will need to bear in mind before entering into negotiations with one another:

The other party will possibly modify their position. If your aims are not different their is no need for you to negotiate. A possible partner who refuses to modify their position has made negotiation impossible – you take it or leave it: buying a box of matches in a shop, say, or filling your car with petrol. Only when the other party is likely to make some kind of concession is there the possibility of negotiation. In return for working late tonight your boss might be persuaded to give you Monday morning off or let you add another day to your holiday entitlement.

You expect an acceptable outcome. You may not expect to get everything that you want, but you could be quite happy with any foreseeable compromise. The boss is known not to want to set a precedent about giving formal time off in lieu, so perhaps you won't get that Monday morning off. On the other hand your holiday flight leaves at a ridiculous time and it would be convenient to leave off work early once your desk has been cleared. If this is the outcome, you will have achieved something you want whilst the boss has not conceded publicly held principles.

You have less than a hundred per cent power in the situation. When your power is nil you are not really in a position to negotiate, unless you can convince the other party that you actually have some power that you do not possess. If you are purchasing goods from a supplier who is the only one on the market you have to pay the asking price. Any buyer who negotiates a discount for bulk, cash on delivery or for continuing orders in this situation has done a magnificent job.

Conversely the supplier who makes these concessions has given away profits for no visible present or future return. When your power is one hundred per cent you do not need to negotiate and to do so is to give away your power unnecessarily. There may also be times when you *may not* negotiate. What you are being asked for may be illegal or firmly against company policy. For example, during job interviews your subordinates may campaign against the appointment of a certain candidate on the grounds of sex or race. This is not a negotiable demand, contravening as it does employment law. You need to spell out why it is impossible but you should not offer to enter into discussion on the matter.

For real negotiation to take place, then, the partners must feel that neither of them has all of the power. Naturally this may not be in equal balance. Buyers, for example, are usually held to be in a stronger position than sellers, given an open market. Negotiation involves the bartering of power positions to achieve an acceptable outcome. Thus your boss may theoretically have all the power, since your contract states that you will get jobs done on time *'for the benefit of the company'*. There is no such thing as overtime or time off in lieu. On the other hand you have a certain amount of power which resides in your willingness to do things 'over and above the call of duty' and to put your full effort into everything that you do. A sensible employer will recognise this and will negotiate on that basis, trading off a short-term loss for a long-term gain.

3.1.2 Beginning negotiation

As we saw above, the first thing to establish is whether or not negotiation is necessary. Should law or company policy determine what is to be done a decision can be made immediately. If one party has all the power or is perceived as being totally immovable from their position then there is no point in negotiating, just take the situation as it is or walk away from it. Sometimes you may find yourself defending the indefensible, the position that you have adopted just does not make sense. Give way gracefully, you keep more face by admitting that you are wrong than by entering into a long losing battle.

Next we need to identify clearly who are the involved parties. Sometimes this may not be as easy as it seems. Changing the working hours of the machine room may have an effect on the way that the evening cleaners organise their routine. Demanding personal sign-ons for e-mail may alter the relationship between managers and their secretaries. The purchase of new accounting software, thus changing accounting practises, could have knock-on effects in every section of the organisation. People who are going to be affected by decisions have a right at least to be informed of those decisions. Better still, they should be consulted about them beforehand because *'people are alienated by the giving of decisions without reasons, or with inadequate reasons, because it is treating them as immature, unthinking and unimportant'* (Manchester Open Learning p.29).

Finally, what are the issues involved? At this point we need to make a careful distinction between aims and objectives. **Aims** are our long-term strategy, what the business as a whole is setting out to do. Perhaps we want to expand into other areas in order to diversify and spread the risk of a collapse in our primary market. On the other hand we may be looking to protect our sources of supply so that we are always in a position to fulfil orders quickly.

Objectives are the means that we use to achieve our aims. They are therefore both short term and flexible, to be dispensed with once they prove to be unhelpful. Let us look at the aims set out above and construct a set of objectives to achieve them.

Aim: *To protect sources of supply.*

Objectives: *1) Buy in to primary producers of raw materials.*
2) Control the five companies which are our biggest suppliers.
3) Buy out the maintenance and software company which is responsible for our information technology needs.
4) 'Lock in' as many suppliers as possible to preferential supply contracts.

This is a very expensive set of objectives, so expensive that the company could bankrupt itself in achieving them. Nevertheless, it proceeds with them since it can as yet see no alternatives. The primary producers all turn out to be state-controlled industries which cannot be purchased or controlled, so instead firm contracts are negotiated with them for long-term supplies at preferential rates.

Of the five company suppliers, three are owned by large conglomerates. The other two are purchased at a realistic price, giving the company a certain amount of security in that area. Investigation of the maintenance and software company reveals that the price they are demanding for its purchase is far too high and that it would be cheaper for the company to have a small information systems section of its own. It therefore drops this objective completely and replaces it with another.

Some suppliers are happy to be locked in, since this gives them guaranteed regular sales. Those that are not happy we replace with alternatives which will accept our contracts.

What has happened to our objectives?

1) has been abandoned, but been replaced by an acceptable alternative.
2) has been partially achieved, improving the existing situation.
3) has been abandoned and replaced with a cheaper alternative
4) has been partly achieved and can be fully achieved in the long run.

What is more important than what has happened to individual objectives is that our *aim* has been more or less achieved and at a lower cost than we thought possible. We have been flexible with our objectives as long as that flexibility allowed for greater efficiency or lower cost. Our approach has been like that of a motorist who has driven from London to Glasgow, listening to traffic reports on the radio and quite happy to take detours around areas of congestion as long as the destination is arrived at in the end. It is important to remember that:

- Aims are more important than objectives
- There may be alternatives which are better than the objectives that we have defined
- We should not become immovably attached to our objectives.

3.1.3 Structuring objectives

All the same we do need to have practical staging posts to help us along the negotiating route. The best way of doing this is by setting out our objectives in the negotiation in a structured manner.

Our first set of objectives is the **ideal** outcome. This is what is sometimes derisively called a 'wish list', all those things that we would like to have if our dreams or fantasies were to come true. Obviously this is tempered by the context of the situation, we cannot wish for things that it is not in our partner's power to supply or for things which would mean their total capitulation. We also expect that not all of them will be achieved, we know that in the real world we will have to trade off some in order to achieve others. Nevertheless we write them down clearly so that we know what we would like to achieve and what bargaining counters we have for later negotiation. Research suggests that having high objectives tends to lead to the achievement of high results whilst having low objectives results in low results.

These ideal outcomes can be further broken down into **main objectives** and **secondary objectives**. Main objectives are those which have the highest priority, probably the ones that will bring greatest benefit to the individual or the organisation. These are the bread and butter of the negotiation, perhaps the reason why we have entered the process in the first place. We would need some very valuable concessions from the other party if we are to trade these away. The secondary objectives are the jam on the bread, the optional extras which increase the value of the agreement. These are not as important to us and are more likely to be used as bargaining positions.

Even if we do nothing else, we must establish our **lowest possible position**, those things that we must get in order to have produced added value for our position. Usually this is referred to as '**the bottom line**', the level below which any offer is totally unacceptable. There is a temptation to feel that the bottom line is wholly about money and is completely inflexible. In fact it is often about other things and varies with the changing context. Within many organisations, including many British and American ones, the one thing that a manager may not do is to lose face. The bottom line for these managers may be the **appearance** of a reasonable agreement, even if, in effect, the negotiations have ended in defeat. Countries and companies involved in high-level negotiation may be more interested in security and power than in immediate prosperity.

Similarly, the bottom line can move as new events unfold. A wage negotiator may be asking for a rise of fifteen per cent, with a bottom line of ten per cent. As negotiations begin the government issues guidance on pay rises stating that there is no reason for any increases in income whatsoever. The company also publishes its figures for the previous year, demonstrating that its profits were halved over that period. Conditions of negotiation have changed and the negotiator's bottom line must change with them; perhaps now the figure is revised to equal cost inflation over the previous year.

There are some situations where the bottom line is quantifiable in financial terms. We can perform a cost benefit analysis and state where agreement ceases to be cost effective. In most negotiations, however, estimates of the bottom line are wholly or partly subjective. Take a case where the company is reducing staff. As the data processing manager you are discussing with senior management how many of your staff are to go. What is your bottom line to be? Is it reductions to the level at which you think you can still function as a department? Is it to the level where you can still justify being a department at all, even if you do not function properly? Or the level at which you personally still have a job? These positions have financial implications, but their main thrust is subjective, how far you are prepared to go to protect your department and the people in it.

Our objectives can be set out diagrammaticaly as a 'stairway to heaven':

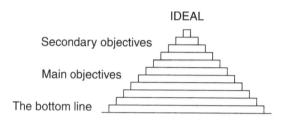

The space between the bottom line and our ideal is the area that we have for manoeuvre, the parts that we can trade off in order that an agreement can be reached.

3.1.4 Alternatives to agreement

The establishment of a bottom line is to make the statement '*I will not reach an agreement that does not give me at least this much*'. Are we sure that this is a sustainable position? If an agreement is not reached, what are our alternatives courses of action?

If we are buying equipment we may be able to go to other dealers (are they cheaper, do they have a better product, are they reliable?). When selling we have to balance the consequences of not making a sale now against the disadvantages of making a sale at any price, even below the basic profit margin. On the other hand, the sale may keep us in business for a few more months by improving our cash flow. Are there competitors who can fill our shoes with our partners just as well? Should we therefore take a loss now in order to tie our partners in over the longer term or can we afford to wait?

The alternatives need to be considered and compared to our bottom line. If the alternative to not reaching an agreement is that we go out of business then this is *worse* than our bottom line position and means that we must reach an agreement at almost any cost, throwing over our basic objectives. Should the alternatives give us a better return in some way, we retain goods that we can easily sell elsewhere for a higher profit than we are being offered, the alternatives are *better* than our bottom line and we can happily accept the consequences of a failure to reach agreement. Alternatives which are *equal* to our bottom line need to be evaluated carefully before being accepted as viable alternatives.

Finally, before formally entering into the negotiating process we need to consider what the *worst* possible outcome might be. By negotiating, we could find that we have less than we had before or less than we would have had should we not have negotiated. Workers in companies that have financial difficulties may find themselves in this sort of position. Should they negotiate on pay and conditions, in the knowledge that they may end up with less than they started with, or should they refuse to negotiate in order to hold on to what they have? If the worst case is that the company goes bankrupt and they all lose their jobs, is negotiation likely to improve or to worsen their situation? Every situation has its own dynamic, but as Godefroy and Robert advise '*it is better not to negotiate at all than to come to a badly negotiated agreement.*'

Although it has already been pointed out that financial objectives are not the only ones, it may do a lot of good to cost out all alternatives. This gives at least some objective assessment of their desirability and allows negotiators room for manoeuvre. Once involved in hard bargaining with the other party it helps to know what the financial consequences of all alternative solutions will be, including failure to reach any agreement at all.

3.1.5 The other party

The basis for a successful negotiation is that both parties are better off after its conclusion than they were before. You may be better off because you now have a high quality laser printer, producing better copy, giving your company a better image and improving sales. The suppliers have made a profit. As we have seen, this calls for a co-operative approach where gains are made by all. Normally this is referred to as a **win-win** situation.

To explain this better, let us take the example of the family fighting about who makes Sunday dinner.

Case 1: The fight goes on so long that dinner time is long past and there is no time to cook or eat the food. Everybody loses. This is a **lose-lose** situation.

Case 2: Somebody finally gives in and makes the whole lot. The cook has lost, but everybody else wins, since they get their meal. This is a **win-lose** situation.

Case 3: The chores are shared out equally with no consideration for preference or expertise. The family gets its meal, but the quality is variable. A **draw**.

Case 4: Everyone picks their favourite jobs or the ones they are best at. Others are shared equally. The result is a four course meal of outstanding quality. A **win-win** situation.

Put another way, the first three cases depend on how the cake is divided up. The win-win outcome depends on being able to enlarge the size of the cake.

Obviously it would help in achieving such an outcome if we could determine the position of the other party in advance. What are their aims and objectives? What power do they have to enforce them?

Sometimes you can answer these questions by simple research. Look up the company in business guides, look through trade literature for references to their past and recent performance, ring up friends who might have dealt with them recently and find out what they know. Even if you do not have access to firm information try and put yourself in the other's position. If you were negotiating for company X, what would your overall aims be? Given those aims, what objectives can you write down that would achieve them? What sort of things would you want and how would you go about achieving them? Given this hypothetical information, what would you establish as your bottom line?

Such a procedure has been likened to a chess player. A good chess player thinks out the opponent's moves in advance, determining what responses will be to given situations and countering them before they even happen. Successful negotiators have laid out their partner's perceived position in advance, with all the arguments that they might use and all the arguments available to counter them. Of course you will rarely cover all of the ground, any more than the chess player will cover every conceivable move. What you are doing is reducing the number of uncomfortable surprises and thus the amount of unplanned moves that you need to make on your own behalf.

We have already noted that the bottom line is not necessarily arrived at purely on the basis of objective considerations such as financial gain. This is particularly true when personalities and power structures are involved rather than pure commerce. Where the bottom line is subjective it becomes far more difficult to identify your partner's position. In personal counselling this is described by the phrase '*the presenting problem is not necessarily the real problem*'.

Take, for example, a small local supplier with a reputation for reliability and quality. These, as well as the nearby location, are factors that make dealing with them highly attractive to your firm. The small supplier may seem unwilling to sell to you at the price you suggest despite concessions you have made, allowing for a sizeable profit. Whatever you suggest the other party seems less and less interested in making a deal, yet they keep quoting price as the determining factor. Since their problem obviously is not price, although they may even believe this themselves, it may be something else. Whilst they are talking you need to listen to the '*music of the message*'; what are they really saying?

In fact the company is worried by the very size of your deal. They see that they will come to depend on you as the main purchaser and be placed in an impossible situation if you choose to withdraw your custom or leave the market altogether. Although they like the present security that your deal brings they are frightened of its longer-term implications. Their bottom line is not price at all, it is long-term survival and it is up to you to spot this before negotiations run into a brick wall.

Where the chess analogy breaks down is that, unlike chess, two negotiators can both win. To facilitate that process your analysis should also take account of areas where you seem to have identical interests or where you can generate solutions which are good for you but also have benefits for your partner. This may involve the suggestion of alternatives which they have not considered or an alteration in your own bargaining position. If you can identify where the interests of your partner lie you have a better chance of fulfilling them and your own as well.

3.1.6 Preparing your position

Now that you have a clear idea of your own aims and objectives and a rather more fuzzy view of those of your partner you are in a position to answer certain basic questions:

- what is the negotiation about?
- what are the different viewpoints?
- where are the areas of agreement?
- where are the areas of disagreement?
- what problems can we foresee?
- what information do we have?
- how can I strengthen my position?

These all come down to the question of information. We may not be able to generate more than vague replies to our concerns about the other party, but we ought to be able to gather full information about our own case. If we are selling a computer system to a client we need to know precisely its range of capabilities and its limitations. We also need to be clear about how quickly it can be installed and what additional costs are associated with installation, training and the adaptation of software.

Perhaps you have a good case; how do you prove it? Prepare the arguments that you find most convincing well in advance and rehearse them thoroughly. Like the chess player you should have your main strategy worked out in this respect with all the counter-moves that you expect fully rehearsed and accounted for. More important is your evidence. Anyone can claim that their system is the best and the fastest, but does it work in practise? You need some kind of proof that yours can do the job. This may take the form of a demonstration, which you need to set up carefully well in advance.

Even then, a demonstration is not real life and you may need more active proof. Sometimes you may be able to arrange for your partners to visit an installation where your product is actually in use, and in chapter six you will come across an example of a company which sold its system by doing exactly that. Where this is not feasible you may have paper documentation, letters from satisfied customers, photographs of the system in action, press reports of your successful installation. The more objective, independent and supportive your evidence is the better.

Since information is power, you also need to seek other information about yourself and your case. Carry out a **SWOT** analysis (strengths, weaknesses, opportunities and threats) using the information that you have to hand, plus any other information you may be able to glean as you go along. Your **strengths** have already been dealt with, they are the arguments that you have in favour of your case plus the documentation that you can bring to bear.

Your **weaknesses** may be personal to you or your team or they may be inherent in your case. Whatever they are, they need to be faced and contingency plans drawn up. Your system may be creaking at the limits of its capabilities given the amount of data your partner is talking about. Are there technical ways of overcoming this problem? Is the other party perhaps overstating the real requirements, which can be fulfilled by a later update if and when the situation arises? You do not want to have invested several days in expensive negotiation only to be blown out of the water by a single awkward question.

Opportunities take the form of what you expect to get out of the negotiation, your aims and objectives plus any incidental benefits that you may gain. For example, negotiating the sale of this system may well put you in a good position with your boss for negotiating a substantial pay rise at a later date. As far as the company is concerned, selling to this client may make it easier to sell the system to others.

Threats may arise from failure to meet a negotiated agreement or from entering into one that has been poorly thought out. In some cases there may be threats involved in the very act of negotiation itself. An insecure manager may find that staff have undermined his position of authority, even though he has still managed to achieve many of his stated objectives. An important question to ask is '*what damage can the other party do to us?*'

3.1.7 The two teams

Individual negotiations are part of everyday business life. Two managers meet over a cup of coffee and work out how their two departments can work together to solve a mutual problem. Let us leave these lower-level problems for a while and concentrate on more formal negotiations, like the purchase of a computer system, which involve large sums of money and a certain amount of technical expertise.

In such a case we are best advised to put together a team rather than to leave everything to one individual. It is unlikely that one individual will have both the expertise in negotiation and the expert knowledge of the area in question. Carrying out the necessary research and preparation tasks could be slow and onerous. Moreover, one person cannot perform at peak efficiency for extended periods; there will be times when alertness decreases or attention wanders.

What is needed is a team that can operate in such a manner that its whole is greater than its parts. As far as preparation goes, the task can be speeded up by having several people researching different areas at the same time. When they come together they can pool their collective wisdom, generating a range of ideas and propose alternative solutions and strategies. However, we have already seen that such advantages are negated if the team becomes too large and experience suggests that between three and five people is the optimum number for an effective negotiating team.

Where we have several team members we can expect that some of them are alert at all times, not allowing anything to pass unexpectedly or without full examination. Apart from areas of expertise, roles can be varied so that members do not become too stale or their weaknesses too apparent to the other side. One role that can be usefully allocated is that of observer, following the actions and non-verbal communication of the other team. Did a proposal cause consternation or discussion? Did the DP manager sigh when the limits of the proposed system were set out by the team leader? Are there some items which are always read from a standard sheet, suggesting that the members are not in control of this information or that it is being imposed from above?

Most teams operate on the basis of ensuring that at least one expert in the subject, preferably more, is backed by an expert negotiator. In the case of selling our computer system we would expect to be able to call on the expertise of members of the development team, who know all about its capabilities. Perhaps, if we are using the system ourselves, we would be able to involve someone whose job it is to work with the system on a daily basis. The other members of the team would be included through the allocated tasks which lead to the building up of a complete information picture.

One problem that may arise is with the attitude of team members to the very act of negotiation itself. As a sub-set of the whole areas of meetings, negotiation suffers from the same range of inherited attitudes: it takes too long, nothing effective comes out of it anyway, the results are often a camel rather than a horse, and so on. Unless you are setting out on a process of staff development and are prepared to accept the consequences you do not want somebody on your team who has a negative attitude to negotiating or who has a negative attitude towards the other party. Wage negotiations, for example, are notorious for a lack of trust and respect between the partners which often leads to needless conflict.

Within the team it is essential that all members should be aware of the issues at stake and fully in control of all relevant information. The display of ignorance by a team member at a crucial point could be devastating, as could a lack of awareness of how one area of information fits into another or into the general plan. Team members also need to be aware of the general strategy to be employed, including when to remain silent. Usually only the team leader is empowered to make any concessions or produce new approaches.

Logically we would expect the other team to be constructed in a similar manner, but we should be wary of assuming too much in this respect. What we need to know from the outset is how much actual power the team has, can it make a final decision? If it cannot, we need to know exactly what its powers and responsibilities are. Even teams with quite extensive powers may need to have their final decisions ratified by other parties, perhaps the managing director, the DP manager or the company accountant. Who these parties are, whether their approval is real or merely procedural and what time scale they may involve is important information that we need before negotiation can properly begin.

Before we leave the question of team formation there is one specialist area that needs to be mentioned. This is the use of representatives to negotiate for individuals or companies. Such a situation is common in industrial relations where trade union members elect or appoint representatives to do their bargaining for them. Some companies employ lawyers in specific situations to represent their interests and to draw up legally binding forms of agreement. Within the information systems world it is quite common for consultants to negotiate on behalf of clients, either alone or as part of a company team, for the supply of hardware and software.

One of the advantages of using a representative is that such a person is detached and may be more objective than the client. Where objectives have become too personal and subjective it is easier for a representative to realise this and to re-order priorities. In the case of a trade union, of course, it would be impractical to have every union member involved directly in the negotiations themselves. Representatives can also be in a better position to float alternative courses of action. '*What if I were to suggest to my client that...*' is a useful bargaining counter to find out whether the other side would be interested in exchanging concessions or moving into alternative areas. Where the client is bargaining directly such a move may be felt to be too dangerous and constitute a firm proposal or weakening of position. The disadvantage of using a representative is that their detachment may mean that they do not fight quite as hard for your interests as you would do yourself, although there are legal safeguards for companies, involving care and professional integrity

3.2 PERSONAL NEGOTIATING SKILLS

Nobody is perfect, but we all have skills upon which we can build and imperfections which we can do our best to hide. The perfect negotiator, besides being a quick and decisive thinker, is also an excellent communicator and works hard to improve the necessary skills. These can be broken down into ten key areas.

1 Thorough preparation

A good negotiator prepares thoroughly, not skimping on any task or area. The case of both parties will have been closely analysed, objectives produced, prioritised and compared and 'worst case' outcomes considered. Opening moves and possible concessions will have been worked out as well as the other party's strategy considered. There is no substitute for hard work, but experience and creativity are added advantages.

2 Knowledge of the subject and processes in hand

Someone at least in the team needs to be a subject expert, even if this means hiring one in for the occasion. However, all team members need to become temporary experts, as far as it lies in their power, of the general area under discussion. This means the sharing of information and careful research and study by all team members. Facts have to be checked before negotiations begin and, if there is any doubt, checked again during adjournments in the proceedings.

All members of the team also need to be aware of the form that the negotiations will take and who has been allocated which roles. They should have analysed their own strengths and weaknesses and taken steps to develop their strengths and to hide their weaknesses within the boundaries of the role they are undertaking. The team leader must be clearly in authority and in control both of the team and of the progress of the negotiations themselves.

3 Thinks clearly and rapidly

A good negotiator is able to sum up the contributions of others within the framework of the negotiations and to fit them into a consistent pattern. This is a skill which can be developed with practice and hard work. Planning and preparation lay out the main areas that are likely to come up, together with the alternatives for action. Contributions from others will usually fit into this framework. Again we can use the chess player analogy, where top class players have memorised as many as the first twenty or thirty moves of past games which involve their favourite openings, plus having analysed alternatives. A similar amount of preparation means that you are filing contributions into categories rather than madly trying to assess their importance.

At some point, though, you will be confronted by something you had not expected and will need to respond to it. With a team approach this is less of a problem. One member of the team will need to respond in some manner, often by '*speaking much but saying nothing*' whilst the others consider the position. Having your ideas and objectives set out before you helps enormously since you do not need to juggle a whole range of variables at the same time. Like a mathematician you will work out your solution logically on paper and arrive at an objective answer. Problem solving is more often about having a clear view of the issues set out in a clear and logical pattern than it is about leaps of creativity.

Also like a mathematician, you will find that with experience you can solve common problems quickly and easily in your head. This is a useful facility to develop, since a rapid response puts the onus back on to the other party, perhaps more quickly than they would like. However, remember that accuracy is more important than speed and if you cannot manage an immediate response there is always the possibility of an adjournment.

4 Expresses thoughts clearly

Again, preparation is the key. Whether you are being asked to outline a topic or the team's position in a particular area you should have carefully prepared what you are going to say, in the same way that you would have prepared a formal business presentation. Indeed, some negotiating procedures may involve the information systems professional making such a full presentation.

Where you are required to respond 'off the cuff' you still have to proceed in the same manner, except that you have only a few seconds in which to prepare. Take your time. Everyone is waiting for you and nothing can happen until you respond. Use this time to go rapidly through basic procedures for making a presentation:

- gather your information
- order your information
- make notes
- consider your audience
- keep your language simple.

Your information, of course, has already been well prepared in advance and you are in total control of it. The pause has enabled you to call it to mind and to order it by jotting down some key words on the pad in front of you. There may even be time to change the running order of your delivery by numbering them slightly differently to the order in which you noted them down. Now, explain each one in turn, using simple, straightforward sentences.

5 A good listener

We have already spent some time enumerating the qualities of a good listener and why listening is so important. In a formal interchange such as negotiation, where you may spend more than half of the time listening to other people and your response is structured by what they say, listening is obviously a primary skill. Manchester Open Learning suggest the following check list for negotiators. Are you:

- Looking interested in what the other person is saying, using supportive body language and facial expressions?
- Using questions to elucidate information and to demonstrate that you have been following the other person's argument?
- Staying on track by keeping concentration and not being distracted by other stimuli?
- Testing your understanding by 'feeding back' test statements to the other person?
- Constantly evaluating the message, perhaps by comparing it against your prepared documentation?
- Neutralising your own feelings, both in respect of the sender of the message and the form of the message itself, in order to minimise subjectivity?

6 Displays sound judgement

Sound judgement is a difficult concept to define. It is more than just getting the right answers, since they can be arrived at by luck or guesswork. Fowler perhaps comes closest to a good definition, by opting for a description of the processes that it involves rather than the outcomes. He describes sound judgement as being the result of a series of analytic skills *similar to those of the management consultant or business analyst in the writing of a complex report in which the key elements of a situation are identified, followed by the pros and cons of alternative actions, leading to a preferred and costed solution.*

Fowler goes on to enumerate the skills that he regards as important, some of which we have already examined. First, the negotiator needs to identify which issues are central and which are merely peripheral, using this judgement to draw up a set of aims and objectives. Next, aids to achieving the objectives are identified, along with possible barriers which may be encountered and alternative approaches evolved to deal with these variables. All available data is gathered and contingency plans are made based on this data. This is, of course, an iterative process which continues until a final judgement has been reached based on all available data. Anyone who has followed this approach may not be right every time but they should show a significant success rate.

7 Honesty

This may seem a peculiar virtue to cite in a situation where deviousness is at least sometimes an integral part. However, we must remember that negotiation is a collaborative venture and there must always be a feeling between the two parties that they can place a certain amount of trust in one another. Playing poker is a good example in this case. We would not expect a poker player to tell us what cards he holds or how high he is likely to go in the bidding. Our opponents will hold out for the best possible result and try to avoid letting us know if they are bluffing or not. This is all part of the game and we expect it. What we will not tolerate is downright cheating, palming cards or marking the deck. Similarly, in negotiations we expect the other party to do everything they can to improve their interests but we would expect them to fall short of straight dishonesty.

Dishonesty is a problem not so much in current negotiations, unless it is discovered before their final conclusion, but in subsequent events. The grapevine is a powerful communications medium and word travels quickly within business circles. A company which cannot be trusted is one that people do not want to do business with. Your aim is to conclude the current negotiations to the satisfaction of all whilst creating a lasting good impression of someone that the other party will want to do business with on a subsequent occasion.

Not that the good negotiator is open all of the time and gives out information on demand, that would be giving away important bargaining power. Instead, the trick is to reveal only as much as is necessary and to conceal the rest without actually lying, to be *'economical with the truth.'* Some of the information that is revealed during negotiations may be disclosed 'in confidence' and this confidence must be respected if your partner is to feel confident of doing business with you again.

8 Persuasive

You may have the best possible case, but can you convince your partner of it? Your knowledge of the subject, the clarity with which you express yourself and the processes you use to form your judgements all come together at this point. The result is a rational position which needs to be set out to the listening public. We will look at some specific strategies for gaining agreement a little later, but for now it suffices to say that you will be more persuasive if your arguments are:

- relevant
- clear
- consistent
- objective
- factual
- applicable to the same events in different contexts.

Only the last needs any extra explanation. Arguments are more persuasive if they can be seen to be more generally applicable. These carry the overtones of scientific laws, which are felt to be both factual and objective, and carry your argument on to a higher plane than the material and the mundane.

9 Patient

Don't rush! The old proverb *'marry in haste, repent at leisure'* applies just as well to negotiation. When a proposal is made, take time to study it. If necessary, ask for an adjournment so that it can be studied at leisure by the whole team and possibly costed out. Similarly, allow your partners time to review proposals that you have made to them, especially if you think that they will find them uncongenial. People need time to allow the unacceptable to become familiar. Nor do they like being rushed into a decision, they may feel flustered and resentful and either not sign or become more truculent in the next phase of negotiation.

Where you have a tight timetable for a successful conclusion, do not reveal it to your partner. Stay relaxed and allow matters to take their course as if you had all the time in the world. Once you reveal your time difficulties you lay yourself open to being pressurised by the other party refusing to make an agreement until right up against the deadline, when you may be forced to make excessive concessions.

10 Assertive and decisive at key moments

We have already looked at assertive behaviour and how it differs from aggression. Being assertive is not appropriate at every stage of negotiation, since for much of the time we are seeking information and trying to arrive at agreement and compromise. However, there may be times when assertiveness is appropriate, either with members of the other team or even with members of one's own. The good negotiator recognises these times and does not shrink from them.

Similarly, there are points in discussions when decisiveness is needed, for example when your partners are making an offer that is well below your bottom line, or when the moment has come to decide that this is the best deal that your side is going to get. Sometimes it is as difficult to say 'yes' as it is to say 'no'. A good negotiator conquers this fear without being too headstrong or too dogmatic.

3.3 FORMAL NEGOTIATING PROCESSES

Negotiation begins from the very first moment of contact with your partner, be it an informal telephone call requesting an outline quotation or a formal handshake in a conference room. Everything that you do must be geared to establishing confidence and an air of working trust within a businesslike atmosphere. Remember that at this stage you are selling yourself and your company's image as much as its products or services.

As in most other kinds of meetings it is helpful to start with a written formal agenda. By convention this is usually drawn up by the hosts or the presenting party but there is nothing to prevent its joint creation by representatives before the meeting or for the visiting party to present their own version. Whoever does this, it is important that you study the agenda carefully first before the meeting begins in order to identify items that have been missed out or ones that are down for discussion that you regard as entirely non-negotiable.

Agenda items can be arranged in a variety of ways according to preference. Perhaps the most difficult to handle is putting the most important items first. This moves discussion straight in to the core of the problem without the distractions of extraneous detail. Once agreement has been reached on the essential items the lesser ones can be picked over at leisure, perhaps even at a lower managerial level. The problem with such an approach is that it may never actually get going, the principal items seeming so huge and insurmountable to the participants that they can make no progress with them.

Another approach is to group together areas where there seems to be agreement and to deal with these first. This allows for a gentle and friendly beginning to the meeting, with the establishment of a working relationship before the hard bargaining begins. Whatever happens subsequently at least some parts of the agenda will have been agreed.

Alternatively matters can be grouped purely by topic, so that they may appear as 'Price', 'Installation', 'Specifications', 'Training' and so on. The attraction of this method is that the areas can be dealt with in isolation, perhaps using a variety of experts who need only attend that part of the meeting. Once one area is safely tucked away work can begin on the next, like writing a modular program. Unfortunately business matters are not that simple. All of the items we used as examples are interrelated and affect one another. Changes in the specification may affect the installation, price and training. Classifying agenda items by topic is not the simple solution that it appears.

Finally, the agenda can be sorted in such a way as to order it by likelihood of agreement, the most likely first, the next second and so on. Again this has the advantage of letting the negotiators into the process gently but may lead to a rather disordered and piecemeal discussion. The first item may be about specifications, the second about installation and the third back to specification again. To get over this a compromise may be established to combine ease of agreement with an amended topic schedule.

How the meeting actually proceeds depends on factors such as the preferences of the chairperson or organiser, legal demands if appropriate, the way meetings have been conducted by the parties in the past, recent contacts between the parties and so on. For example, discussions between a dissatisfied worker and the personnel officer may progress from friendly chats in the canteen to more serious negotiations in the personnel officer's office, to negotiations with a union representative present, up to a full-blown disputes tribunal.

Whatever the form of the meeting it is up to the chairperson or host to state the reasons for the meeting and to outline such facts as might reasonably be assumed to be agreed. As well as setting the tone this also helps to establish that the participants are talking a 'common language' both in terms of what they expect the meeting to achieve and the language that they are using to describe it. We have already noted that the language of information systems, or personnel management for that matter, is not necessarily the language that will be employed or understood by those with whom you will be dealing.

The preliminary period also allows the representatives to establish their respective powers and levels of responsibilities, which will in turn affect the status of the meeting. Representatives who only have the power to gather information and to observe, such as users being given a demonstration of a new piece of software, will obviously be involved in different kinds and levels of discussion to the management team at a subsequent meeting who have the power to make the purchase.

However the process is conducted it can only be defined as negotiation if both parties are ready to make concessions willingly. Moreover, they should expect that those concessions would be fair and equal according to the aims of each. Negotiation usually progresses in six clear stages:

1. Defining of the issues
2. Defining initial positions
3. Presenting the arguments
4. Exploring the possibilities
5. Defining proposals
6. Defining an unambiguous agreement.

3.4 WORKING TOGETHER

Now that discussions have begun it is important that a member of the team keeps a record of what is said, even if there is a formal system of recording the minutes. Making your own notes keeps you in control of vital information and helps with your decision making processes. Where minutes are not kept you also need to make sure that areas of agreement have been properly recorded to prevent them being over-looked later. Taking notes is also an aid to concentration and ensures that you are listening actively.

Both parties need to begin by clarifying objectives: what do they see as the problem in hand and what do they see as possible solutions? Where information is lacking or is unclear you need to ask detailed questions, establishing your understanding by confirmatory questioning such as: '*Am I right in thinking that what you feel you need is...?*' Assess whether non-negotiable issues, such as delivery dates, are really that immovable. Some deadlines turn out to be wishful thinking rather than firm dates; often the builders have not finished with the new office block in time for the installation date that has been set.

With points of agreement established somebody has to make the first move towards compromise. Do you wish to be proactive, to take the initiative, or to be reactive, to respond to the actions of others? The proactive negotiator again takes a clue from chess, where it is generally accepted that to be white and to make the first move is to have an advantage since white is always one move ahead. Similarly, in negotiations to make the first move is to begin to define the parameters that will bind the discussion, particularly in the definition of the upper limits. It also signals to your partner that you have enough mutual trust to risk making the first proposal.

Although the advantages of this approach are clear, there are some pitfalls. Your position must be clearly worked out in advance or you risk pitching your offer at the wrong level; too low and the deal is to your detriment, too high and your partner may just break off negotiations in disgust. Also, there are expert defensive players who specialise in playing black, teams who are renowned for hitting on the break, and this applies equally to negotiating teams. However, unless you come across one of these it is to your advantage to make the first move.

During the ensuing discussions you should be looking to expose flaws in the argument or to reveal errors of fact. How you do this is vital to the relationship with your partner. Your objective is to maintain a spirit of co-operation, not one of antagonism and polarisation of views. Concentrate on the arguments rather than the personalities, the people will still be there long after the arguments have been discarded. Egoism and point scoring have nothing to do with the issues at hand.

As for your own arguments, it is vital to make it clear what the benefits are for your partner, rather than for yourself. Only introduce new issues if they are helpful to the matter in hand, otherwise they can be left until later in the meeting or for general discussions afterwards. In the same way that you used questions to make sure that you understood your partner's position you need to ensure that they understand your proposals. Append brief summaries to your suggestions ('*briefly to recap on what I am suggesting*') to clarify the main points of the proposal. Naturally you will expect to be asked check questions in turn.

The formulation of any proposal that you make should make it clear that it is the result of listening to your partner. Making them sound like the other person's proposals is even better: '*From what Mr. Jones has been saying on delivery dates we could perhaps agree to tie them to the architect's final approval of the building work. I would like to make a formal proposal to that effect to the meeting.*' This isn't my suggestion at all, it comes from your side! Godefroy points out that '*the feeling of participation in formulating a proposal is the single most important factor when the time comes to accept or reject a proposal.*'

3.5 MOVING TOWARDS AN AGREEMENT

At all times we need to bear in mind the hidden agenda of any negotiation process, the tacit agreement between the parties that they will both be able to leave the negotiating table with their minimum requirements satisfied, and more than those if possible. While strengthening your own case you should still be seeking common ground and working towards that final agreement.

Much of the time will be spent listening rather than talking. You are trying to find links and to make suggestions that will aid progress, sending verbal and non-verbal signals that are entirely positive. Listen particularly for verbal messages that hint at subtleties of meaning or changes in position. Has the formulation moved from '*We cannot consider this proposal*' to '*We cannot consider this proposal* **at this time.**'? If so, this proposal can be left on the table until other matters have been dealt with and discussed later.

In negotiation we are all the time looking for possibility of movement ourselves and to encourage movement in the other party. Some people find it difficult to be seen to change their mind or their position, they see it as a sign of weakness and they need to be helped over this barrier. At any point proposals and agreements have to be phrased in such a way as to avoid loss of face by either party. Providing concessions, however minor or enforced, allows the other person to walk away from the table with dignity. So, instead of telling your partner '*Now you have given in over the price we can move on to delivery and installation*' you could reformulate your sentence as '*Thank you for being so helpful over the question of price; I'm sure that we can do everything to accommodate you when it comes to delivery and installation.*'

The first sentence tells everyone that your partner has capitulated, the second says that an agreed solution has been reached and that concessions will be made in return on other matters. In the first sentence you are gloating and scoring points; in the second you are keeping negotiations open with a willing partner. Your public manner will help your partner to support agreements that might be some way from the ideal.

Introducing suggestions themselves is best done through the use of hypotheticals such as '*Have you thought about....*', '*Without commitment, what if we were to suggest...*' or '*Suppose we were to suggest...*' At this stage it is best to avoid being too specific in order to get broad agreement to the proposal rather than to get bogged down in specifics. Thus: '*Could you concertina the time you will need for installation, without increasing the cost, if we were to be able to move delivery time back a short while?*'

Notice that the condition has been placed first whilst the possible concession has been put at the end of the sentence. This is because the natural reaction is to respond to the end of an utterance rather than its beginning. Since you want your partner to say 'yes'', the part to which you expect agreement is placed at the end. Also, it is the concession which leaves the lasting impression rather than the conditions that are attached to it.

Once a compromise has been agreed the details have to be dealt with. How short is the 'short while' that delivery is to be deferred? What sort of shortened time scale can we expect for installation. There is a temptation to avoid or postpone intricate matters in the initial euphoria of having agreed broad areas but it is in the neglect of the detail that commercial lawyers make their living. Certainly it is possible to leave lesser detail to the end of the session or to delegate it to a lower body but it must be resolved before the negotiation can be said to have finished and an agreement signed.

Throughout the negotiations and particularly before breaks in the discussions, it is useful to summarise how far the meeting has got. This helps to keep track of progress and acts as a motivating factor for both teams, who can see that progress is actually being made. Summaries also help to identify areas of misunderstanding, where the listeners' perception of what has been agreed is not that of the summariser's.

Despite the fact that you are constantly searching for agreement there may be points on which you cannot move. These will be questions of your basic interests; once abandoned only negative results would flow from the current negotiations. Both your language and your tone of voice must signal to your partner that these are non-negotiable areas. Your tone should be clear, sentences short and to the point and the words firm. 'We have to stand by this'; 'We must stand firm on this point', rather than 'We may not do this' (personally I would like to but somebody else is stopping me), or the soggy 'I'm terribly sorry, but....'

A good negotiator will not accept this at its face value but will ask you to give reasons for your intransigence, since they may be illogical or turn out to be avoidable in some way. Your reply must again be clear, rational and firm, especially since these will have been matters that you will have spent some time considering since before formal negotiations began.

Similarly. if you disagree with your partner you need to lay out clearly, rationally and firmly why that is so. At the same time emphasise the points on which you do agree, reaffirming your co-operative purpose and narrowing down the area for discussion. Disagreements can easily become heated. Avoid becoming aggressive, it only has an adverse effect on your partner, causing rejecting and defensive behaviour. Stay calm yourself whatever your partner's behaviour; staying calm helps you to think more clearly. This will help you to concentrate your reasoning on the other person's arguments rather than on the person. As a last resort, when matters are becoming heated and progress appears impossible, call for an adjournment of the meeting in order to allow tempers to cool and ruffled feathers to be re-arranged. Whatever you do, do not be intimidated or rushed into an agreement by a desire to avoid disagreement or a wish not to offend the other person.

3.6   FINAL SOLUTIONS

Normally a solution can only be reached by both parties making concessions. Someone who is not prepared to make concessions is not really negotiating, they are engaging in a test of strength that demands a winner and a loser. On the other hand, concessions should not be all one way or made lightly. Fowler sets out the position neatly:

> *'In commercial negotiations it may also be taken as a universal rule that there should be no concessions without conditions. Get something back for anything you have to concede even if, because of an unequal power position, the condition may not have the same value as the concession.'*

In this final stage it is important to try and avoid questions of principle, citing instead precedents and stressing the benefits to your partner (who will take it for granted that there will also be benefits for you). This is a time for offers and opportunities rather than for threats and disagreements. All the time you will be emphasising the features, benefits and quality of your services over the competition, factors that will obviously sway discerning partners.

On your own behalf you need to stay flexible, stressing your willingness to make concessions as long as they do not conflict with your own interests. This constant series of adjustments and re-adjustments is typical of negotiation, trading off what is more valuable for you than your partner against what is more valuable for your partner than for you, as in the following examples:

Give	For
Low initial price	Long-term commitment
A fast sale	A discount
Acceptance of the other manager's claim for resources now	A bigger resource cake at a later date
Agreement to lower specification	Advantageous backup contract
Higher price	Longer than normal training
Higher holiday entitlement	More flexible working hours

Whatever concessions you make or added features you offer be careful to cost them first. In simulation exercises students tend to give away all sorts of added benefits and guarantees (most often about training) without first considering what this will do to profitability. If the other side will only agree if these are present and the cost to you is uneconomic then it is better to let go of the discussions and agree to part.

One of the signals to the conclusion of an agreement is an increase in bluster, announcements that all of this is completely impossible and that we cannot sign an agreement that looks like this. Keep calm, keep quiet. Your partner is getting used to the situation, allowing the idea of the agreement to take shape. There is no need for you to badger and to urge what has already been agreed. Simply wait, allowing them to let off steam.

As we come towards a final agreement we may find ourselves faced by added difficulties from our partner. The first of these is to know what to do about non-executive negotiating teams, that is those who do not have the power to conclude an agreement. Since you followed the advice earlier in the chapter about establishing your partner's exact position this will not come to you as a surprise. Negotiation has continued since you have realised that these are still people worth convincing and that they will return to their base with glowing reports and perhaps even a draft agreement. Where there are areas of executive power, agreements can be closed if only as preliminaries or of a limited nature.

Some negotiators deliberately leave a sting in the tail in order to try and extort last minute concessions. Just as you are both reaching for the pen to sign the contract they will seek to throw in another item or to return to a matter already concluded. Despite the fact that your taxi is waiting outside or that your train leaves in five minutes you should strongly resist the pressure. It is always a mistake to negotiate under duress, whether of time or power. Instead, concentrate on the issues in hand, summarise the agreements that have already been made and emphasise that an agreement has been reached. By all means refuse to be rushed, there will always be another train!

In the information systems area the more common demand is not from a subtle professional negotiator but from the small business user, perhaps introducing information technology to the business for the first time. Almost inevitably the client picks up more and more information from the analyst's conversation or by reading trade literature. Slowly it becomes clear just how much information technology can do, how it can permeate every part of the business. As time goes on the client's stated needs in the area become larger and larger, the wish list becomes immense.

Such a client demands patience and understanding. An unscrupulous analyst or sales person can bankrupt a small business simply by selling it everything that the owner desires. Instead negotiations might take the form of explaining to the client why this particular piece of hardware is not appropriate at this time and would not, after all, enhance the profitability of the business. The concession in this case might well be the promise that add-ons can be made at a later date as they become necessary, leaving a viable business that will be a valued customer for the analyst or the sales person for many years to come.

Despite all your efforts there may come a time when a deal just cannot be reached. In a simple case of buying and selling the normal solution is just to walk away from the deal. Some cases, though, demand that some conclusion is reached. This is usually the case when the partners are locked-in to one another by an existing agreement or by the nature of their relationship. Divorcing couples, for example, need one another in order to be able to settle the divorce; management and workers have little choice but to continue in some sort of relationship; companies held together by a maintenance contract may find it legally impossible to break the broad agreement whilst not being able to negotiate terms that will make it work.

The solution is usually to bring in some third party in order to mediate between the parties. This may take the form of a subject expert or of a specialised mediation service. In civil engineering, for example, companies are often bound by time penalty clauses in their contracts. However, changes of design by the commissioning organisation, weather conditions and geological formations can all cause delays beyond the control of the contractors. It is therefore common practise for them to hire freelance specialist engineers who record these delays, assign them a time value and negotiate time extensions with the original client. Similarly, where there is disagreement between two companies about the daily operation of a maintenance contract an expert third party can be brought in to mediate.

Where this fails or is inappropriate, organisations such as ACAS operate as intermediaries between the parties, although they have no statutory powers to enforce a settlement. Legislation in Britain over the past fifteen years has made it possible for companies and individuals to apply for mediation through the courts rather than to have to engage in prolonged and extensive litigation. The court will appoint a mediator whose judgement is binding on all parties. Such has been the success of this system that it is now used even in multi-million pound disputes.

3.7 CLOSING THE DEAL

Many negotiations will drift calmly and amicably towards a close. All issues will have been covered and resolved and all that remains is for the chairperson to review the agreements that have been made and ensure that they are correctly recorded. Others, usually industrial negotiations or discussions which involve sales, may involve one side putting pressure on the other to finalise the deal. A certain amount of manoeuvring is inevitable at this stage.

Try and finalise your agreement when all parties are feeling excited, perhaps after having negotiated a particularly difficult point. Again, review the agreements that have been made and have them 'signed off' by the other party, either as a firm 'yes' or a simple nod of the head. (*And we did agree to the first week in March as the delivery date, didn't we?*) This instils the habit of agreement, so that it becomes almost automatic. Any other questions that you ask should assume that the other party is going to agree (*Do you want to draw up an agreement yourselves or are you happy to use our standard one?*).

You now want your partner to sign. To do this, use a similar sort of 'non-no' question, such as: '*Shall we sign this now, or wait until after coffee?*' The question is not about whether you are going to sign, only whether it is immediately or in fifteen minutes. Even if the response is along the lines of '*I'm not sure we have fully explored the question of ...*' there is still the implicit agreement to sign, probably fairly soon.

Even at this late stage one or other of you may feel dubious about signing. You may feel that you really cannot move any further, that your partner is being intransigent and blocking progress. If you have made your final offer your tone of voice and delivery should reflect this. Perhaps you can make reference to the pressures that are on you from elsewhere. Be careful if you are going to do this that those outside pressures should be **concrete** in form ('*I have instructions from my departmental manager that I may not offer more than....*'), that they are **visible** to your partner. 'The shareholders' are not only invisible, they are also not **credible** within the framework of the negotiations, since their power to influence individual business decisions is minimal.

Should you be in the opposite position of having a partner who is wavering about concluding, then bring out that last concession that you have held in reserve. This does not have to be a major one as long as it provides your partner with enough to be able to accept the full package. As with other concessions it can be as much about perceptions and self-image as about finance or quality. If agreement still cannot be reached all that remains is to pack up and go home, or at least to appear to pack up and go home. Often the appearance is enough to convince the other party that the time spent so far cannot be allowed to go to waste.

Now that agreement has been made, get it formalised quickly but calmly, without talking too much. This can take several forms, as set out below:

- Partial
- Detailed
- Verbal
- Written
- Contractual

Under British law even verbal agreements are held to be legally binding, especially in the area of a commercially negotiated price agreement. The problem, of course, is proving their existence and detailed content, so that a full written agreement should normally be your final objective. At the same time there may be a range of details that also have to be finalised. This may include an implementation programme, where a network has to be installed, for example, when the two parties need to integrate their operations. An implementation programme should lay out clearly who is responsible for each phase of the operation and on what time scale.

Major projects can also involve the setting up of a joint implementation review team to monitor the progress of operations. A similar body was set up by the teams involved in the Channel Tunnel project and they are also a feature of major industrial negotiations. Joint review teams may be the site of further negotiations about minor matters or instances of interpretation as well as dealing with unforeseen circumstances that may arise.

Negotiating teams, particularly where they are acting as representatives, also need to report back to their sponsors at the end of negotiations, producing a report of what was agreed and why. Trade union representatives, for example, would be expected to report back to their membership and recommend acceptance of the proposals. A sales team that has just sold a full network to a major client needs to set out the full agreement and implementation plan to aid sourcing, programming, installation and testing by the relevant departments.

Your partner has at last signed. You do not crow and tell them how much more you were prepared to offer or how much more they are paying than the company down the road, at least if you want to do business again. Instead you congratulate them on what a good deal they have got and how their business will be improved as a result.

Everyone should be able to leave the room in a haze of mutual congratulations, perhaps in some cases cemented by extended social contact later. As a general rule, make a polite but rapid exit, there is little to gain by hanging around until the post-agreement euphoria has worn off.

After installing a system an information systems professional carries out a post-implementation review in order to confirm that all has gone to plan, that processes have been carried out efficiently and to time and that the system does what it has been designed to do. Similarly you also need to carry out a post-negotiation review. If you are a professional negotiating team you will need to carry out a process review, to assure yourselves that the negotiation was carried out in the best manner possible and that you got the most from it that you could.

On the business front, someone from the team needs to keep in touch with your partners to ensure that all is going as it should, perhaps that sub-contractors are doing the work that they were meant to, that a formal contract has been drawn up and sent on time, or that invoices and payments have been correctly despatched. Most important of all, whatever goods and services that you have contracted for must be delivered and to the agreed time scale. No amount of wonderful negotiating technique will keep you in business if you cannot come up with the goods afterwards!

3.8 OTHER NEGOTIATING MEDIA

Not all negotiating is done face to face. All or part of it may be done by means of correspondence or telephone. One of the jobs of the DP manager or the IS consultant may be to analyse the information technology needs of the company in detail and to produce an **invitation to tender**. This sets out clearly and precisely what the company wants, giving technical specifications that need to be followed. For example, an NHS Trust Hospital on split sites may wish to standardise its IT usage based on a network which links the various sites. A consultant would be employed to carry out a full systems analysis, specifying hardware and software needs with target and minimum performance levels and times. The conclusions are collated into the invitation to tender document which is sent to interested companies.

Companies respond with a tender document which will set out how they intend to fulfil the needs of the Trust, over what time scale and at what cost. Often the company is not able to match requirements exactly and it is the task of the tender writer to explain why this cannot be done and also why the non-compliance is not a problem since the company can compensate for this in other ways. In effect, the Trust has laid out its objectives and the tendering companies are making counter-proposals which they hope will be acceptable. The Trust is in the special position of negotiating with several companies, whilst the companies are only negotiating with the Trust and working blind insofar as the competition is concerned, putting them in a disadvantageous position.

Where a range of companies respond, an initial analysis will be carried out to match their design specifications against those required by the Trust. Cost is an obvious factor along with closeness to the original specification. Tendering companies which have not offered concessions to compensate for their shortfalls in some areas may well be eliminated at this stage. This emphasises the care that needs to be taken over the phrasing of such documents. Also, where a tender is accepted, it is itself acceptable in law as a formal contract (together with any subsequent amendments to it) and needs to be drawn up with that in mind.

Once tenders have been recognised as acceptable a series of face-to-face meetings and demonstrations may take place. Alongside these there may be a series of letters and fax messages which clarify or request information on points of detail, all of which constitute part of the negotiating process. On simple contracts a letter may be the sum of the negotiation. You request a price for the goods or services, which you find to be acceptable, and send a letter of confirmation along with the cheque.

Similarly, a lot of work is done over the telephone, since this is quick and saves time. Telephone conversations also tend to lead to quick settlements, one way or the other. The longer the conversation the easier it is for one of the parties to say 'no'. This is because it is harder to look someone straight in the eyes and refuse a request than it is when not in their presence. On the other hand, short conversations are more likely to elicit a quick 'yes'. Perhaps it is the unexpectedness of the call and the fact that it is an interruption of other activities combined with the abstract format of the contact which inclines us to deal with it rapidly. There may also be some sort of media influence on us, the image of the decisive business tycoon dealing rapidly and decisively with matters over the phone.

All this suggests that it is better to be the caller than to be the callee. If you cannot avoid being the callee, try to keep the relevant file to hand or play for time while you fetch it. Whatever happens it is important not to negotiate from ignorance or when you are rushed. Prevaricate while you arrange your thoughts, perhaps even inventing an important business contact in your office which forces you to ring your caller back later, thus reversing the roles.

3.8.1 Everyday negotiation

As we noted right at the beginning of this chapter, for much of the time people are engaged in negotiations at home and at work. Most of the qualities and procedures laid out in the preceding pages are applicable to this form of negotiation, with a few additional comments.

Within your place of work the constant interplay of personality and working practices may bring you into conflict with your colleagues. How you deal with these depends upon your position within the formal and informal power structures of the organisation and the real and perceived status of the parties involved. Like any negotiation it remains important to establish your own power base by being fully informed about the situation, whether it is a matter of personnel relations, inter-departmental rivalry or a dispute over which make of hardware to purchase. Even if decisions are made for what you consider to be the wrong reasons you will have put forward an informed, rational and reasoned argument which you can point to later if things go wrong.

Your position can be established initially by the circulation of a report or document which sets out the issue and how you believe it may be dealt with. This puts the question into the public domain and enables full discussion to take place both formally and informally. When negotiating with colleagues it is important not to let your judgement of the position be clouded by judgements about the person. Dislike of a colleague does not invalidate the argument, any more than a colleague that you like is always correct. Believe in your case, but be prepared to consider everyone's point of view.

Finally, watch out for the imposed obligation. This is where a colleague does you a favour or set of favours for no apparent reason. A backlog of obligation is being built up so that at some later date you will find it much harder to refuse should a favour or concession be asked in return. If at all possible, refuse the favour so that you are not put in an invidious position later.

The rules for personal negotiation are the same as for any other sort:

1. Define the issue
2. Define your initial position
3. Present your argument
4. Explore the possibilities
5. Define the proposals
6. Define an unambiguous agreement.

Above all, remember that negotiation is about finding an acceptable agreement with a business partner, not pursuing an ultimate personal victory over an enemy.

3.9 BEING ASSERTIVE

The American constitution states that it is a self-evident truth that all men were created equal. Western societies make much of their democratic structures whilst at the same time praising leadership and hierarchies. How can the ordinary person insist on equality of regard and treatment within occupational and social structures that are often built upon rank, power and status?

The answer is to act assertively, to claim the rights and privileges that are due to you as a person and as an actor within a given role. As a manager you may wish to defend others within your department against unfair criticism from outside, whilst at the same time reserving the right to apportion blame where it is due. A consultant might have a client who does not approve of the way the current task is carried out, perhaps feeling that a range of interviews and the generation of meaningless diagrams is merely a way of prolonging the task and increasing the fee. Only bad feeling, and perhaps even the withdrawal of the contract, will result if the accusations are not dealt with. A programmer might feel that the work assigned is consistently menial, yet is still carried out promptly and to a high standard. Despite this there are no words of praise, nor do the assigned tasks become any more interesting.

3.9.1 The passive response

'Why should I say anything? He never listens to anything I say. It won't get me anywhere and I will just be labelled a trouble maker.' Here is an actor who recognises that he is never going to get anywhere but who wants to blame everyone else except himself. The other person perhaps remains unaware that there is any problem or feeling of resentment, that what are regarded as perfectly acceptable actions by one party are seen as impositions by the other. On the other hand, it may be that it is well known that you do not complain about things and will do any job, however unpleasant, that is assigned to you. Other people take advantage of this, passing you the worst jobs.

The passive response means that people can act towards you as they wish, they know that there will be no resistance or retribution. It is difficult for you to achieve your goals, since others ignore your rightful requests and ambition in the furtherance of their own. The department head cannot defend the staff, the consultant is forced to drop proper analysis techniques in favour of a 'quick and dirty' solution, the programmer carries on with menial tasks for a whole career, never achieving advancement.

Somewhere in your organisation dwells an ageing example of passivity, hanging on until retirement, refusing to make complaints because *'it never does any good'*. This person is obviously frustrated and unhappy, the world has passed by. Apart from the regular moan session they tend to have become inhibited and withdrawn, perhaps even anxious. The passive person has had a lifetime of avoiding confrontation of any kind and as a result has had personal and employment rights violated over and over again, allowing others to choose what should be done rather than making a choice themselves. It has been a quiet life, but a frustrating one.

3.9.2 The aggressive response

By contrast the aggressive actor may have got on famously within organisations (although this is by no means universally true). The aggressive person has clear objectives and will do anything to achieve them, including trampling on the rights of others. When other people can be bullied out of making choices that are sensible for themselves they will be. Any attack on an idea or a belief will be translated as being a personal attack and will be met either with defensive bluster or a full-blown belligerent personal offensive of the type *'I don't need to take comments like that from a person like you.'*

Where these people have moved into management they operate by a system of 'divide and rule', setting subordinates against one another in the fear that any cohesive action will be turned towards the manager in the end. Criticism is diverted by humiliating the other party or by angry and hostile behaviour. Subordinates may find that the response to their work is highly unpredictable, varying even from day to day.

These people tend to become isolated and alienated. For many their sense of self-worth is so high that this is not only bearable but expected, since the dislike of others is interpreted as the envy of inferiors. At some stages of the business cycle the aggressive individual may be of positive worth to the organisation. Setting up a branch in a new area, sorting out a part of the company which has become too cosy and inefficient, conducting an aggressive 'one off' sales campaign may all be times when an autocratic and confrontational approach could be of use.

In the day-to-day run of a smooth-running business the aggressive approach is counter-productive. The outcome of this kind of behaviour is to break the lines of communication. In ancient Greece nobles were chosen to carry good news, only persons of lowest birth to carry bad. This was because the messenger was associated with the news; the noble was feasted and entertained for the good news, the bearer of bad was put to death. Who wants to be the bearer of bad news to the aggressive manager if the response is personal anger and hostility? Who wants to discuss how well the current contract is progressing (perhaps with comments on that individual's part within it) if the result is hostility and a claim for all the credit when matters are discussed with higher powers?

Teams in particular function less efficiently under aggressive personalities. Members see their role as that of 'rubber stamping' the ideas of the leader and cease to make contributions. Although groups tend to improve their operation when they perceive their leader as having power (and thus being able to translate their decisions into action) we should not equate power with aggression. A powerful leader may well spend large amounts of time listening to others and considering their contributions before coming to a decision. Power is used to implement that decision. The aggressive individual alienates both supporters and competitors, making the implementation of ideas that depend on others that much more difficult.

3.9.3 The assertive person

So far we have defined assertion negatively, by illustrating what it is not and the disadvantages of non-assertive behaviour. The assertive person is neither a doormat nor a raving autocrat; what are the positive qualities of assertion?

Assertiveness is about being respected as a person and operating both morally and efficiently with others. It improves the communication flow in inter-personal situations and allows interaction and negotiation to proceed calmly and effectively. That does not mean that you will always get your own way or get others to do what you want, but it does mean that you will feel at the end of the day that your position has been considered and that you have done your best in the situation. You will have made your own choices, rather than have them thrust upon you, whilst respecting the rights of others to make it.

Bloom, Coburn and Pearlman set out their own 'bill of rights' for the assertive person:

- to be treated with respect
- to have and express your own feelings
- to be listened to and taken seriously
- to set your own priorities
- to say NO without feeling guilty
- to ask for what you want
- to ask for information from professionals
- to make mistakes
- to choose not to assert oneself.

Let us translate these into a firm example, that of the consultant whose client is upset about how the task is being carried out, and see how assertion differs in its approaches and effects from passivity and aggression.

Being treated with respect. The client has a perfect right to question how you are doing the job and spending the company's money. How this is done is another matter. You should expect to be addressed properly as a fellow human being who will treat the other person in the same way. In turn you should treat your client with respect and recognise that this is a real concern, not merely a tactic to reduce the consultancy fee. Meet objections courteously and set out clearly the reasons you have for operating in this way. Give as much information as you can in the situation, perhaps even bringing in books or articles on your next visit which show the real cash advantages of thorough analysis over the 'buy a box of kit' approach.

Have and express your own feelings. Being assertive does not mean just having or showing positive feelings. Everyone has negative responses and has a perfect right to them. The consultant may feel annoyed and hurt that the client is questioning what is being achieved. By all means let this show, but not in an aggressive or blaming manner, more as a statement of fact, as an objective observation. '*I am hurt that you should think that I am not doing my job properly. Perhaps this is because you have never been shown what the analysis process involves. Let me show you on this diagram.*'

Be listened to and taken seriously. The analysis has been done and you have delivered your conclusions to your client and the other partners in the company. In the discussions that follow you have to be clear that your findings are purely objective, that they have been arrived at by following professional standards and that they are in the best interests of the company. No amount of dismissive comments, perhaps even aimed at your age, sex or background, should deflect you from your task. Any irrelevant comments or attempts to use humour to denigrate your work should be pointed out as such. Openers such as '*My dear young woman, how do you expect...*' need to be publicly countered if the discussion is to proceed on the proper footing: '*Please do not refer to me as 'my dear young woman.' I am a fully qualified systems analyst with a degree in computer science and five years' experience in the profession.*'

Set your own priorities. All organisations have their own objectives. Good ones recognise that the people who work for them also have objectives and priorities of their own and attempt to work with them in order to maximise worker satisfaction, which they believe will spread into productivity and efficiency. Inevitably these two sets of objectives may come into conflict; some individuals or organisations may totally ignore the fact that you have your own priorities.

Our consultant has two small children and wishes to spend as much time with them as possible. The working day breaks at three-thirty for the children to be collected from school and recommences at eight in the evening when they go to bed. The client expects everyone to work nine until five and wants the analysis concluded as quickly as possible. What the client cannot do is to over-ride the consultant's priorities. Nor can the consultant ignore the client's proper feelings. This is a case for negotiation, where both parties respect the fact that the other has legitimate concerns which must be respected. Neither is aiming to 'win'; what is wanted is an amiable compromise.

Say NO without feeling guilty. There are times when you need to refuse a request from someone else. A subordinate may be asking for leave, your children may want a toy you cannot afford, your client may want you to break off some other business to deal with a pressing problem. All sorts of pressures, financial, moral, emotional, may be brought to bear. You answer still has to be 'No'. Bloom asserts that, because of their conditioning, this is far more difficult for women than for men and that when they do refuse such requests they spend much more time feeling guilty about it. This is a case when rational action is subverted by external pressures and where assertion keeps us on the right track both in our private and our public lives.

Ask for what you want. Do you ask people for what you want, what you think you ought to want, or what you think you might get? If you are not honest and state your legitimate requirements, how can anyone fulfil them for you? When your manager asks what company car you want, come straight out with your request. At the worst you have established a bargaining position, at the best you may even get what you want!

Ask for information from professionals. Traditionally, professionals such as doctors, teachers and lawyers have not encouraged questions from outsiders; they have regarded a statement of their professional judgement as being sufficient. Over recent years this has changed radically. As an IS professional you are in the double position of being someone who must explain processes and decisions and as one who can expect others to act in a similar way towards you.

The consultant can expect to receive full help and co-operation from the company accountant and solicitor about relevant matters such as health and safety law. Whilst working for a client the consultant might also expect to be given information from local authorities about planning applications or from the Inland Revenue about requirements for tax returns. Where required these should be in the form of a full interview rather than just a short letter. In this case the consultant is required to be assertive on behalf of the client.

There may also be occasions when services or goods do not come up to standards or expectations: the software will not load properly on to the PC, delivery dates have not been met, the statement of the company's tax position from the Inland Revenue is incomplete or unclear. A polite but firm complaint is in order, asking what the company is going to do about the situation. In many cases you may have legal rights or rights guaranteed by government charter or professional code of practice; if you do not assert them you cannot be said to have them.

Make mistakes. Everyone makes mistakes, no-one is perfect. Admit to your mistakes and put them right as quickly and completely as possible. Do not allow people constantly to bring them up against you. Naturally, if you are making too many mistakes you need to re-examine your whole attitude to the task in hand.

Choose not to assert oneself. There will be times when all you want to do is to drift along with the tide, to let other people make decisions for you, to recover from the battering you have received from the world. Our consultant has got home from a hard week working for that difficult client and just wants to be organised and cosseted, making no decisions of any significance. Since that is a deliberate choice, an assertion of priorities, then it should be respected.

In some situations to act assertively may involve you in personal risk. Being stopped by traffic police, for example, calls for behaviour which is verging on the servile, especially if one is in the wrong. Similar encounters where there is a gross imbalance of power may call for you to remove yourself from the situation with the least damage rather than to assert your rights. Also, personal relationships may not be able to support an excess of assertive behaviour, especially from both parties simultaneously. Taking too many risks is not wise.

3.9.4 Assertive communication

In the previous section we looked at how you might assert your general rights. Let us look now at the sort of the approaches in communication that we might use in order to achieve our ends on a day-to-day basis. Lyn Porritt identifies eight activities which form the basis of assertive communication:

- give information
- state reality
- give praise
- make constructive criticism
- accept praise
- receive criticism
- state feelings
- confront others.

Let us take the example of a DP manager who is dealing with a junior programmer who is not performing to an acceptable standard.

Give information. The interview cannot proceed unless the data is shared by both parties. What exactly is the behaviour that the manager is complaining about? How was it made known? Are there other people, such as colleagues or clients, who have also made complaints? Is there a company policy or set of performance criteria with which the programmer has not complied?

State reality. What is the real situation? Have there been muffled complaints or are people calling for the programmer's dismissal? Does the work that is being done have to be regularly checked because of the high number of mistakes?

On a more general level, a consultant was called in by a small retail outlet to analyse its procedures and to make suggestions as to how information technology could improve its operations. After two weeks of analysis the consultant terminated the process and delivered a judgement to the owners, much to their immediate distress but to their benefit in the long run. Because of its position and the general drift of consumers away from that type of product the business just was not viable, however much its procedures might be updated. Any extra investment would just be throwing good money after bad. The owners found the judgement difficult to deal with at first but after some time accepted it as valid and regarded the consultant's fee as a sensible use of their resources.

Give praise. In all walks of life people perform better if they are praised for what they do well. No-one likes to feel that everything that they do will be criticised or that their good work passes unnoticed. Inspirational leaders produce a feeling of self-worth in their followers, implying that they have set their own standards that they have to live up to.

The manager dealing with the junior programmer needs to find areas of praise, to show that everything is not black. Perhaps mistakes have been decreasing recently, punctuality has improved or the person has shown willing by applying for an updating course in a particular area.

Give constructive criticism. All criticism must be constructive, it must contain the seeds of improvement and change. Our junior programmer is first told what is being done well and only then what room there is for improvement. Suggestions for change are better if they come from the other person, who then has a feeling of ownership over them, even if they have been sparked off by prompting from the manager:

> *'What about structuring your programs, will that help to eliminate some of the errors we were discussing?'*
>
> *'Yes, perhaps if I were to look at Jackson structures again then that would suggest where I have been going wrong. I'll talk to some of the others as well and ask them what methods they use.'*

Accept praise. Everyone needs praise, including you. Accept it graciously, you have earned it and have a right to it.

Receive criticism. Similarly, as we noted earlier, everyone makes mistakes. Do not be defensive about them. Accept them, rectify them if possible, but do not become defensive or act aggressively towards people who point them out to you. Receiving criticism is a form of listening technique: you have been given information and people have made statements of reality about you and your performance. Evaluate what you hear and act on the data accordingly.

The junior programmer may feel that many of the current problems are the result of lack of support and assistance from the manager. Although this clashes with the manager's own assessment of the situation it is important to accept that this is the way that the programmer feels and to realise that this feeling has to be dealt with. The manager may also be moved to check whether others feel the same way and, if so, to change behaviour accordingly.

State feelings. Say how you feel about the situation. This allows the other person to open up and to be honest about their own feelings. Perhaps the manager, who appointed the programmer in the first place, feels disappointed and let down or is led to question how such a mistake could have been made. Despite the dangers of such open behaviour, for example the other person may respond with personalised aggression, the gains in terms of placing the discussion on an open footing far outweigh them, especially for someone secure in their own feelings of worth.

Confront others. In the area of assertiveness confrontation does not imply conflict. Instead it is a behaviour which involves giving honest feedback to others, even if they find it unpleasant. *'This is the way that others see you...'* can be a shock to the system but is necessary if reform is to take place. A business consultant may need to tell a client that the client's products are seen as shoddy and overpriced by the public. The client needs to change either the product or its image. The message may hurt but until it is received the business cannot progress.

On a personal basis the same may be true of our analyst. *'Your colleagues see you as lazy, unmotivated and incompetent. If I were to sack you they would be very happy. The conversation we have just had has done nothing to dispel the impression your colleagues have given me. What do you think we can do about the situation?'* This is being brutally frank, but the manager has still left room for manoeuvre, the programmer is encouraged to suggest strategies for change, perhaps to make a completely new start.

3.9.5 Conclusion

Acting assertively is about retaining your personal respect and identity whilst allowing others to retain theirs. In the majority of cases it is not only the most moral but also the most effective way of proceeding. Assertiveness opens up communications channels and keeps them open despite the efforts of others to diminish them.

For the information systems professional, acting assertively helps to build up trust and respect with both colleagues and clients as well as improving job efficiency. Data and business systems are removed from the arena of emotions and social conditioning and placed firmly into the objective domain where they belong. A passive or an aggressive systems analyst is a contradiction in terms.

CHAPTER 4
Oral presentations

INTRODUCTION

There are a whole range of reasons why oral presentations are made within a company or to organisations outside it. Many of them are to do with selling in its broadest sense, that is selling an idea, a solution or a corporate plan, as well as in the narrower sense of actually selling equipment or services. Some organisations require applicants for jobs to make a formal presentation on a given topic to the interview panel. In this case the product that you are selling is yourself.

Other presentations may be on implementation issues. The fact of implementation has been decided, we now need a policy and structure of how to go about it, which is what you are about to present to your audience. Obviously, even at this stage your plan needs to be 'sold' to the audience in order to gain their full commitment. In the example of changing over systems cited in Chapter 1, Emma had to convince her audience that she understood their current working practices, understood the new system and had worked out the most painless way for the staff to integrate the two.

A third form of presentation is the slick demonstration of equipment that is to be found at computer trade fairs. Again, this is a form of selling, one that relies upon the quality of the product and the ability of the demonstrator to use it. Technicians and operators may be called upon by sales personnel to give lower-level demonstrations to prospective clients or to help set up demonstrations that they will use. Personnel in DP departments are nowadays called upon to give presentations to potential users when new systems are introduced, which themselves shade off into the training area.

The examples above are not exhaustive, nor are they meant to be. Since there are many purposes for presentations, the presenter must be prepared to adapt style, content and level depending on the situation. Creativity and competence need to go together.

4.1   THE PURPOSES OF PRESENTATIONS

We may find it strange that companies bother with oral presentations at all. After all, they tie up key personnel for a considerable amount of time, cost the company money and rarely lead to any immediate practical outcomes. In an ideal world the analyst would prepare the report, submit it to senior management, who would promptly read and annotate it, rapidly discuss it among themselves and make a decision. Also in an ideal world the lecturer would prepare a set of lesson notes, give them to the students at the beginning of the year with a set of assignment and examination dates and leave them to it.

Be honest. How many students would read the notes, finish the course or pass the examinations? Not many. Other matters would get in the way, their motivation might be lax, they may not have been trained to such a highly disciplined mode of working. Managers are no different, in that they have competing demands on their time which may lead them to deal with topics only when forced to do so. The analyst or DP manager cannot rely on that report having been read. Even if it has been read, what is the guarantee that its implications have been understood? Like the lecturer checking back on the student's performance and understanding, the IS professional needs to ensure that the management fully understands this particular complex area of expertise.

Nor will managers spend large amounts of their or the company's money unless fully convinced of its necessity. Written reports do not answer back or explain difficulties. Yes, you can put your questions and objections in a memo, but how long will they take to be answered? How do you know if others have the same difficulties? Will you understand the answers when they eventually arrive? Much quicker and more efficient, then, to put those concerned together in a meeting and let the author(s) of the report justify it to them. This may also shorten the gap between presentation of the proposal and implementation, a gap which many companies from the sixties onwards had felt was growing unacceptably longer.

4.2   CONTENT

You are setting out in your presentation to gain both the agreement and active support of your audience. They may be asked to change working practices, to buy a new system or just to give you a good mark for your assignment. Whatever your objective, you have a solution that you wish to sell, a product that the audience is going to buy.

It must be a good product. In other words, you must have done all the preparatory work thoroughly. If you are trying to get the company to buy a new system you must have thoroughly investigated the company itself, identifying what is needed and why. The present system had to be reviewed in order to ascertain its shortfalls and the hardware and software solutions thoroughly researched. All conclusions must flow logically from your investigation. Final proposals need to be socially and financially feasible. If you have something to demonstrate you must be thoroughly familiar with it. Not only that, like any good salesman you must be convinced that your solution is the best possible one for your client.

Top class salespeople sometimes manage to sell inferior goods. They do not sell inferior goods to the same client twice. If you want to keep your job or retain your credibility as a consultant you need to do the groundwork well. However suave and professional your presentation may be, the over-riding question asked by the audience is always 'how good is it from a technical/business point of view?' Gross errors of fact, gaps in the investigative process, demonstrations which do not work will destroy the most elegant presentation.

On the other hand, a reasonable solution can quite easily be disregarded if it is not well presented.

4.3 THE AUDIENCE

If you look back for a moment to the models of communication laid out in Chapter 1 you will notice that most of the emphasis is put on the sender of the message. It is the sender who makes choices about what material to select, how it is encoded, what channel and medium are to be used, and so on. The sender does this in the light of what is known about the receiver, what codes and jargon the receiver uses, what medium is preferred for picking up messages, what are the individual and social limitations on reception of the message.

The inference we might draw from this is that **'the audience is always right'**. If the audience does not receive the message for any reason, then it is the sender's fault. In a normal presentation this should be the case. The audience are at the presentation because they want or need to be there, they have an intrinsic interest in the subject matter. Failure to communicate is thus the responsibility of the speaker.

4.4 PLANNING THE DELIVERY

You already have a preparatory script, your written report. Although the audience may also have a copy you cannot rely on them having read it. Your job is to extract the salient features from that report and present them in as simple and logical manner as possible. The old salesperson's motto KISS (*Keep It Simple, Stupid*) is applicable here, remembering that what is simple to a computing audience may be highly complicated to a general one.

Normally you will have a limited amount of time in which to make your presentation, anything from five minutes to one hour. Your first task is to reduce the material in your report to manageable proportions, given the background of the audience. For example, if you are presenting to the management of an auctioneering company you do not need to go in to detail about auctioneering in general or the background of the company. You do need to emphasise simple technical details such as ease of backup, response times and data handling capabilities. Exercise your professional judgement in the light of the business context.

The simplest way to proceed at this point is to take a 'magic marker' pen and a copy of your report. In the light of the remarks in the previous paragraph, read through your report marking off the points and comments that you could not possibly do without. Most new presenters will then be left with twice as much material as they need. Hard decisions have to be made at this point about what is left out, but remember that you can always refer listeners back to the report for any detailed discussions of a point and for statistics or background information.

Another way of planning your presentation is with the mnemonic W5H, which stands for: Who, What, Why, When and How. This is particularly useful when discussing systems implementation but it can also be used for more general presentations, where 'How often' becomes *How much?* Such an approach ensures that you cover the rationale for the study, the data that was unearthed, the solutions proposed and the time scale of their implementation.

Whichever method you have chosen, you should by now have got your material down to a manageable size. At this point it has to be ordered, fitted into the overall structure of your presentation. Remember that most of the time you are involved in a selling exercise, you are trying to convince your audience to accept your solution to the problem. Your audience should not face any unexpected surprises. If you have ordered your material and your arguments well they should themselves be coming to an identical conclusion to your own well before the end of the presentation. This is known as '*selling as you go*', a gentle leading of the prospect towards the proposed goal. Nasty intellectual jolts tend to throw the hearers out of their mood of conceptual acceptance and push them into a feeling of opposition.

4.4.1 The script

Making a presentation can be frightening. Some people never get over their nerves and go in fear and trembling for days before performing. Others are 'naturals', just as some people are born actors. Most of us are somewhere in between. We are all nervous, which is what starts the adrenaline moving in our system and helps us along, but we do not allow that nervousness to get in the way. It is our attitudes towards our nervousness which determines what sort of script we use.

Most members of an audience hate the prepared speech. Poor readers deliver it in a dull monotone with their face pointed at the floor or lectern. When the reader misses the place there is an embarrassed silence accompanying the mad search to find it again or to recover a sheaf of papers which have fallen to the floor. Even a good reader can be thoroughly thrown off stride when hit with a difficult question from the audience. How is that to be fitted in to the general flow of the text? Finally, rather than listen to someone else read most people would much rather go through the text themselves and then ask questions afterwards; it is quicker. Such a procedure also negates the whole object of an oral presentation.

Reading also raises questions in the listener's mind about the competence of the presenter. This person does not appear to be in control of the material and lacks confidence in its presentation. How, then, can anything that the speaker says be believed? Perhaps such an impression can be redressed slightly in the final question and answer session but it does nothing for our objective of '*selling as you go*'. Another rule from the salesperson's manual states that '*the customer does not buy the product until he accepts the salesman.*' You are selling yourself and your competence to the audience in advance of any findings or recommendations that you may have. Reading a script places a barrier between you and your audience and delays or even prevents your acceptance.

Similar objections also apply to learning a script off by heart. Some cultures use this as a basic form of learning, where children in school 'repeat their lessons'. Unwanted questions can ruin the flow, even to the extent that the presenter has to start again all over from the beginning. If this is part of your own culture you need to look at ways of adapting the skill you have learnt in the light of these criticisms.

Some highly experienced presenters seem to work completely without notes. This is not to be recommended. Even teachers of many years experience still have their lecture notes lurking about somewhere, even if they do not refer to them very often. They are an emergency backup system which only the foolhardy would do without.

What type of notes you use is a matter of choice and of what suits you best. Tony Buzan in *Use Your Head* suggests a sort of dendritic structure for note making which students often refer to as 'spidergrams' or 'mind maps' (Fig. 4.1).

Although these look complicated at first sight they are actually quite logical and easy to use. Each main branch is a topic, with sub-topics coming off them. The speaker follows the system through, expanding on each area in turn. With only one sheet for the whole presentation the speaker can easily switch attention from one area to another, if there are questions from the floor or if a section needs to be omitted for any reason. Building up such a diagram is also quite easy for similar reasons. It quickly becomes evident where information has been missed out or where it is incomplete and this can be added to the diagram.

Slightly less effective but easier to use in the early stages is the old set of filing cards. These can be held in the palm of the hand, are easy to read and prepare and are unostentatious in use. Use one for each topic or sub-topic with brief paragraph headers on the card. Demonstrations or use of visual aids can be clearly marked so that they can be used at the right time (see Fig. 4.2). Although you do not gain the overview that is implicit in Buzan's method the ease of use compensates for this. One word of warning: keep the cards in your hand all the time, otherwise the audience may become more interested in how many you have left than in what you are saying.

Many teachers and lecturers now use visual aids as a form of notes. Section headers are placed on overhead projector transparencies which the lecturer 'talks over'. This is quite acceptable in the teaching situation, where the teacher may have over twenty hours to prepare each week, but is not best professional practice, especially if you are giving a 'one off' presentation to an important client. Visual aids are too important for their general impact to be dissipated in this way. There is plenty of other vital information that your audience could be concentrating upon.

Notes should be brief, effective and unostentatious. You should be able to refer to them when need arises, especially if you are intending to do a complicated demonstration. Hiding behind a huge sheaf of papers may do much for your nerves but little for your credibility.

4.4.2   The voice

Like any actor, your voice is your main weapon. Words, arguments, examples, even demonstrations are all mediated through the power of your voice. At the very basic level you need to be speaking loud enough and clearly enough for your audience to hear you. Once that has been achieved you need to use your voice to persuade the audience of the overwhelming certainty of your case.

Some people speak quietly. Others pitch their voices quite high, which makes them difficult to pick up in certain circumstances. Whether due to physical characteristics or to social conditioning, as some feminist writers such as Dale Spender claim, women's voices tend to be both lower in pitch and quieter than men's. Female presenters therefore need to make a conscious and continual effort to overcome this problem. 'Continual' is important in this context because it is no good starting off loud and then trailing away into inaudibility as sometimes happens.

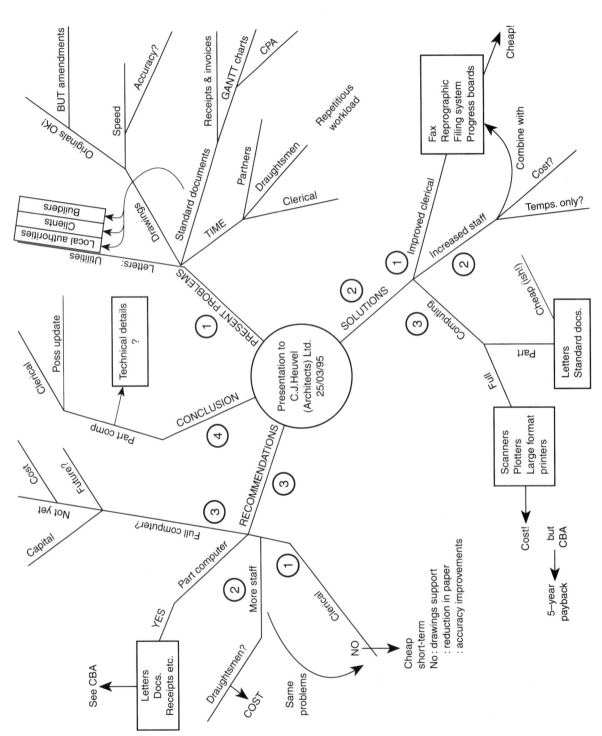

Fig. 4.1 An example of a 'spidergram'

PRESENTATION TO C.J.HEUVEL (ARCHITECTS) LTD.
Sale of integrated computer system (LAN possible?)
 	
       1 Introduce   self
                            company
 	
      2 Structure of presentation
                   needs
                   system features
                   accounts
                   technical details
                   updating
                   costs
 	
1 of 4 FB/95
	ohp company logo

3 Features: Wordprocessing   standard letters
                                     forms
 	
             Spreadsheet
 	
             Database   clients
                                suppliers
                                utilities
                                sites in progress
4 Accounts not required in system BUT
             quick
             accurate
             updates receipts
                       invoices etc
 	
2 of 4 FB/95
	ohp example
	
	DEMONSTRATE
	example from N.F.
	presentation
	NO new data
	
	DEMONSTRATE
	use receipt & show
	update of all
	ledgers

5 Technical   speed
                       storage
                       back-up
                       printers
                       LAN features
 	
6 Updates   scanners
                       plotters
                       dedicated software
 	
3 of 4 FB/95
	drawings from N.F's
	system – hand round

7 Costs   simple system ONLY
                 avoid specifics on full system
                 stress price negotiation for full system
 	
8 Recap   what all this will do for you
 	
4 of 4 FB/95
	manufacturers'
	promotional
	material

Fig. 4.2 A keyword prompt sheet

Another common fault is to drop one's voice at the end of a sentence or phrase. This leaves the audience groping and straining after the full sense of the previous utterance when they should be paying attention to the current one.

Once the problem of audibility has been conquered we can now start to use the voice as a more delicate weapon. If you listen to a good actor, teacher or presenter you will notice that the tone and timbre of the voice is subtly modulated. A soft monotonous tone is soporific for the audience and ineffective for the presenter. You can use your voice to point up important or challenging parts of your presentation ('*Now*, *we come to the question of cost effectiveness...*'), to express doubt ('*Were we given the full details of this operation?*') or even to wake up a rather dozy audience!

Such variations in your delivery make for interest in your audience. They also stress how well you are in control of your material and how enthusiastic you are about the subject and the solution that you are offering. The verbal 'fillers' that we came across earlier, such as '*like*', '*you know*', '*um*' and '*er*' have no place in a well-prepared presentation. You have no need to grope for the next word or idea or to prevent a member of the audience from interrupting. Presenters who use minimal notes are particularly liable to this error. During outstandingly poor presentations you may catch yourself counting the '*ums*' rather than listening to the sense of what the speaker is saying, an example of bad coding and transmission leading to minimal reception.

4.4.3 Language

Keeping within the audience's linguistic codes and technical competence has already been mentioned. Once this has been observed the speaker still needs to look closely at **how** the ideas are expressed. Most word processing programs nowadays contain methods of analysing the complexity of written messages and we will be looking at some of these in the next chapter. Suffice it to say that the use of long sentences and complex words makes a communication more difficult to absorb. This is particularly true of oral communications where the audience has to move at the speed of the presenter and is not able to turn back the text and review bits they did not understand.

Practically, this means that you need to keep your sentences short and use simple words wherever possible. There is no room for the presenter who is, in Disraeli's famous words, '*inebriated with the exuberance of his own verbosity*'. Nor is there for the amateur comedian. People who are naturally funny tend to be paid for it, those who are not can be a public embarrassment. Although humour can add force to a point or lighten up proceedings it is difficult to use and even teachers of long standing have often pared their year's delivery down to the same three jokes. Student presentations which try to use humour have a very high cringe factor.

4.4.4 Timing

Usually you will have a time limit into which to fit your presentation, although you may have some say in the duration. A client may ask you '*how long do you need*' or '*when would you like to do this?*' There is a temptation to bend over backwards to please the client at the expense of the presenter. Especially if you are demonstrating software you need to give yourself enough time in which to demonstrate its features plus time in which to extol its benefits and to take questions. The result of that sum is the **minimum** time that you require. Any less and you cannot do the job, leaving the scene wide open to the opposition.

That said, you now need to use your political skills in order to put the client in the best mood. Avoid busy times of the day or week or times when the client is impatient to go off elsewhere. Mornings tend to be better than afternoons in that both you and the client are fresher and more receptive; after lunch on a Friday must be the worst time of the week! If possible make sure that you have no appointments for the rest of the day, so that you can follow up any commitments or decisions made as a result of your presentation. This applies to internal company presentations, too, since there may be matters that need clarifying, project teams to consider or delivery dates to discuss.

In larger companies your delivery date may be constrained by the availability of the conference room or the regular meeting of the appropriate committee. Smaller companies rely more on staff availability and exterior pressures from customers. Needless to say, it is up to you to be flexible.

You now have a date, a place, a room, a time and a duration. First, check out the room. Does it have power sockets, are they in the right place? Does it black out? Can you project onto the wall or do you need a screen? Are computer facilities available? Do they need to be booked? Are they reliable? Is the room large enough for your audience, or is it too large for the few that you expect? Sometimes you will have to give a presentation 'blind', without having seen the room or the equipment. In this case you should telephone the organisers well in advance, setting out you requirements and finding out what is available. Your conversation should be confirmed in writing well before the presentation date.

Whatever room you use it should be well ventilated and the seating arranged so that all of the audience has a good view of the speaker and of any visual aids that are to be used. Seating should be comfortable enough not to cause irritation to the sitter but not so comfortable as to cause drowsiness. Refreshments are often provided on these occasions; it is best to get them out of the way and the cutlery removed before your presentation begins. Someone refilling a cup or splashing coffee all over the table can be most off-putting to presenter and audience alike.

Good oral presentations have a very simple structure:

- Tell people what you are going to say
- Tell it to them in detail
- Give a resumé of what you have told them

Naturally you do not use exactly the same words for each of the three sections!

Tell them what you are going to say

Here you need general introductions and comments on the purpose of the meeting. ('*My name is Frank Boyle and I am here today to introduce to you the new accounts package developed by Sybiz.*') We need to know what the structure of the presentation is going to be. ('*As you can see from the flip chart here, this presentation will be divided into six parts, which are....*') Perhaps you can also organise some form of impact to drive home the need for the meeting. ('*Your accounts system is currently held on paper, which is heavy, cumbersome and prone to accident*': throws sheaf of 'notes' into the air, which drift everywhere.)

Tell it to them in detail

This is the main body of your presentation. For an analyst it will contain a short description of the methodology involved in researching the report and a brief overview of its findings. It is in this section that the analyst will include any problems and requirements, information gleaned from interviews, data flows and logical data structures and financial and social constraints. From this it is logical to move on to preliminary conclusions and recommendations, including whatever business options have been proposed, with their related cost-benefit analysis. It is a useful tactic to pause at the end of a section or after a particularly telling point in order to give listeners time to assimilate what you have just said, to allow it to 'sink in'.

By the end of this section the audience should have a clear idea of what is being proposed, why, and how it will be of benefit to the company. In the case of a demonstration they will have been taken through the main features of the product in a logical manner which relates to the needs of the client.

Give a resumé of what you have said

Although you have been 'selling as you go' this is your main hook point, the time when you try and achieve commitment for your proposals. Remind the audience of the problems and difficulties you began with and give a brief overview of your solution, how it will address the problems and what are its tangible and intangible benefits. A comparison against the problems and requirements list is useful at this point, followed by a sharp statement of the benefits that the audience will gain from accepting the proposal. Visual reinforcement will leave a lasting impact on viewers of this key point. For example you might end with: '*Here are this year's ledgers and receipts.*' (hand on large pile of documents). '*Here is the same information prepared using our new accounts package*' (holds up single floppy disk).

Questions

Despite the councils of perfection about considering your audience given earlier, in practise there are bound to be listeners who want to clarify certain points or point out apparent inconsistencies. Time should always be left at the end of your presentation for questions of this sort. They should be dealt with as honestly as possible. If something was outside your remit, say so. If you do not know the answer to something, say so in the most politic manner possible: '*I don't have the figures on that with me but I can look them up and let you have them within the next couple of days.*'

Every audience has its member who is freaked on technical detail and the latest developments of technology. Do not get sucked in to talking about detail with this person, who will never admit to having got something wrong, leading to a long discussion which causes you to completely lose the rest of the audience. *'That is a very interesting point, perhaps we could discuss it in detail afterwards'* is a useful ploy at this point. Nor is the end of a presentation the right time to be entering into detailed negotiations about contractual matters. If you are offering training as an added extra, discussions of costs, timing and place are a matter for later, unless they have been part of your presentation.

When you take questions is a matter of choice, often dictated by individual circumstances. Generally speaking, the smaller and more intimate your audience the more prepared you should be to take questions 'as they come'. With greater formality and an increase in size of audience questions will be delayed until the end. Generally, try to leave all but the simplest ones to the end anyway. There is a tendency for them to disrupt the flow of the presentation and to tie the speaker down in irrelevancies and lead down unproductive cul-de-sacs. Certainly, inexperienced speakers or those in hostile environments should try to ensure that questions only come at the end of the presentation.

As a general rule, split the timing for your presentation into four parts:

- Introduction   10%
- Body of talk   70%
- Conclusion   10%
- Questions   10%

Questions can be open-ended, depending on the situation. You may find that you can be involved in sessions which last as long as two hours, including many detailed and searching questions. These are often the ones which involve the company spending money!

Arrive well in advance of your time so that you can arrange the room, order your notes and sort out all of those last minute problems that always arise. Even if you can, do not visit your own office first; there is bound to be something which urgently demands your attention and which will force you to arrive late and flustered.

4.4.5   The delivery

You have scouted out the room to be used, prepared the content of your presentation, formed it into a logical order and produced a set of visual aids. What do you do next? The answer is that you **rehearse**, as frequently as necessary. Like an actor, you need to be familiar with your lines and their delivery as well as being confident that they fit into the time allowed. Imagine listening to a radio soap and finding that it finishes five minutes early because there is not enough script or the actors have rushed their lines!

Rehearsals are best done with an audience, your colleagues, perhaps, or the long-suffering members of your family. Get them to put up their hands when you say things they do not understand, or to ask particularly searching questions. Remember that your delivery in rehearsals tends to be quicker than during 'the real thing', so do not be too worried if you are below target (10% is quite reasonable). If you are spot on target or slightly over, either remove parts of your script or mark off parts towards the end which you can miss out if necessary. Watching yourself on a video recording can be a salutary experience and is an excellent preparation technique.

Once all is smooth and well-timed you are ready for your performance. In normal speech we talk very quickly and elide one word into another untilonewholephrasejustbecomesonehugeword. Presentations need to be clearer and slower than this because they are a lengthy monologue which has to be made as easy to follow as possible. Again, listen to actors on radio or delivering a long speech on stage or screen. Their delivery is very precise and about 80% the speed of normal speech, without being strained or stilted.

Your actual style of delivery should help you gain and keep rapport with the audience. Referring to listeners by name attracts and keeps people's attention as well as indicating your involvement with the organisation. (*'Jack's department was particularly helpful in supplying us with statistics on this', 'Mr. Davies mentioned earlier over coffee that he was experiencing difficulties with...' 'Thank you for the question, Henry, you have picked up on a very important point.'*)

Eye contact with an audience is always difficult, but essential. Avoiding eye contact makes you appear shifty and insincere, staring at people makes them uncomfortable. On the other hand, too much directed eye contact acts as an invitation for people to interrupt, something which it has already been suggested should be avoided. The answer is a generalised sweep on the same level as the audience's eyes but without lingering on any particular individual, thus giving the impression of involvement with the audience but without lingering too long or personalising the delivery. When mentioning Jack, Henry or Mr. Davies it is useful to achieve eye contact with them.

Nervous presenters often make the mistake of presenting to the back wall. Instead, fix on an area just behind the shoulders of the audience (try to vary which member of the audience you use) and fix on that. Naturally, with experience you will move away from such props and achieve proper eye contact and a more confident manner.

Most of us have little mannerisms which take over when we are nervous. In class some teachers are always fiddling with a whiteboard pen or piece of chalk, others constantly take off their glasses or drum their fingers. You will need to control any mannerisms during your presentation, or at least hide them so they are not noticed. (Fiddle with the chalk behind your back, drum your fingers on a soft surface...) Otherwise the audience will spend more time watching your mannerisms than listening to you. Smiling is permitted (however nervous you might be) and is a wonderful way of bonding the audience to you. Remember that you are your own best visual aid and it is the way you act, dress and deliver your presentation which makes the most lasting impression on your audience.

Like all meetings, the presentation has not finished until everybody has left the room. Despite the formal end of the question session you are still on the spot, still selling yourself and your solution. When appropriate shake hands with your audience and see them on their way. Only when that is done can you perform the last job of cleaning up the room: erasing the whiteboard writings, removing the flip chart, taking away the hardware that you used. You can then go back to the office and wait for formal written agreement of your proposals!

4.4.6 Group presentations

Where a team has carried out an analysis or developed a system a group presentation may be appropriate. These are much more difficult to organise but are proportionately more satisfying to get right.

All of the foregoing features of presentations have to be taken into account. Central items such as content, structure and responsibilities need to be agreed by the team as a whole well in advance and times for rehearsals fixed to allow for changes to be made. In addition strong contingencies have to be made for illness or non-attendance for any reason. All members of the project team should have an overview of the project as a whole (there is something wrong with both team and project if they do not) and should be able to give a general overview of even the most technical areas. Project teams have been known to write out individual scripts which are available to the whole team to read in advance and which could be read in a member's absence. Such methods are not ideal but are preferable to gaping and suspicious holes being left in the team's argument.

Student groups tend to present in a 'modular' manner. That is, they divide up the work strictly into the appropriate number of sections and move linearly from one to the next. No doubt they wish to share the load equally and make sure that assessors have no problems with assigning marks to individuals. At a company level the modular system allows room for specialists to make recognisable inputs into the discussion. A modular system has drawbacks in that:

- material may be omitted
- material may be repeated
- members of the project team may not be familiar with all areas
- non-appearance causes problems
- the presentation may fragment if there is no coherent underlying structure.

The alternative to the modular structure is a 'spinal' presentation. The spinal presentation depends on a link person who introduces and concludes the presentation as well as perhaps linking individual contributions within it. This takes skill and expertise on behalf of the link person and, to a lesser extent, of the other presenters. However, it does give the impression of the working of a well-oiled machine and a team that is fully in control of the situation. Because the link has an overview of the whole project the person can help out at times of crisis or fill in for absentees. Such a method demands more from the participants in terms of time spent on rehearsal and planning, which is no bad thing in itself but may place extra demands on the manpower of the organisation. The features of a spinal system are that:

- it has a highly professional 'feel'
- the presenters have total control over their material
- absences can be ameliorated reasonably easily
- it is harder and more time consuming to set up.

Whatever system you choose the timing for each person must be very strict to fit in with the overall pattern. The audience's attention should be clearly focused on one person at all times. Other members of the team need to clear the area quickly and efficiently and remain as 'invisible' as possible with no extraneous fidgeting, movement or chatter when others are presenting.

4.5   USING VISUAL AIDS

We human beings are visual animals. As hunter-gatherers on the great African plains we hunted our prey by sight and searched in hidden places for roots and plants. Even now we find our mates primarily by sight and spend large amounts of time trying to make our exteriors as attractive as possible. Information can also be ingested quickest by visual means, even if we often need to have a verbal explanation to tease out the subtleties involved. A picture is indeed worth a thousand words.

Using visual representations in oral presentations is done for a variety of reasons. First, it can add clarity and precision. We have already noted that words can be ambiguous and prone to error. A visual aid gives confirmation of what is meant, perhaps clarifying and solidifying the presenter's statements. Second, it allows us to present information which would be indigestible if simply read to the audience. A series of system specifications or the figures in a cost/benefit analysis would be examples of this.

Third, we can present information which cannot be effectively transmitted by words at all. Instead of describing the Mona Lisa you could present a slide of the painting. A data flow diagram is meant to be a visual conceptual model and should be presented as such. Sales figures can be presented either as a table or as a series of graphs. A new computer program might be presented to an audience as a series of 'screen dumps' on an overhead projector, as a series of stills on a VDU or even as the real thing, using a ceiling-mounted projector.

Within information theory redundancy of information is a cardinal sin. Information should be presented once only, in order to avoid clogging the communications channels. Human beings do not work in that way. We rarely remember something that we have only been told once, unless it has been strongly signalled to us that it is of overwhelming importance (then we repeat it to ourselves several times as a substitute for the telling). In a short presentation you have little time for redundancy, of telling the audience the same things in several different ways. Instead, you can use visual aids to reinforce your message, keeping them in front of the audience's eyes for a long period.

Finally, visual aids are used to fix the attention of the audience and to stop their attention wandering. Humans need visual stimulus, which they rarely find in fixing on the speaker alone. Attention tends to wander and has to be constantly re-captured. Good visual aids do this, keeping even unmotivated audiences reasonably on track.

4.5.1   Choosing visual aids

Your choice of visual aids is limited by:

● the information that you wish to convey

- the time you have available
- the availability of equipment
- the size and configuration of the room
- the size of the audience
- the facilities available in the room
- finance.

Obviously, if you are giving a five minute talk on the difficulties you encountered in installing version 3.6 of a piece of software to three colleagues your scope for using visual aids is strictly limited. On the other hand, if you are running a stand at a computer fair at Olympia, giving a series of hour long presentations on your company's new CASE tool, then you would be expected to have a continuous series of visual stimuli for your audience.

Some of the companies for which you work may have a limited supply of equipment. For example, only larger firms will have a room with enhanced screen facilities for VDUs and few firms have film projectors any more. Similarly, you may find yourself giving a presentation on a company's premises where there is no room which blacks out, making the use of slides impossible and the use of the overhead projector quite difficult. Many larger companies and conference venues now have specialist presentation suites with a range of up-to-date equipment and full technician support which considerably simplifies the presenter's job. Even here, though, you need to phone up well in advance to check what is available and that it is compatible with whatever equipment you will be using.

In Fig. 4.3 you will find a chart of the most commonly used visual aids for your reference. Some added comments are also in order.

Flip charts

Flip charts are large pads of paper, clipped at the top to an easel. The user writes on them as clearly as possible, flipping each entry over to reveal the next. Presenters often use them to display information that they want to keep in front of the audience for a considerable length of time, such as the order of the presentation or the problems that an organisation is facing. In the latter case, another aid, such as an overhead projector, might be used simultaneously to deal with each individual point.

The flip chart can be used in rooms which have no fixed board for writing on or for displaying the same sort of information that might be presented on a board but only allowing part of it to be revealed at any one time. This is useful in a sequential presentation where the presenter wishes to surprise the audience, to pull them along with the steps in the reasoning or to force them to come up with their own answers before giving them the presenter's solution.

Charts can be prepared in advance but have the advantage that they can be added to either during the presentation or in the light of new information. In management seminars flip charts are also used as feedback devices, where participants write down their problems or solutions for comment, or as the basis of continuing exercises.

CHOICE OF VISUAL AIDS FOR ORAL PRESENTATIONS

	FLIP CHART	WHITEBOARD	35mm SLIDES	OVERHEAD	VIDEO	FILM	VDU UNIT	SOUND TAPE
CLARITY	Good in small rooms if well prepared	Good if writing large enough	Excellent, depends on room quality	Good in small rooms with top quality	Good, especially with large format monitor	Excellent if equipment good	Good if enhanced	Poor
EASY USE	Simple, quick modification	Takes practice Quickly modified	'Carousel' type simple	Simple	Excellent	Lacing can be a problem	Needs practice	Excellent. Can use with slides
LIMITATIONS	Not visible at great distance	Messy and 'unprofessional' appearance	Poor manipulation	Low print quality, too crowded	Poor manipulation	Loses quality easily. Poor manipulation	Small screen ineffective	Room and equipment limits acoustics
PERMANENT	Can be	No	Long, physical life	Yes	Yes	Yes, but quality degrades	Yes, on disc.	Yes, degrades
MAKING	Simple	Simple, even 'on the spot'	Needs photo skills; quick printing	Simple, beware need for design skills	Difficult, needs professional help	Difficult, needs professional help	Takes time, otherwise simple	Needs help for top quality
COST	Very cheap	Very cheap	Printing cheap. Moderate cost for help	Very cheap	Cheap tapes. Expensive help	High cost Expensive help	Very cheap if equipment available	Cheap tapes Expensive help
TECHNOLOGY DEPENDANCE	Nil	Nil	Moderate OHP backup	Moderate, keep spare bulb	Complete	Complete	Moderate. OHP backup	Moderate OHP backup
COMMENTS	Pre-prepared Silent Use at any time	Pre-prepared Silent Use at any time Turn back on audience	Noisy, hot Must be in order 'Professional' feel to best use	Hot and noisy Portable Few problems	Top class quality only Integration difficult	Old technology. Fussy use Integration difficult	'Medium is the message' High impact	Few uses in IS area

Fig. 4.3 Matrix of commonly used visual aids

Presenters can use them to record the comments of their audience or as a sketch pad on which to illustrate their replies.

From a company point of view, flip charts are cheap and easy to use. They need no specialist equipment except for a few felt tip pens and are not susceptible to breakdown. For small rooms and small audiences they are ideal and although they are 'low tech' their extensive use in management training makes them acceptable as a professional visual aid.

Whiteboards

Whiteboards have overtaken blackboards in colleges and training departments, ostensibly for health and safety reasons. They have many of the advantages of the flip chart, being cheap, easy to use and free from technological malfunction. Added advantages include the amount of information that can be displayed on them and the ease of making additions or corrections. Because of their size they can be used even in large lecture theatres.

On the debit side, whiteboards are cumbersome to use. Unless you are able to gain access to the room well in advance and write up your information on the board there is the problem of ignoring one's audience. You are faced with the choice between ignoring the audience completely while you write up your comments or draw your diagram on the board, or of talking to the audience with your back to them. In the latter case you are trying to do two things at the same time. This is a recipe for disaster; you lose audibility by talking at the board whilst being impolite to your audience at the same time.

Teachers and lecturers spend hours learning how to use a whiteboard, trying to keep the writing large enough to read and preventing it drooping away across the board. Its apparent ease of use is a trap for the unwary! If you are using a room with a whiteboard in it make sure that you clean it before you begin; however boring the material on it may be the audience will invariably prefer it to what you are saying. Carry a set of your own whiteboard pens, just in case, and check them before leaving your home base. The ones that you find in the room are sure to have dried out.

The whiteboard is not a permanent record of what was said, nor is it as versatile as the flip chart. Having said that, it is useful as a jotter when answering questions and it never goes wrong.

Slides

Slides have all the advantages of the photograph. They make us think that we are getting a full view of the place as it actually is, usually in full colour. For this reason many companies have collections of slides which they use for promotional purposes. The best of these are very good indeed and help the audience to understand, say, the layout of a parts section or the conditions of a 'goods inwards' bay. Double projection, that is using two sets of equipment to project two pictures simultaneously, is a useful technique for comparing two related objects or for 'before and after' comparisons. This demands very careful rehearsal and preparation.

Should you be a reasonable photographer you can also produce slides yourself. If the point you are trying to make is that at peak times the current system is so slow that it causes huge queues as customers wait for their purchases to be processed then the best way to make this point is by a photograph of those same queues. If stores are a mess, piled high with a huge range of stock which could obviously be reduced with a computerised system, then a clear photograph of stores will back up your point. Some of the best presentations use slides to illustrate background material with which the audience is not familiar. For example, a talk on constructing an historical database on windmills for an educational foundation was enlivened for the audience by a set of slides of the windmills in question.

Slides are cheap to produce, although the top class equipment for projecting them is less so. You need a room which blacks out well, especially on sunny days, and a good surface, either a screen or a clear wall, on which to project them. An extension lead is a useful accessory. Remember to label your slides and to place a red dot in the bottom left hand corner (this becomes the top right when you project so that your slide holder should present a consistent row of red dots). Always run through all of your slides beforehand to check that they are the right way up; *never* rely only on the dots.

If you are producing your own slides remember that you need to obtain permission first. This may take some time, especially with companies who are security conscious. Slides are rarely developed by local photographic companies 'in house' and are sent back to the makers of the film for processing. You therefore need to allow several weeks for delays and re-shoots. Slides which are of poor quality should not be used. If in doubt about your own abilities get a skilled amateur or a professional to take them for you.

Slide projectors are hot and noisy. You will need to raise your voice in order to be heard clearly and make sure that ventilation is increased. Bulbs do blow on slide projectors, so you will need to have a spare handy, or two if you are using double projection. If your automatic control lead is not long enough you may need to engage someone to change slides for you, using an agreed signal.

Slides are cheap, can be prepared in advance, are portable, have high impact and are easy to use. Setting up is slightly fussy and areas of application are limited. They cannot be altered or manipulated during the course of the presentation.

Overhead projectors

Overhead projectors were developed to replace the whiteboard because of the latter's limitations. These, you will remember, are: lack of portability, lack of permanence, difficult to pre-prepare and the necessity of turning away from the audience when using it. The projector itself can be carried from room to room, whilst the slides will fit into a briefcase. Many professional presenters use ring binders and plastic 'envelopes' in which to keep their overhead transparencies.

The transparencies themselves are sheets of acetate on which the presenter writes or prints the desired image. Nowadays this can be done direct from a PC onto a laser colour or monochrome printer. Be careful to use the right sort of acetate, as the ordinary ones tend to melt in the printer. Ink jet printers need their own special acetates, which have a more 'laid' surface for the ink to take on to. Some users find difficulty with ink from inkjet printers running or smudging. Computer-generated acetates are obviously a boon to the presenter who no longer has to draw diagrams, set out statements of accounts or write up spreadsheets by hand.

Take care when preparing the layout of your acetates. There is only a limited amount of information that your audience can take in at any one time, so that a crowded screen can be counter-productive. The exception is where you deliberately reproduce an example of poor presentation in order to make a point. Otherwise your document needs to be rather sparsely laid out in order to gain maximum impact. Print should be large and clear. The bigger the room you are using the larger your print should be, and the larger the projection area you use. Check your print for clarity and quality and try to use a new toner cartridge wherever possible.

Colour can be added by hand if you do not have access to a colour printer, though this should be done as neatly as possible. Charts, diagrams, graphs and screen shots are a much better use of overhead visuals than lists of figures or mere words; listeners can be referred back to your main report for detailed information. Systems analysis diagrams are popular subjects for projection and should be used sparingly. In general you should put up each screen for at least half a minute and talk through its significance. ('*As you can see, this is a profit and loss account*' is *not* a good way of presenting visual information.)

With this in mind, how would we use a logical data structure? Our first diagram might be of the structure as a whole in order to give an overview, despite its rather complex nature. We would take the audience through the main boxes in order to illustrate the relationships involved. The next slide might take the early processes only, so that they might be viewed in greater detail whilst still keeping the overall structure in mind. Use a sheet of paper or piece of card to reveal each step and to prevent the audience from moving ahead of you.

A similar approach could be evoked with an organisation chart, using overlays. The first slide gives a structure down to departmental level. Another is added over the top to show the breakdown within departments, then a third which adds the relationship to external entities. Thus the whole is seen in terms of its parts without too much information being presented at any one time.

When using an overhead projector, check first that your slide is correctly lined up on the wall or screen and that it is in focus. Remember that you should face your audience at all times, so indicate and point to areas on the chart itself, not on the screen behind you. A simple pointer should be used, such as a pencil, which can also be rested on the screen whilst you talk on that particular point. This is also a useful tip if you cannot control your nervous shakes.

The projector should be mounted in such a way that the glass screen is level with the top of the desk. Should you have to mount it on top of the desk or table remember that you are probably cutting off somebody's view of the image. You can either check with the audience where the best place is for you to stand or move around frequently so that everyone has a chance to see. Again, the older type of overhead projectors are quite noisy, so switch them off when not in use and during question sessions, unless the question involves information from one of the slides. You do not need to turn off the machine when merely changing slides. It is a good idea to number your slides in case of accident and this also helps your audience to identify them when asking questions.

Assuming that you do not need to buy the projector, overheads are cheap and easy to use, although printer quality acetates are dearer than others. Quite high quality can be achieved and the slides will last almost as long as you wish. Bigger rooms present minor difficulties as does the possibility of blowing bulbs. Otherwise this is an excellent and well-proven method of presentation.

Video

Quality video production is expensive. Think in terms of a minimum of one hour spent making each minute of film and you will see how quickly the costs mount up. At a time when Channel 4's budget for an hour of television was £30,000, Levi jeans were spending £100,000 on a two-minute commercial. Any video that an organisation presents will inevitably be judged against those professional standards and found wanting if they fail to reach them. Consequently, companies tend to employ production companies when needed.

You are more likely, then, to be using either an excerpt from an existing product or some sort of 'home movie'. Uses of existing products cover the whole range, from business features in magazine programmes through to excerpts from comedy shows which illustrate a particular point, such as fear of computers. Anyone who tapes such items 'off air' should check the position as regards copyright first before using them in public.

Unlikely as it may seem, some effective presentations have been mounted using small amounts of 'home movie' footage. One in particular involved a hire shop where the computerised logging and payments system was not operating as it should. The footage was shot without sound, allowing the speaker to talk over the images and give extra information. A general view of the store illustrated the speaker's contention that one of the problems was the sheer range of items on display. Further footage gave a 'real time' view of how an item was loaned out and the paperwork involved before it could leave the shop. This enabled us to feel that we were the customer, impatiently waiting for the printer to come up with receipts and conditions of hire.

In this case the presenter was able to achieve a reasonable enough quality for the audience to be able to follow. The short duration of the video and the sensible decision to abandon sound reproduction allowed the audience to forget its usual demands for high production standards.

Video is useful in short bursts which are integrated into the general presentation. It has high impact and can convey visual information quickly and in an exciting manner. You will need to have all your equipment installed and working well before the presentation begins and the video tape wound through to the correct spot so that there is no extraneous footage or embarrassing gaps in the presentation. Most people nowadays can operate a video recorder, though you should be aware that malfunction is likelier than in any of the methods discussed so far.

Film

Outside of the cinema, film is old technology. Even here it is being replaced by videotape despite its alleged superior quality of tone and colour. Film is more difficult to use, can only be exposed once and not reused and needs to be processed in the same way as slides. From the presenter's point of view it is also more difficult to use. It has to be laced into a machine, although most are now semi-automatic, and played through complete without stopping or talking over the images. Even modern film projectors are noisier than video players. Only the use of archive film justifies the use of such inappropriate technology nowadays.

Video display units

The Canadian communications theorist Marshall McCluhan coined the phrase 'the medium is the message.' By this he meant that the way the message was presented altered your basic understanding of that message, and that good communications came about when message and medium were in complete congruence. Naturally, for workers in the information systems area the perfect medium for transmitting messages is through the computer and the visual display unit.

Older readers will remember the days when VDUs were linked to television screens so that presenters could work on-screen in front of an audience. The limitations were linked to the television technology of the day, with insufficient definition, low point size of the print and problems of reflected light. Modern technology has done away with the television and allows the image on the VDU screen to be projected directly on to a wall or screen in full colour.

Advantages of such systems are obvious. You can demonstrate the program you have written as it operates, exhibit your company's new accounts package, show where the glitches are in a commercial product or take a class of trainees through a package screen by screen.

So what are the problems? It is relatively expensive to buy and install. Once installed it cannot be moved around, so that only one room can be used. (Given the speed of technical advance it is reasonable to expect a portable version to be developed within the next few years.) More importantly, it involves a complete reliance on the technology. Once the system goes down for whatever reason, such as a corrupt disk or a spilled cup of coffee, you have no presentation. The solution is to have your presentation backed up on to overheads, which can be brought to light at moments of crisis.

Despite limitations of price and mobility it seems likely that this will be the preferred method of presentation within the information systems community for the foreseeable future, combining as it does the advantages of the overhead projector with that of other aids such as the slide projector and whiteboard.

Sound tapes

Anyone who has ever recorded an interview with a client knows the problems associated with sound tapes. Although easy and cheap to use at a basic level the reproduction quality depends on far too many variables to make them dependable. The quality of the tape itself, the recording instrument and the microphone all have a significant impact. The conditions under which they are used also raise difficulties. Variations in distance of speakers from the microphones, exterior noise and interference and equipment malfunction all cause difficulties. These are compounded by further equipment problems on playback and the poor acoustics of most rooms in which they are used. Even commercially produced tapes can be ruined by these latter difficulties.

It is, however, possible to produce good quality recordings by using quality equipment under controlled conditions but it is rarely worth the effort. Some companies still use tape-slide packages as do many art galleries. This involves setting up a commentary on a sound tape and implanting an electronic pulse at points where a new slide is to be shown. As long as slide and commentary are kept synchronised such a system works well and many are still in use a decade or more after they were produced.

Unless you are going to get a lot of usage from it this sort of package is not worth the effort, especially as it involves the purchase of specialised equipment. Although more portable than a video and television, a tape-slide package leaves you totally reliant on the technology.

Handouts

The great advantage of handouts is that, once produced, they have no reliance on technology whatsoever. Their disadvantage is that they are difficult to use.

Let us start with handouts that are going to be used during a presentation. There are virtually no limits as to what might go on them, although large amounts of text tend to be disrupting. For a small audience of up to half a dozen you can give out handouts as you go, fitting them to the stage you have reached in your presentation. Larger audiences produce distribution problems and you can find yourself well in to the next section before a group of fifty or so have handed round the papers. This is very disruptive.

With a larger group the secret is to staple the handouts together in sets and give them all out at the beginning. If you do this you also need to keep the audience in step with your presentation by fixing their attention firmly on the paperwork and not letting them rush ahead. For this reason you should let larger audiences have the handout only at the end of the session as a kind of *aide-memoire*.

Computer companies use handouts as promotional material for the clients to take away with them, so much so that visitors to computer fairs can be seen staggering under the weight of bulging plastic bags. How much of this gets read and how much used to light the family barbecue is a moot point. For the speaker in front of a small but committed audience, handouts still remain a cheap and effective means of leaving the listeners with a list of the main points covered and the recommendations flowing from them.

4.6 CONCLUSION

Oral presentations are a common form of business communication. They enable information and ideas to be passed swiftly to a large number of people, with immediate controlled feedback from the audience to the presenter. Within information systems they are used extensively to demonstrate new hardware and software systems, to sell products and to enhance the information flow through the company.

When preparing an oral presentation you should consider

- the quality and accuracy of what you have to say
- the nature of your audience

- how you are to organise your material
- your use of notes, including demonstrations
- the language in which your presentation is encoded
- the clarity and audibility of your voice
- the timing of the presentation as a whole and of its constituent parts
- the choice and use of visual aids.

Once you have prepared to the best of your ability, **rehearse** your presentation until it is as near perfect as you can make it. This will give you the smoothness and confidence that you need to impress the audience with your ability and competence and the quality of your product.

CHAPTER 5
Writing reports

INTRODUCTION

Reports are a standard method of conveying information within and between organisations. They also operate as check mechanisms to ensure that work and processes have been done and that analyses of operations have been carried out. Employees who have been sent on courses or conferences at the company's expense may be asked to report on their activities and to assess their value.

Although oral reports can be delivered to large numbers of people all at once, the written report has the advantages that it can be read at the recipient's convenience and can be retained for further reference. Research reports, for example, may end up in the company library or published in specialist journals.

For consultants in information systems the end product, the deliverable to the client, may well be the report alone. The consultant could be asked to review systems, to report on training matters or to evaluate hardware and software for a particular purpose. However well these activities may have been carried out in themselves all the client has in return for the fee is the report. If the consultant's report is poor, unreadable or unrepresentative of the skill and effort invested in the work it is unlikely to convince the client to follow its recommendations or to retain the consultant for any follow-up business that might occur.

For example, the review of the system might recommend that it is to be updated and expanded. Follow-up business could involve the purchase and installation of the new system and training of the users. There might be new programs to be written. This amount of work would be quite lucrative to the consultant but will only follow if the client is convinced of the consultant's expertise as demonstrated in the original report. An inability to write a good report can cost money in terms of commissions and promotion.

Even at what we might term the operative level there is still a need for the production of minor reports on matters of health and safety, working practices and so on. Some reports are basic presentations of such things as sales statistics or staff absenteeism, providing the basic data which might later be incorporated into a full-scale management report. These shade into structured responses and memoranda, which will be dealt with towards the end of the chapter. For the moment let us concentrate on the large-scale management report itself, which may include feasibility reports for systems analysis and in-house reports on hardware and software.

5.1 THE AUDIENCE

Whatever the subject, objectives or purpose of your report the most important consideration is its audience. Who are you writing for? Is your primary reader the head of the DP department, with twenty years' experience and a Ph.D. in Business Information Systems, or is it a self-employed printer with almost no knowledge of the computer world? The approach and language that you use, the illustrations that you give, the assumptions that you make will differ widely between the two.

The majority of reports are commissioned, either explicitly or implicitly. The request by the head of the DP department for a report on specified software is an example of an explicit commission. Writing a report on that conference you attended because that is what everyone in the company is expected to do is an example of an implicit commission. Writing a feasibility study for a client as part of your systems analysis (even though the client has no idea what a feasibility study is) can be seen as falling somewhere between the two. You must be clear in your own mind of the identity of the commissioner and the relationship between you.

The aim and parameters of the report should be clearly established between yourself and the client. If your brief is to log the existence and whereabouts of all of the PCs in the organisation, what are the objectives of the exercise? It could be to prevent theft, in which case serial numbers and official 'ownership' within the organisation might be important. On the other hand, it might be part of a drive towards standardisation and greater control of hardware by the DP department. In this case, we might need to establish the capacity of the equipment and the functions for which it is used.

As usual there is a certain political undertone to the negotiations that you undertake at this point. Your commissioner may not be completely forthright about the true objectives of the exercise, yet you need to establish what data is likely to be considered relevant and what will be irrelevant. Although you might be guided by inferences that you make in negotiations at the end of the process it is still imperative to get your brief clearly laid down in writing. This is frequently enshrined as formal terms of reference.

Terms of reference lay out clearly the exact area that a report is to cover and consequently determine the amount of time that will be spent preparing the report and the depth to which it will have to go. For the independent consultant this is essential information as it determines the contract price that will be quoted and the availability of the consultant to carry out work for other clients.

If we take the previous example of the location of PCs within the company, our terms of reference could be as follows:

From:	Leon Russell, Systems Manager, Delta Products Inc.
To:	Geoff Hamilton, Hamilton Computer Consultants Ltd.
Subject:	Terms of Reference for investigation of PC availability within the company.

The Terms of Reference for your investigation should include the following:

1. Identification of all PCs owned by the company.
2. Identification of all PCs by make, description and serial number.
3. Current normal location of all PCs.
4. Current actual location.
5. Responsible party by department, job title and name.
6. Uses to which each machine is put.

> 7. Date of purchase of each machine.
> 8. Matching of machines to purchase invoices.
> 9. Identification of discrepancies between invoices and located PCs.
> 10. Recommendations for a policy of PC usage within the company.

This exercise was actually carried out by a consultant for the new owners of a company which had had several owners over quite a short time and which was trying to improve its overall efficiency.

The first five points are unobjectionable. Company property has to be identified, if only for inventory purposes. Once identified it can then be located at will and lines of responsibility for its accessibility and maintenance drawn up.

Point six is clearly related to point ten. Mr. Russell, newly appointed to the post by the holding company, obviously has something in mind, whether it is the replacement of stand-alone machines by a network or the introduction of company standards of software and hardware we do not know. What we do know is that this is likely to be very difficult and time-consuming. Not only do we need to find every machine we also need to interview its user or users and get from them a clear statement of how and why the machine is used. Mr. Hamilton has to take great care at this point over costing his services or, depending on the size of the organisation, negotiating with Mr. Russell that only a representative sample of machines should be surveyed.

Points seven, eight and nine Mr. Hamilton rejects out of hand. Besides being somewhat outside his area of expertise (they are best handled by an accountant) they may involve employees being involved in legal action. Not only does he feel that this is not in the best interests of good industrial relations, he also does not want to find himself involved in legal process and industrial tribunals. Mr. Hamilton is also dubious of the amount of co-operation he will receive from the workforce if it is felt that he is involved in a quasi-legal investigation.

He therefore goes back to his clients and re-negotiates his terms of reference, including a delivery date for the report:

From: Geoff Hamilton, Hamilton Computer Consultants Ltd.

To: Leon Russell, Systems Manager, Delta Products Inc.

Subject: Terms of Reference for investigation of PC availability within the company.

Following our recent conversations I confirm that the Terms of Reference for our investigation should be as follows:

1. Identification of all PCs owned by the company.
2. Identification of all PCs by make, description and serial number.
3. Current normal location of all PCs.
4. Current actual location.
5. Responsible party by department, job title and name.
6. Uses to which each machine is put.
7. Date of purchase of each machine.
8. Recommendations for a policy of PC usage within the company.

> The company will provide full access to all parts of the company premises and all company employees at all normal working times. The report will be delivered in full to Mr. Russell on or before 25th March of this current year.

You will notice that point seven has been retained. Mr. Russell insisted on this in order that he could immediately identify the antiquity of each machine, which would give him a rough guide as to its continued utility to the company. The original points eight and nine have been deleted. Mr. Hamilton now knows **who** is going to use his report, he has a good idea of **why** it is being prepared and has negotiated **when** it will be delivered. He has also established full authority for his investigations.

In this example Mr. Hamilton's job is simplified by the fact that he is preparing his report for one person. More often reports end up on the desks of several people with a variety of wants, needs and backgrounds. The accountant may be interested in the cost-benefit analysis and totally ignorant of the technical specifications. A production manager may just want the job done with the maximum of benefit and the minimum of disruption. The personnel manager wants to establish quickly what changes are to be made and what this means in terms of recruitment and training. How can the report writer satisfy all of these people at once?

The keyword here is **clarity**. All reports need to be written in as clear and unambiguous language as possible with technical jargon included only when absolutely necessary. Where technical or highly specific information has to be included then it should be relegated to an appendix, with a simple digest appearing in the main text. Thus our self-employed printer may be told in the main text that what is required is the fastest and most powerful machine available in order to cope with the large amounts of graphics and text manipulation that will be used and that this will cost in excess of £X. Full technical details of the various systems (which the printer currently does not understand) will appear in the appendix rather than interrupting the flow of the narrative. The client can then use this information when purchasing the new system or for cross-checking its validity before commissioning the consultant to purchase and install it.

A more complex report will deal with information in a similar manner. All of the sections will be in clear English, with specialist areas in the appendices. Thus the accountant can study the figures in detail, the personnel manager can look at the training needs analysis, and the production manager can have both a report on the technical specifications of the new computer-controlled system and a GANTT chart setting out the timetable for its installation and implementation. None of them should have any difficulty in reading the text of the main body of the report.

Our difficulty lies in establishing what might constitute an area of difficulty. When writing for others within the broad area of information systems the answer is relatively simple. You are entitled to assume that your readers know as much as you did before you began researching your report, unless you happen to be an expert in that particular field. However, we all know that there is more knowledge lying dormant in our brains than we can readily bring to mind. If pushed we might be able to state Ohm's law or the second law of thermodynamics but perhaps the method of solving simultaneous equations is eluding us for the present. This is especially true of information which we do not use regularly or which we did not learn thoroughly in the first place.

If the report writer is making a point that leans heavily on the sort of information that 'everyone knows' it is as well to remind the audience of it just in case. The reader can then progress steadily through the argument without any undue racking of brains or recourse to reference books. On the other hand, the head of the DP department does not need to be given an organisation chart of the department with the report (although this would be included if the report had more extensive distribution). Nor does our printer need to be told how artwork gets from the drawing board to the finished printed page.

Another associated problem that arises is in the meaning of words and concepts. 'Everyone knows' what a bus or a ring is, until they try and explain it to a non-technical outsider. Try explaining clearly what a 'fourth generation language' is, how it differs from a third generation one and how it can be described as a language at all. If you undertake this task seriously you will find that you are not totally clear about the answers to these questions yourself. At least you are now in the position that you have recognised an area of ignorance and can take steps to rectify it.

The relevance of this example for the project writer is that the writer needs to take care over accepting that words and concepts are clearly understood by writer or reader. Making an attempt to lay them out clearly in writing can be beneficial in that it may identify such areas of ignorance or confusion. An analogy to this is in systems analysis, where the analyst draws up diagrams of the existing system, partly in order to check that the analyst's understanding is coherent. Clearly, setting out the constituent ideas in a report has a similar function. You are clear that you understand them and have set this out for your readers. Even if they do not agree with your definition for some reason (too broad? too narrow?) they at least know what it *is* and can operate within your conceptual framework.

Exactly what appears in the report comes down to a matter of judgement by the writer of the expertise and current level of knowledge of the readers. Whilst not teaching grandmother to suck eggs the writer needs to give a clear view of defining principles and the progression of the argument towards its final conclusions. Though brevity may be a virtue, clarity is an even greater one.

A problem which afflicts the outside consultant is that of **culture**. Culture in this context is used in a sociological sense of a set of received values by a group or clan. Information systems professionals have their own sub-culture, as do nurses, teachers, insurance agents and printers. Occupational sub-cultures may share a common educational background or view on society which other groups do not have. For example, a nurse will fight to give the patient the best possible care and treatment regardless of cost, whilst the insurance agent will be balancing the client's means against the amount of private medical care that can be provided. The teacher will value human contact over contact with machines; the printer may feel that layout and correctness are more important than the content of the article that is printed. Although these may be seen as stereotypes there is no doubt that employees experience a distinct 'culture shock' when transferring between occupational areas.

For the computer consultant the difficulty is to be able to stand apart from the IS culture and temporarily to enter into that of the client. Where the IS professional values speed of response and a variety of facilities in a program the user may prefer a more human interface (despite its adverse effects on response times) and a clear layout of a moderate number of simple tasks. In salesperson's terms, the IS person is concerned with the computer's features, the user is concerned with its benefits. To be of greatest benefit the consultant has to empathise with the client in order to be able to communicate at the same cultural level.

As in all communications, in report writing the audience is always right. If they have not understood, then it is the writer's fault in some way. Readers need what you have to say, in a way that they can understand. If this means regression to a form of technological baby talk, then so be it. Define your terms, define your technical language and keep everything as simple as possible.

5.2 WORD PROCESSING

Over the last ten years or so word processing has virtually destroyed the old mechanical typewriter industry. The benefits of on-screen editing, text manipulation and electronic storage have converted even the most conservative and sceptical of writers and businessmen. Some companies could not handle the volume of business that they need in order to remain profitable without using word processors, whilst others have eliminated whole departments or sections in favour of the computer.

Magazine and newspaper publishing has been revolutionised by the use of modems and scanners. Editors now send off their layouts to printers on floppy disks, perhaps automatically downloaded from the disks sent in by contributing writers. Smaller circulation magazines, such as 'fanzines', might even be laid out and printed directly by the editor using a desk-top publishing program.

For a few hundred pounds anyone can now be in possession of an advanced desktop publishing system complete with printer. Possession of this software does not make the owner a designer any more than possession of a gun makes you a marksman. Like a gun it needs to be handled with care and only used in appropriate circumstances.

Despite pressure on college resources, students on information systems courses are expected to word process their assignments. Informal research revealed that some seventy per cent of second year students owned their own computer and slightly over twenty per cent had a dtp application of some sort. None of the eighty students questioned had had any design training.

In this section we will be concerned not with the mechanics of using a word processor or dtp package (information which you can glean from the manual of the system you are using) but with considerations of layout and audience friendliness.

5.2.1 Page layout

The two most commonly used forms of layout for reports are Block layout and Indent layout. Block layout uses a strict left justification, that is all the words at the beginning of a line are against the left hand margin. Paragraphs are signalled by leaving an extra line at the end of each. This is slightly more common in the IS area and in the presentation of formal reports, as in the following example:

For quick location within a chapter, the chapter number and title have been included as a footer on each page. This allows the reader to navigate quickly through the book.

The quick reference guide allows the user to overview the menu bar listings and shows the location of all functions. Empty pages have been left in the back of the manual for user's notes.

(Block layout using both left and right justification.)

Indented layout indents the first word of each paragraph by a standard amount, usually fixed in advance by use of the tab key. No line is left at the end of the paragraph. Indenting is seen in some quarters as a more 'traditional' style and tends to be preferred by the professions.

We all know that the more hands a communication passes through the more likely it is to be distorted. This is partly because of distortions and noise in the transmission process, where details are poorly transmitted or not received properly (as in 'Chinese whispers') and partly because we interpret and paraphrase information that comes to us in order to fit it into our own conceptual framework and to be able to understand and memorise it better.

Even when this is done from the best of motives it can still result in the message being changed from the intentions of the sender. The greatest problems arise when neither sender nor receiver realise that such changes have taken place.

(Indented layout, with left justification and right 'ragged edge'.)

In both cases there is discussion about right justification, the aligning of all text down the right hand side, as opposed to 'ragged edge'. Although justification is associated with block layout and ragged edge with indenting there are no rigid rules. Justification operates by the computer squeezing or compacting space so that the characters fit exactly on the line. With smaller font sizes this is imperceptible. Larger fonts, however, with a fewer number of characters can look distorted and the spaces between characters appear uneven. You may sometimes have come across this in newspapers, where some lines have a 'sat on' appearance or where the opening up of the text has left irregular 'rivers' of space running down the page.

The objectives of using justification largely emanates from the desire for conservative layouts, where alternatives are clearly signalled by introducing new paragraphs.

Where this necessitates fewer characters in mathematical ratio to the line size, especially if characters are emphasised by larger fonts, distortion of text can result, thus offending the reader's aesthetic sensibilities.

(Fully justified text in larger type, illustrating the excessive opening up of the space between words, leading to large amounts of white space, forming into 'rivers' within the text.)

More important from a reader's point of view is the daunting impression of a solid page of text justified down both sides. A ragged edge can open up the space and allow in some fresh air visually, besides being much easier to read. On the other hand, justification is felt to add seriousness and solidity. Whichever system you use, be consistent. Do not mix them in the same report.

The overall layout can also be improved by allowing generous amounts of space around the page. The type is allowed to breathe and does not feel heavy and threatening. Block layouts in particular need this kind of treatment. Again, it must be consistent throughout the document.

How you organise the page space depends on the general layout and binding of the document. However, there are some general guidelines to observe. Try to make your foot margin roughly twice the depth of your top margin. This helps to anchor the text to the page, preventing the impression of it sliding off the bottom which can occur when the foot margin is too small. For documents printed on both sides of the page the inner margins (that is, the ones nearest the spine of the document) should be half the width of the outer margins. When opened, the document will then present us with three equal vertical margins.

The exception would be in cases when you deliberately wish to leave a large margin, perhaps for notes or comments, or where the binding of the document necessitates extra space on the inner edge. Such would be the case where the document is stapled vertically or where a ring binding system is used. Having to force apart the binding in order to read the text can be most frustrating for the reader and can quickly ruin the binding.

Even in this case you need to establish a sensible mathematical ratio between the margins. Something like two or three to one would be appropriate. This is the kind of layout that the Inland Revenue now use for their information documents, formal but easy to read and with plenty of space for additions by the reader.

You may be able to adjust your page to allow for the introduction of columns, as in a newspaper layout. Don't. Readers of business reports expect to have lines that cover the whole width of the page; the convention is that writing in columns is more 'light weight'. What you might do instead is to reduce the length of your standard lines slightly to produce a line which has a standard word count of around ten to twelve words per line. This makes the document easier to read without offending conventional sensibilities.

5.2.2 Spacing

The text itself can be spaced in two ways. The size of the letters can be altered and the space between the lines can be adjusted.

Traditionally, letter size is measured by points. There are seventy-two points to an inch, so that twenty point type is quite large, whilst six point is rather small. You might use twenty point when preparing a set of overhead projector transparencies for an oral presentation and the six point for labelling on a complex diagram. Reports would usually be written in ten or twelve point, with a preference for the latter.

Note that increasing the point size of type increases its width as well as its height. Changing font sizes can therefore have untoward effects on the rest of your layout such as right justification and page breaks.

Line spacing on word processors can be expressed either in millimetres or in half lines. Experiment with the settings on your particular system until you are happy that you have the right balance between space and type. Some academic reports, such as Ph.D. theses, demand double spacing so that comments and insertions can be made between the lines. Business reports tend to have single or one and a half line spacing. The line spaces themselves are described in terms of pitch sizes. Most printers work to a default pitch size of 6 (that is six lines to the inch) although this can be altered should you wish.

Within the text itself you need to operate a standard spacing system. Printers' conventions are slightly different to those used by typists. Since reports in the past would usually have been produced by the latter we will deal only with typists' conventions, in order to avoid confusion.

Words must be separated by a single space between them. Any following punctuation, such as a full stop, comma or question mark, comes directly after the previous word, with no intervening space. Use two spaces after the end of a sentence. The sentence will be marked by either a full stop, exclamation mark or a question mark. Any punctuation *within* a sentence, such as a comma, colon or semi-colon, should be followed by a single space.

5.2.3 Identifying text

The simplest identifier in any report is by page number. These can be set automatically on even the simplest word processors, which will also allow limited choice of positioning. Large documents which use facing pages (such as this book) tend to have the numbers situated in the top or bottom corners. Smaller and single-sided documents are more likely to centre the number at either top or bottom. The main part of the text should use Arabic numerals, with roman numerals reserved for appendices.

Smaller documents, which are for that reason not likely to be securely bound, may have footer messages at the bottom of each page. These vary from the simple 'continues' to identifiers such as 'Page 6 of 8', and are particularly helpful in meetings where the document may be dismembered in order to facilitate discussion and is subsequently reassembled. Some companies insist on the document reference initials appearing on each page, usually in the bottom left section of the footer.

Again, larger documents such as books, may have added headers on each page, perhaps with the title of the book on the left and the chapter heading on the right. Reports can be enhanced by headers which contain information such as title and author, the originating company or the target company/company logo. The temptation to overload the header should be avoided, since it can become visually heavy as well as taking up valuable space and printing time.

5.2.4   Typefaces and fonts

Most modern word processors will give a choice of at least six typefaces, some even more. Disks can be purchased which will extend the number to over fifty. In practice most people never need more than one or two, such as Helvetica or Times Roman, which are familiar and easy to read. Specialist styles such as Deco or Bauhaus (which has no capital letters!) are best avoided in favour of the plain and simple.

Besides being fun it is also useful to print out a standard text from your machine in all the typefaces and fonts that it offers. From this you can then make a choice depending on your personal design preference and the readability of the typeface. You will also see that some appear larger than others, even though they have the same nominal size. Do not worry about this, it is in the nature of the typefaces themselves, but it is something to take into account when deciding which typeface to use. Remember that the legibility of the printed page is a function of:

- the size of the type
- the length of the line
- the spacing between the lines.

Recently script typefaces have been appearing on some machines. These replicate the features of handwriting and are used in textbooks, for example, to indicate that the letter illustrated has been handwritten. A few organisations also use them to get over the feeling of the impersonal nature of machine-generated letters. Few would regard scripts as formal enough for use in report writing and they are best avoided.

Emphasis can be added within any typeface by the addition of such features as emboldening, italics or underlining. Of these **emboldening**, used within measure, is perhaps the most useful. It can be used for major headings, for numbering sections or for emphasising particular words. Used to excess its purpose is undermined and it can give an unhealthily spotty appearance to the text of the sort which is rife in promotional material from public relations consultants.

Italics are less aggressive than bold or even normal text, so much so that some writers use them to replace quotation marks or to indicate that a foreign word is being used. Because of its gentler appearance italic is used to indicate difference rather than emphasis. Thus it is unusual to use italic for headings except at a very low level.

Underlining is fast disappearing from the printed page, being replaced by emboldening. Underlining words causes them to lose their visual shape and makes them harder to read as well as digging in to the visual space between lines. With letters which have descenders, that is letters which descend below the line, underlining cuts into the actual word, as in <u>grey</u>, <u>employer</u> or <u>opportunity</u>. Where a document is to be copy typed it may also cause confusion, since underlining is a signal that the words should be typed in italic.

CAPITAL LETTERS are an additional way of adding emphasis. In a properly printed word-processed document they have no advantage over emboldening when used as part of the main text. They can serve an important function by indicating a hierarchy within the header system, where main headings might be consistently designated by using the upper case.

If you have access to a colour printer you may be tempted to use colour to emphasise certain parts of your report. Technically the use of colour does not add emphasis at all. Since black type on white gives the greatest contrast on the printed page, the use of colour is for differentiation, in the same way that italic is often used to differentiate different types of information. Because of this lack of contrast you may find it necessary to use greater areas of colour in order to gain an effect. Too much colour, or too many, within the text is disorientating and is best avoided. Its use in diagrams is another matter and will be dealt with later in this chapter.

Whatever system of emphasis you use, do so sparingly. If everything is deemed worthy of emphasis then nothing seems more important than anything else.

5.2.5 Widows and orphans

Having made overall stylistic judgements about typefaces and page layouts there still remains one more decision for the report writer to make before entering text. This is that state of what is referred to as 'widows and orphan'. Widows and orphans refers to the unsightliness of having only the first line of a paragraph appearing at the bottom of a page or only the last line of a paragraph appearing at the top of another. Traditionally printers have regarded this as bad practice and have tried to avoid it.

Word processors cope with this quite happily as long as they are set in advance. You do need to check, though, that they will justify the page vertically in order to compensate for the smaller number of lines. If not, you could be left with a series of pages of grossly irregular lengths, which is far more unsightly than the problem that you were seeking to avoid. Keeping your paragraphs fairly short, besides being an aid to readability, also helps the computer in dealing with vertical justification.

Even with a pre-set system you need to beware of headings. If you leave a line space after headings the word processor will treat these as individual paragraphs and you may well find the heading on one page and the text relegated to the next. This is embarrassing as well as being unsightly.

5.2.6 Text offsets

Whole paragraphs or substantial sections of text can be indented for emphasis or ease of reading. Although these should be used with caution they are an excellent way of breaking up substantial areas of text which might otherwise appear forbidding to the reader. Many of the text offset systems appear as standard on the menu system or style bar of word processor systems. The best approach to them is through the system manual, assuming that it gives examples. If it does not, then experimenting with sample text is the next best solution.

Most of the variations you will be offered by your system will be based around either full or hanging indents, so we will deal with both of these briefly.

> A **full indent** pushes the whole of your text in from the left for a fixed number of tab spaces. This saves you having to type return at the end of each line and then tab in on the next, with all the problems that alterations and insertions could cause. Instead, an indent format retains all the features of normal word processing, such as the wraparound facility and full justification if required.

Indenting might be used if the writer wanted to draw attention to direct speech by an interviewee or a substantial quotation from an authority on the subject. Like other forms of emphasis it should be used sparingly, preferably according to a system which quickly becomes transparent to the reader. Some layouts allow indenting from both left and right, further setting the paragraph apart from the rest of the text.

A **hanging indent** starts the first line of the paragraph in the usual place but then indents all subsequent lines by a standard amount. This is not quite as forceful as a full indent and might be used when attention is being called to a paragraph which yet remains a full part of the main argument rather than illustrative material.

Bullets and **numbers** are similarly used with indents to indicate lists or summaries within the main text. They help the reader both by lightening the page and by providing quick reference points. Numbers are best used rather than bullets when a specified number of points have been referred to in the text (*'There are four reasons why the company should buy this particular system....'*). Otherwise bullets are quite sufficient.

Tables are best created on other applications, such as spreadsheets, and imported in to the document. If the table is quite small or you do not have access to other applications, then they can be created by the word processor. Do not create your spacing by using the space bar, since this can be difficult to manage with any degree of precision. Use the tab key instead, which ensures that all spaces are of exactly the same length.

5.2.7   Headings and numbering

A formal report requires that readers should be able to find their way around it simply and efficiently. On a straight-through reading each section should be clearly signposted in a way that indicates its relative importance and status. When sampled, each section of the report must stand out clearly so that it can be accessed, skimmed or ignored as required. At other times sub-sections of the report may be referred to in detail, making it imperative that they can be readily identified by all users. A numbering system is essential if all of these requirements are to be fulfilled.

Numbering systems can be as sparse or as detailed as you or your company wish. Heavily bureaucratic organisations demand that virtually every sentence or statement is numbered. Organisations whose reports are more discursive (such as social services departments, for example) tend towards a system which numbers only main headings.

A sensible compromise is to take your numbering system down to two decimal points only, as in this chapter. Any greater subdivision interferes with the flow of the text, producing a dreary document. Paradoxically, shorter documents which set out succinct instructions may have more complex numbering systems than longer ones.

Numbering systems might also be combined with headings and indents, although the latter is beginning to go out of fashion as being too cumbersome and time consuming for modern tastes. A hierarchical heading system may involve printing the main section heading in bold capitals with a double spacing beneath. The subsidiary headings would be in upper and lower case but with no space left underneath. Lower level headers might be in ordinary type or in bold with the text running straight on (although this latter is an unlikely solution in a business report).

A few organisations still demand that an indent be added for each sub-point in the numbering system. Thus, a section beginning 4.1 would not be indented at all. Section 4.1.1 would have a single indent, 4.1.1.1 would have a double indent and so on. As well as being environmentally unfriendly in the excessive amount of paper that it uses, this system can lead to idiocies such as only having a few centimetres of space available in which to locate the text of some lower sections. Avoid such a system if you possibly can.

There are no hard and fast rules about constructing your hierarchy of headings and numbers. Just remember that the objective is to present a pleasing layout which the recipient will find easy to read and use. Mixing systems, such as by introducing centred headings in an otherwise left justified document, is a grave mistake.

5.2.8 Spelling, grammar and style checkers

In the early days of typewriters it was found that efficient operators were too quick for the machine. Their nimble fingers sent up the metal rods to which the characters were affixed so quickly that they became entangled and bent. To slow them down the alphabetic keyboard was replaced by the one we know today, the QWERTY keyboard, which is harder to use and takes longer to learn.

Even the best typists made mistakes and each one had to be laboriously remedied with correcting fluid or, in the worst cases, by re-typing the whole document. A well equipped secretary always had a dictionary in which to check the correct spelling of words, since mistakes were very costly in terms of time.

With word processing mistakes are nothing but a pin prick. Indeed, it is claimed that if you are not making mistakes, then you are not typing fast enough. Certainly the computer can ingest and process words far faster than even the best typist can input them. Despite this some users still operate as if they were using a typewriter and fail to take advantage of the word processor's unique advantages.

Most important is the automatic spell checker. These now come as standard, complete with an updating facility to cope with the special needs of each user's vocabulary. Rather than carefully checking each word as it goes into the document, as a typist had to do, the user of a WP system inputs the whole document and instructs the system to check it at the end. This speeds up input time enormously and even with correction time at the end stills produces great savings.

Users who have difficulties with spelling or who have clinical disabilities such as dyslexia find that spell checkers allow them to produce acceptable documentation with ease. Gross errors at least should now be a thing of the past.

However, a word of caution. Spell checkers are not perfect. First, they offer the user a choice of operations: to change the word highlighted, to leave it as it is or to choose from a list of words similar to the one on the screen. The user still has to make a choice, and for this a good dictionary is essential. Similarly, if the system allows you to build up your own dictionary of words you must ensure that the ones you add are correctly spelled or else you will merely be compounding your own errors.

The other difficulty with spell checkers is that they only indicate that they recognise the word in question as having a standard spelling. They do not tell you whether or not you are using the correct word in that context. Simple examples include their, they're and there, or were, where, wear and Ware.

Grammar checkers help with this, indicating that there is a range of possibilities available and asking whether you have chosen the right one. (You can imagine the fury of activity that ensued from grammar checking the previous paragraph!) Better versions will not only ask you if you are sure that you have maintained correct usage but will also supply you with the rule, in case you had forgotten.

As well as being informed about your grammar you can also receive useful information about your paragraph and sentence length and the readability of your text as indicated by the FOG index (see later). Indications can also be derived of the proportion of active and passive expressions.

Style writers operate along similar lines but tend to have a greater range of functions and be more interactive, allowing the user to adjust for type of communication (formal, informal, academic), sentence and paragraph length or even your use of sexist language. If you are deliberately writing in a certain way, producing a report which demands the passive voice for example, you can instruct the program to ignore that analysis type. Similarly, rule explanations can be turned on or off. Better programs give a graphical presentation of sentence length with the ability directly to access ones that are too lengthy.

Style writers usually come with integral spell checkers and thesaurus; with grammar checkers these come as additional external functions. A thesaurus allows you to vary your language so that the same words do not keep appearing, dulling the sense and impact of the text. Thus 'error' in the following passage appears too often:

'There are too many **errors** in your work. These **errors** should be eradicated and an **error**-free text produced.'

After appealing to the thesaurus for help we might rewrite it in the following manner:

'There are too many **inaccuracies** in your work. These **mistakes** should be eradicated and an error-free text produced.'

Beware, though, of being too mechanical in the replacement process. 'Inaccuracy' is not an exact synonym for 'error' and some of the other possibilities (fault, slip, mistake) might be more appropriate. Sometimes there is no alternative for the word you are using. Checking my thesaurus against 'access' gives me a choice of : entrance, entree, entry and ingress, none of which fits into the instruction 'First access your database.'

There are three accusations levelled against electronic style aids:

- They encourage all users towards a dreary norm which allows for no differences or creativity
- They are time consuming and take the users away from more pressing tasks
- They induce a false sense of security.

Let us take these in order. Certainly grammar aids encourage uniformity of good usage, but then that is what teachers of grammar have been seeking from their students for centuries. Good systems are interactive and allow users to accept or discard suggestions. If you want an exceptionally long sentence or a single sentence paragraph your style checker alerts you to their existence, it does not alter them against your will.

There is no doubt that grammar checkers are time consuming. Whether the use of that time is cost effective is a decision that you have to make. Computer users have been known to sit for hours trying to fathom out how to use a comparatively obscure function in a program which they may never use again. Contrast that with the urge to perfect a report whose acceptance may save the company thousands of pounds. Writers have to make their own decisions about when the quest for perfection becomes uneconomic.

As for grammar aids inducing a false sense of security, it is certainly true that students in particular react with a look of incredulity when handed work back with the comment that its grammar is not up to commercial standard. '*But I used the grammar checker*' is a standard response in these circumstances. The problem is one of education, in companies as much as in colleges. Report writers have to be made aware that the computer cannot do it all for them, it is for them to make choices and to apply rules and guidelines in an intelligent manner.

No matter how good your spell checker, grammar checker, thesaurus or style checker may be it is still essential that you carry out final assessment of your report in the old-fashioned way, probably on a paper draft copy. Carefully read through your text and check for errors with the help of a dictionary. If necessary, give the completed text to somebody else to read before printing the final version. When it comes to a judgement of the report by the readers it is you who are the responsible originator, not your word processor. You are the final judge of style and correctness and your final proof reading is vital.

5.2.9 Printing

The output of electronic documents often depends as much on the equipment available to the individual or organisation as upon any aesthetic decision by the author.

Assuming that you do not have a great choice over the exact type of printer you are using there are still some considerations to be borne in mind.

Very few people are able to proof read a document effectively from a VDU. Most of us are more efficient with a hard copy which we can scan and write on. Where appropriate use your printer's 'draft' mode for such copies. This is cheaper and quicker. For students, colleges are increasingly insisting that all printouts on laser printers are paid for, although dot matrix printouts are still free. It therefore makes sense to print out proof copies on the dot matrix printer and only final copies on the laser. If your college is amenable, assignments printed on a good quality dot matrix printer should be quite sufficient.

Good quality dot matrix printers are now the equal of old-fashioned typewriters and their printout is quite adequate for everyday in-house reports and college assignments. Remember that they are more economic to produce compared to other systems.

For reports that are in the public domain and where a high level of presentation is a significant factor then ink-jet and laser printers are the obvious choice. Both produce excellent results and the falling prices of printers has brought them within the reach of the average user. Ink jet printers are cheaper to buy, especially if one wants to use colour. There still remains the problem of smudging, caused by the ink being literally sprayed onto the page and having to dry before being touched. This is particularly true when large fonts, with consequent large areas of ink, are being used. Acetates for use on overhead projectors are also more expensive for ink jet machines.

Colour copiers are now widely available at astonishingly low prices. There can be no doubt that colour, handled judiciously, enhances the appearance of a document. Diagrams, graphs and even text can gain more impact when presented in this way and the commercial advantages of colour printing are obvious.

5.2.10 Conclusion

Whatever system of layout, presentation and production you use is up to you. What you need to remember is that your objective is to give the correct impression to your intended reader. The documents should be easy to use and pleasant to read. Important points need to be emphasised but this can be done with subtle methods such as hierarchical headings as well as with emboldening or increased type sizes.

Experiment with a variety of presentations, but remember that those experiments are for your private information and are not to be carried out on documents that are intended for use by others. Keep your general structures simple, in terms of typography and layout. Any departures from your basic system need to be clearly justified. If in any doubt, don't do it!

As in the writing and presentation of projects as a whole, clarity and simplicity are the watchwords, taste and restraint are important. Leave complex effects and multiple columns for the newspapers and magazines.

5.3 AN EXAMPLE REPORT FORMAT

It is important to realise that what is suggested in this section is not the only possible way in which a report can be presented. Many organisations have their own expectations for project contents and layouts and the one given here is an example rather than a tightly prescriptive blueprint. Nor is every report large enough to be given the full treatment. As mentioned earlier, very small reports can be set out in memos or on standard forms. Examples of this include equipment status reports, monthly reports on reported faults and accident reports.

You will need to decide whether or not a full report is needed and, if it is, discover if the college, company or department has a standard format. Further decisions will need to be made about deleting sections, given the size or destination of the report. A six-page report probably does not need a contents page; a report to your head of section is unlikely to need a glossary, and so on. You need to be as selective in your structure as in what text is to be included in the report itself.

The elements of a report can be selected from the following:

Title and title page	System description
Author identification	Research findings
Circulation	Discussion of findings
Authorisation	Conclusions
Target dates	Recommendations
Contents	Glossary
Terms of Reference	Acknowledgements
Summary	Bibliography
Introduction	Appendices
Methodology	Index
Literature survey	

5.3.1　Title and title page

Every report, even if presented as a memorandum, needs a full and informative title. Brevity is a virtue in this case as it aids indexing. *'Investigation of the Business System at Baileys (Martham) Ltd.'* is quite sufficient. Should you feel the need to be more descriptive then a single sentence subtitle will suffice.

The title page itself should be uncluttered and neatly laid out. The title is normally centred on the page, even if other information (see later) is offset to one side. It is useful in laying out the title page to remember the theory of the 'golden section', which defines the most pleasing ratio to be that of 1.6:1. As far as page layout goes, this means that your eye prefers to enter the page about one third of the way down and about one third of the way across. You therefore start your title one third of the way down the page, rather than at the top or half way down, with supplementary information placed one third of the way from the bottom. If indented, it should be centred around one third of the page width.

Like all general rules the golden section is merely a guide. However, for those with no pretences to be designers it is very helpful.

5.3.2 Author identification

Simply, this is your name (or names if it is a group report). A mere name may not be enough, though, for a variety of reasons. For students, especially in these days of large classes, identification by group is important so that the report does not get lost or mixed with other reports. For consultants who are not self-employed the name of the company needs to be added as information to the recipient (why should the head office know that J. Smith has been carrying out a systems analysis on behalf of his company, Netherwood Associates Ltd.?) and partly to establish intellectual ownership of the report.

Intellectual ownership is quite a new concept which has developed with the information industries and which is related to copyright of books and visual materials. A report prepared by a consultant is a valuable article for which the clients may be paying large amounts of money. It is protected in law like any other piece of valuable property and its ownership needs to be protected. Generally ownership resides in the author, except where the author is an employee and is preparing the work on his employer's behalf. Thus Geoff Hamilton (trading as Hamilton Consultants Ltd.) owns the report he produces. J. Smith, working for Netherwood Associates Ltd. does not own his report, it is Netherwood's property.

Students who are being funded by their employers to undertake research or to take a college course still remain employees. Any research findings or articles produced over that time or as a result of their further training remain the property of the employer, unless otherwise specified in the contract of employment. Most employers are pleased to waive their rights in return for consultation and acknowledgement in the text.

5.3.3 Circulation

Many companies use a photocopied circulation list which is appended to documents that are sent around sections or departments for their perusal. This is to ensure that all concerned see the document and that none are missed out. In this case the report writer does not need to specify the recipients in the text. A circulation list helps management, in that they know who else has read the report or who has a copy, so that a base line for discussion has been established.

At other times the circulation of a report may be deliberately limited. A business consultant carrying out analysis for the directors of a small company has been commissioned to produce a full report 'warts and all'. Perhaps this includes a SWOT analysis (Strengths, Weaknesses, Opportunities and Threats) and a review of company staffing given a variety of business and economic scenarios. The directors would be most unhappy if this information were to pass into general circulation. Competitors could make use of it to make inroads into the company's business; confidence in the company could be eroded should its weaknesses be made public; staff could become disaffected if preliminary discussions of redundancies were made known.

Our company tries to prevent this by limiting the circulation of the analyst's report. Should a copy fall into the hands of outsiders the company is in a strong legal position when it comes to the information it contains being disseminated to others. Failing this, compensation may be obtained through the courts for any business losses incurred or for the use of intellectual property which has been illegitimately obtained.

Within a company similar considerations may arise between discussion documents and final reports. Discussion documents (like a government Green Paper) set out alternative courses of action, sometimes with the author acting as 'devil's advocate', in order that they should be considered by the appropriate sub-group. The DP manager might, for example, set out in a report to his team the arguments for dissolving the department, re-deploying its members across the company and installing a small help desk facility. The objective is to force colleagues in the team seriously to consider their objectives and re-examine their position within the company. Imagine the chaos if that were to arrive on the desk of senior management masquerading as a full operational report!

Reports such as this are therefore very clear as to their circulation and carry clear messages such as '*For discussion only*' or '*First draft, not for circulation outside the DP department*'. A misdirected report can be a veritable time bomb.

5.3.4 Authorisation

The authorisation of the report sets out who requested it. A letter of authorisation may be included in the appendices. For internal reports the authorisation indicates that the writer has been using time properly at the direction of a line manager or senior committee. In the case of consultancy work the authorisation indicates that the consultant was properly appointed by a responsible person within the company.

5.3.5 Target dates

Most reports will have been commissioned with a target date in mind. This may be the meeting of an internal committee, the beginning of the financial year or a handing-in date for a student assignment. Writers need to be clear about the urgency of their report and of the date of any deadlines which may be set. Missing that vital committee may mean that hardware cannot be purchased until after the next meeting of the committee; a consultant's report on the installation of new systems may need to be acted upon while suppliers' special arrangements are still current or before the end of the financial year in order to make the most of the tax situation. Students who miss deadlines may fail their units or modules as a result.

It is therefore important that the document contains both the scheduled completion date and the actual completion date. As long as they match up the writer has done all that can be expected and cannot be held responsible for subsequent delays.

5.3.6 Contents

Turn to the front of any good text book and you will find a lengthy and informative set of contents. It will include chapter number and headings, and numbered sub-sections.

Each sub-section will have page numbers attached down the right hand side. This helps the reader check what topics have been covered in the report and where to find them if quick reference is needed.

The writer needs to judge at what point the report begins to be large enough to need a contents section. A rough guide is that anything over six pages or three sub-sections needs one, smaller reports do not. Over about twenty pages a contents page becomes essential.

5.3.7 Terms of reference

Terms of reference have already been touched upon in the commercial context. For academic reports or reports where the author is operating independently they are still important but operate slightly more fluidly. Here they are a road map of the area to be covered and, like a road map, they serve to indicate the range of routes that an investigation might take. If a road is blocked the driver may need to take a detour; if a motorway is too crowded the driver may prefer instead to travel along a minor road.

Thus a student investigating the use made of expert systems in local business and commerce may be forced to adjust the terms of reference for the final dissertation when it is discovered that the range of systems in the local area are particularly various. To cut down on the scope of the work the phrases *some local companies*' or '*major applications of expert systems*' may be inserted. Again, after looking closer at what is available the student may be struck by a single novel application which can be explored in detail. In both of these cases a change in the terms of reference will have to be negotiated with the student's supervisor.

Again, the extent of the terms of reference increases proportionately to the size of the report. Larger reports may have as many as ten or a dozen numbered sections, complete with a short rationale of the need for the report and how this judgement was arrived at.

5.3.8 Summary

In larger companies senior managers may have several large reports crossing their desk every week. If they read all of the reports in full precious little other work would get done. Some reports may come to them out of courtesy, others 'for information' so they can keep track of what is happening within the company. Managers in specialist areas may need to keep track of what is happening across the company without needing to go into too much detail.

The summary helps all these people to grasp the basis of the report and to decide whether or not they need to read it in greater detail. In effect it is a précis of the general findings of the report together with the main recommendations and, as such, may also act as a reminder of the findings to someone who has not read it for some time. In academic circles the summary can also be used as an abstract and be published as such in professional journals. Summaries rarely exceed five hundred words in length.

5.3.9 Introduction

Summaries are a management tool, introductions are a stylistic device. They serve to establish the context for the report, why it was conceived and under what circumstances it was written. Reading the report we discover what the problem was, how it arose and what the objectives are in the current work. You need to arouse the interest of your reader, leading steadily into the main body of the work. This is that gripping first paragraph that you were taught to write in essay classes at school!

5.3.10 Methodology

In scientific reports this is a vital section, laying out how the researcher went about setting up the experiment. Business reports depend more on the analysis of existing data rather than the discovery of new information, so that methodology is consequently of less importance and the space devoted to it proportionately smaller. Some may even omit this section completely and insert a single sentence on methodology in the Introduction.

However, especially in larger projects, there may be circumstances where a programmer may need to state such things as that the program has been planned using object-oriented design or by Jackson structured programming or the analyst may declare that SSADM version four was used, including interviews with all key staff and with full reiterative sequences. Where expected processes may have been omitted, such as full prototyping or testing, this would be the place to declare and justify the fact.

5.3.11 Literature survey

Here we are in the realms of academic reports or theoretical research. The literature survey tells us what has been written on the topic and is still regarded as current. Even in academic reports the literature survey would be quite brief, giving a quick resumé of the authorities on the subject and the gist of their argument. The reader now knows the base from which the writer is beginning and upon which the continuing research builds. Around five hundred words is usually adequate for the literature survey.

5.3.12 System description

Describing the existing system is an important part of business analysis and may constitute the major part of an analyst's report. In a small business the analysis would be of the complete company; within a larger one the area studied is likely to be a sub-set of the whole. Whichever it is, the system description must always place the area it is dealing with within the context of the overall business objectives of the company.

The reason for this is so that the analyst sees the whole wood and not just the trees. It is easy to be seduced into thinking that one particular area or section is the most important in the company and to forget what the company as a whole is there for. To quote Don Yeates:

'A particular challenge for analysts...is to keep the business requirements as a focus instead of getting hooked up on technological solutions. It is very easy, for example, to take a messy and cumbersome manual system and produce instead a messy and cumbersome computer system.'

Only when the overall business objectives have been laid out can the existing system be placed in its context and the job that it does described. A company which has an existing computer system needs to set out precisely what it uses the computer for and why. Only at this point does it become obvious that the technology is being under-utilised, mis-deployed or is failing to produce significant benefits for the company at large.

A description of technological systems follows on from a description of the business system in which it is embedded. Such a description may in itself provide pointers to problems such as under-utilisation of systems. For example, an examination of computer usage within National Health Trusts revealed a variety of systems and IT applications within the National Health in general and even within specific Trusts. As a result efforts were made towards rationalisation of patient booking systems, culminating in the installation of HISS systems during 1994. While it is too early to judge HISS in its entirety it has at least led to different hospitals on geographically diverse sites but within the same Trust being able to interrogate patients' records and to arrange treatment and admission almost immediately.

The age of a system, its concentration in one part of the organisation, the paucity of software, multiple entry of the same data and the inability of users to access data being used concurrently by others are all difficulties which can become apparent as a result of a technological description. Beware of confusing this with the business system. Your company PCs may be old and slow as far as you are concerned but if they do the job they were designed for in a reliable manner that the users are happy with they are fulfilling their business objectives. Having the brightest, shiniest, fastest kit is not a business objective. Having one that does the job properly is.

5.3.13 Research findings/evidence

In effect this is the information that you have found out, the meat of your report. In smaller reports it would also include the system description. You might present the results of your questionnaires and interviews in a general format such as *'Sixteen of the twenty people interviewed said that they regularly experienced problems with entering data on the screen. When questioned, twelve of the sixteen claimed that the data boxes were not large enough for the amount of data that they needed to enter.'* The full statistics will be available in a later appendix.

Note that you are not yet discussing this information, nor making recommendations. You are like the prosecutor at a trial, bringing pieces of evidence to the jury's attention in a structured manner. The chronological collection of this material is irrelevant to them, they only need to know how it fits together into a coherent pattern. You are writing a report, not a diary.

Your evidence should be presented in a manner that is fair, balanced and restrained. The reader expects to have an intellectual encounter, not an emotional one.

Set your information out clearly in numbered sections and sub-sections, with one flowing into the next. Lead your reader along gently, with reminders if necessary, of how each piece of evidence relates to others or to general areas of theory which you may have laid out in previous sections.

5.3.14 Discussion of findings

If you have done your job properly your readers will now be getting ahead of you. It will be obvious from your evidence what the problems and difficulties are and what other companies or academic authorities have suggested to be the range of possible solutions. Nevertheless, at this point you need a pause for consolidation, to discuss the significance of what has gone before. Thus the prosecutor may have made it clear that the bloodstained knife was found in the accused's room and that it had the victim's blood on it. The jury still needs to be told that the possession of the murder weapon suggests that the accused either committed the murder or knew exactly who did.

In our previous example of screen entry, the reader needs to be told that the screen design is no longer efficient for the users' needs. The size of data boxes particularly is obviously far too small.

Or is it? Remember that we are discussing the findings, not merely re-stating them. Have we considered that there is a training problem and the users are inserting the wrong sort of data? Is there an 'overflow' facility that they do not know how to use? Was the application designed for this sort of use in the first place? Why do the other respondents to your interviews not identify this as a problem?

Because of the lack of feedback inherent in writing a report you need to provide your own, to ask your own difficult questions. If these questions are not asked then the reader can feel dissatisfied and reject your findings as inconclusive. Somehow you must bring yourself to be your own audience and to question the validity of your findings and judgements.

5.3.15 Conclusion

The prosecutor finally sums up, based on the evidence already presented. At this point no further evidence can be admitted, no more discussion allowed. Again your readers could be well ahead of you, since you have presented and discussed your findings in such a clear and accurate manner. Our input screens are not only too small, they often contain duplicate information and are badly designed from the point of view of the users who have to enter data at different points on the screen. Few are the reports which would not require a conclusions section by the person who is the expert in the matter – yourself.

5.3.16 Recommendations

In the conclusion you told your reader what is wrong, now you need to say what can be done about it. Do we go for a piecemeal redesign of the data boxes or do we re-design the whole screen? An alternative might be to scrap the whole system completely and to start again from scratch. What exactly are you recommending, and why?

Your recommendations flow clearly and irrevocably from your findings, which may involve you in a certain amount of repetition as you re-deploy your arguments in favour of your preferred solution. Do not worry about this. Here is your sales pitch, where you tell the reader that to re-design the screens would cost only slightly less than buying in a brand new application, which would also allow you to export the data onto spreadsheet and database, a task currently done by hand. Your conclusions state the problem, the recommendations give the solution.

5.3.17 Glossary

The need for a glossary has already been mentioned. Where you have introduced technical terms that the reader cannot be expected to know or may have forgotten or where acronyms (such as SSADM, VDU, DFD, etc.) have been used they should be explained in a glossary. The existence and extent of the glossary is related to the knowledge and experience of your perceived readership.

5.3.18 Acknowledgements

Acknowledgements are necessary where individuals or institutions have given substantial assistance in the preparation of your report. It may be a company which has allowed you to come and watch a piece of software operating on their system, or a colleague who has assisted with a particularly complex programming problem. Academic reports sponsored by companies, or where the writer has been released by the employer in order to complete the course or compile the report, usually contain acknowledgements to that company.

5.3.19 Bibliography

A bibliography is a structured list of all the books and periodicals that you have used. There are several standard methods of presenting bibliographies and the organisation for which you are writing will normally have its preference, which you should respect. Whatever the structure of presentation all systems present relevant information, which for books would be:

Author
Date
Title
Publisher

An example of this would be:

Yeates, Shields and Helmy (1994), *Systems Analysis and Design*, Pitman Publishing.

Magazines and periodicals necessitate extra information:

Name of periodical
Edition (if not dated)
Page numbers of article

For example:

Rogers and Roethlisberger, 'Barriers and Gateways to Communication', *Harvard Business Review*, July–August 1952, pp.46–50

The bibliography enables the reader to check your sources of information and its currency. Title and author enable the book to be found through reference systems. Interested readers can go to your sources and gain extra information that you have not had space to include or, in the case of academic studies, confirm that your work is original and has not been plagiarised from others. Publishers often have specialist areas which give added credence to their authors' writings. Thus Cambridge University Press have a high reputation for academic works on history, Routledge for philosophy books and Pitman for business.

Other publishers have been established to reflect the views of the owners. These include Good News Press (owned by a religious organisation), Pluto Press (owned by a radical political party) and Progress Publishers (at one time controlled by the communist government of the old Soviet Union). Thus an unwary student could well take as authoritative a statement that information systems only have a function in as far as they create wealth for the ruling class, irrespective of the needs of the majority of the population, who are slowly declining into economic slavery, or take seriously an argument that computers are an instrument of the devil designed to hasten Armageddon. Well-informed readers can adjust their critical faculties to take account of such bias, even where the writer has remained unaware that any exists.

In the area of information systems, currency is of key importance because of the rapid changes in technology. Because of the time scale involved in the writing and publishing process the information contained in books can be up to two years old. Thus a book published in 1990 may be using 1988 information and the reader would do well to be wary of any judgements based upon it. Commercial magazines are much faster means of communication since both writing and publishing time are proportionately shorter and corrections and updates can be more easily included. Some publishers take work on floppy disk or automatically downloaded from the writer's computer via modem for both books and magazines, further cutting down the time spent on the printing process, if not on research and writing.

Academic journals, however, can also take years to publish, because of the intense scrutiny that the articles have to undergo. Academic referees are invited to give their opinions of the articles, that they are based on valid research and draw logical conclusions from that research, and in extreme cases to replicate any experiments described in the article.

Books and articles in some areas date much more slowly than others. The Rogers and Roethlisberger article cited above is still interesting reading and makes points which can be applied today. Within quantum mathematics there is still theoretical work from the last decade which awaits application. Thus currency does not always equate with modernity.

5.3.20 Appendices

An appendix is not a dustbin. It is a place where detailed information is stored for those who may need to make use of it. The appendix clears the main text of cluttering detail, such as the statistical analysis, records of fault calls over the period, or detailed technical specifications of hardware. Returned questionnaires, manufacturers' literature or the full text of the Data Protection Act should not be included. Instead we would have a table of statistics, detailed technical specifications and a digest of the DPA as it affects the company in question.

Each appendix should be numbered and titled. Where your appendices are extensive each should have its own page numbering system, probably using roman numerals. A smaller amount of material, up to around a dozen pages, can be numbered continuously. All appendices should appear on your contents pages, together with their page numbers.

5.3.21 Index

An index will only be necessary for major reports which probably also have a wide circulation. Indexes allow the reader rapidly to look up information that is more detailed than that held on the contents pages. With computerised indexing systems their production is much quicker than it used to be, but they are still time-consuming. and take up time which would be better spent improving the gathering and presentation of your basic information.

5.3.22 Conclusion

There are twenty-one sub-sections included above for possible inclusion in your report. Rarely, if ever, would you include all twenty-one. Your terms of reference, authority for the report, target dates, circulation and methodology will often be condensed into one page or paragraph. There may be no literature survey, glossary or bibliography whatsoever. Think of these twenty-one sections in the same way as the icons at the top of your computer screen, as facilities to be employed as the need arises, not as a straight-jacket into which to fit everything that you write.

5.4 MIND YOUR LANGUAGE

Reports reflect, and reflect on, their writers. Quite apart from the content the writer is also judged on presentation, grammar and punctuation. Among others, HRH the Prince of Wales has been critical of the standard of written English in business and elsewhere. Whether or not it is true that the standard of English is not as high among school leavers as it used to be, the constant attention given to this matter indicates the importance that is attached to it by the business community.

As we have seen in earlier chapters, language is inseparable from meaning. We use language to convey our ideas, to persuade, to inform. It is a means to an end, and if we will those ends we must do our best to improve the means we use to achieve them. There is no point in alienating a business audience by flouting the rules of grammar and spelling. Nor should we weaken our case by failing to have the linguistic fluency to express it in the best possible manner.

Reports are not noted for their readability. Shearring and Christian cynically remark that if the serpent in the Garden of Eden had used the language of the average report Eve would never have realised that he was talking about fruit at all and we might still be living in a state of bliss! Experience suggests that the situation has changed since Shearring and Christian were writing. Certainly government publications are now vetted for the clarity and simplicity of their language and large organisations such as General Motors, the armed forces and IBM all provide communications courses for their employees.

While such an improvement is welcome we should not run away with the idea that reports are the site for beautiful stylistics. Nor should they be. They are functional documents which have a specific and limited audience. Writers of reports need only to ensure that their reports are:

- clear
- simple
- correct

This is more easily said than done. However, some general rules can be laid down as guidelines.

5.4.1   Sentences

Sentences contain a subject, an object and a verb. The subject tells us who did the action, the verb tells us what the action was and the object tells us the destination or result of the action. Reading novels you will find thousands of exceptions to this rule. When reading reports you should find very few. This is because the novelist is involved in examining language or in how language is used in colloquial speech. The report writer is trying to convey complex ideas simply and easily; linguistic complexity merely serves to muddy the water.

If a sentence does not have a verb it is not a sentence. Beware, though, of words ending in -ing. Generally these are parts of verb forms :'I **was** walking', 'I **am** eating', 'I **had been** sleeping' and so on. Note that these all have what is called an auxiliary verb with them formed from either the verbs 'to be' or 'to have', which are indicated in bold in the examples. Words which end in -ing but which do not have an attached auxiliary verb are **not** verbs but verbal nouns or gerunds. The following examples have been taken from student work:

'**Being** the best programming language for the job.'
'**Giving** justification for, and the reasons behind, the inclusion of objectives, criteria and range statements.'
'**Working** through comprehension, understanding and the ability to use the material in new situations.'

None of the above are sentences, because they have gerunds but no finite verbs in them.

One way to consider a sentence is as the bearer of one idea. If you want to qualify that idea it should be done in a separate sentence. The qualification is a different idea and deserves a sentence to itself. The consequences of following this rule would be sentences of around twenty to twenty-five words, ideal for easy comprehension. Computerised style checkers such as 'Stylewriter' will automatically check your work for sentence length and advise you of ones which are too long. If you do not have access to such a facility, check your text for any sentences in excess of two lines long.

Having said that, a report that only contained such sentences would be choppy in feel and difficult to read. A complicated idea might sometimes demand longer sentences. Shorter sentences can be used for effect at key points to bring the reader up short. ('*We cannot afford this*', after descriptions of stock wastage, for example.)

What you need to avoid is sentences which go on forever, with increasing numbers of subordinate clauses. If in doubt, keep it short. The quotation below illustrates the difficulties of understanding caused by complex language and lengthy sentences:

> '*It is relatively easy for a process during execution to generate invalid address references (i.e. addresses outwith its own memory space); this can frequently happen with low or high level languages where, for example, a process bug has generated array subscript values greater than the bounds of the array. A good deal of programming nowadays involves manipulation of dynamically allocated data accessed using address variables. It is relatively easy to produce erroneous address references in these circumstances. Hopefully, such errors will be detected during program development and not in live running, but in either case it is important firstly that the erroneous memory reference does not succeed and secondly that we learn that the attempt has occurred, even if it results simply in the aborting of the process.*'

Some word processing applications will allow you to apply a **FOG index** to your writing. This stands for '**frequency of gobbledygook**'. It is a way of assessing texts for ease of understanding and is a function of sentence length and number of complex words. To calculate your average sentence length for yourself, take a number of passages of around one hundred words from the text and divide by the number of sentences, to give the average sentence length. Then count the number of words in your samples of three syllables or more. Divide by the number of samples to obtain an average. Calculate:

Average sentence length + Average number of 3+ syllable words

Multiply the result by 0.4 and you have the reading age of the material. This is the age at which the average reader could be expected to understand the grammar of the text that you have analysed. A popular newspaper, aiming at as wide an audience as possible, has a reading age of about seven or eight. An upmarket newspaper with a more educated audience will come out at around fourteen and a university textbook at around eighteen to twenty. The example used above is from a text book mainly aimed at university lecturers and postgraduate students and has a FOG index of 19.6, which could easily be improved by shortening the current average 34 word average sentence length.

Note that this only indicates grammatical complexity, not the difficulty of the material or the concepts deployed. Although *The Times* has a reading age of only fourteen, one would still expect the average schoolchild of that age to struggle with the ideas that it contains. The book quoted above deals with complex issues which take it into a further realm of difficulty, even when reduced to simple sentences.

5.4.2 Paragraphs

Paragraphs are whole ideas or arguments. If you have three reasons for choosing to program in Turbo Pascal rather than COBOL you have either three paragraphs which discuss each reason or one paragraph containing all three. The choice is yours, depending upon the depth of your argument.

Remember that, except in special circumstances, a paragraph contains more than one sentence. But it does not continue for more than ten lines. Lengthy paragraphs are hard on the eyes and difficult to follow on the page, making the reader's job more difficult.

Well-written reports have the subject matter of each paragraph encapsulated in the first sentence of each. This enables readers who are in a hurry to skim read, looking for the basic ideas, perhaps as an *aide-memoire* before the meeting at which the report is to be discussed.

5.4.3 Active or passive?

There are two schools of thought about the use of the personal pronoun 'I' in reports and the consequent use of the passive voice. Companies vary in their preferences and as an employee you will have no choice but to follow standard company usage. Consultants may please themselves but should be aware of the preferences of their clients.

The impersonal mode is the most commonly used form of report. At its extremes this consists of suppressing all forms of personal pronouns whatsoever. Thus I, you, he, we are never used. In order to perform this feat the writer must turn all verbs into the passive voice and all people into job titles. Let us take an example from a student project:

> *'Mr. Smith, the Managing Director, told me that he had no idea as to how the pricings on the stock were worked out. He said that this was done as a result of discussions between Mr. Hendry and Bob Ottley. When I asked them about it, they said that they didn't really discuss it in detail but kept to the old prices unless there had been a recent large rise in raw material prices which Mr. Smith had told them about. This did not seem to be to be a very efficient way of fixing prices.'*

Proponents of the 'impersonal' school of writing argue that such a paragraph lacks objectivity and logical consistency. Prices are not fixed by Mr. Hendry and Bob Ottley as individuals but by whoever has the role of chief accountant and production supervisor. Moreover, a certain amount of elitism has crept in, where the accountant is mister, whilst a mere supervisor is referred to by his christian name.

Above all, the analyst has taken a central position in the enquiry, whereas the analyst's job is to fix the facts firmly and make recommendations on that basis. The facts are there to be discovered and revealed by an objective observer. This objectivity must be retained in the language used, as in the re-written version below:

'The Managing Director stated that detailed pricing was fixed in discussions between the chief accountant and the production supervisor. Upon questioning, both made clear that formal discussions rarely took place. Prices were maintained at the old level unless information came from the managing director of large price rises in raw materials. This does not seem to be an efficient way of fixing prices.'

Here is all the information, set out simply and in a logical manner. The judgement in the last sentence might perhaps have been held over for a later section, but otherwise the paragraph is unexceptional.

On the other hand, proponents of a more 'personal' form of writing argue that the second example is clearly dishonest and suppresses information which might be significant. First of all, it might be true that the actors, Messrs Smith, Hendry and Ottley and the analyst, act as they do because of their roles. What is not true is that every managing director or every analyst would act in exactly the same manner. There are individual differences in their approaches and it may be that these differences are having an effect on the company. Few managing directors, for example, would distance themselves so far from pricing policy, nor would many accountants be so blasé about production costs. In the end it is Smith or Hendry who are the actors in this situation, not some disembodied managing director or accountant.

There are other clues which are suppressed in the second version. The use of Mr. Ottley's christian name reflects the relationship between him and the accountant, he is clearly the subordinate. It may also reflect the way that he manages the shop floor, where his success or lack of it is important for the company's survival. From the language of the first version the analyst does not appear to have used a very structured approach to interviewing (*'when I asked them about it...'*) and the reader may wish to follow this up. The second version eliminates the suggestion of any possible looseness.

Most important of all is the elimination in the second version of any feeling of humanity or the existence of a human agency. The report might as well have dropped from the skies. Proponents of 'personal' writing declare this to be a dishonest impression. The report was compiled by somebody with all their human failings and preconceptions whose mere presence in the organisation may have produced changes and skewed the results. Judgements and conclusions were arrived at by that individual acting on the data that had been discovered, not by some impersonal machine which had access to all possible data.

From a stylistic point of view there is a tendency for impersonal writing to be stodgy and dull. Personal writing, on the other hand, can be egotistical and emphasise people rather than processes. Information systems professionals should be able to write in both styles should the occasion require it.

5.4.4 Tone and style

Tone of voice in speech has already been discussed in previous chapters. The same principles apply to writing, in that the tone of the communication carries additional information or strikes a particular chord in the recipient. A letter which begins with the words '*Dear sir, Unless...*' is calculated to raise the hackles of most readers, whereas '*Thank you for your last letter*' is at least an attempt to start things off on a polite footing, however bad the subsequent news might be.

As a public document a report should be serious in tone, even at the expense of being dull, setting out its information and arguments clearly and ambiguously. The sort of comments and jokes that one might write in a letter are to be avoided, as is any emotive language. Although you are trying to be persuasive it is the strength of your argument that counts, along with the data that you have uncovered.

To this end you need to avoid ambiguity, using words to clarify rather than to confuse. Simple words are to be preferred over complex, short sentences over long. Precision helps. If you know that 67% of all users have bought this application say so, rather than using vague phrases such as '*a majority of...*'

Creative writing, with its appeal to the aesthetic and the emotional, emphasises the use of adjectives and adverbs. Business writing, emphasising the material and the logical, has little need for them. To describe someone as '*a very successful businessman*' adds little to '*a successful businessman.*' Nor does the word 'disastrously' in '*the profits have dropped disastrously from £320 million to £5 million*' add anything beyond an emotional frisson best kept for the popular daily newspapers.

An interesting exercise is to go through a report that you have written crossing out all adjectives. You will find that you will only be required to replace about five per cent of them in order to retain your original meaning.

5.4.5   Slang and clichés

Slang is a forceful and vigorous addition to the language. It may constitute new coinages, imported phrases or be a remnant of the local languages and dialects from which our current standard language grew. Used in the correct context it can aid communication and establish personal links, signalling that the users are part of one linguistic 'club'.

However, in written business communication it is best avoided. Slang alienates many linguistic traditionalists, especially those who are not privy to its gestation or use. If it is current only within limited circles, be they geographical, professional, to do with age or leisure preferences, it has a tendency to obscure rather than to illuminate meaning. Slang terms also have a tendency to change their meaning rapidly, leaving the sense of a passage marooned behind them.

For example, in late-nineteenth-century France artists felt themselves cut off from polite society, to be at the very edge of acceptability. They identified themselves with others in this position such as beggars, prostitutes and the insane. An artist who seemed to be going further in his art than his contemporaries was Vincent van Gogh, who was referred to approvingly as '*a complete madman*'. Later historians have misinterpreted this slang use of the word and used it as evidence that van Gogh was insane rather than merely suffering from physical abuse of his body allied with epilepsy. History has been changed by a word.

At the other end from slang is the cliché. This is a word or phrase that is overused, virtually mouthed without meaning. *'It has to be said that the company is hanging on by its fingertips. Once we have a level playing field we can get ourselves on an even keel.'* Quite apart from mixing metaphors from football, sailing and mountaineering, the speaker has said very little. *'Times are hard'* would have sufficed.

Pomposity is another vice to be avoided. The use of high flown phrases to say simple things might be acceptable for businessmen, politicians and the military trying not to give any information away to the press, but they are not appropriate for the efficient report writer.

'Your board is taking careful cognisance of the matter'. *'We have had free and frank discussions about this'*. *'As of this time the executive is developing ongoing parameters for optimising decision making.'* Besides been ugly, obscure and pedantic these phrases bore the reader with their predictability. What is wrong with *'We are looking at this'*; *'There was a row over the matter'*, or *'We are looking at better decision-making methods'*?

Finally, be wary of translating from speech directly on to the page. You may refer to 'punters' in private, but on the public page you will write 'customers'. *'He say he were now going down the city'* needs to become *'he said that he was going into the city centre'* in order to avoid accusations by the reader of provincialism and ignorance.

5.4.6 Grammar and punctuation

There are many books on grammar and punctuation and several of them are listed in the bibliography. The subject is far too wide for us to be able to do it justice here and readers with particular queries or difficulties are advised to refer to the specialist literature. For the majority of business writers the best way of improving style and usage is through extensive reading of technical literature and of whatever other writings one finds entertaining.

5.5 CHARTS AND DIAGRAMS

Charts and diagrams are an important aid to explaining and understanding complex information. They help the reader to understand trends, perceive organisational strategies and track data flows. A business analysis would lean quite heavily on statistics of production, output and profitability. Production and installation analyses might have floor plans, cabling diagrams and GANTT charts. Systems analysis deals more in the area of entity life histories, logical data structures and data flow diagrams. Whatever sort of chart or diagram is most appropriate to your particular report there are still some basic rules that have to be followed.

The old cliché tells us that *'a picture is worth a thousand words'*. What it does not tell us is **which** thousand words. Turn to any newspaper that is handy and you will find pictures on nearly every page. What you will also find is that each one also has a short caption below it. The function of the caption is to instruct us how to 'read' the picture. Very rarely is one allowed to speak for itself and indeed the same photograph might be used by the newspaper in order to give radically different messages. The grand new building project can be highlighted one year as a sign of progress and prosperity, whilst exactly the same photograph can be used the following year when the building company has gone into liquidation as a symbol of over-reaching pride and financial mismanagement.

All visuals, therefore, need to be clearly labelled, together with an accompanying explanatory text. `We need to be told what the chart or diagram is about, what the symbols refer to and what the whole thing means. It is the writer's responsibility to identify clearly the data and to indicate how it can be turned into information.

5.5.1　Tables

Tables are a basic way of recording and presenting numerical information. Scientific observations, trade statistics, even the familiar bank statement are examples of the tabular presentation of data. Like all forms of communication, tables are not 'innocent', they do not suddenly appear from nowhere. Some human has decided what data is to be collected and how it is to be recorded and presented. Choices have been made as to how and where that data was collected in the first place.

At this point we need to distinguish between primary research and secondary research. **Primary research** is where basic information is generated by the researcher, perhaps by conducting experiments or interviews, constructing questionnaires or by participant observation. When writing up the results the researcher has to be very clear about what the methodology and its underlying assumptions were in order to inform the reader of the validity of the data gained and its limitations.

For example, if we investigated the business operations of a computer sales company every Wednesday for six months we would have some very interesting data. What we would not have would be a full picture of the company. Wednesday was chosen because it was the quietest time of the week, the research thus causing least disruption. Do people operate in a different manner when under the stress of ringing telephones and irate customers? Do those carefully planned procedures suddenly become slow and tedious at peak operating periods? A good researcher will recognise such limitations and inform us of them along with the raw data.

Secondary research uses data that has already been produced. The British government has a Central Statistical Office, which publishes information such as the *Business Monitor* and the *Monthly Digest of Statistics*. *Kelly's Directory* provides detailed summaries of financial performance in their 'Key European Enterprises'. This and data from many other sources is reliable and valuable information, used by analysts, governments and enterprises the world over.

As respectable as it is, it was still produced by primary researchers using data that was based on a whole range of underlying assumptions. Organisations such as the Central Statistical Office always set out clearly the limitations and assumptions involved in their data, sometimes along with a 'health warning' where it has been gathered under adverse circumstances, such as the refusal of a government to release economic data as being too sensitive. Other sources are not as fastidious and secondary researchers have to take particular care when analysing data from parties who have an interest in its interpretation and use.

One example of this is in company take-overs. The target company publishes statistics to show that they have been growing steadily and that return on capital for shareholders exceeds the average. On the other hand the predator company uses its statistics to show that it is a major international company whose spread of investments and products provides shareholders with security for their money. Both companies try to prove that the underlying value of their company is much greater than had previously been recognised, in order to push up the value of their shares on the stock exchange and increase their value in relation to the other.

On a more personal level, take a look at the advertisements in PC magazines. Some companies will use statistics to show that they are the largest single manufacturer and seller of that product in the country (*'You can rely on us, we are the market leaders and least likely to go bankrupt'*.) Other will claim that they are the fastest growing company in the area (*'Buy our products, we are obviously ahead of the others in development of new technology.'*) No-one is telling lies; the data is available for all to see.

Whether your report is based on primary research or on secondary research the readers need to be clear about how your data was gathered and what limitations it has. In the case of secondary research they also need to know where the data came from and what its currency is. Most government statistics, for example, are rather dated because they usually rely on a large number of companies and organisations providing statistical returns, which then have to be collated and ordered by statisticians. Because of their thoroughness the results have a high degree of reliability but may be many months old by the time they are published.

Thus any statistical table needs to be accompanied by extra information:

- the source of the data
- its method of compilation
- any limitations to its validity caused by the method of compilation
- its currency, over what period was it gathered
- any events which may have occurred since then which affects the data
- the reliability of the data source.

Frequently much of the data that you possess will be surplus to requirements. If you want to inform your readers of the number of computers imported into the country, there is no point in using the whole page which also includes dishwashers, CD players and televisions. As long as you are not distorting or suppressing evidence there is nothing wrong about being selective about the data you present. Indeed, this is to be encouraged, since the removal of redundant or irrelevant information will aid the reader's understanding of the table as a whole.

Within a report each table should be numbered to allow for ease of reference. Within the table itself make sure that all information is clearly labelled and that quantities and time spans are indicated. If you have to use abbreviations a key should also be included.

5.5.2 Graphs

Tables have the virtue of being able to present large amounts of statistical data in a coherent format. However, they lack impact and interest for the general reader, who may prefer the more visual approach that graphs provide. Graphs also allow trends to be shown and direct comparisons to be made.

What type of graph you use depends on the type of data you are using and the uses you wish to put it to. A simple line graph will allow you to indicate the changes over a period of time of a continuous process. A monthly chart of the importation of computers from abroad would be a simple example of this. The monthly sales by a company, so beloved of cartoonists, is another. Troughs and peaks in the line indicate a cyclical or seasonal pattern of sales, information which helps us to plan production schedules and sales drives.

Line graphs are not efficient at showing comparisons between different factors, especially if the lines overlap or there are large variations in scales. Bar charts are a more efficient method of doing this, especially where the application used allows the use of three-dimensional effects or of colour. The example in Fig. 5.1 is taken from a report which examines the administrative uses of computers in schools and the feelings of the head teachers who were expected to use them.

As you can see, the researcher has managed to present several pieces of information succinctly and in a manner which allows the reader to make immediate and useful comparisons. She has clearly labelled the graphs themselves as well as the three axes and has included explanatory text in order to reinforce her point.

You will note also that her use of labelling has eliminated the need for keys. This means that the reader is immediately in command of the relevant information without

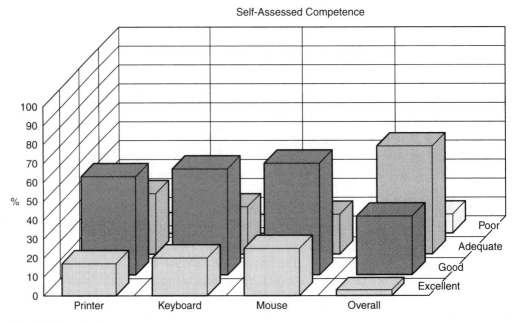

Fig. 5.1 Bar chart

having to look elsewhere. If abbreviations and keys are unavoidable then you must include them, but it is always worthwhile reconsidering the presentation of your information in such a way that they can be avoided.

Although bar charts are conventionally presented in a vertical format there are times when a horizontal one has more impact or is easier to read. In the example of Fig. 5.2 the placing of the text along the left hand side allows us to read it with ease and obviates the need for a key or for complicated forty-five degree text insertions.

Processes can be illustrated and organised by the use of GANTT charts and critical path analysis. Again the idea is to present the information in an easily accessible visual form but it should also be backed up by text explaining key points, such as that the cabling has to be installed before the mainframe and terminals are put in place. You may feel that such statements would just be stating the obvious but corporate history is full of examples of times when the obvious has been completely overlooked, with expensive consequences.

If your graphs are being produced automatically, by a spreadsheet package for example, you have the advantage of being forced to use a standardised format. Writers who produce their graphs by hand or through design packages need to establish their own standards in order to achieve stylistic coherence. Although producing graphs freehand is more difficult it does allow the writer the freedom to play with different modes of presentation, such as using a square pie chart instead of a round one, introducing colour or using rows of dots rather than a solid bar.

By all means experiment with methods of data presentation. At the same time keep in mind that the object of the exercise is to present information clearly, quickly and honestly to the reader. Data can be distorted by unwary or unscrupulous writers and you should make yourself aware of the major pitfalls.

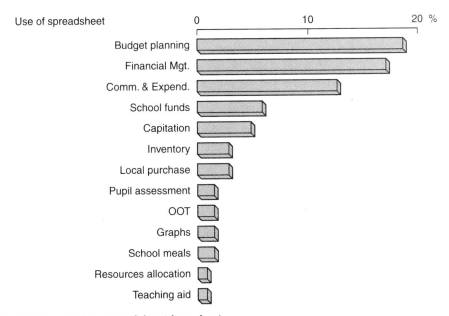

Fig. 5.2 Use of the spreadsheet bar chart

Prime among these are the use of inappropriate scales and the axis which does not begin at zero. Let us imagine that we wish to show the growth in the commercial use of computing. Naturally we would not take our time graph back before about 1940. Our graph would show a slow but steady rise until the early 1980s, when the graph grows steadily steeper. The period from 1990 on our graph shows much slower growth as the result of the world recession. If we were to take this period alone and alter the scales of the axes we could give quite a different impression. By making the vertical Sales axis much longer and the horizontal Time axis much shorter we have produced the impression of a healthy sector, rather than one caught like most others in difficult economic circumstances.

In a similar manner the graphs in Fig. 5.3 seek to illustrate how changes in the bank rate affect house building. Notice that the axis for the bank rate does not start at zero, thus emphasising the height of the graph and exaggerating the effects. This is a typical example of the 'false zero'.

Graphs should be integrated into the text as much as possible, ideally embedded in the discussion to which they relate. Alternatively they can appear on the facing page for double-sided texts or on a subsequent page for single-sided reports. In the latter case be careful to make your page numbering sequential. Each graph should be numbered according to a transparent and logical system. Where significant data has been extracted from a more detailed chart, the chart itself should appear in full in an appendix.

Graphs and charts can enhance the quality and usefulness of your reports if they are used and presented properly. Along with techniques of planning and statistical analysis they add another dimension to data and its application. See Figs 5.4 and 5.5.

5.6 SMALLER REPORTS

5.6.1 Memoranda

Memoranda are a standard method of communication within business organisations of all types. They stand in the gap between the long formal report and the short verbal instruction. Unlike the report they are short and can be generated quickly; unlike the verbal message they are formal, a matter of paper record and can be used to convey complex information. Memos are never used for communicating outside the organisation, when a formal letter or fax would be sent.

However complex the information may be, the memo should only cover a single topic. This might be instructions to a subordinate, a summary of work undertaken, a request for information, advance notice of important events such as meetings, the implementation of new regulations or organisational changes, or a commentary on possible courses of action. Charts, statistics or formal detailed instructions might be appended.

The memo can have quite a wide circulation and for that reason should not contain anything of a confidential nature. The usual practice is to address the memo to the main recipient or recipients, with copies to others who might be interested. The sender keeps a copy as a record of what was said and to whom. Because they have a short period for which they remain relevant memos are always dated and referenced.

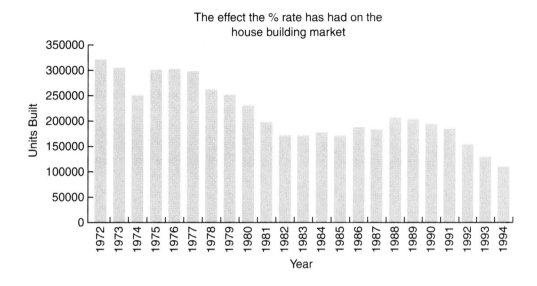

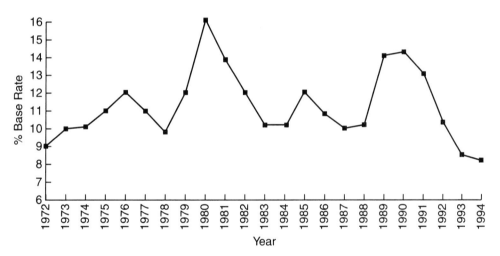

Fig. 5.3 Two connected graphs illustrating the connection between the bank rate and house building

Convention suggests that they are not signed, since the name of the sender appears in the header. A few companies demand that memos be initialled by the writer (after all, anyone with access to company note paper can generate a fake memorandum) and that important ones, such as those authorising financial expenditure, be signed. In this case no space should be left between the last line of the memo and the signature, to prevent subsequent unauthorised insertions.

Larger companies have standard memorandum forms printed which contain headers for the required basic information. Most word processing packages either have

SINGAPORE

YEAR	1960	1965	1970	1971	1972	1973	1974	1975	1976	1977	1978	1979	1980	1981
Pop $\times 10^3$	1634	1880	2075	2113	2152	2193	2230	2263	2293	2325	2353	2384	2414	2481

TRENDS IN AIRCRAFT FREIGHT CARRIED 1977-91

Units: Million tonne-kilometres

Source: Table 2211 + Table 2208 — Euromonitor Int-Euro Market

Country	1977	1979	1980	1983	1985	1986	1987	1988	1989	1990	1991	% 77-91
Singapore	248		554.1		981	1111.8	1256.8	1398.3	1640.1	1652.5		601.9
ratio wrt 1987	0.1973265		0.44		0.78	0.88	1.00	1.11	1.30	1.31		0.48
airfreight/Pop	106.66667		229.54		359.21	398.64	441.76	482.17	555.59	550.28		203.90
ratio wrt 1987	0.2414598		0.52		0.81	0.90	1.00	1.09	1.26	1.25		0.46

TRENDS IN AIRCRAFT PASSENGERS CARRIED 1977-91

Units: Million passenger-kilometres

Source: Table 2207 — Euromonitor Int-Euro Market — 1991

Country	1977	1979	1980	1983	1985	1986	1987	1988	1989	1990
Singapore	7869	0.00	14719	0.00	21741	22876	24947	28062	30466	31600
ratio wrt 1987	0.32	0.00	0.59	0.00	0.87	0.92	1.00	1.12	1.22	1.27
airpassengers/pop	3384.52	0.00	6097.35	0.00	7960.82	8202.22	8768.72	9676.55	10320.46	10522.81
ratio wrt 1987	0.39	0.00	0.70	0.00	0.91	0.94	1.00	1.10	1.18	1.20

IMPORTS – EXPORTS FOB

Units: Million tonne

Source: UNCTAD 1993

Country	50	60	70	75	80	85	86	87	88	89	90	91
Singapore Export	1006	1136	1554	5376	19376	22813	22495	28686	39303	44678	52729	
Import	1069	1332	2461	8134	23589	26285	2513	32559	43872	49675	60787	
Total	2075	2468	4015	13510	42965	49098	25008	61245	83175	94353	113516	
ratio wrt 1987	0.03	0.04	0.07	0.22	0.70	0.80	0.41	1.00	1.36	1.54	1.85	
Imports-exports/pop		1.51	1.93	5.97	17.80	17.98	8.97	21.53	0.68	31.96	37.80	
ratio wrt 1987		0.07	0.09	0.28	0.83	0.84	0.42	1.00	0.03	1.48	1.76	

MERCHANT SHIPPING
GOODS LOADED + UNLOADED IN INTERNATIONAL SEABORNE TRADE 1977-91

Units: Million tonne

Source: Table 2215 + 2211 — Euromonitor Int-Euro Marketing Stats & Europa Yearbook 1977, 82

Country	1977	1979	1980	1983	1985	1986	1987	1988	1989	1990
Singapore										
loaded	24.284	31.388	32.412		59.237	67.116	71.304	84.168	75.9308	81.5668
unloaded	40.471	31.39	48.55		59.24	67.12	71.30	84.17	87.308	106.224
total	64.76		80.96						163.24	187.79
ratio wrt 1987	0.91	0.44	1.14		0.83	0.94	1.00	1.18	2.29	2.63
loaded-unloaded/pop	27.85	13.17	33.54		21.69	24.06	25.06	29.02	55.30	62.53
ratio wrt 1987	1.11	0.53	1.34		0.87	0.96	1.00	1.16	2.21	2.50

Fig. 5.4 Chart of Singapore tourism and freight

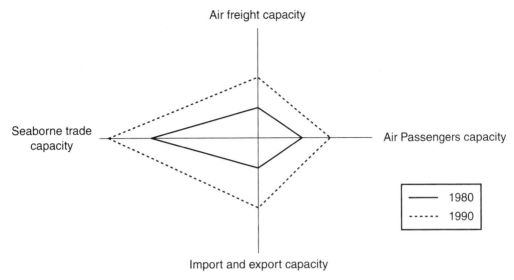

Fig. 5.5 Graph of Singapore tourism and freight
(*Source*: Euromonitor Int/Euromarketing Stats. 1994)

standard memorandum layouts or allow you to construct your own. Generally you should include:

- sender's name
- sender's reference (which usually incorporates the typist's initials if not physically written by the sender)
- main recipient's name
- recipient's reference
- other recipients who are receiving the memo for information
- date
- subject of the memorandum.

A typical company memorandum might look something like this:

Our ref: LR/mt/VT4
Your ref

From: Leon Russell
To: Victor Thomas
cc.   All heads of department; Chief Accountant

DATE: 27 October

SUBJECT: CONSULTANT'S REPORT ON PC INVENTORY

Following our brief discussion this morning, let me confirm the following:

1. The consultant is to be given free access to all parts of the company.

---

2. All machines of whatever vintage, whether operational or not, should be available for his inspection.

3. All documents detailing the permanent or temporary whereabouts of PCs should be made available to the consultant.

4. The deliberate withholding of information about PCs, their usage and where-abouts, will be regarded as a serious disciplinary offence irrespective of the grade or length of service of the employee.

We can only guess at the nature of the brief discussion that preceded the sending of this memo, but Mr. Russell has certainly made clear to his heads of department, and to one in particular, that he will stand no interference with the work of the consultant. Given the tone of the letter he is also making matters clear for any internal action or industrial tribunal which may result.

The memo is set out clearly and briefly. It is on one unitary subject, divided into four sub-headings. As a director Mr. Russell can be as sharp in his tone as he wishes. Any subordinate replying to the message would do well to take the sage advice of Anderson *et al.*: '*If time permits, write your memo today and leave it on your desk until tomorrow. It may seem different when you give it a cold look the next day.*'

5.6.2 Minutes

As we noted in Chapter 2, all meetings should have both an agenda and a set of minutes. The minutes record what was said, what was resolved, what action is to be taken and who is to take that action.

5.7 AN EXAMPLE REPORT

The report which follows is an abridged version of a forty-six page report produced by a computer consultant for a firm of auctioneers. Names of companies and figures have been changed to maintain commercial confidentiality. Following the submission of the report, the partners and senior members of the firm were given a twenty minute verbal presentation by the author, followed by questions, which lasted ninety minutes. In the end the company purchased the package and commissioned the author of the report to oversee its installation and testing. The new system is now in operation and is running according to expectations.

1.0 SUMMARY

The present system has obvious problems, inhibiting growth and profitability. Special sales have been identified as the major growth area. These sales demand an improved computer system to support them. At the same time manual operations could be automated into an overall system.

Eight auctioneering packages were originally identified but only two reached the company's specifications. These were:

TRACE by R.Mayes and Company
AUCTIONEER by Auctionmaster Business Services

Both systems were demonstrated by the companies on Hereward's premises and both were seen in action at other auction rooms.

This report recommends the purchase of AUCTIONEER for its superior operating system, the ease of customisation to Hereward's requirements and the high level of support offered by Auctionmaster.

2.0 TERMS OF REFERENCE

1. To evaluate the present system.
2. Identify areas where problems exist and which could be solved by the installation of a new computer system
3. Evaluate existing commercial auctioneering software.
4. Recommend the purchase of a new system (if appropriate) within the following parameters:
   a. Installation to begin no later than July of this year
   b. Purchase and installation costs should not exceed £20,000

3.0 METHOD OF INVESTIGATION

Software was researched through promotional literature and a shortlist drawn up. One company from the shortlist was found to be in liquidation. Demonstrations were arranged of the other two and visits were made to other auction houses to see them in action.

A further visit was made to Auctionmaster to evaluate their accounts software.

4.0 COMPANY BACKGROUND

Hereward Auctioneers were established in 1849 as an agricultural auctioneer. By 1985 agricultural sales had been overtaken in value by general stock. Some land was sold off to pay for an extension to the existing auction rooms, with associated driveways and customer parking. In 1990 only poultry and eggs were left in the agricultural area on site, whilst farm sales continued elsewhere.

A small computer system with bespoke software was purchased in 1990. In 1992 'special sales' were introduced. These sales deal with items of specialist interest and range from farm machinery to period furniture. Because of this items are likely to be of higher value than those in the general sales.

At the same time the company had also expanded into commercial and residential estate agency as well as their other agricultural interests of estate management and surveying. This part of the business is operated from an office complex in the centre of town which also serves as the company's main office.

The company plans to expand its buildings for storage, helping to increase its throughput at special sales. Increased computerisation may be needed to support this expansion as there is presently no computerised stock handling system.

5.0 THE PRESENT SYSTEM

5.1 Overview

The auction house earns its money by selling vendor's goods at a commission on a sliding scale of 7.5% to 15% depending on value, and taking a premium from buyers. The buyers' premium is 5% plus VAT on the hammer price.

Ordinary sales work on a single week turnaround (excluding the book keeping):

- Saturday and Monday, taking in lots
- Tuesday and Wednesday, cataloguing
- Thursday, produce auctioneer's sheets. Buyers' viewing.
- Friday, sale day.
- Saturday and Monday book keeping

For special sales, taking in begins ten days in advance, meaning that extra goods have to be stored and for a longer period.

5.2 The Computer System

Auction rooms: a 386 SX 25 with 2 Mb of memory and a 40 Mb hard drive. Acts as a server to two dumb terminals each with a 9-pin dot matrix printer. Operates a bespoke auctioneering package.

Accounts: Amstrad PC1512 with dot matrix printer, running Sage Book-keeper.

Main Office: 386 SX 25 as above, with bubble jet printer, running DTP system and commercial database.

5.3 Taking in

Lots are booked in by company staff in the week prior to the auction. Vendors' details are taken and entered on the computer. Reserves are set for each item.

Unique lot numbers are assigned to all items. Each area of the sale has its own range of numbers. Numbers are linked to the vendor's name and this information is entered into the computer, along with the estimate and the reserve. The computer indicates missing lot numbers and these are investigated. Lots subject to VAT are flagged by the computer.

Catalogues are produced for the antiques section using the DTP facility. Details of all lots are printed off onto the auctioneer's sheets.

Registered buyers are given a permanent buyer's number. Casual buyers are issued a number on the day of the sale. There are over three thousand permanent buyers (numbered from 0001 to 3999) and around two hundred casual buyers each week. Casual buyers' numbers run from 4000 to 9999.

These numbers are used whenever a buyer makes a purchase in any of the sale rooms. The auctioneer only has to write down the four numbers and there is no confusion between buyers with similar names. All of the numbers are held on manual files which have to be accessed every week.

Commission bids are left with the company by buyers who cannot attend the actual sale. The bid is entered on the auctioneer's form along with the buyer's number and his assistant does the bidding on the buyer's behalf. Once the sale is over the forms are returned to the office where they are filed with the other forms in alphabetical order of surname.

5.4 Sale Day

When a sale is made the auctioneer enters the buyer's number and the hammer price on his sheet which he gives to his assistant, who marks the item as sold. The assistant marks any commission purchases with the buyer's number. A runner takes the sheet to the office, where the details are fed into the computer. Some eager bidders manage to beat the sheet to the office when they are coming to pay for their lots and they are asked to wait until their details are processed.

Vendors can collect their money immediately all of their lots have been sold, even before the vendor has paid, so the accuracy of details entered on the computer is vital.

Egg and poultry sales are completely manual. Some buyers may have made other purchases as well, causing an overlap of manual and computer systems. This is done through a separate statementing system.

5.5 Post Sale

Once all details of the sale have been entered, the computer produces a balance sheet which includes all unpaid invoices. Problems are caused by buyers coming in to the office to pay as the final invoices are being printed out. Cheques are printed and despatched to vendors. Any debts are identified and compared to the 'aged debtors' file, which is also supplemented by unpaid invoices from the current sale.

Sale details are kept on the main system for six weeks due to the limited disk space. After that time they are backed up on to floppy disks for storage and kept for seven years for tax and VAT purposes.

6.0 PROBLEMS WITH THE PRESENT SYSTEM
6.1 General

There are several systems operating on two different sites:

- Sale administration operates both manually and on computer. Interaction between them demands a further set of forms.
- Auction accounts: all accounts are kept manually.
- Desk top publishing: although compatible with the main system the machine is on a different site.
- Database: is used for auction room details but is on the other site.
- Archived information has to be typed in separately.

6.2 Sales

- With so many buyers on the system access to individual details is slow.
- Paying out to vendors is slow and complicated.
- Collecting back payments involves both manual and computer systems.

The filing operation for the buyers' numbering system needs ten box files to contain the records and the indexes. The system is slow and unwieldy, despite being the main reference system for tracing buyers' accounts and for general accounting purposes.

6.3 The Existing Computer

The design specification of the present system is exceeded in eighty percent of sales. Extra terminals cannot be added.

There is no backup documentation or reference manuals. As the company which wrote the software no longer exists there is no outside support for the system. Serious problems have been encountered with:

- Data integrity
- Invoicing
- Setting up sale parameters
- Archiving
- Carrying over information from sale to sale
- Response speeds, especially on sale days

There is no disaster recovery mechanism in the event of hardware failure. No stock control facility exists on the system. This will be needed when the new buildings are completed. At present commission bids have to be transferred by hand from the invoices to the system before the buyers can be contacted to pick up their goods and arrange payment. Commission bids have to be distinguished from 'unpaids' by a manual search.

7.0 REQUIREMENTS FOR THE NEW SYSTEM
7.1 Software

1 Easy input, deletion and manipulation of lot, buyer and vendor details
2 Information can be carried forward from sale to sale
3 Locking system to allow for data manipulation from one terminal only
4 Capable of printing both full and selected information
5 Automatic calculation of commissions on fixed sliding scales
6 Transfer information onto a DTP system for catalogues
7 Print auctioneer's sheets with full information
8 Automatic totalling from auctioneer's sheets
9 Simple correction of inputting errors (e.g. wrong buyer's number)
10 Print all buyers' and vendors' statements with full details
11 Highlight previous unpaid invoices for buyers
12 Ability to handle part payments
13 Print cheques for vendors
14 Generate financial summaries
15 Handle full accounting details and procedures

16 Hold up to 8000 items of stock
17 Generate bar codes

7.2 System

1 Installed and commissioned by supplier
2 Training provided by supplier
3 Full documentation to be provided
4 Relational database capable of holding information as specified
5 Capacity for up to 10 usable screens with independent capability
6 Graded status password capability
7 Tape streamer for backup
8 Parallel server for disaster recovery

8.0 SOFTWARE RESEARCH

8.1 Initial Research

Eight companies were identified as producing auctioneering packages. Three companies no longer exist and three were not able to offer accounting software. This left two companies offering appropriate systems:

TRACE by R.Mayes and Company
AUCTIONEER by Auctionmaster Business Services

8.2 TRACE

A modular system running on a concurrent DOS operating system. The company does not supply modified versions to individual suppliers. No manual is supplied but there is a hotline system.

Three modules can be run concurrently, but not on the same machine. The package integrates with Sage software for the accounts.

8.2.1 Deficiencies of TRACE

- Cannot automatically identify buyers with unpaid invoices
- Does not itemise buyers' purchase invoices
- Cannot cope with Hereward's large number of permanent buyers without significant data redundancy
- Version updating does not cover archiving procedures
- Carrying lots forward to the next sale is awkward, but not impossible
- Hereward would need to change its auctioneer's sheets to fit the system

8.2.2 Usability of TRACE

The system would solve the majority of Hereward's problems, but not all. Some existing paperwork and procedures would need to be changed.

8.3 AUCTIONEER

A unified system running on UNIX. The accounts ledgers are offered separately. Full customisation of the product is offered, though this may cause initial installation problems.

8.3.1 Deficiencies of AUCTIONEER

- The database is not resident
- Invoice and statement layouts cannot be easily changed
- Minor modifications to auctioneer's sheets would be necessary
- Stock control is approached differently to Hereward' standard method

8.2.2 Usability of AUCTIONEER

There is a full disaster recovery system, a telephone hotline and user manuals. Two full days training is offered as part of the overall price. Good feedback has been obtained from current users. The database difficulty is not a major problem.

This is a comprehensive and speedy package, offering all that Hereward needs in all areas.

9.0 COST BENEFIT ANALYSIS

9.1 Costs

The company must be aware that there are costs beyond the mere purchase and wiring of the system, itself some £15,000 (including VAT). These include:

- new stationery
- time in setting up and copying in existing data
- time lost to staff training
- time spent producing hardware and software specifications, test plan and post-implementation review
- disruption to the staff
- stress caused by changing the system
- disruption caused to customers while the system is 'bedding in'
- time spent entering details to the system that are presently dealt with manually

9.2 Benefits

1 The system could identify bad debts quickly and efficiently. Numbers and length of debts could be cut, improving income and cash flow
2 Bad debts are increasing. A new system could reverse this trend
3 Special sales could be increased in number and in content
4 Stock control could be implemented in the new building
5 Automated book keeping will enable the existing staff to cope with the increasing work load generated by more special sales
6 Savings in staff time in entering and manipulating data
7 Catalogues can be produced quicker and distributed to the trade sooner
8 A faster and more efficient service to all customers

10.0 CONCLUSIONS

Hereward has five major options
1. Continue with the present system
2. Extend the present system
3. Purchase TRACE
4. Purchase AUCTIONEER
5. Have a bespoke system written for the company

Option 1 is not viable if the company is to extend its business. The system is heavily overloaded at present. Although a 'no cost' solution it is also a 'no gain' one.

Option 2 is similarly not viable. Extra machines would slow the system even more. There would be cost but minimal gain.

Option 3 is a serious possibility and would cover many of the company's requirements.

Option 4 is a serious possibility and would cover many of the company's requirements.

Option 5 was found to fall outside the financial parameters set.

The choice of system rests between TRACE and AUCTIONEER. The main differences between the two systems are:

Operating System TRACE uses concurrent DOS, which is old but cheap. AUCTIONEER uses UNIX which is fast and adaptable but more expensive.

Disaster Recovery TRACE has no disaster recovery system. AUCTIONEER uses a second machine for disaster recovery.

Database TRACE has an integral database but massive data redundancy. AUCTIONEER has a separate database with easy access and no data redundancy.

Check back debts TRACE cannot do this.

Company support Auctionmaster (AUCTIONEER) were willing to help at all times and to discuss matters with Hereward. R.M.Mayes seemed only to wish to sell their standard system.

11.0 CONCLUSION

That the company accept the quotation from Auctionmaster Ltd. for the supply and installation of the AUCTIONEER system.

That the company retain an independent consultant to oversee the installation and operation of the new system if they intend to 'go live' in an accelerated time scale. That full testing and training be done before the system is to go 'live'.

12.0 APPENDICES

Appendix A Glossary of Terms
Appendix B Full System Requirements
Appendix C Annual company turnover 1990–1994
Appendix D Quotations and correspondence with companies
Appendix E Forms used in the current system
Appendix F Data Flow Diagrams and Logical Data Structures of the current system.

CHAPTER 6

Interviewing

INTRODUCTION

Interviews are a very powerful tool for information gathering within a business environment. As soon as a company grows beyond the one-person business there are automatically information and perspectives which are hidden from some of the workers. Obviously the larger the company, the greater the problem. If there is information that others have that you do not then the simplest solution is to ask them. A series of questions becomes a full-blown interview.

We all think that we know about interviews because we come across them so frequently. Television news and current affairs programmes rely on them for introducing 'the human interest factor' into the show. Magazines usually carry transcriptions of interviews with media personalities or those 'in the trade' as part of their normal format.

Because of this familiarity we regard interviews as being somehow normal and unproblematic. Want to find out? Just ask a few questions! If it were that simple we would have no need of elections, opinion pollsters would just extrapolate the results from a few thousand sample interviews. Results of general elections in Britain in recent times have shown just how inaccurate opinion polls can be. Similarly, companies could forecast the likely size of market for a new product by simple market research.

A useful cautionary tale is that of the Sony Corporation, who questioned customers on whether they would buy a tape recorder which played but did not record. They received an overwhelmingly negative response but produced it anyway. The Sony Walkman went on to become one of the biggest selling items of the age. These examples are not meant to negate all market research or all interviews but to indicate that difficulties abound in this area. If we are going to make decisions on the basis of interviewing other people we must be careful to budget for the incipient errors in the procedure and to build in high levels of quality control.

6.1 PERCEIVING OTHERS

People are not computers. They do not operate according to the rules of logic. Or, more accurately, they have a whole range of logics within their makeup, some of them incompatible with the others, which are brought to bear at different times and in different situations. Thus a respondent may quite happily tell you that the system that you have just installed is wonderful, is very easy to use and is just what the whole section was looking for. The respondent will then proceed to ignore it totally, allowing it to sit gathering dust in the corner of a room.

The respondent may be entirely honest in the answers that have been given. What we have not discovered is the deep-seated fear that, if the program lives up to all that has been promised of it, the respondent may be thrown out of a job. We have discovered the 'top-level' logical thoughts; we have not discovered the underlying feelings and emotions. When it comes to end users implementing systems these can be even more important than technical competence or the efficiency of the system.

Interviewing has at its heart the basic assumption that we can gather information from others by asking them questions. As we have already seen, there are problems and caveats attached to this assumption, most of them to do with the complex nature of people.

The American sociologist Erving Goffman made a convincing case for seeing individuals as actors on the stage of life. They control the messages they give off in an effort to control the responses of others, to control the way that others see them. '*It will be in [the individual's] interests to control the conduct of the others, especially their responsive treatment of him... Thus, when an individual appears in the presence of others, there will usually be some reason for him to mobilise his activity so that it will convey an impression to others which it is in his interests to convey.*' In other words, we manipulate social situations whenever we can.

Most human beings want other people to like and respect them. They therefore carefully send off the appropriate messages to the interviewer. Take the despatch section of a large food company as an example. There have been problems recently with getting lorries out on time and with the correct loads. You have been asked to investigate the reasons for this. The despatch manager will take care to make it clear that none of this is the fault of that department but is caused instead by illnesses among the workers and inaccuracies in the computer-generated loading schedules. On the other hand the head of data processing tells you that the schedules cannot possibly be wrong because great care was taken over writing and testing the program that generates them and there has been no difficulties at all over the last two years since its implementation. Both managers fear that they will be blamed for the shortfalls and their future prospects damaged. To say that they are lying is to go too far; they are just concerned with presenting themselves in the best possible light.

A related problem which is familiar to researchers is the question of whether changes are brought about by the sheer existence of an interviewer. Being asked a series of questions is not a natural state. If someone on a train started to question you in this way you would soon become wary and begin to seek to avoid the questioner. Such an artificial situation may thus produce artificial responses. Market researchers are aware of the problem, especially when it concerns respondents giving opinions. There is a tendency for some respondents to try to please the questioner in order to give the answers they think they want to hear. A questioner with large IBM stickers on the back of the clipboard might get completely different responses when these are replaced by Apple logos.

This problem is made more difficult by the dynamic of the interview situation itself. Most interviews are inter-active. The interviewee may need to ask questions from time to time in order to clarify what the interviewer meant or to query whether the questions meet the objectives originally laid down. Many interviews even take on the format of a conversation, with all the interchange and elucidations involved. Consequently interviewer and interviewee are constantly changing places; in Goffman's terms they interchange constantly between actor and observer.

Another way of setting out the dynamic of the interview situation is to use the simple matrix known as the **Johari Window**. This provide us with four boxes:

1. Things we know about ourselves and others also know about us or could easily find out. Examples of this are our name, sex, status in the organisation, address and so on.
2. Things we know about ourselves but which others do not know about us. This includes our inner emotions, fears, view of our self and character, lusts, loves, ambitions and so on.
3. Things that others know about us that we do not. We know the kind of impression we try to make on others, what we rarely know is what kind of impression we actually make on them. This is quite apart from telling traits such as body odour and bad breath.
4. Things neither we nor others know about us. This might include phobias or those inner capacities which are not tapped until the situation arises, if it ever does.

Let us go back for a moment to our food distribution company. What we know about the two managers involved is entirely contained in box 1, the public aspect. As interviewers we need to know that the head of data processing is overwhelmingly

	What you know about me	*What you don't know about me*
What I know about myself	1 Status Job Appearance	2 Fears Ambitions Motivators
What I don't know about myself	3 How I appear to others, etc	4 Fears and neuroses Behaviour under stress

Fig. 6.1 Johari Window

ambitious and will do almost anything to get ahead in the company. It might also be a help to find out that the despatch manager, despite a gruff exterior, is overwhelmingly shy and also feels it to be grossly immoral to put blame onto others. These are all matters which fall in to box 2 and which we need to be aware of because they may skew our conclusions if allowed to go unremarked. Since they are hidden, however, how are we to make allowance for their effects?

The great Cambridge philosopher Ludwig Wittgenstein gave a rather pessimistic answer. Inner states, such as pain, love, ambition, fears, are completely unknowable. This is because we can never get inside someone else's head, we can never feel someone else's emotions. He compared them to a child's private possession, a beetle that he carries around in a matchbox. So precious is the beetle that no one is ever allowed to look at it. For all the verbal descriptions I give of my beetle, how can you be sure that yours is the same as mine? How can you be sure that you see colours the way I do (you may be colour blind), or feel pain the way I do (there are some diseases of the nerves which prevent people from feeling pain at all). A logical progression from this is that we cannot even be sure that I feel the same emotions as you at all, my emotional box may be completely empty.

If we need to know about what our interviewees are keeping secret in order to counteract possible bias, doesn't Wittgenstein's answer render that impossible? If you are a philosopher searching for absolute truth, perhaps it does; if you are an analyst who has to get the job done anyway there has to be a more pragmatic solution. The way ahead is signalled by Sigmund Freud: '*When I set myself the task of bringing to light what human beings keep hidden within them, not by the compelling power of hypnosis, but by observing what they say and what they show I thought the task was a harder one than it really is. He that has eyes to see and ears to hear may convince himself that no mortal can keep a secret. If the lips are silent he chatters with his finger tips; betrayal oozes out of him at every pore. And thus the task of making conscious the most hidden recesses of the mind is one which is quite possible to accomplish.*' Lawrence Ferlinghetti made the same point in his poem 'Underwear':

I saw the governor of Alabama on TV the other night.
He must have had tight underwear
he squirmed a lot.

Whilst things are not quite as easy as Freud makes out there are still plenty of visual clues which help us run a truth check on what others say to us. Most people, for example, find it difficult to look others straight in the eyes and tell them a lie. The tendency is to look elsewhere at these times. Your interviewee might blush or clench his fists in anger at some point. His speech may become hesitant or he may start to perspire. These are all signs of stress and tell us that there is more to be communicated than is actually being said. Exactly what is being missed out, we cannot be sure, but the signals are there that we should be digging deeper at this point.

6.2 PREPARING THE INTERVIEW

Before embarking on any pattern of information gathering it is useful to set out what sorts of information you need and what is the best way of finding it out. This might also involve the production of an informal critical path analysis to determine what order activities should be in. For example, it would be helpful to understand how the company determines its stock levels and places orders with suppliers before investigating the procedures when deliveries are made, since delivery verification procedures may depend on whether and how ordering details are held on the firm's computer.

As mentioned above, this may involve the analyst in extensive document gathering, perhaps resulting in the production of preliminary diagrammatic representations of the system. Once this has been achieved the analyst is at least some way towards understanding the broad parameters and purposes of the system. At this point apparent ambiguities, replication of processes and data redundancies begin to become obvious. Questions are forming in the analyst's mind; broad outlines have begun to coalesce which need to be filled in with significant detail. The more background information that is absorbed at this point the better and deeper the questioning will be at the interview stage.

6.2.1   Key personnel

As well as identifying what information is needed our document search is also likely to have identified the holders of that information, thus narrowing down the scope of subsequent activity. In theory, everyone in the organisation should be interviewed in order to build up a thorough and complex view of the organisational structure and culture. In practise this is impractical and unnecessary. Given time constraints the analyst needs to reduce activity to key personnel. These fall into three groups:

1. The system owners
System owners may be heads of department in which the system is used or was developed, or the director of a small company whose system is being investigated. These are the decision makers as far as that system is concerned, little could be initiated without their consent. They are also key political players in the investigation.

System owners have access to an overview of the organisation that personnel further down the ladder do not have. They may be privy to development plans, changing company objectives and a sense of how a variety of systems fit together to form the whole. Without this overview it would be difficult for the analyst to gain a comprehensive high-level view of the organisation.

Within the organisation system owners are also gate keepers. The analyst may only be allowed access to other personnel through them, especially where the sense of hierarchy is a strong one. Interviewing system owners is thus a matter of political manoeuvring as well as of information gathering. Doors have to be opened, other key personnel identified and a sense of trust established before the analysis can continue. Getting the system owners on your side is therefore vital.

2. Information holders
These will have been identified in your preliminary analysis. Wherever there are points to be elucidated, gaps to be filled in, structures that do not cohere it is likely that you

can identify a key person as holding the information that you want. Where this is not so, other information holders can usually direct you to a source.

Often information holders will be identified by their post in the organisation. The stores manager will be the one to tell you about stock levels, the DP manager will tell you about hardware purchasing, the personnel manager will tell you about recruitment. Where information is found to be held in unexpected places (as when the stores manager is solely responsible for the purchase of computer hardware) this becomes a matter to be probed during interview.

Remember that information holders are as likely to be at the bottom of the hierarchy as at the top. The key player in the sales organisation is as likely to be the clerk who takes and processes the individual orders as it is the departmental head. Trust to your information analysis rather than to the company's organisation charts.

3. System users

In the fifties and sixties many companies introduced systems of work study. The idea was that working practices would be carefully studied with a view to making them more efficient, the workers more productive and the companies more profitable. As with so many good ideas the practise did not measure up to the theory. Much good work was done but it was undermined by unscrupulous employers using work study as an excuse for cutting pay and by union suspicions that the results would be used to justify redundancies.

Some work study practitioners also did their cause little good by seeing themselves as objective scientific investigators observing fixed systems. Processes were timed, the results recorded and analysed. The outcomes were disappointing. One important factor had been left out of the equation, the operators of the system themselves. These were the very people who knew most about how the process actually operated, what were its strengths and weaknesses.

Nowadays those operators are as likely to be sitting at a VDU as they are working a pressing machine or on an assembly line. The work study engineer has been replaced by the systems analyst but the danger still remains that the expertise and experience of the operator can be overlooked by an unguarded emphasis on strategic planning and higher level operations. Where systems exist to make the work of the users simpler, or even possible in some cases, it makes sense to check with as many of them as possible that it is delivering all that it promises.

Within organisations there may also be a hierarchy of users. Where software has been brought in the DP department may be its first users. They have to adapt it to local needs and maintain it on the company network. In the company at large there may be a range of users who need that particular application as an aid to their work but who have no knowledge of its structure. The analyst needs to interview representatives of both sets of users, since they may have conflicting views. The software that is easy to install, adapt and maintain may, after all, not support enough functions for the end user's purposes.

6.2.2 Setting aims and objectives

An interview can be likened to any other information systems project. We begin with a project initiation document, continue through analysis and implementation and conclude with a post-implementation review. In terms of interviewing this means:

- an **issue review**, in which the reasons for using the methodology are established
- setting out **aims** that the interview will help you to achieve
- establishing **specific objectives** which will be met over the course of the interview
- tying in **performance criteria**, which will indicate that your objectives have been met
- setting out **methods** that will be used during the interview
- **reviewing your performance** in terms of performance criteria and interview methods.

We have already dealt with the **issue review** in the sense that our document gathering has indicated for us the gaps in our knowledge and the detail that needs to be filled in. The nature of the information required will indicate that an interview is the most appropriate way of acquiring it. For example, we may want to know about actual procedures, rather than paper ones, or the attitudes of users towards the existing system. It is at this stage that we consider what problems may arise during the interview, perhaps as the result of resistance by the interviewee, and take steps to minimise them.

Our **aims** indicate what the purpose of the interview is to be. In the examples above we have set out our general aims, which cannot by their nature be settled by any one particular interview, although we should have achieved them by the end of the interview process as a whole.

By contrast the **specific objectives** are tightly tied to the interview itself. These should be limited and achievable. Yeates et al specify that they should contain a **time**, an **action** and a **deliverable**. Thus our interview with Janet Smith may have the following objectives:

1. to ascertain which procedures the interviewee uses
2. to ascertain in detail how those procedures are used
3. to identify the interviewee's opinions on those procedures
4. to identify deviations of actual procedures from theoretical procedures
5. the above to be clearly recorded in an interview schedule
6. one hour to be allowed for the interview.

Objectives one to four constitute our actions (ascertaining and identifying), objective five is the deliverable and objective six is the time scheduled

The **performance criteria** are intimately tied to the objectives. They tell us what counts as having achieved each of the objectives and act as a check list in the final review. It is all too easy to set up a mental set of criteria, which can be easily forgotten about or altered after the event. A written set of criteria cannot be avoided. In the above example our performance criteria might be set out in question form:

- Do I know all the procedures used by the interviewee?
- Could I replicate each one in detail using the information that I possess?
- Do I know the interviewee's full opinion of the procedures?

- What proof do I have that this is the *full* opinion?
- Do I have a list of non-standard procedures?
- Does this correlate with information from parallel interviews in the same set?
- Is an interview schedule available?
- Start and finish times of interview are recorded and indicate time schedule kept.

Process in interviews can be as important as content, since it is the process which helps to ensure that peak efficiency is reached. You therefore need to set out what **methods** you intend to use during the interview. In our interview with Janet Smith we may use a standard questionnaire as the basis for our initial questioning, since there are several people doing similar work to her. We might also ask for a demonstration of some of the procedure that she uses as a cross-check on her verbal descriptions. Existing procedures might be described in terms of a data flow diagram, so we could use this as a yardstick by which to judge how far her actual procedures are from the theoretical norm. Such approaches have to be planned in advance, especially where there is a tight time schedule.

Reviewing your performance should be a normal procedure in any form of business activity. How can you know what you did well and what you did less well unless you reflect upon it? We can improve our mechanical performance to a limited extent purely by practise and repetition but it is only by intelligent reflection that we can move forward onto a higher level. By looking back at each interview we can glean information about ourselves and our performance.

In this process, look first at the performance criteria. Which of them were not achieved? Is this a regular event? For example, your interviews may frequently go on longer than you planned. In this case either your planning is awry or, more likely, you are not structuring your interview in such a way that it fits into the time allowed. Are you speaking too much, are you allowing your interviewee to be too discursive, do you fail to stop the interview running away down blind alleys, are you unable to bring the interview to a solid conclusion?

Perhaps you are failing to get a full picture of the procedures that the interviewee undertakes. Is this through lack of preparation? Would the use of a data flow diagram help? Are you not being sharp enough in your questioning? Is your implied approach too informal, leading to a lax attitude in the interviewee? The review will not give you the answer to these questions, but it will cause you to ask them and to set up an inner analysis of your strengths and weaknesses.

6.3 SETTING UP THE INTERVIEW

As we have established, interviewing is a complex and demanding intellectual activity, almost as much so for the interviewee as for the interviewer. Participants have to devote their whole concentration to it if its success is to be maximised. Given that we now know who we are going to interview and why, how do we go about establishing our structures?

6.3.1 The time, the place

Most of the time you will find that you need to book your interviewee. This might be as simple as *'have you got a few minutes to spare now?'* through to *'can we compare our diaries for the coming week?'* Once you have made your appointment you must stick to it, unless unavoidable problems come up. In that case you will need to cancel the original date as soon as possible, preferably in person. If you have to leave a message then you should follow this up with personal contact as soon as possible. No interviewee should ever be 'stood up' by an interviewer with no prior warning.

Try to allow as much time as possible for your interview; think how long you expect the interview to take and then double it! This allows for particularly loquacious interviewees as well as stopping you both getting nervous about that urgent meeting you have to go to afterwards. As you gain more experience you will be able to gauge your time keeping more accurately but at first you should err on the side of caution. Naturally you may encounter pressure from companies about the amount of time you are taking up. Stick to your guns. Time spent now getting the analysis right is saving three times that amount in re-writing your system.

Where to interview is far more difficult. In an ideal world you will always have a specialist interview room available. This will be comfortable, well lit, pleasantly ventilated and with few visual or aural distractions. Generally, the facilities available will only approximate to this ideal and you will have to adapt them to your purposes. The standard office is quite good, especially if you can have telephone calls diverted for the duration of the interview. Few people can resist answering the telephone and its mere ringing causes tension.

Sometimes you will be faced with having to interview workers at their work stations. Try to move them elsewhere if at all possible, unless it is essential that the processes they operate are demonstrated on-screen. An interviewee at a work station is a worker first and an interviewee second; your objective is to reverse these priorities, thus removing potential interruptions and distractions. Your eventual destination may not be perfect, either, but should be a discernible improvement.

For example, a student was analysing the feasibility of installing a system into a bus and taxi company. She tried hard to interview the owner of the company in his office but they were continually interrupted by the telephone which the owner compulsively answered. In the end she gave in and took him across the road to the local pub. Despite the juke box and the gaming machines she was able to get her interview completed.

6.3.2 The context

Both parties have to be clear at all times that a formal interview is in progress. Employees of organisations in particular have to have the purpose and parameters of the interview set before them. The employee needs to know the status of the interviewer and the terms of reference that have been set, otherwise personal and professional confusion will arise. On the professional level the interviewee needs to be clear what information may be divulged: are sensitive financial matters to be dealt with? does the interviewer have security clearance? does this interview have anything to do with performance monitoring? is it confidential?

In Fig. 6.2 you will see an internal memorandum issued by a senior manager to all staff in advance of an analyst undertaking interviews with staff. You will notice that the senior manager is clearly identified, as are all members of staff affected. The purpose of the exercise is set out ('*Examining our requirements for our new commercial computer system*') as is the time-scale of the exercise. The analyst is named; seven basic questions are presented and deliverables identified. Staff are given an idea of how long the process might take ('*some minutes of your time*') and how their input will be used ('*in any specification for the new system*').

Staff now know the areas that questions will cover and have been reassured that the analyst has a clearly defined role, which will be to their benefit in the long run. Confidentiality is not a question in this case, although it is clear that this is an exercise emanating from management and under their control. Staff who receive this memo are clear that they are expected to collaborate fully.

The Midwich Thame memorandum, then, smoothed the way for the analyst to operate on the professional level she anticipated. On the personal level she needs to introduce herself to the interviewee in such a way that she is seen as both professional and independent. As we saw earlier, people carry piles of emotional baggage and insecurities around with them which colour their experience of the interview. In an age of structural unemployment paranoia, will always be with us; the analyst needs to be both objective and reassuring.

On a similar line, the interviewee needs to know when she starts and stops 'performing'. What is said in the interview is fair game, it counts as data and may be reported, either by name or anonymously. Once the interview is over what is said is social rather than work and is not ascribable. Not that the analyst may not use it, for it may be what the employees in general really feel, only that its source is privileged in the same way that a journalist's would be.

6.3.3   Recording and transcription

Interviews need to be recorded in some form for a variety of reasons. First, as a transcription of what is said to aid you in bringing together all the relevant data for your subsequent report. Memory is not reliable enough to be trusted in this respect.

Second, the interviewee has a right to expect that what was said, at least in its broad sense, if not in its entire details, has been recorded accurately and views correctly and fairly represented. In short interviews you should have enough time to check your notes with the interviewee. For longer ones feedback may be delayed some days, perhaps taking the form of the delivery of a formal written document or diagrams and a follow-up interview.

Finally, the interview record is a public record in the same way as all the other documents: data flow diagrams, context diagrams, logical data structures and so on. They constitute part of the data that has been gathered and will have to be checked by readers of your report or by others on your project team. From this point of view it is important that the interview should be written up as soon after it takes place as possible, together with any comments, queries or need for further action that you have identified as a result.

MEMO   MIDWICH
                                                      THAME

                                                      ———

                                                      Gilray Road
                                                      Diss
Subject   System and other reports   Norfolk IP22 3EU

From   Roger Pulford   ———

To   All Staff

Date   15 April 1994

Reference   RWP/MIDAS01

Copy to   Emma Pearce

As the next stage in our examination of requirements for our new commercial computer system, Emma Pearce has been tasked to spend a short time with everyone during the coming two weeks to discuss the current use of computer-generated and other reports.

Answers will be required to the following questions:

1   What reports do you use?

2   To what use do you put these reports?

3   Are these reports used or amended by any colleague?

4   How regularly are these reports printed or screen displayed (eg daily, weekly, monthly, on demand)?

5   Are these reports computer-generated, word-processor produced, or only screen-based?

6   What are the short-comings, if any, of these reports?

7   Is the report structure or design in need of improvement?

A sample or photocopy of the first and last page of each report will be useful to Emma.

Some minutes of your time for Emma will be appreciated. The answers to these questions, and any suggestions, will be used in any specification for the new system.

Fig. 6.2 Midwich Thame memo

It is only polite to ask the interviewee whether you may take notes. Those who object will have to have the purposes of note taking explained to them and the fact that they will be agreed by both parties before being printed up. Should the interviewee still not agree, you are left with having to write up as much as you can remember immediately afterwards. This record must then be treated with care as not being 'first grade' information. How and what to record of an interview is analogous to deciding what to record of a college lecture. You do not need every word, on the other hand you have to be careful not to pare it down so much that nuances, subtlety and perhaps the whole meaning get lost. Lectures and interviews are similar but they are not identical. The lecture lasts an hour or more, the interview may be as short as ten minutes. Lectures involve tens or hundreds of people, interviews are normally confined to two. Lectures are one-way communications, interviews have a more conversational structure.

These differences affect the way in which we take notes, particularly in the use of the tape recorder. Small desk-top recorders with built in microphones and reasonable recording properties are available nowadays from most electrical retailers and are used by magazine journalists in particular. Rechargeable batteries are standard in many of them, getting round the old problem of trying to find a new set of batteries at short notice.

Tape recorders have the overwhelming advantage of recording every word that is said, plus the intonation that goes with it. They also free the interviewer's hand and mind from the task of taking notes in order to concentrate on what is being said, identifying gaps or inconsistencies in the flow. However, they do have some problems. First, there are still some people who do not like speaking into a machine. They prefer the personal touch and their wishes need to be respected. Second, there is the possibility of malfunction. Either machine or tape can malfunction (there is nothing that compares to removing a tape after a long interview and finding metres of it dripping from the cassette!) and microphones can be overwhelmed by extraneous noise. Fortunately such malfunctions are rare nowadays but it is always advisable to take some skeleton notes as a backup to the machine.

The third and most difficult problem with tape recorders is the problem of transcription. Somehow you have to remove the data from the tape into your report. This can only be done by laboriously replaying the tape and typing in what was said, either word for word or in some truncated form. To transcribe an interview in full takes about twice the length of the interview whilst to gather just the gist of it takes about one and a half times. Referring to portions of the interview can also be time consuming as one cannot scan a tape as one does the printed page. All this apart, tape recorders are still most people's choice for use during lengthy formal interviews.

The alternative is to take notes at the time. Where precision of record is not a primary objective this is still a reputable method, especially if you develop some form of personal or international shorthand system. Not that you can write all the time, or all the interviewee sees is that growing bald patch on the crown of your head. Your jottings have to be intermittent, to allow eye contact and for rapport to develop.

Pen and paper are cheap, easy to use methods for short interviews and for less precise occasions. They do not put people off if used with discretion (*'Do you mind if I make a quick note of that?'*) and can be 'turned off' at will when the interviewee requests it.

One of the ways of getting round the main limitation of pen and paper, that the interviewer has to write and think at the same time, is to use a standard form or set of questions. The seven questions mentioned in the Midwich Thame memo above could be used by Emma on a standard form, one for each interviewee, which she could then use. Thus, recording straightforward replies becomes almost automatic, freeing her mind for the next question or to detect areas of difficulty.

Where information is more complex the making of notes may need to be suspended altogether for a time. Listen to the explanation, try to make sense of it. When you have done that, check your understanding by feeding back the information to the interviewee. Once it has been agreed that you have got things right you can proceed to make your notes, but not before. From time to time you may ask your interviewee to pause so that you can make notes. Trying to write and listen at the same time invariably leads you to do neither efficiently.

6.3.4   Listening triads

Such concentrated listening takes practise and training. A useful exercise is the one known as 'Listening Triads' which, as its name suggests, needs three participants. Each person chooses a topic, which may be from a pre-prepared list or something chosen from the participants' interests. Around ten minutes is set aside to make notes ready for a three minute talk.

When the notes are ready a running order is agreed. The person designated the first speaker delivers the presentation to the others. The one designated the first listener takes in as much of the presentation as possible, but without taking notes. At the same time the third person, the referee, records as much in note form as possible.

Once the speaker has finished the listener feeds back as much of the talk as possible, taking care not to alter, interpret or misinterpret what was said (although summarising is allowed). Both speaker and referee act as a check on the accuracy of the listener's account. Each participant takes it in turns to be speaker, listener and referee.

As you can see, this mimics closely the problem that interviewers have of listening carefully to extended explanations and then preparing a summary that is satisfactory to both parties. A refinement to this exercise is to divide the presentation into three parts, between which the listener is allowed to make notes. At the end of the listening process these can be used for feedback. Again, interviewers would use this technique when conducting an extended interview with pauses at intervals for note taking.

6.4   WHAT QUESTIONS?

Interviewers should never go into an interview 'cold'. As well as the preparatory material discussed in section 6.2 they should also have mapped out what sort of questions they need to ask. In very simple cases this will lead to the preparation of a standard interview schedule which can be used on large numbers of respondents. This is the sort of schedule that market researchers use, where all the questions have been mapped out in advance, often with standard multiple choice responses.

These are an effective way of getting replies from a large number of people quickly and in a format that is susceptible to quantitative analysis. Respondents could fill the schedule in themselves, except that the presence of an interviewer ensures a one hundred per cent response rate and cuts out facetious answers.

Such research deals predominantly in what is termed '**closed questions**'. These are questions which have a simple standard response. '*Do you own a computer?*' allows only yes or no as a response. Slightly more complex answers might ask you to grade your computer's performance from one to ten, where one is terrible and ten is '*couldn't be better*'.

Closed questions, despite their seeming objectivity, have certain drawbacks. A prime factor in their efficacy is the precision with which they are drawn up. Market research companies spend vast amounts of time trying to eliminate the equivalent of '*have you stopped beating your wife?*', and allowing for regional, racial and contextual variations. Pilot studies are carried out in order to be able to test the wording and the ordering of the questions, not always with perfect success. Analysts who are merely using their interview schedule as a backbone to the interview can easily overcome this problem by discussing with the respondent what sort of response is called for.

The second problem lies in the nature of closed questions themselves. They have been drawn up in advance by teams or individuals who have a lesser or greater knowledge of the area they are investigating. What questions they ask is a function of their knowledge and of what results they expect to find. The results they get will be those following from the knowledge and questions that they started with. If the interview started off with the wrong view of the situation the results are likely to remain there.

Open questions get over this problem. '*What sort of improvements would you like to see made to the company's training policy*' allows the respondent to put forward original ideas which the researcher has not so far considered. Similarly questions such as '*What difficulties have you encountered whilst using the company's PCs? How would you suggest they be overcome?*' gives us much more usable information than '*Please rate the performance of the company's PCs on a scale of one to ten.*' Open questions produce new data and previously unconsidered approaches, enabling the analyst to take a more rounded view of the problem and perhaps to indulge in some creative and lateral thinking.

Despite this, open questions should only be used sparingly and in appropriate situations, for they are time-consuming and difficult to quantify. If the fifty employees of the company each give different responses to the question about the training policy how are we to compile that into a meaningful report? How long is it going to take to interview them all while they recount their personal experiences with training, or the lack of it?

What we need to achieve is a perfect balance between open and closed questions. We need to use open questions when the response is likely to give us information that we had not considered before, closed questions where an answer is crucial to the direction the interview will take or where the results need to be quantified. Such a simple example might be:

Q: Do you own a personal computer? (Closed)
A: Yes.
Q: What make is it? (Open)
A: An Opus 486.
Q: Do you have any problems with it? (Open)
A: It is a bit slow accessing large files.
Q: I have got something that will solve all that. Would you like to try it? (Closed)
A: Yes, of course.

The salesperson makes sure that the prospect is a computer user with a preliminary closed question, uses open questions to gain information, then finishes with a closed question in order to gain commitment from the client. An analyst researching the production of reports might go through a similar process:

Q: Do you produce any reports during your work? (Closed)
A: Yes, several.
Q: Are any of them on this list? (Closed)
A: Yes, these three.
Q: Do you produce any other kinds of reports that are not on this list? (Closed)
A: I have a special monthly report for the sales manager.
Q: Could you tell me all about it and let me have an example, please? (Open)

The analyst has produced the quantitative information that is needed with the closed questions and has used the open question to uncover new information which had not so far come to light.

Whatever type of question you are using it is important not to be limited by your interview schedule. Consider the answers that you are being given. Are they consistent? If not then they should be interrogated. Do they seem to point to a deviant method of working within the company culture? Is this sub-culture common or confined only to this respondent? Do the replies point to the existence of a sub-process in the data flow which has not so far been mentioned? All these would demand the use of supplementary questioning, as would an answer which the analyst did not understand. Coming out of a high-level interview merely with a few ticks on an interview schedule means that all parties have wasted their time.

If closed questions are difficult to formulate, open questions are even more so. They need to be formed in such a way to allow the respondent full rein but within the limits of the inquiry at hand. '*Tell me everything about the company*' is so far-ranging as to be useless. '*Describe the processes you go through when a customer phones through an order*' confines itself to one area of the business and makes it clear what the interviewer wants to know whilst at the same time leaving space for the interviewee to be as expansive as necessary.

A useful tactic is the use of **multiple choice questions**. Not to be confused with portmanteau questions (see below) these allow us to clarify matters by forcing the interviewee to make clear decisions, perhaps putting requirements into an order of importance. So we might ask: the client: '*Which is more important to you, the fast response time or the ability to hold all the data that you have specified?*' or '*You have* *identified the slowness of the customers to pay their bills and the rises in suppliers' prices to be the primary causes of your cash flow problem. Which of these two would you say is costing you the most money?'*

We have already mentioned that it is impossible to take notes and to listen at the same time. Open questions, with their more discursive responses, call for attentive listening and an intelligent use of non-verbal communication. On the one hand, the interview may be throwing up a whole host of questions in the interviewer's mind which need to be formulated as follow-ups to the original question. As we will see later, this is a dangerous time for listeners as they tend to be listening to the workings of their own minds rather than to the speech of the other person.

On the other hand, we may be getting too little response from the interviewee. Responses may be minimal or stop short of a complete description. It is important that the interviewer is paying as close attention as possible to all the available information, both verbal and non-verbal. Is the other person nervous? Are they trying not to give away certain information for some reason? Is the person just shy? Are you regarded as a threat? Are your questions formulated incorrectly, causing puzzlement in the interviewer? An interviewer whose head is down taking notes will find difficulty in observing enough behaviour to be able to resolve these questions.

Questions that have been prepared in advance are quite easy to handle. If you have probed sufficiently well your respondents may produce answers which you wish to examine further, inventing the questions as you go along. This is the most exciting time in an interview, when you take off into uncharted territory. It is also the most dangerous and the time when your questions can drift in to danger areas.

Portmanteau questions are ones where everything has been thrown in, as in a travelling bag or portmanteau. Because there are so many questions the interviewee does not know which one to answer, or even be able to remember what they were. *'Do you find that the speed response of this system is insufficient for your needs, or is it that the screens are badly laid out, leading you to make too many mistakes, or is the problem one of entering the data in the wrong areas over a long period of time?'* If you want three pieces of information, ask three questions.

Leading questions are ones where the interviewee is merely asked to agree with a formulation by the interviewer. *'Wouldn't you agree that this system is far too slow?'* is a typical example. The interviewee politely agrees, never having thought about the question before, and fails to give any personal opinion, since it seems not to be called for. Leading questions are closed questions with only one answer rather than two. They may be useful for a salesperson attempting to get agreement from the client but they are not part of the armoury of the committed analyst.

Non-questions may take the form of a long and rambling statement by the interviewer, followed by a significant pause, into which the interviewee is expected to insert some sort of answer. Alternatively, the question may be so packed with subsidiary information that its purpose can be elusive. For example: *'If we consider the installation of a new system, as I suppose we must, given the current difficulties with the present one, added to its antiquity and difficulty of use, especially on days when there are large numbers of clients, which as you know is often on Wednesdays and weekends, although of late that has not been so bad...'* and we haven't yet got to the question!

One other procedure that an analyst might consider does not really count as questioning at all. This is the request for a demonstration. Our analyst might follow up questions about the production of reports by asking the respondent to demonstrate how the operator goes about producing the monthly report for the sales manager and what existing information it utilises. When researching a company's telesales the analyst might ask the salesperson to demonstrate what procedures are gone through when a client phones in an order. Better still, the analyst could observe the processing of a real order and question the salesperson about it afterwards.

6.5 LISTENING

Listening has been referred to as '*the forgotten skill*'. It is, after all, something that we do every day, why would anyone ever imagine that we do not do it well? Certainly we listen to others or to the radio or television for long periods of the day. What we rarely do is to listen in the highly concentrated manner that is required in an interview. Much of the time we drift in and out of listening, formulating thoughts, ideas and speech of our own.

What we are concerned with in the interview is not just listening but **positive listening**. This is the art of giving oneself over completely to the speaker, taking in all that is said, encouraging the speaker to give freely of all the relevant data and feelings on the topic and reflecting on the data that we receive (although not in a way that prevents us from taking in what is currently being said).

If you reflect on the way that you interact verbally with others you will observe a whole range of behaviours in yourself which are dysfunctional as far as active listening is concerned. A lot of the time we listen with only partial attention, our other senses roving around picking up messages from elsewhere which are of more interest. This is probably an ancient survival mechanism, not getting so interested in one event that danger can creep up on us unawares.

We also let our view of the person doing the speaking colour what we hear and how we receive it. In the opening chapter research was described which indicated that we rate intelligence by such things as accent, appearance and perceived background. As we need to be aware that people are judging our communications in this manner we should also take care that we are not doing the same thing. Do we dismiss what is said to us by a mere clerk, a temporary employee or someone with a strong West Indian accent? If we do, we are judging the speaker rather than the message, always a dangerous thing to do.

Frequently we are guilty of **partial listening**. This may take several forms, but its central feature is that the listener only listens to a part of what is being said. For the rest of the time the listener gives the appearance of listening but is in fact involved in some private inner dialogue. At its extreme such behaviour is triggered off by a decision that the speaker cannot have anything of interest to say or that it is likely to be totally opposed to all that we believe. The first reaction may be the result of the sort of stereotyping illustrated in the previous paragraph, the second could be awoken by an unfortunate remark by the speaker. If an interviewee were to make grossly insulting racist or sexist remarks at the beginning of the interview the unwary interviewer might leap to the unfounded conclusion that someone like this cannot have anything of use to say. Our value judgements have got in the way of our listening.

Another form of partial listening is that of **completion**. In normal conversation, with its elisions, absences and breaks in continuity, we often have to complete the speaker's meaning, making linguistic leaps to complete sentences and ideas. We become so used to doing this that we assume the general meaning of what someone is saying and then cease to listen, perhaps using the time to plan our own contribution. When interviewing a group of people who all do similar jobs we need to be particularly aware that we are likely to be seduced into partial listening by the assumption that they will all tell us the same things.

Not all interviewees are confident or skilled communicators. Some think or talk slowly, others have limited vocabularies to express their ideas. It is easy to get impatient with such people, to become bored with listening to them or to discount their experience. Our brains operate three times faster than we can speak. When listening to a simple or poorly constructed message it is easy to become bored and seek other tasks with which to occupy ourselves. Good listeners learn to empathise with the other person, allowing for the lack of communication skills and recognising that they do not invalidate the speaker's ideas or experience.

Information systems professionals often find that the people that they interview lack a vocabulary that enables them to describe their feelings or experiences with information technology in a precise and structured manner. This is not unusual or unexpected. Motor mechanics have similar problems with their clients, as do printers, insurance agents and town planners. Each has specialist techniques, equipment and vocabulary which the general public may not have learnt.

In this case it is the interviewer's job to use a **reflective listening** technique. Reflective listening involves the interviewer reformulating what has been said and reflecting it back to the interviewee. Note that this is a restating of the information, not an interpretation of it. You are attempting to get the speaker's ideas into a meaningful format, not set up a dialogue on their value. Such reflection might be prefaced with phrases such as : '*What you said is...*' or '*You seem to feel that...*' making it obvious that the interviewer is trying to be helpful rather than being judgmental. Specific examples of reflective listening applied to interview technique are given elsewhere in this chapter.

This can all be summed up in a set of do's and don'ts:

DON'T
- make early assumptions about the course or content of the interview
- be mislead by early impressions, prejudices or stereotypes
- interrupt the speaker
- allow yourself emotional responses
- lose patience with slow or poor communicators

DO

- listen to what was actually said, not what you thought was said
- listen for key issues, not mere facts
- take notes
- empathise with the speaker
- keep as much eye contact as possible
- use non-verbal communication to show interest in the speaker and to pace the speed of the interaction.

Non-verbal behaviour begins with an alert body posture which conveys that the interviewer is interested in what is being said. The simple nod encourages the speaker to continue, whilst a puzzled frown or quizzical look is an invitation to expand on a point that is being made. From time to time an '*um*' or '*yes*' or '*uh-huh*' shows that the interviewer is still listening and wants the speaker to continue. Gestures can be used to call for a slight pause whilst notes are taken.

The two behaviours to avoid in this context are those of **over-response** and **apparent listening**. Over-response is the overdoing of non-verbal clues until they become a disturbing mannerism which put the interviewee off rather than acting as encouragement. Apparent listening is the fate of bored professionals who have perhaps heard it all before. Their response mechanisms click on to automatic, putting their '*yeses*' and '*ums*' in the right place irrespective of whether or not they are taking in the information. The first behaviour distracts the sending of the message, the second distracts from its reception.

6.6 INTERVIEW PROCEDURES

Interviews are two-way processes that are under the control of the interviewer. Both parties need to feel satisfied with the result; the feeling in the interviewer that as much has been discovered as is necessary or possible and the feeling of the interviewee that information and opinions have been valued. They also need to feel satisfied with the process. For the interviewee this is aided by the feeling that the interviewer has taken the time to acquire background information and has structured the interview in a logical manner, but not so strictly as to remain a slave to structure at the expense of being able to follow important new areas which may reveal themselves.

6.6.1 Effective behaviour

In order that the interview can be effective the interviewer needs to take positive steps to open up the process, to indicate to the interviewee that this is a two-way process in which the interviewee's contribution is of prime value. To do this a range of behaviours are employed in order to draw out the interviewee.

Inviting asks the interviewee to make a contribution. Usually this is employed in the early stages of an interaction, as a starter. Simple questions such as '*tell me about how the ordering system works*' or '*what difficulties are you having operating this package?*' may be enough in themselves to produce all the necessary information for a short interview.

At some stage the interviewees may demand help or information themselves. This demands that the interviewer moves to the **giving** phase. Sometimes this may be initiated by the interviewer at the beginning of an interaction, by making clear the agenda for the interview or describing its background and why the interview was needed. As we have already said, the interviewee has the right to expect feedback after the interview has finished in order to agree what has been recorded. In longer or more complicated interviews the feedback may come at stage points in the interview itself, confirming understanding before progressing to the next stage.

Interviewees frequently demand information or reassurance from the interviewer. *'Is this the normal presentation of a screen?'*, *'Do other people have problems with this, or is it just me?'* are typical examples. Such questions are part of the implicit contract of care and interest between interviewer and interviewee: *'I will give you all the information that I have as long as you regard my wants and needs as a person and support me as best you can.'*

As a partner in the enterprise and an expert in the immediate area under review the interviewee can be expected to have thoughts and ideas about that area. As we mentioned above, one of the weaknesses of the work study movement was that poor practitioners tended to ignore that expertise. Instead, good interviewers encourage **proposing** by their interviewees, who may in fact be the very users who will have to operate the system that will be implemented.

Systems analysis particularly stresses the involvement of users in carrying out systems reviews. The National Computing Centre (NCC) notes on SSADM calls for their involvement as part of the analysis team: *'It is important that those carrying out the review include the responsible users'*, although it is recognised that in small systems this is not always possible. In all cases the NCC insists that analysis is *'carried out by the analyst working in consultation with the responsible users'*. Consultation involves both giving by the analyst and the opportunity for proposing by the user.

A related activity is **suggesting**. This involves the interviewer making suggestions about possible procedures or plans of action. Some interviewers use this as a manipulative activity, planting ideas in the minds of subordinates, who then accept them as their own for implementation, rather than ordering the subordinate to make the change. Suggesting is claimed to be nearly three times as effective as ordering.

One would hope that suggesting is used more directly by an interviewer, as a way of eliciting opinions on alternative courses of action. As far as possible, the courses of action should be business oriented rather than matters of technical detail. *'What do you think about linking accounts and ordering together?'* leads to a discussion on the desirability of changing the way we operate. *'What do you think of using Sage rather than Pegasus?'* could lead us into an unedifying discussion of detail, which may also be based on hearsay and prejudice rather than knowledge.

In our society, we tend to treat new proposals with scepticism. This may be the result of centuries of successful scientific approaches, emphasising the constant testing of hypotheses to destruction. A report writer naturally uses this sceptical approach but for several reasons the interviewer might well proceed differently. Since the interviewer is part of a co-operative process with the interviewee it is useful for the interviewer to empathise, to 'get inside the skin' of the other person. As well as empathy the interviewer wants to show that the other's contributions are valued and worthwhile.

This calls for an activity we have come across before, that of **building**. Instead of being critical of the interviewee's suggestions they are built upon, added to. The interviewer suggests how they might work in principle, how the ideas could be built upon in a wider context. Both actors concentrate heavily upon finding reasons to support the ideas and proposals put forward, creating a kind of intellectual 'added value'. Although the suggestion may not be acted upon in its entirety later it does indicate what can be achieved by any given solution and it may also have features which can be included later in the process.

We have already mentioned the need for **testing** during the interview process. Testing demonstrates that listening has taken place and that the interviewee has been valued. It involves the interviewer feeding back all or some of the information gleaned to the interviewee. This gives the interviewer a chance to test for understanding of what has been said and gives the interviewee an opportunity to correct mistakes. Testing may also take the form of **confirming**, reformulating the interviewee's statement in your own words, in order to check that you have understood it, and of **summarising**, where a longer detailed exposition or discussion is reduced to its main points.

Finally, the interviewer signs off with a **closing** procedure. This might be signalled by a previous procedure, such as a final testing phase, or an invitation to continue or close the discussion such as *'That is as far as I think we can go. Is there any topic that we haven't covered which you think is important?'* Closure might also be effected by a series of closed questions, indicating that interaction is about to come to a close. Where appropriate you need to suggest further action, such as returning interview forms for checking or making appointments for a further meeting. Remember that time keeping should always be one of your interview objectives and an effective closure procedure is your prime weapon in achieving that objective.

6.6.2 Taking control

Unlike a conversation an interview has a senior and a junior partner. It is the senior partner, the interviewer, who sets and controls the agenda and makes decisions about its progress. The interviewer signals opening and closure and determines the direction the interview takes. To do all this you need to be in control of the process, including handling the unexpected.

You should already be armed with a set of preliminary questions and perhaps a whole interview schedule. Your objectives tell you what information you are seeking to find and what will count as success at the end.

Begin the interview with a general introduction both to yourself and to the interview process:

'Good morning, my name is Janet Smith from Optimum Computer Services, you may have had a memo about me from the managing director. As it says on the memorandum, I am looking at how the company's telesales service operates with a view to making it more efficient. The interview should last about half an hour. I have a set of standard questions that I am asking everyone, then there will be the chance for you to tell me your feelings about the system and perhaps even take me through some of the processes.'

Janet has firmly introduced herself, the project and the form the interview will take. She has presented the authority for the investigation, set out the length of the interview and presented a rough **agenda** for its conduct. The interviewee might ask a set of questions at this point and Janet will be as reassuring as she can be within the realms of honesty and commercial confidentiality:

'Well, I can't promise you that there will not be changes in the telesales department as a result of this report. But the department certainly seems overwhelmed with work and my main concern is to make it possible for you to handle that even more efficiently than you do at present.'

She now begins the questioning with a **preliminary** set of questions. These were probably drawn up as a result of initial research. In general they will be aimed at producing hard facts or confirming data that the analyst already has. Full questionnaires, structured questions and closed questions are the usual approach at this point. In some situations this may be the full extent of the interview.

Usually, though, enough questions are raised for the interviewer to proceed to the **probing** stage of the interview. We are concerned now with information more than with mere data. We want to know: how, when, where, what, who and why. At this point the system under investigation should be opened up to us, not merely described:

'You say that when an order is confirmed you enter the details on the screen and also a shorter form of the details on a notepad for later collection. Can you tell me why you have to do that?'

There are a range of factors which may lay behind our probing questions. We may wish to probe for:

- undisclosed meanings
- undisclosed information
- clarification of statements
- confirmation of understanding
- agreement to observations

An interviewer would do this by using **reflecting** or **linking** questions. A reflecting question echoes back a key word or phrase to the interviewee, as in *'Inefficient? Can you tell me in what way?'* As well as demonstrating active listening this encourages the interviewee to go on to make unprompted and open comments. Linking questions are not quite as immediate. They usually come at the end of a section of speech when we are moving off in a slightly different direction:

'When you were talking about the backup details on the notepad you said that it is more efficient on some days than on others. Could you elaborate on that?

Another technique of reflecting is the **unfinished statement**, where the interviewee is invited to volunteer the completion: *'Then the system of extra paper recording is...'* may be used to finally confirm the viewpoint that we have suspected that the interviewee has held all along, be it *'a waste of time'* or *'the only way we have of making this* *useless computer system work.'* Beware of giving too much information in your contribution, though. You may be trapping the interviewee into saying something just to be polite and to please you.

Nor should you feel that talking or asking questions are the only activities in an interview. **Silence** gives a chance for thought and reflection on both sides. Interviewees need time to gather their thoughts together and to put them in an acceptable form. Do not be too quick to rush in with a clarification of your question or to assume that the other person has nothing to say on the matter.

Silence and significant pauses can also put pressure on the interviewee to reply. The rules of the game are known. If the interviewer is not speaking it is the turn of the interviewee to make a contribution, the obligation is there to do so. This *'pressure of silence'* is particularly useful with unforthcoming interviewees or at difficult periods in the interview, perhaps when reaching for deeper levels of disclosure.

After a period of probing for information the interview may pass to a deeper and more personal level, seeking opinions and views from the interviewee. Some of these may already have been gained as part of the previous activity but others may need to be followed up. This is a particularly difficult stage since it usually involves personalities rather than procedures or technology. On the one hand, investigation in this area may help to explain why an otherwise commendable system does not appear to be working. On the other, personal factors may be beyond the scope of your investigation or your ability to influence the situation.

6.6.3 Bad interviews

Most interviewees are ready to help you. They see your intervention as one that will ease their problems and make life easier for them. In hard times employees realise that making the company more efficient keeps up profits (or at least reduces losses) and allows it to continue employing its staff. There will be times, however, when your presence will be resented and co-operation will be at best half hearted.

Some of these may be cases where members of staff are working out their notice or where they feel that your intervention will lead to staff reductions. As mentioned earlier these fears may be well founded. People fear change; the analyst is an agent of that change.

With luck, you will have been warned of problems in advance and perhaps you have taken the precaution of asking beforehand whether you can expect any particular difficulties. If not, you need to spot resistance early on in the interview and to take steps to deal with it.

Effective interviewers preface the formal part of the interview with a firm handshake and a smile, followed by a short period of introductory social chat. This is not only polite, it helps to break the ice and establish an early rapport with the interviewee. A handshake may be formal but it also establishes contact by breaking the taboo against touching; a smile breaks down barriers and further reduces the level of formality. Preliminary conversation allows you to judge the other person's mood or attitude towards you. Monosyllabic answers, a refusal to volunteer anything of their own or a tense and set look to the facial muscles all indicate that you are about to encounter resistance.

Your preliminary comments about the purpose of the interview and the uses to which it will be put should help to defuse a certain amount of antagonism, especially if you allow space for the interviewee to question you about them. This helps to establish an open relationship. Beware at this stage of making promises that you cannot keep or reassurances based on insufficient data. How the company implements your recommendations will rarely be under your direct control and you should make this clear.

Reluctant interviewees will use a range of tactics, either consciously or sub-consciously, to subvert your interview. These are related to those behaviours that we have examined in the section on meetings and include:

Blocking. A simple device which takes the form of facetious or mocking answers and comments on the professional competence of others. Such behaviour may be frustrating for the interviewer but usually has its roots in real events. If the comment is that '*the system is as much use as a chocolate teapot*' do not let things rest there. '*How has that shown itself? Have you got any recent concrete examples?*' Work on the interviewee's professionalism and feeling of self-worth: '*That must be very frustrating for you. How exactly does it prevent you doing your job? How would you do things yourself?*'

Interrupting. As we noted earlier, someone who is interrupting is not listening properly to the whole of the message. It is an indication that the message or the messenger, or both, is not valued. Allow the interrupter to finish, listening carefully to what is said (after all, your question, or another interesting one, might be answered by accident). If your question has not been answered, re-phrase it and ask it again. Using a reflexive technique helps here: '*you said earlier that...*' puts the onus back on to the interviewee, who will find it difficult to interrupt himself!

Attacking. If you touch on a raw nerve your interviewee may become verbally aggressive, evidenced by an increase in the amount of emotional language, an increase of volume in the speech or by a changed tone of voice. A fight of whatever sort is not a productive interview and you need to take steps to defuse the situation. Remember that it takes two to fight; unless you respond in kind it cannot continue.

When confronted with aggression animals either fight, fly or exhibit some appeasing physical activity. Monkeys, for example, present their hinder parts to the aggressor as a sign of submission, dogs roll over on to their sides. Since in the interview situation neither fight nor flight are appropriate, some sort of softening behaviour is called for. This takes the form of **openness**, revealing feelings and information to the other person. It might take the form of admitting to being the author of the program which is being so heavily criticised and expressing willingness to learn from mistakes, or giving extra background information about oneself, the parent company or the particular project in hand.

Disagreement. In some ways disagreements are one of the things you are searching for. An employee who thinks that things are not being done well can be a valuable resource in your analysis, more so than the one who merely accepts the status quo.

What we are looking for is not just disagreement for its own sake ('*this lot always gets everything wrong, they'll never change*') but reasoned disagreement. Where disagreement takes place it should be listened to and noted but not confronted. Confrontation has a way of becoming self-perpetuating and can take over your interview. Besides, the interviewer's job is to gather information, not to make judgements.

6.6.4 Triangulation

A scientist conducting an experiment will not be satisfied by just one set of results. The experiment will be repeated, perhaps several times, in order to ascertain that it works consistently. Variables will be investigated in order to demonstrate their relative influence on the final result.

Users and makers of maps carry out an analogous process. They fix positions by taking a series of known reference points and taking a bearing on each one. Where the bearing lines intersect indicates our present position. This process is known as triangulation.

Given the vagaries of human response it is imperative that we, like the map maker and the scientist, cross-check our information. In some cases our standard procedure helps us to do this. An initial overview of documents and procedures produces a series of check questions with which we begin our interview. If a range of interviewees at different levels of the organisation all give us the same confirmatory information then our triangulation is complete.

Feelings and opinions, however, are more difficult to triangulate. These only become apparent in the course of interviewing and are usually of a delicate nature. Nevertheless, if they affect the operation of the system we have to follow them up in the most politic manner possible:

> '*It has been suggested to me that some supervisors are less efficient than others in collecting and collating the written confirmation slips. Have you ever had problems with this?*'

Note that no names have been mentioned, partly to avoid embarrassing the interviewee but also because you do not need to know. Any system which depends on a variable form of voluntary action by a participant has a loss of efficiency and should be revised.

Where no triangulation is forthcoming you have the choice of:

- re-interviewing in order to probe the reply further
- discarding the information as a 'rogue response'
- recording the information with a warning to the reader.

Naturally the first option is the best but it may not always be practicable for reasons of time or access to the interviewee. Discarding any information is always a questionable practise, leaving the analyst open to charges of lack of thoroughness in gathering it in the first place or of censorship in not making use of it. The final solution may be to mention the dissenting voice in such a manner as to avoid appearing either to doubt the interviewee or to cast suspicion in other quarters:

'One respondent suggested that lack of efficiency among supervisors in collecting the paper reply slips was causing difficulty. Despite further questioning this was not confirmed by any other respondent.'

6.6.5 Participant observation

When it comes to finding out about a system nothing beats having to operate it yourself. As already noted, design methodologies such as SSADM suggest that users should be an integral part of the analysis and design team. Where this is not possible it is open to the analyst to move backwards and become a user, if only for a limited amount of time.

Naturally this would probably not be for any extended period. The opportunity might arise when interviewing an operative, when the analyst could ask to carry out the operation a couple of times in order to 'get the feel of it'. If time allows, more extended periods could be spent under supervision carrying out each task. The analyst is then in some position of strength when asking questions or making observations as well as being able to establish better rapport with the interviewees.

Besides being an aid to information gathering, participant observation is also useful in empathising with actors in the system. It is all very well being told that it is frustrating having to wait for the next screen whilst an irate client is on the telephone, quite another to experience it oneself. The proponent of 'lateral thinking', Edward de Bono, once proposed a way of clearing up industrial pollution by forcing companies to take in materials such as air and water from the areas that they had themselves polluted. Getting programmers to operate for a few days on the shop floor with the systems they had designed themselves might lead to less polluted systems.

6.6.6 Using graphical representations

Most design methodologies emphasise the use of graphical representations in order to make sense of the existing system. Whether this is the use of rich pictures, as in the soft systems approach, or the logical data structures of hard systems methodologies, the analyst is still called upon to generate visual representations in order *'to verify that the analyst's perception of the system is sound'* (NCC).

The diagram in Fig. 6.3 was prepared by a colleague who was investigating the problems of a public service corporation. In its format it lies somewhere between a soft systems methodology and one of Buzan's spidergrams. In practice, it was presented to the clients in A3 format and each linkage carefully explained. Once each individual response function had been covered the analyst was able to bring the system as a whole under scrutiny and to draw conclusions from it for the corporation.

Within other systems methodologies, such as SSADM, the analyst would draw up diagrammatic representations of the system and check them through with the user. This has the dual function of verifying that the analyst's understanding is complete and correct and of drawing the user into the process. At first this can be a slow business but becomes quicker as the client begins to understand the conventions used. Do not rush your client but allow the diagrams to sink in. This will save time if you need to return for further interviews or clarification.

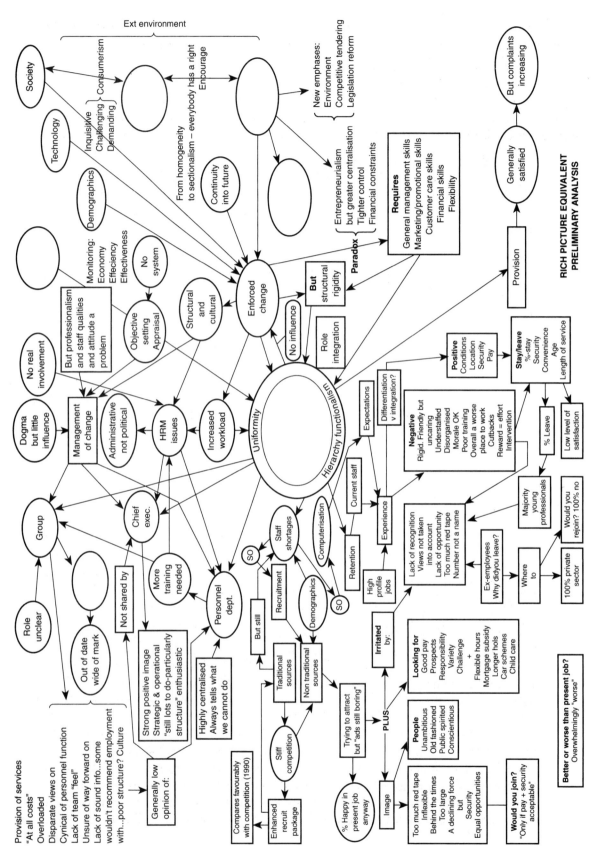

Fig. 6.3 Rich picture equivalent

6.7   MANAGEMENT INTERVIEWS

So far we have looked at interviews which are specific to information systems. All employees and managers will at some time be involved in management interviews, the appointment, sustainment and possible severance of staff. In management interviews our data may not be so much hard facts as observations, opinions, perspectives and character judgements. Our aim is to maintain the efficiency of the overall system through the human actors within it.

6.7.1   Employment interviews

Most of the procedures that have been advocated in this chapter apply equally well to employment interviews. We will deal with these briefly from the point of view of the interviewer, with a few asides meant to aid the potential interviewee. After all, the manager who is recruiting today could be the job applicant tomorrow!

Like any interview the first job is to draw up a set of aims and objectives. The aims may have been set out already in discussions leading to the preparation of the original job advertisement. On the other hand some eighty per cent of jobs are never formally advertised, so that you may need to sit down and write your aims from scratch. Naturally the aims follow from your business objectives and fulfil long-term rather than short-term needs. Why are you employing a DOS-based programmer when your company is moving to a UNIX system next year?

With your aims firmly fixed you can move to specific objectives. These should be prioritised in some way. Either you could put them in descending order, say of 1 to 10, or group them in three sections: essential, desirable, possible. This provides a preliminary matrix for your use, where any candidate who cannot fulfil all the requirements in the 'essential' section is immediately eliminated.

Be careful not to include only technical considerations in your objectives. The new employee will no doubt be required to work with other colleagues, with users and possibly with the general public. Anyone who proves impossible to work with or who alienates your clientele is a liability rather than an asset.

In many cases your 'essential' category will have been signalled by the job advertisement. Your initial research will take the form of comparing applications to the requirements that have been set out. Many firms, however, use the advertisement as a form of 'wish list'. If you look at these in the computing press you will see requirements for several years of experience, top level skills in at least two programming languages, acquaintance with a whole range of applications and a readiness to accept the lowest possible salary. Such companies are wasting everybody's time by not suggesting to readers what is absolutely essential. They are also putting off potential high quality applicants who lack one or two of the myriad qualities asked for.

In the same way that the selector makes an initial choice by comparing company needs to candidate applications, the candidates need to look closely at company requirements before filling in the application form. A standard letter of application is of little use at this point beyond providing a platform from which to build. Each application must be tailor-made to the company, attempting to meet all their wants and requirements in the same way that you would build any system for a user.

Applicants who do not meet all the essential requirements are rejected at an early stage. If this leaves too few candidates to form a short list the post must be re-advertised. With too many candidates the list can be reduced by moving on to those who fulfil the 'desirable' objectives. Although subjectivity can never be entirely removed, concentration on objectives at this stage ensures that all short-listed candidates will be worthy of selection.

The interview itself can progress according to our standard procedure. Candidates will be set at ease with polite introductions, an introduction to the interview agenda and general social enquiries about their journey and so on. Introductory questions will be tied to the application form, checking that the information given is correct and allowing the candidate to 'warm up'. Once this is over the interview moves in to the probing stage, finding out exactly how much experience the candidate has had and how deeply knowledge of certain areas extends. As in any interview it is the business of the interviewer to encourage the interviewee to talk, using all those techniques of unfinished sentences, requests for clarification and pressure of silence mentioned above.

For the candidate this is the most trying time. There is an agenda, the interviewer's list of priorities, of which the candidate is not aware. All that interviewees can do is to stay alert, answer questions as straightforwardly as possible and show themselves in the best light. In this respect positive answers are preferable to negative ones. For example, a candidate might be asked about knowledge of PASCAL: *'No, I've never used PASCAL, but I have had a lot of experience with both COBOL and C++. I'm sure that I can learn to use PASCAL quite quickly if I have to.'*

Interviewers are impressed by candidates who are alert, show interest and are loyal to their previous employers. No-one likes to employ staff who are likely to do the bare minimum, slouch around the office looking bored and who 'bad mouth' the company to outsiders. Showing interest can be done by researching the company and its operations in advance, either through company directories, the trade press or by personal contact. At some point the interviewer is bound to ask *'Why do you want this job'* or *'Why do you want to join this company'*. A reply along the lines of *'I was so impressed with the accounts I read of the system that you installed for Woodshire Health Authority'* is far more impressive than the standard *'Because you seem such an interesting company'*.

Student candidates are often at a disadvantage because of their lack of experience. Interviewers also have difficulty with such candidates because they have so little employment experience upon which to hang probing questions. To counter this, it is always worthwhile to take major projects or dissertations to interviews, where they can provide props and centres of discussion for both sides.

Non-verbal communication plays a vital role in job interviews. Researchers have claimed that the majority of these interviews are decided within the first two minutes, that is before the social niceties and setting of agenda have been properly concluded. If this is true then the interviewers are not doing their job properly, failing to screen out personal prejudice, stereotyping and managed impressions delivered by the interviewee. Again, a check list of criteria is invaluable in asserting objectivity.

For the interviewee it is important to manage those first two minutes by dressing appropriately and giving off an air of polite confidence. Adopt an alert posture in your chair and avoid being flippant in your answers. Like the interviewer you should also be listening carefully and show this by using reflective replies: '*As you mentioned earlier, this is quite a small company, but from my point of view that has the advantage of allowing me to show what I can do.*' Engaging openly and honestly with the interviewer makes the interview easier for both parties and acts as a point in your favour.

Once the interview is over the interviewer can study the set of objectives compared to the candidates' performance. No-one would ever suggest that the decision should be made in a mechanical way from the objectives matrix. On the other hand, these were the criteria that you drew up in an objective fashion based on the company's business objectives; you must have very sound reasons, not just a hunch or an unreasoning prejudice, for dropping them now. If in doubt, you can recall candidates for extra questions or defer making a decision until you have checked back with referees or previous employees.

If you still cannot decide, the answer may be a cost-benefit analysis. How long is the candidate likely to stay, will you get good service? How adaptable is the candidate to new ideas or places? How much will the candidate cost? Will extra training be required? What are the benefits that your company will gain from this candidate?

Similarly for applicants, the objective in an interview is to pre-empt this phase of the interviewer's decision making. Like any salesperson you are selling the features and benefits of the goods, in this case yourself. Your features (a first-class honours degree, ability to program in COBOL, experience with UNIX systems, solid employment record, ability to communicate to a high level) should all have been ascertained by the interviewer. If they weren't, then you make sure that you mention them yourself.

Your benefits (code always fully documented so that it can be easily and cheaply updated, good interviewing technique so that customer's needs are ascertained quickly and efficiently, recently moved back into the area as a pleasant place to bring up young children so expect to stay with the company some while) need also to be brought to the interviewer's attention. Just as the interviewer has a set of objectives it does no harm for you to have a written set of points that you want to make sure you make during the interview.

A minority of interviewers still persist in introducing extra stress to an already stressful situation, by the use of aggressive interview techniques, interruptions and so on. There is considerable research to show that these methods are in fact ineffective in choosing appropriate candidates except when they mirror exactly the situations that candidates will encounter in the work situation. If you do find yourself in such an interview all you can do is to try to stay cool and recognise that it is a deliberate strategy. Although difficult, you still need to remind the interviewer of your features and benefits, without which the company would be considerably poorer.

6.7.2 Assessment and development interviews

A structured review of performance has been standard in large organisations for many years. Though varying in detail they have broad similarities in approach. Usually the appraisee fills in a self-analysis questionnaire which also allows a certain amount of individual comment. The immediate supervisor or line manager also fills out a questionnaire on the employee's performance. These two documents form the basis of the discussion between appraiser and appraisee.

Some companies still see these interviews as the territory of the Personnel Department (or the Human Resources Division as some are now known). Others claim that, because assessment is heavily biased towards job performance, it needs a manager experienced in that particular area. In smaller companies with no HRD there may be no choice.

While HRD professionals may be limited in their approach through lack of expertise the IS professional needs to beware of being too directly instrumentalist in approach. Human resources are very valuable in the information industries and have to be husbanded and developed like any other. At the assessment and development level the interviewer needs to probe beneath the surface of job competence to the level of feelings, thoughts and aspirations below.

The gathering of such information allows the manager to take prompt and remedial action in times of difficulty and to maintain confidence in better times. The junior programmer may be happy with the job at present but does not want to stay a junior programmer for too long. The manager's job is to establish this feeling and to find out in which direction the employee sees career development moving. If the employee can be helped and supported the company has a satisfied and committed worker for many years to come.

Where performance is not up to standard an assessment interview is important in finding the underlying causes. Assuming that your staff were recruited with integrity, lack of performance cannot be due to lack of competence, especially if there has been a notable falling off over some time. Wherever possible, probe for underlying reasons for such a change. Although you may feel that personal difficulties are none of the company's business you still need to know why your employee is under-performing and how that can be changed or managed. Helping someone through the trauma of a messy divorce may be more cost-effective than employing an unknown replacement. Finding out that the employee has grown to detest programming may lead to a quick and amicable agreement to part company. If you have not got sufficient information you cannot make a properly informed decision.

When carrying out an assessment or development process you should:

- Identify performance by observation and reports
- Seek a contribution from the employee
- Identify any problems which may exist
- Propose a range of solutions
- Discuss them with the employee and, where possible, agree a solution
- Take decisive action.

6.8 CONCLUSION

Good practice in information systems has moved to the stage where professionals are expected to spend eighty per cent of their time information gathering and planning and only twenty per cent of their time on installation and coding. The result is said to be a huge reduction in the time spent in 'debugging', faster installation of workable systems and fewer faults and call-outs. All of these reduce overheads and consequently increase profits.

Since interviews are a central methodology in all major systems analysis methodologies it is essential that you develop your skills in this area. Without them you cannot be said to be a fully developed IS professional. With them, you are poised to take advantage of the spread of information technology across the whole spectrum of users and prepared to take on new responsibilities in the field of management.

Like most skills, interviewing is best improved by practice and reflection on your performance. Trying to dodge something you find uncongenial may be effective in the short term but does nothing to increase your long-term performance. However good or bad you are at interviewing, work at your technique on a regular basis, perhaps with colleagues, and you will see a steady improvement which will set you on the way to being a more rounded professional.

CHAPTER 7
User documentation

Try a simple exercise. Walk into any large bookshop and locate the 'computing' section. Then count the number of books on sale that are guides to *specific* hardware or software, books with titles such as '*An Idiot's Guide to Excel*'. Depending on the amount of stock the bookshop holds, you could find anything up to fifty or more titles. All of the machines and the software that these books refer to come complete with their own free manual, yet owners are prepared to go out and spend extra money on another manual.

Some colleges go even further and employ people to write manuals especially for their students, who rarely get to see the manufacturer's version. There is no reason to suppose that students are less intelligent or less acquainted with information systems than the public at large, yet still commercial manuals are not thought to be appropriate to them. Why is this?

7.1   DEFINING THE PROBLEM

One explanation that is frequently given is that most computer hardware now originates in the far east. Manuals have been written in Korean or Japanese and then translated into English, or an approximation of English. On the other hand, few people complain about maintenance manuals for Japanese cars and manuals originating from English-speaking countries seem just as bad as their Pacific competition.

Another explanation is that the wrong people write the manuals. In the days of the domination of massive mainframe computers, documentation was written by engineers and programmers for other engineers and programmers. They knew one another's level of expertise, spoke the same specialist language and, given the limited number of manufacturers in the market, probably had a good working knowledge of each others machine.

With the advent of the PC the market fractured. Manufacturers proliferated as did software. More importantly, so did users. Government statistics suggest that over half of the homes in Britain have a PC of some sort. Small shops, single person businesses, doctors, designers and delicatessens all use computers. These people are being given manuals written by software engineers who have no conception of what it is like to come to the subject 'cold', with no background knowledge at all. Software engineers are still writing for software engineers.

A third explanation blames the problem on the companies selling the products, especially those at the bottom of the market. Money is spent on developing a product which may have a limited shelf life. To spend extra money employing technical writers to write extensive user manuals is to cut into both time and profit margins. Better to get the whole thing done quickly in-house and get the product on the shelves. Yet why is it that even expensive products from reputable companies still need commercial manuals to explain their manuals?

Each of these three arguments contains a grain of truth but none of them is sufficient to explain the problem entirely. Enough market research has been done over the last ten years to convince companies that an effective and comprehensive manual is an important selling point for hardware in particular. It is certainly not want of will that has been the problem, there must be something in the general approach that is causing difficulties.

Systems analysis gives us a clue to what this might be. Within systems analysis we first assess the business needs of the operation before investigating either its efficiency or its technological needs. If we do not know what the organisation's objectives are, how do we know whether it is fulfilling them or whether they could be fulfilled more effectively? Similarly with a piece of hardware or software. What does the individual user want to *do* with it, what are the objectives of its use? Or in soft systems terms, what is the transformation that is to take place?

The other question that systems analysis leads us to ask is: who are the **actors** in the system? These are the people who are actually going to use it to bring about those business objectives, the end users. Without their competence and co-operation the system does not work. Thus a system is only as good as its users make it, whatever its other qualities in terms of program design and coding.

The analogy of the motor car is very apt in this context and we will use it frequently throughout this chapter. Some car owners enjoy what is under the bonnet, they love tinkering with the machinery and talking about technical details. A larger number merely undertake routine maintenance and take their car to a specialist garage for any more pressing problems. They may not know or care how the engine operates or how the electrical wiring is laid out. What they want to do is to drive from A to B in reasonable comfort and safety in the expectation that their car will start every time and not break down at unforeseen moments. The owner's manual tells them how the lights, windows and other functions operate. When they buy a new car they expect to be able to operate it with the minimum of fuss. The car is a tool to be used.

Business computer users have many of the same attitudes. A minority are interested in what goes on inside the machine and are quite prepared to talk about it with anybody that will listen. Most business users could not care less. They want to produce form letters, set up accounts or forecast profits as quickly and as easily as possible without any roadblocks in the system or losses of data. The computer is a tool to be used.

You may object that this example refers only to naive users, not to those within the information systems area. However, it applies even here. We are now quite used to the demand that documentation be produced as we go along, that systems work uses a standard methodology or that programmers use standard design methodologies. These exist so that the procedures can be checked before implementation and so that the system or program can be maintained by other members of the team. Documenting in this way makes the assumption that the writer will not be the user of the system, it builds in the potential user from the design stage.

If we do this for those who are going to **maintain** the system, should we not do it for those who are going to **use** the system? A motor car is designed with the comfort and convenience of the driver in mind, the same should be true of IS products.

We therefore need to build the user in from the beginning, to allow for user documentation from the first stage of the investigation process, through the programming to the final implementation. With a major project carried out by a large team it may be possible to include a technical author from the beginning. In smaller projects the analysts and programmers will be their own writers and develop their skills in this area. It cannot be emphasised too strongly that a program may only be as good as its user documentation. If the user cannot operate the program or bring out its full potential then the programmer has failed.

User documentation is an integral part of information systems operations. It is not an added extra to be bolted on at the end, it is to be considered from the very beginning of the project. Time spent on enhancing the quality of documentation is rarely wasted. From a company's point of view it can reduce the amount of money spent on training and education, operating as a form of Open University text. A good manual will contain useful and pertinent information which will help the user perform the job function self-sufficiently and remedy the initial performance problem caused by lack of information,

7.2 THE USERS

As in all forms of communication we need to start from a consideration of our target audience, since this will inform the style and the tone of our writing. We need to consider:

- the level of IT sophistication
- the employment experience
- the level of education or training
- the attitude to the message
- the attitudes of the business sub-culture
- subject specialisation.

If our audience is a reasonably homogenous one then our task is much easier. Writing the manual for an accounts package aimed at qualified accountants means that we can make informed assumptions about their employment and subject specialisation, their level of training and the attitudes of accountants to electronic systems. A determined writer would track down a sample range of accountants and talk to them about their work and attitudes as well as the package that is being developed. (One would hope that the development team have already undertaken a certain amount of research among potential users which could be further utilised.)

More difficult is writing the manual for an accounting system to be used by the general public. Here our audience can be literally anybody, from a family that wishes to keep an eye on the monthly budget to a whole range of small businesses and voluntary organisations. How can we target such an impossibly wide range of people?

The solution is to produce a multi-layered manual which is aimed at all levels of product usage, based on the user's level of IT sophistication. To make matters simpler, users can be arranged in five categories:

1. The Beginner
2. The Novice
3. The Learner
4. The Expert
5. The Accidental User

7.2.1 The beginner

The beginner does not have a clue. This is probably a user who has just unpacked the newly-delivered computer from the box and is staring at it in bewilderment wondering how it all fits together. Beginners are the sort of people who need to be told what software is and that it has to be loaded into the computer before anything else can be done. They are frustrating and disorientating to work with.

We were all beginners once. The problem is that we have forgotten that we once knew nothing and have only a hazy memory of how we progressed to our present state. Writers of user documentation are in the same relationship to the beginner as is the proud parent taking out son or daughter for that first driving lesson. The parent finds it hard to believe that the pupil does not know about putting the key in the ignition, operating the clutch or where the signals are; they have become second nature to the experienced driver. Experienced computer users find it difficult to unlearn what they know and put themselves in the shoes of the absolute beginner, they have a problem with empathising with the client.

Like the learner driver the computer beginner does not see the system. Each part, each operation, is a discrete entity unconnected to any other. Excitement of discovery may be interlaced with blind panic and fear of making a mistake. Any trainer will tell you stories of beginners afraid to touch the keyboard '*in case I break something*'. Such users have no understanding of the system and may not even pause to think about the existence of a system at all. Their horizons are limited to the next key press; they spend more time consciously considering how to use the system than in thinking about what data they want to enter or what operations they want it to perform.

Some users stay in this state for a matter of minutes, others may remain in it for months. When Eastern Counties Newspapers was computerised in the mid 1980s one sub-editor almost lost his job because he could not get to grips with the new on-line system. Only several intense tutorial sessions with colleagues saved him from a humiliating exit.

What beginners need are very simple instructions on the lines of '*how to get started with...*', which shows them how to set things up and how to take the first steps. It is important that these steps are crowned with success and that by the end they can perform simple operations.

7.2.2   The novice

Once some understanding has been achieved the beginner passes to the novice stage. The novice has achieved some level of understanding and realises that there is a system underpinning what is going on. More importantly the novice can undertake simple tasks and begins to look towards a widening of skills and competence. The novice, though, is still heavily dependant on support systems such as instructors, manuals or on-line help systems, perhaps still keeping the book open while performing even the simplest operations.

More sophisticated users slip almost immediately straight into the novice phase when confronted with a new piece of software and progress quickly on to the next stage. Novice users tend to be more task-oriented than beginners. They have got over any fear of the system and are beginning to query what it can do for them. Consequently they may set out to perform specific tasks rather than working through the manual in a sequential order.

7.2.3   The learner

Learners have reached the stage of understanding the context of the system. They now see commands as being linked and as forming part of a coherent whole. We might liken this to the learner driver who can deal with clutch and accelerator smoothly, whilst looking in the rear view mirror before signalling and moving off.

At the stage the user is becoming independent, trying to build up a knowledge of the whole system, or at least the functions that are directly useful. Common operations are performed from memory and without much conscious effort. Some less common ones may be performed with quick reference to the manual or to a help screen whilst others may never be used or investigated at all. Many users remain at this stage, which might be likened to the experienced driver who has little interest in further exploring the workings or potential of the car itself.

7.2.4   The expert

Not all users progress to the expert category. Those who are driven by a need for knowledge for its own sake may investigate an application fully. For others, as long as the needs of the moment are being fulfilled that is quite sufficient.

An expert uses the full system to its complete potential. The system itself is seen as the abstract concepts and ideas which lie behind the material operation on the computer. When it comes to use, the expert's handling is virtually automatic, although even here there may be functions which are very rarely used and the expert will need to refer back to the manual. They may well be the people that other users refer to rather then consulting paper sources.

7.2.5   The accidental user

Accidental users do not use the application very often. Inland Revenue regulations for companies with a turnover of less than £10,000 exempts the company from using a qualified accountant for their annual accounts, so that the owners only need to put simple accounts onto a spreadsheet once each year. This might be the only time that the spreadsheet is used, so the details have to be looked up each time. Accidental users quite naturally are often not prepared to invest time or effort in little used applications. Only when they become convinced that their usage will be regular rather than accidental do they step onto the ladder that leads from novice to expert.

Any of the other groups can easily become accidental users, perhaps by change in occupational role or by completing one task and moving on to another which does not need the previous skills. Operating a computer application is not like riding a bicycle, we do forget, or at least regress in our level of knowledge.

7.2.6 Fitting documentation to users

Each of the five kinds of user has different needs from the documentation and uses it in different ways. At the same time, the beginner who bought the system last year may be the expert user this year. Our single manual must take account of the levels of user and the fact that a single user may progress through all levels. The users are not static, manuals should not be static either.

Let us take as an example Henry Jones, a beginner who has just bought a PC with associated software for his small art materials shop and gallery. Friends have been telling Henry for years that he can make his business more efficient by using a computer. Sales from a successful exhibition have left him with some spare cash. An advert for a PC with bundled software caught his eye and he decided to take the plunge. Now he is the proud owner of a 486 machine, a collection of software discs and a whole lot of paperwork. Henry is at a loss. Where should he start?

Henry has two problems. He needs to get the PC up and running and he needs to make it productive in terms of his business as soon as possible. Fortunately, the writers of the manuals have considered the problems of people like Henry at the outset.

Rather than being an immense tome the manual for this system is a series of booklets, each one carefully headed and numbered. Henry is immediately reassured; this means that he does not have to read five hundred pages of computer speak before he can begin. He starts with '*How to use this manual*', which explains about different levels of users and instructs him, as a novice, how to relate the documentation to his own situation. The first step is to begin with '*Setting up your computer*' which tells him how to link all the hardware together, how to load the software, how to make backup discs from the masters and where to store them 'just in case'. The process finished, Henry puts that booklet away, perhaps never to refer to it again. However, it has served its purpose, his first encounter with the machine has been a successful one.

Henry now has a choice. There are a whole series of booklets, each one associated with one piece of software, with the title of '*How to get started with...*'. These give step-by-step instructions of how to open the application, what it looks like and what it can do. By the end of an hour Henry can type a letter (the layout is rather poor, but never mind for now), set out a simple spreadsheet, or begin using the database (as long as he wants to follow the model in the booklet). This has taken him through to the end of the beginner stage and the PC has begun to earn its keep.

Over the next few days Henry builds in confidence. He no longer has to refer to '*How to get started with...*' for every operation that he performs. Moreover, he is beginning to experiment. The layout of his letters needs to be improved. He wants to put the names of his customers on the database and then generate labels for the invitations to the next exhibition's private view. Although he has tried out the pull-down menus he finds them rather terse in their descriptions and is afraid of doing something wrong.

Naturally he turns to the documentation, especially to the booklets labelled '*All about....*'. By now he is rather impatient, he wants to get things working, without having to read through unnecessary text or wading through procedures that he is not intending to use. He has little interest in understanding the system, or at least not yet. What he wants to do is to move straight onto the production stage. Henry has become a typical novice user.

Fortunately the manuals labelled '*All about....*' have been written with novice and learner users in mind. The writers have carefully organised their information according to a series of criteria:

- Chronological order
- Order of importance
- Frequency of need
- Order of difficulty.

Chronological order takes account of the way that a normal user would step through the system: a document would be opened, for example data would be entered, data would be corrected, the document would be printed. Obviously the detail and the order would change with each application. Organising the information in this way helps the new user to become familiar with the application whilst simultaneously doing something productive.

Order of importance structures the information within each section. Broad applications are described first and strongly signposted, whilst lesser detail would have less prominence and come later in the text. Possibly the numbering system or use of typographical features such as emphasis or font size would reinforce this division.

Frequency of need places operations that are done most often at the beginning of the manual or the beginning of a section. This is not the normal method of writing manuals. For example, setting out a document layout for a word processing application usually appears before the section on printing a document, despite the fact that printing is done nearly every time the application is opened whilst new document layouts are created quite infrequently. The novice or learner user would need to refer to printing information much more often, at least in the early stages.

Order of difficulty places easy operations first and more difficult ones later. Our users need to do simple things first, to walk before they can run, and not be put off by coming across what are, to them, incomprehensible instructions. Henry's manuals have a separate section for '*advanced uses of....*' towards the end of each.

You will, of course, already have noticed that some of these criteria may be mutually incompatible. Some frequently used operations may be very difficult. Do you put them at the beginning or at the end? Printing is usually placed at the end because that is where it comes chronologically, do I really place it near the beginning on grounds of frequency? Naturally you have to use your own discretion on these matters, balancing up the weight of individual criteria in each particular instance, perhaps drawing up a matrix for each operation and weighting it against the four criteria used.

Now that Henry is moving into the learner stage he is less worried about the order of information within the manual. This is because he has ceased to read in a connected manner, relying instead on specific sections that he has located through the contents page and the index. He is using the menu system far more frequently now and may even be getting some information from the on-line help in the package. The manual is used to obtain specific information about specialised operations or ones that he has not used before. Perhaps this means reading as little as half a page each week. What frustrates him now is not the strange workings of the computer but his inability to find detailed information in his manual.

Henry is hooked on his machine and tries to find out everything about it that he can. The spreadsheet, database and word processing packages are used to their full capacity by this new expert user. When there is a procedure that he has not used for some time, perhaps related to his quarterly VAT returns, Henry might need to remind himself exactly how it is done. For this he uses the booklet entitled 'Quick reference', which has all the main procedures laid out in a truncated format specifically for the expert user. Much of this information also appears on-line. One of Henry's friends has the same information but on file cards instead of in a booklet. These list all the commands in the system with what they do, as well as a 'backwards' listing of all the tasks and the commands used to fulfil them.

Thanks to the range of manuals Henry is able to make full use of his computer at the various stages of his development. He also has an efficient resource which he can use when he takes on a new assistant to help him run his increasingly profitable business. Henry's informal tuition plus the manuals will quickly make the assistant familiar with the system.

Let us recap on the various sections that have been provided with this computer:

- *How to use the manual, giving guidance for users at various stages of knowledge*
- *How to set up your system and get everything working*
- *Getting started, a quick tutorial guide for immediate use*
- *Full operating details, that can be dipped into at any time and in any order*
- *Quick reference for expert users, to jog the memory.*

This manual is unusual in that it comes as a series of booklets. Most manuals are still unitary books of various sizes. Whatever format we choose we still need to cater for a range of users, or the same user at different stages of development. Although it would be ideal if the users read carefully through the manual and learnt everything there is to know about the system first, people do not operate in that way. They are impatient to get started, after all that is why they have their machine in the first place. Once started they will skip around the manual looking for the bits that will help them.

Users will be motivated to varying extents, but they will at least be curious and seeking to become competent as quickly and easily as possible. Some will be easily put off by their inability to perform simple tasks or to understand the instructions given to them. This means that the language used should be as simple as possible and all instructions in a logical order. Many users will have rushed ahead to do a task and failed. The manual needs to support their attempts at rectifying their mistakes, which themselves provide a valuable learning experience. Like a good teacher, a good manual should be unobtrusive, allowing the learners to believe that the amazing progress that they are making is down to their application and ability alone.

7.3 STRUCTURE

The first task of any manual writer is to understand the system thoroughly. In a larger system this entails involving a professional writer from the start. In smaller systems the author of system and manual will be the same person and in an ideal world will be equally well equipped for both tasks.

7.3.1 Analysis and planning

Whoever is to write the manual needs to carry out design tasks in advance, as a good programmer would before writing a program and for the same reasons. We are aiming to achieve a system which displays:

- consistency
- speed
- no duplication of data
- ease of use
- replicability
- ease of maintenance.

In the context of a manual **consistency** would refer to the layout of the whole product and of individual pages. The user would expect headings to indicate relative importance throughout. Similarly, actions by the user would be clearly and consistently marked, as would information that appears on screen. This might be indicated by all actions being printed in **BOLD** and upper case, while key presses are indicated by being contained in a box. The user will need to be able to distinguish at a glance what functions are designated as operator input and which are machine response.

Because the majority of users will be skimming the manual or only referring to specific parts we need them to do this as quickly as possible, to encourage **speed** of use. This involves the building in of reference aids such as a table of contents or an index. The index would be as extensive as possible, with linking structures within it. Some manuals use coded tabs for easier access to specific sections, aiding generalised scanning.

Data duplication can be avoided by referencing between sections and by ordering data in the manner set out in the previous section. If processes that are more important or more frequently used are set out as separate operations early in the manual they will precede subsequent operations which depend upon them. Users can be referred back to these sections if needed. Avoiding duplication of data keeps down the size of the manual, preventing it becoming too daunting to the user and minimising printing costs.

Like any tool, computer hardware and software should be as **easy to use** as possible. The manual is an extension of the product and the part that enhances its user friendliness. Brockmann defines the purpose of a manual as:

'to ease interaction between software and those who manage, audit, operate or maintain it'.

It must therefore itself be easy to use. This is facilitated by its general layout and use of graphics, the style in which it is written, the use of vocabulary and the avoidance of jargon and the use of analogies taken from outside the field of information systems. Ease of use would also refer to how well the manual could be used in practice, on a crowded desk, for example, or in a situation where many people might be using and abusing it.

Replicability suggests that we are likely to need more than one copy. The more copies that are generated the more pressing these considerations become. A small operations manual in three copies could be printed out directly on the office laser printer. Larger in-house manuals might be photocopied, with consequent loss of print quality. Commercial manuals demand a professional printer and hard decisions about binding and the use of colour. The cost of the manual is part of the cost of the whole project and needs to be built into the budget from the beginning.

Nowadays successful commercial projects can go through a whole series of updates. With in-house projects, bugs may be removed, improvements made, functions added. What are we going to do about the manual when these things happen? We make decisions about how and when we maintain the program, we also need to decide what we will do about **maintaining the manual** as well. The simplest answer might appear to be to throw it away and to start again. However, this is to ignore the amount of time and money that has already been invested in it. Good planning will have already considered the problem and perhaps decided on clear sections for the manual which can be replaced by regular printed updates. Choices about format and binding can facilitate simple replacement.

7.3.2 Determining the content

We have already seen that manuals need to be divided into different sections for different levels of user. For the sake of simplicity we can divide manual organisation into two areas: Tutorial and Reference.

Tutorials are aimed at getting the user started and able to do a reasonable range of tasks. These would be expected to cover the most frequently used functions and the main applications of the product. The writer needs to predict what the tasks are that the majority of users would be expected to perform and to write instructions and exercises which will see them through these tasks. Such a selective and task-oriented approach is ideally suited to what we might call 'closed' products, such as dedicated accounting software, where the range of possibilities may be limited. For more 'open' software it serves as a short-term introduction only.

The writer needs to begin by compiling a list of standard tasks that a new user might wish to perform and ordering them by frequency of use, etc. Each one then has to be described in detail, specifying:

- what the task is
- in what circumstances would it be carried out
- what actions begin the task
- what are the specific chronological steps involved in carrying it out
- what actions end, complete or sign off the task
- if there are any hardware or software variations that might change the actions.

General software, which is designed for a whole range of machines, is particularly susceptible to variation when used on different hardware.

For the longer term the user needs a **reference** manual. This would be encyclopaedic in the range of material that it covers as well as going into great detail. Where appropriate it might also be quite technical, allowing the user to understand the underlying concepts of the system. A reference manual would also avoid being too prescriptive about the uses to which the system could be put. By all means make suggestions but do not imply that these are the only possibilities. The user may have wants and needs that you have never considered which could be catered for by this system. 'Open ended' software such as spreadsheets and databases are only limited by the imagination of the user.

Some in-house documentation in particular might need to specify the specific technical functioning of the system, describing the micro-level of the system. This would be a case of the designer talking to other designers who are concerned with the maintenance of the system.

7.3.3   Speaking to the user

A recurring theme of this book is the importance of always considering your audience. In any form of written communication, where feedback is slow or absent, the needs of the audience are paramount.

As we noted earlier, computer documentation was originally written by programmers, for programmers. Since much of it was software-oriented as well, rather than being function-oriented, this was not a huge problem. Even today there is still space for peer-to-peer communication about technical matters, as we noted above. The introduction of programming standards and design methodologies have to a large extent made technical documentation easier to compile and to follow.

More often, the users of computer manuals will not be information systems professionals. Their language will not be that of computing but of the law, of graphic design or health care. They may want to get to grips with another tool to help them in their work or hobby, they do not want to have to learn another language in order to have to do it. For many of them the task involved in coping with computer jargon is as daunting as translating a manual from Japanese or Russian would be for you. Given that many users see the manual as an important factor in purchasing a product it should be as inviting as possible.

Previous chapters have already stressed the importance of using appropriate language for the audience you are addressing but it is worth going into further detail at this point.

As far as manuals are concerned, particularly in the tutorial section, jargon is to be carefully avoided. '*Boot up the computer*' or '*insert your boot disk*', for example, are totally opaque messages to the uninformed user, however much they may be part of your everyday language. The manual writer's difficulty is to remember back to those days of complete ignorance, before any acquaintance with information systems at all. This enables you to identify what is new to the user in terms of the concepts involved and the language needed to express them.

As far as possible the tutorial section does not introduce the user to any new concepts at this stage. All tasks are expressed in the terms of the application, of file storage or accountancy, for example. If you can achieve that, and it is not always possible, then there should be no need to use IS jargon at all, since all procedures will be capable of being expressed in non-specialist language. Your computer can be started rather than booted, files can be taken out rather than accessed, you can stop using your machine rather than logging off.

At the same time it is reassuring to the user to be shown on paper precisely what should be appearing on the screen. This enables direct comparisons to be made for both layout and information and opens out what can be quite dense text. What we are trying to do with the manual in this case is to replicate that most effective form of support, one-to-one tuition. The feeling should be of the author standing next to the user, calmly going through each operation as it appears on the screen. Except, of course, that the author's voice comes from the written page and that the screens are both on paper and on the VDU as well.

Screen shots both increase interest and provide emphasis for the text. They inspire confidence that all is well and that the instructions are concrete and accurate. Sometimes they may well replace or simplify explanations and discussions and serve to clarify technical points. Research suggests that purchasers are particularly attracted to manuals with an extensive use of screen shots, implying that this is how users feel that they learn to operate IS products best.

There is some disagreement about the appropriate tone to adopt in a manual. Some manuals employ a light conversational tone, bordering on the flippant. Others are more businesslike and straightforward, whilst a third set are almost military in their terseness and use of strict functional language. Given that each manual performs several functions there is room for each of these approaches, in the right context.

A **conversational tone** is best suited to the beginner's introduction. The user needs settling down, to be reassured that nothing untoward is about to happen and that nothing will be too difficult or will get out of control. Again, the user needs to feel that there is a knowledgeable friend in the room who will deal with all problems efficiently and kindly. No assumptions will be made about any previous knowledge of computing or of the specific application. There will be plenty of examples and analogies drawn from everyday life, such as comparing disk maintenance to clearing out a filing cabinet or moving text around a document to 'cut and paste' using scissors and glue. For example:

'The ruler line at the top counts the characters and tells you where the margins are. The other symbols tell you where your TAB stops are. The oblong is called the CURSOR. This marks the current typing position. All these features have a parallel in a standard typewriter. These parallels are...'

There is a tendency, however, to become too 'folksy' in this style and to descend to banal humour. Quite apart from the fact that humour does not translate very well, even from American English to British English, it does not last. A joke is funny once but tends to pall on reading the same passage for a third or fourth time. The same is true of a tone which is too offhand and flippant. Many people find this infuriating, contrasting the tone of the message unfavourably with the seriousness of the task in hand. The role model here is that of the approachable teacher rather than the snappy media presenter.

The **business tone** is most appropriate for the main reference section of the manual. *'Let us now get on with the job in hand,'* it says, implying that there are serious tasks to be done. It is a functional tone which allows us to set out processes in a logical manner whilst leaving opportunities for explanations and technical comments. Like a business report the use of words will be unadorned and functional, whilst still allowing for examples and analogies since new users will still need this kind of support. Depending on the perceived preference of the user personal pronouns (*we do this, you should do that*) may be eliminated, to be replaced with a more direct command format (*press F2 key; re-format the disk*). Some users may prefer one to the other. Where they cannot be surveyed efficiently the simple solution is to adhere to internal company standards. The following example comes from an internal company document produced to simplify a more lengthy and complex manual:

To **PRINT** a document:
  1)   View it before printing by:
       From the Menu choose **PRINT PREVIEW**
       Make any corrections needed
  2)   From the Menu choose **PRINT**
       Select the required options: Number of copies
                                   Print Range
                                   Draft or Document quality

A **military terseness** works best with the expert section of the manual, the reference cards or quick reference section. Given the complete absence of explanation or examples, operations are reduced to the minimum number of words possible, existing purely to jog the memory like the keywords we use when giving an oral presentation. Because of its lack of explanatory power this style is not suitable in situations where the user is learning something new or has not completely grasped the operation. A simple example of this style might look like this:

DIR [SIZE]   for file size
SHOW   disk space available

| **SHOW [DIR]** | free directory entries |
| **SHOW [DRIVE]** | drive characteristics |

Whatever the tone, or tones, adopted in the manual it is important that the language and the terms used are consistent. The 'Enter' command is always Enter, it never changes to 'Return' (or vice versa); 'Clear', 'Erase' and 'Delete' must always refer to three distinct operations rather than being interchangeable synonyms for the same one.

When writing your manual try as much as possible to:

- use the active voice
- use personal pronouns at the beginner and novice stage
- use short sentences
- eliminate subordinate clauses
- make your headings informative.

7.3.4 Improving reference

Whereas in a business report we can make the assumption that the reader has read it from the beginning we cannot do so in user manuals. Many users will simply have dipped into areas that are unfamiliar or have skimmed through sections in order to reach the part that they need. Therefore there will be people who have not come across the explanation for any abbreviations, acronyms or specialist terms that you have used, since they missed your original explanation when they first appeared in the text. It is therefore imperative that a glossary is appended to the manual for easy reference.

Good **glossaries** concentrate on the definition of terms and expressions and not on procedures, which are held in the main text. Any definition given must be explanatory in terms drawn from general usage, not as an internal definition. Internal definitions leave the reader none the wiser, as in the following example drawn from the on-line Help of a major spreadsheet package:

'Cannot resolve circular references.
There is a circular reference and the Iteration option is not selected in the Option menu's calculation dialog box. Circular references can only be resolved when iteration is selected.'

Quite apart from any other problem the user may have with this message, the basic concept 'circular message' is nowhere defined except in relation to itself. This is neither a good help message nor a good glossary entry. Although in a report the glossary traditionally comes towards the end, with a manual you might consider placing it at the beginning, where it will catch the user's eye and be signposted as having similar importance to the contents pages.

If glossaries help us to make sense of material once we have skimmed or randomly accessed a text, the **index** helps us in that random access process. A good index:

- is exhaustive
- is precise

- uses the words the user employs
- cross-references entries.

An ideal index would contain every procedure that any user would ever wish to perform. Instead of having to read through chapters or sections the user should be able to turn straight to the index and be directed to a precise page. The compiler of the index has to consider two sets of words. First, there are the terms that have actually been used in the manual. These may include the trade terms that you have incorporated because professional users will naturally use them and because you wish to introduce newer users to them, so that they can understand what trade professionals are saying. The other set of words are those that the beginner will use when starting with the application. Thus, as we noted earlier, the beginner will use words such as start, open and close, rather than boot, access and log off. Both language sets must be included in your index.

Good indexes also employ extensive sub-references and cross-references. Sub-references are specific references which appear under a topic heading. They help the reader to determine which specific page reference is needed, thus:

CHARACTERS	129
changing width	87, 89
deleting	15
double width	89
with accents	52

Cross-references help the reader with that tricky problem of knowing how to classify the problem in hand. How do we know that our label is the one that the index uses? A good index will make copious use of cross-referencing, signalled by the phrase 'see also'. Thus a random trawl through the help facility produces the following section:

DATA FILE INFORMATION:
    see also: Form letters
                   Mailing labels
                   Merged documents
                   Printing envelopes

If we were to look up 'printing envelopes' we would be similarly cross-referenced to 'data file information'. In this way the user should never be at a loss for the title of a topic or for alternative locations for information.

Nowadays, standard word processing packages include an indexing tool, which makes the work of compiling an index much easier. Like a spell checker, though, it is an aid rather than a complete solution. You will still need to check both from the text and from the index for complete accuracy. Start first from the index. Take as many entries as you can and check them back into the text. Where you have time and are compiling a commercial product this will mean checking all of the entries. If time is pressing, especially with an in-house or student product, a random sample will have to suffice.

Next, take a series of pages at random. Choose two or three items from each of them and check whether they appear in the index. Did they appear under the title you were expecting? If not, that title should be included in the index as well. Any items which cannot be found should be added to the index. If there are a large number of additions or amendments you will need to review your whole indexing strategy.

7.4 LAYOUT

From the point of view of typography and layout we can regard the manual as a special type of report. Some features, however, are specific to manuals and these will be dealt with at greater length.

7.4.1 The printed page

Since users will often have to juggle the manual on their lap or on a crowded desk the typeface has to be particularly clear.. This means using a good size font with a clear and unfussy type face. Clarity is also aided by allowing plenty of space, probably with exceptionally wide margins. The wide margins are valuable for the addition of notes and comments by the user as well as reducing the line length, thus improving readability, and making the product more manageable. Remember that it is easier to write notes on the outside of the page than near the spine and incorporate this in your design. In general the text should not be right justified, since the ragged edge breaks up the solidity of the text and makes it easier on the eye.

Colour is a valuable aid to users, as long as it is used properly. We have already seen that the greatest contrast on a page is between black and white. This means that colour is not an aid either to emphasis or to comprehension of the text. On the other hand it can be used effectively to aid search procedures. At the cheapest level different coloured card can be used as front sheets for the main sections, making the divisions easier to spot. The next step up is to use card with tabs, on which are printed the section titles. Over time these become worn and dog-eared, but for a cheap internal product with a short shelf life this may not be a consideration. Fully indented pages, like those of a telephone index or an address book, are less liable to bending or tearing and will last a considerable time.

More expensive products use colour by tinting the edges or the surrounds of pages rather than just the header page. Readers quickly learn the colour code system, enabling them to move rapidly around the document. A similar tactic, but at less cost, is to use tinted paper, perhaps a light grey, for the tutorial section and the expert reference, leaving the main reference manual printed in white. This does not, however, help with navigation around the main reference section itself. Whatever method you devise, based on cost and ease of use, keep in mind that your objective is to aid the user and that anything that does that is to be welcomed.

From this point of view it does no harm to look at as many manuals as possible. Look at the way that they use typography, layout, graphics and colour. Ask yourself how these features help you to use the manual better and quicker, is the information easy to assimilate and easy to access? Dip into the manual at random and see whether sections are 'free standing' or whether you need to refer back to other parts of the book. If you do, is the reference clearly signposted, has your skimming been anticipated by the writer? Whenever you come across something which helps you in writing your own manual, adopt it. When you come across layouts and so on that are unhelpful, try to analyse why they do not work and learn from them so that you do not repeat the same mistakes yourself.

7.4.2 Graphics

In 1988 IBM published their version of DOS 4, complete with operating manual. Out of 460 pages eleven carried graphics of some sort, three of them being concerned with messages about disks. By 1994 Compaq were providing seventeen booklets with their PC, each one packed with graphics of various sorts. Was this merely a change in fashion or a real qualitative change in the production and presentation of manuals?

If we return again to the motor car analogy we can clarify the point. Imagine buying a workshop manual for your car that has no graphics or diagrams at all. Everything is described in words, from instructions about where to top up the engine oil down to how to change the gearbox. For some people this could be a reasonably useful manual. As long as you have a high degree of literacy, an extensive existing knowledge of car mechanics and strong motivation towards the internal combustion engine then a verbal description might suffice. The rest of us might well give up and look instead for a garage that is not too expensive.

The most popular series of car maintenance manuals in Britain today consists of pages of informative diagrams and photographs. Written text is reduced to a minimum, with the only word-based pages being introductions to chapters or fault-finding tables. When complex operations have to be performed the various operations are broken down into their component operations, each one illustrated by a photograph attached to a small amount of text.

Half of the population of Britain have access to a computer in their own home. More than half of the workforce are regular or casual users of computers. For the vast majority of the population, irrespective of employment, education or background, the computer is a part of everyday life, much as the motor car is. Our use of graphics should therefore parallel the non-elitist graphic approach of car maintenance manuals and for much the same reasons.

Try a simple experiment. Pick a simple piece of machinery, such as a tea-maker or a washing machine, and write instructions on how to use it. Give these to someone who has not used the machine before and ask them to operate the machine purely from your instructions. Next, repeat the process but using only pictures and diagrams. Time how long your subjects take to get to grips with the machine and how many mistakes and false starts they make. The subject using the pictures and diagrams will learn to use the machine quicker, making fewer errors. Any technical message can be made clearer or simpler by using a diagram.

Quite apart from their effectiveness, graphics appeal to users in their own right. They increase interest as well as comprehension. One of the reasons why *The Times* newspaper changed its famous front page was that the solid mass of type was so unappealing to the casual buyer. The readership profile was becoming older and older and the general circulation declining. People like pictures. Start from what the consumer wants, then adapt it to provide what the consumer needs. In the case of graphics the manual writer is fortunate in that the two coincide.

Not that we should throw in just any old picture. A good diagram will contain a sufficiency of information but with no extraneous detail. Pare down information to the essentials needed for the task in hand. Use flow-chart techniques to clarify lines of procedure and to make clear to users the precise ordering of tasks.

Remember that your users are unlikely to be experts in the information systems field. They will be insurance agents, nurses or clerks. Where possible, translate technical terms and explanations into simple similes taken from personal experience. IBM do this when discussing files and directories:

'Compare files and directories to the structure of a tree. The root directory is the directory you are in when you start DOS on your system.... When your information needs grow and you want to branch out and create other groups of related files you can form directories called sub-directories.'

Back this up with an appropriate graphic (Fig. 7.1).

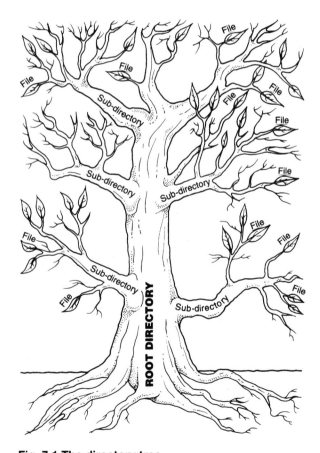

Fig. 7.1 The directory tree

A simple use of graphics that has become almost standard over the last few years is the representation of processes or key presses by the use of 'buttons' in the text. These are icons which represent a key from the keyboard. They have the function of indicating that a response is demanded from the user, usually that a key press is required. When adding buttons to your text it is helpful if you do so including what designers call 'a dropped shadow'. This adds three dimensionality to the button and makes it pop out from the surface, giving immediacy and interest to the page (Fig. 7.2).

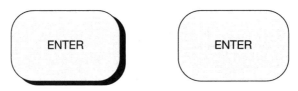

Fig. 7.2 Dropping a shadow

To sum up, graphics should be used as extensively as possible in manuals because they:

- are attractive to the buyer/user
- add interest and variety to the presentation
- make abstract processes visible
- make the explanation of technical details simpler and clearer
- evade problems caused by variations in the user population in terms of literacy, education and motivation towards the technology.

When using graphics, pay attention to:

- including only the essential details
- explaining by using similes from everyday life
- including brief text explanations if this helps further with the explanation
- adding three-dimensional effects for greater impact
- locating the graphics on the same or facing page to the associated text.

7.5 BINDING

7.5.1 Choosing paper size

Paper is generally sold in standard sizes starting at A1 (594 × 841 mm), which is what an art student might use for a large life drawing. The next size A2 is produced by folding an A1 sheet in half; A3 is half of an A2 sheet and so on. Most offices will use A4 (210 × 297 mm) sheets for their letters and internal documentation. Standard reprographic machines are set up for A4 paper, usually with A3 as an optional extra.

It would seem logical to print your manual on A4 paper and there are advantages to this, especially if your product is designed to be cheap and to be reproduced in small quantities. Running off half a dozen copies on the office photocopier is the ideal solution as far as cost effectiveness is concerned.

This solution does have its drawbacks. Desk space is usually severely limited and users find it difficult to accommodate another large document as well as the VDU and their working notes. The large size of A4 does also mean that the line length can be difficult to follow (15–20 words), allowing the eye to stray off on to the next or subsequent line. Shorter line length, allowing ample space for notes, a larger font size or even double columns can compensate for this. This size of manual is hardly ever seen for commercial manuals. The amount of desk space that they take up when opened out and their formidable appearance tend to frighten off most users.

Another solution would be to fold the A4 sheet in half to produce an A5 (148 × 210 mm) sheet. An A5 sheet forces a much smaller line width, about ten words, and takes up less space on the desk. Even when the book is opened out the maximum space it can take is that of one sheet of paper. If the paper is folded rather than cut two pages can be photocopied at a time, cutting down on printing costs. Be careful! You need to work out beforehand exactly which sheet backs on to which or you can get into a dreadful muddle. The production of an initial paste-up version before embarking on a print run is recommended.

Your manual can be printed to whatever size you wish, but remember that the printer will charge you for the whole sheet of paper, including offcuts, so the more of the sheet you can use the better. This usually means operating to standard sizes.

7.5.2 Binding permanent documents

Along with the size of page to be used the method of binding has to be considered. This will be determined partly by the conditions of use and partly by the likelihood and frequency of updates. The greater the number of users and the greater the frequency of use the more sturdy the binding will need to be. A manual that is liable to frequent updates will need a binding and organisation to facilitate those changes.

The simplest method of binding is by using the office **stapler**, either in the top corner or inserting two or three staples along the left hand edge. Pages can be turned relatively easily and the method costs only pence. Stapling is an ideal method for a system that has a very short life, few users and will only be used 'in house'. Its poor appearance makes it unsuitable for commercial products. Pages tend to pull away from the staples after even a short time and they rapidly become dog-eared and unappealing. The number of pages that can be bound together in this manner is strictly limited.

Slightly more sophisticated is the method of **side stabbing**, where large staples are used along the spine. Tape is often glued on afterwards to hide the unsightly staples and add strength. Documents are limited to around one hundred and fifty pages and large margins have to be observed in order to allow for the binding process. Some colleges still use this method for binding student dissertations as it is cheap and moderately durable.

A related but more sophisticated method is known as **saddle stitch**. This involves using double-sized sheets and folding them down the middle to produce a double page. Each double page tucks in to the 'saddle' formed by the others to build up the completed product. It was suggested earlier that a desk-sized A5 manual could be formed in this manner from standard A4 paper. The final product is held together by a couple of staples from the outside page to the inside page through the spine. Because of the folding process the document is made up of multiples of four pages.

The majority of weekly magazines are put together using saddle stitch. It is quick and easy to do and stands up to a reasonable amount of use over a short time. As you might expect, it is cheap and easy to produce, although its appearance is not impressive enough for a full-blown system manual. A company might use this method for 'extras', such as Compaq's 'Safety and Comfort Guide' which comes with its PCs.

Depending on the thickness and quality of the paper, saddle stitched products resist laying flat on the desk when opened, a problem when both hands are engaged with the keyboard. Whatever their quality they do not stand up on a shelf, bending and sliding down, so they are difficult to store. Like any system which uses staples there is a limit to the number of pages that can be bound together. Any document over forty-eight pages will need to be constructed with more than one section, whilst sixteen pages is recommended as the maximum for non-printers to produce.

All of the previous systems are confined mainly to 'in-house' products. By contrast '**perfect binding**' is a respectable commercial method and the one used to bind this book and most paperbacks. Single sheets are lined up and clamped together with a film of plastic glue and a stronger card cover around the outside. Books of any size that are perfect bound stand up well on bookshelves and are easy to store. This method is not recommended for books of less than 48 pages as the glue may not hold.

Because of its cheapness and ease of production this method is still the most popular among producers of computer manuals, if the evidence of the booksellers' shelves is to be believed. The overwhelming problems for the user of this form of binding is its durability and the unwillingness of the pages to lie flat. One problem exacerbates the other. Because of the stiffness of the glue, pages have to be persuaded to lie down. Sometimes, whether due to excessive glue, poor binding or an impatient user, the book is bent too far at the spine and the bonding is weakened or broken. Once this happens pages are liable to fall out (although this is much less of a problem than it once was). Even when the spine of the book has been mistreated in this way the pages still have a tendency to turn at unwanted times when left unattended.

Having said that, you will find plenty of books in your nearest library that are perfect bound and still in good condition. Not least among these is BT's Yellow Pages, which in some areas exceeds a thousand pages.

Another popular system is the use of **comb binding**. This involves punching a series of holes along the spine of the document and inserting a plastic or wire grip or grips. Many offices use this sort of system for documents which are produced and distributed in-house. Even commercial companies, including IBM, bind some of their commercial manuals in this manner. It is simple, quick and cheap to produce as well as being reasonably durable. The greatest advantage of this system is that it allows the pages to lie flat on the desk whilst the reader is engaged with the keyboard. Because of the variety of ring sizes virtually any size document can be bound in this manner.

Comb bound documents have only slight disadvantages. The pages do not turn particularly well or smoothly and it is easy for the careless user to rip them. A set of comb bound books do not sit well together on a shelf. The comb spine is wider than the book, which forces them outwards off the shelf, and the combs can intertwine with one another and become difficult to detach. This can be overcome to some extent by pasting a strip of card over the spine or by binding the rings inside the outer cover. With no vertical stiffening the book tends to slump on the shelf, but again this can be avoided by using a stiffer outer cover.

7.5.3   Binding changing documents

All of the binding methods we have looked at so far are for documents that do not change, or which will be completely re-issued when changes take place. Other documents may need to be changed on a regular basis as updates, corrections and improvements are made. Some products are sold with optional extras, which the purchaser can add on at a later date. It would be expensive and annoying to have to supply or buy a complete new manual each time a further option is purchased.

The common solution is to use a loose leaf system with an associated **ring binder**. Pre-punched holes allow the pages to be clipped into the binder. They can be removed for ease of use or replaced by updates. Additions can be inserted at the end of sections or chapters and directions for those optional extras added in at the end, or wherever the user feels is appropriate. Coloured tab cards can be incorporated for ease of navigation around the document. The pages will lie open on a desk or be removed and clipped into a document holder next to the VDU. Better still, if the user needs to refer to several sections at a time or over a session they can be removed and spread around the desk for easy reference.

Some companies go to the trouble of having their own ring binders produced, complete with company crest and title on the front cover. These are still quite cheap and relatively impressive. Commercially, software manufacturers tend to prefer the smaller A5 format as this fits neatly into the boxes in which their products are packaged. The boxes themselves fit onto shelves well, overcoming the tendency of ring binders to squeeze themselves off shelves because of their wide spines.

With all these advantages it seems strange that not all manuals are of this type, but ring binding does have its own problems. Most important, the punched holes tend to wear badly and finally pull through. This can be repaired by using reinforcers, although heavily used pages eventually become permanently detached. As these also tend to be bread and butter sections, rather than areas subject to constant upgrade, manufacturers tend not to have replacement pages in stock. Using a larger number of holes (within reason) reduces the problem, as does the use of better quality paper or card.

Another difficulty is the updating itself. What happens to your numbering system if pages 92-94 are replaced by eight pages instead of three? Where this is likely to be the case good manual writers will already have taken notice of the problem. A manual which is going to change frequently needs a referencing system which is related to its internal contents rather than page numbers. If we take the IBM DOS 4.0 manual as an example we find that Chapter 3 is referenced as follows:

Chapter 3 Redirecting Input and Output	**59**
Input/Output (I/O)	59
Redirecting I/O	60
Filtering and Piping I/O	61
FIND (Searching files for lines of text)	62
MORE (Displaying output, one screen at a time)	63
SORT (Sorting information by letter or number)	64

What happens to this when sections are expanded, running over to subsequent pages, or new functions are introduced? As the system stands we find ourselves either renumbering the whole manual, leading us to changing the contents pages and index, or introducing anomalies such as page 61d or 63f. Let us first change the reference system that we are to use:

Chapter 3 Redirecting Input and Output	**3**	**Orange**
Input/Output (I/O)	3.1	
Redirecting I/O	3.2	
Filtering and Piping I/O	3.3	
FIND (Searching files for lines of text)	3.4	
MORE (Displaying output, one screen at a time)	3.5	
SORT (Sorting information by letter or number)	3.6	

Chapter 3 has been retained as such (although we do not need to retain the numbering system at all if we expect radical changes) with a colour-coded frontispiece or paper edging to aid access. Instead of being referenced by page number the subsections have been referenced by section. By the time we reach DOS version 4.2 our actual manual might look something like this:

Chapter 3 Redirecting Input and Output	**3**	**Orange**
Input/Output (I/O)	3.1	
Redirecting I/O	3.2	
Filtering and Piping I/O	3.3	
Examples of use of piping	3.3.1	
Replacing using filtering commands	3.3.2	
FIND (Searching files for lines of text)	3.4	
MORE (Displaying output, one screen at a time)	3.5	
MORVAR (Displaying output in multiple screens)	3.5.1	
SORT (Sorting information by letter or number)	3.6	
Advanced SORT commands	3.6.1	

Each page would be individually identified by section (3.2, 3.3.2, etc.) rather than by page number. The contents page needs to allow for additions or emendations by allowing extra space between lines, by providing a blank 'changes' page or by periodic reissues.

This may seem a bothersome procedure but if it is written in from the beginning as part of the document design it is little more trouble than standard page numbering. Identification by section is also a viable option where tabs or colour coding are used.

7.5.4 Packaging

How you package your manual will depend on the budget allocation. Given that you should allocate resources to areas of a project in percentage terms, the greater your overall budget for the entire project the more you have to spend on the manual. Remember that the manual is a marketing tool as well as an aid to users and should reflect the quality and investment cost or the product with which it is associated.

A manual which will stand alone on bookshelves needs an attractive cover like any other book. Do not try to design this yourself, except as a rough indication. Find an experienced designer who will know all about the aesthetics and technicalities of print layout. Talking through your rough design will show you the wisdom of this decision, as improvements are made and alterations occur because of the print methods chosen. With a long or expensive print run the designer's fee will come out as pence per copy.

Where the budget does not stretch to employing a designer other cost factors are also important. As the primary raw material, paper needs to be chosen with care. The company wants the reader to feel that the manual is an important and authoritative document, a message which is often conveyed by the choice of paper. If this is the case then you need to discuss with your printer what is the most expensive paper you can afford. You are looking for paper which feels pleasant to the touch, does not have high reflective qualities when used in artificial light and which has a low degree of opacity.

Low opacity in a paper means that the type on the other side of the page does not show through and confuse the eye. Very thin papers, such as newsprint, have greater opacity and tend to be more flimsy, hardly a good choice for a well-used manual. Glossy papers have a smooth feel to them but tend to reflect light, particularly artificial light, which makes them hard on the eye when used for lengthy periods. Matt papers take light easier and often have a more tactile quality.

Like any other commodity paper varies in quality even within the limitations set out above. Some matt papers are pleasant both to the touch and to the eye, whilst others have a 'reconstituted' feel to them, like thin chipboard. For a short print run the printer's costs will be relatively high per copy, so that the price of the paper will not be significant. In this case, use the best quality paper that you can. With a lengthy print run the printing costs are spread much more thinly across a large number of copies, so that material costs are more significant. You will need to think seriously about economising on paper quality, within the limits of functionality and attractiveness.

Basic documents can, of course, be produced on the office copier. Standard copy paper is light, rather flimsy and not very opaque. However, it is very cheap. If all you want is a single-sided document that will last for a couple of months then this is quite adequate. The quality of the product will depend on the quality of the copying machine, but any copying process will result in some deterioration of quality from the original.

Therefore, if your print run is to be very small, there is nothing better than to take your copies directly from a laser printer. No intervening processes are involved and modern machines are reliable enough to be left to produce collated print runs for long periods of time as long as someone remains in the same room to cope with minor upsets. Costs are reduced to the minimum: the price of the paper, the toner cartridge and the electricity.

Another factor which governs the choice of paper and packaging is **the environment** in which the product is to be used. Some documents will find themselves in sticky, dusty or oily environments. Even the standard office can be a dangerous place, more keyboards having been ruined by spilt coffee than by any other single cause. Where problems like this are likely to occur talk to your printer about using coated paper or card which will not take staining as badly and may even be wiped down gently. The manual cover can be coated in a thin plastic film to save it from wear.

One solution that has been used for many years in engineering workshops is to have a ring binder system where each page has its own plastic envelope. The pages can be removed from the binder by oily hands, which never touch the paper itself. For the duration of the operation the reference page can sit on a workbench or coffee-stained desk before being returned to its binder. The binders themselves are also more resistant to tearing than is punched paper and can be more easily replaced. Although this increases initial costs it does increase durability.

So far we have assumed that manuals are to be bound vertically, like a standard book. However, this is not the only, or even the optimum, solution. Ring binders evade the question altogether by allowing us to remove individual pages and clip them onto a document reader or lay them on our lap. Manuals which are permanently bound do not allow us to do that, but they can be designed with office usage in mind.

What we want is a book that will keep its page without having to be bent back or held down with weights, can be referred to quickly from time to time, will resist smears and stains and will take up the minimum amount of space, just like a good recipe book! And like a recipe book we can design clearly for use. For example, we can bind our book horizontally, like a reporter's notebook. Thus it only takes up half the immediate desk space, the turned part being tucked away against the VDU screen or under some other document. Alternatively, we can take our cue from some recipe books, which are designed to stand up like mini easels or flip charts. This allows us to station the manual alongside the VDU, taking up the minimum amount of space whilst being right next to the subject to which it refers and leaving the document holder free for work in progress. Why not go the whole hog and cover each page in a plastic film?

7.6   ON-LINE MANUALS

If the computer is such a powerful communications tool that few businesses can afford to be without one, the ideal way of explaining how it works would seem to be through the computer itself. As part recognition of this argument new commercial systems usually come complete with an on-line help system. When the user reaches an impasse with the machine or is unsure what to do next F1 will provide access to a complete tutorial which will not have to be bound or printed and which will not take up valuable desk space where grubby fingers and coffee cups will degrade it.

Yet even when it is available many users will studiously avoid using on-line help. Why should this be? Part of the reason lies in the social nature of the human animal. A large number of people prefer to be shown how to do things by other people. However imperfect the explanation may be, the personal contact compensates for inaccuracies and mazy explanations. Moreover, the user can try the task out while an instructor watches and corrects mistakes as they occur or answer questions, despite their being phrased in obscure or non-computing language.

The other way we are taught in our society is through books. They are substitutes for the human presence but also have advantages in their own right. Books are portable, they can be carried around from place to place and read at the owner's leisure. They can be left open on a desk and referred to in between tasks, or thumbed through in order to find extra information using a straightforward indexing system. New information can be sought by flicking quickly through the pages, picking out relevant diagrams or key words. If one proves to be insufficient the user can have several open at the same time without them getting in the way of what is shown on the VDU. Finally, the user can pencil in notes or comments to the page, building up a conceptual overview of the task in hand.

How does on-line help compare to books? First, it is a new technology and therefore suspect in some quarters, although more committed users prefer it for that very reason. Furthermore, it is only available when using an appropriate terminal; the user has problems spending an evening at home brushing up on the computer commands.

On a day-to-day basis other difficulties reveal themselves. A user is having difficulties using the application and calls up the help screen. This at least partially covers the data that is being used, making it difficult to compare the two screens. The user probably has to take notes of what is said, because the help screen will disappear once the decision is made to return to the original data. If the information has to be written down anyway, what is the advantage of having it on the screen?

If the user needs to cross-reference the on-screen information this has to be done by closing the first screen and moving on to the next. Only one screen or one set of help data can be opened at a time, unlike with books where several pages of the same book can be accessed almost simultaneously or pages from different books left open on the desk. Obtaining the correct screen depends totally on the efficiency of the help system's indexing and the variety of 'normal language' options that it offers to the non-specialist user. Flicking through topics or pages does not compare for speed or efficiency with a standard book, nor is there a facility available for the personalised writing of notes or comments. Such are the disadvantages of on-line help that they led John Brockmann to write:

'If on-line documentation is not at least ten times better and easier to use (than books) from the user's perspective it is not going to be successful'.

In the five years since Brockmann made that comment important changes have taken place in screen design. It is now possible to minimise screens so that several pieces of data can appear at the same time without masking one another. Thus a user trying to mail-merge from a database could hold the target letter, sample data and the instructions about merging the two, all on the screen at the same time. In principle it is possible to view several help screens simultaneously, although the small size of the VDU screen is itself a limitation.

For an on-screen system to be effective it must emulate as far as possible the advantages of a paper-based system whilst utilising the best features of electronic data processing. The introduction of lap top and palm top machines has made the computer more portable, certainly between office and home. 'Windows' and other icon-based user interfaces allow for multiple access to data and help screens, whilst screen design has accommodated itself increasingly to the needs of the user. Brockmann reports the development of hypertext systems which can incorporate notes and cross-references entered by the system user.

On a more particularised level, the VDU still presents sensory problems. A full screen only represents half a sheet of A4 paper, thus giving us less information at any one time. Resolution of individual letters tends to be poor, a mere sixty-three pixels per letter compared to a thousand pixels for a letter in a laser-printed document. In some systems the lines on screen are insufficiently leaded, that is the space between lines of text is too small. This causes the two lines to blend into one another visually, making it difficult to follow the text. As a result, users take over 25% more time to read text on a screen than they do on paper. Few people are able to proof read documents directly on-screen, having to print out a proof copy first.

None of these difficulties are insurmountable, as long as we take them into account from the beginning and plan our help screens around them. We also need to decide who our help system is for and what they need.

Absolute beginners do not use the help function. Most of them do not know that it is there or, if they do, what words they should use to interrogate it. In the same way that we include a tutorial as a starter for beginners in a paper-based system we also need to supply an on-line tutorial which is separate from the help system. This will take the user through common actions in the system, using a range of example screens and operations. Since beginners feel safer with paper-based systems the two tutorials will be virtually the same, engendering confidence in both the system and the user's ability to use it.

Since we have eliminated beginners from the help system proper our task has been simplified. We are now dealing with users who have at least a modicum of skill and confidence in their use of the system. They are using on-line help to cut down the time needed to reference procedures and are reasonably confident that they will understand the result. To help them, the indexing system needs to be as broad and as informative as possible, with an emphasis on 'natural language'. If the first try does not work the user will feel that it is quicker to scan the manual than to try and second-guess the writer's linguistic processes. As an example of this, try looking up barrel makers, authors and software manufacturers in the Yellow Pages. They are all in there, but you have to exercise a certain amount of linguistic dexterity to find them. Your users may not have either the dexterity or the patience that you possess.

Once entered, the user's enquiry should be cross-referenced for width and depth. For width, users are given related topics, on the basis of a 'see also' comment in a standard index. Depth is introduced into the system by the use of hierarchical screens (Fig. 7.3). Each level is embedded in the level above, enabling users to jump around between screens in the way that they would do if flicking through a book.

To do this efficiently needs an approach which owes more to the concept of cue cards than to the continuous prose of a standard manual. The user wants everything on any given topic to be displayed at once on a single screen. This means operating with single pages which contain an absolute maximum of 200 words and usually much less. Because of the difficulties of detailed reading, on-screen paragraphs will be of a maximum three or four lines, with obvious blank spaces between them. Readability will be improved by using ragged rather than justified edges.

If all the text is to be displayed on one screen, scrolling is not an option, however complex the message. Instead, break the message down into sub-sections which can be displayed as discrete entities. Again, this enables the user to move quickly and efficiently through the document. Use page numbers as an additional aid, but remember to confine them strictly with sections rather than to number your whole system. Thus your screen header will read:

'Indexes: Cross-referencing   Page 3 of 7'

The first time through the user might read all seven pages. On subsequent visits pages will be flipped through quickly before the specific matter of reference is reached.

The help screen itself needs to be carefully designed with the user in mind. Given that black on white is the optimum colour combination for comprehension all screens should use this combination. Bordering off the window is sufficient to separate help from the main text. The text itself should be in a clear typeface with shorter than normal ascenders and descenders (the parts of the letter which rise or fall above the line, as in g, h or p). This prevents lines bleeding into one another and allows the user to read the message quickly and with the minimum of error.

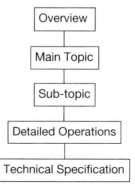

Fig. 7.3 Hierarchical screen structure

For the improving user your objective is to produce an on-line system that will be quicker to use than getting up from the desk, fetching the manual and looking up the operation in hand. As the improver becomes more expert your system comes into its own as a quick reference system whose electronic base makes access faster and more efficient. Like most high-performance technology, the efficiency of on-line help improves exponentially with the expertise of the user. An on-line system therefore needs to incorporate the same features as a paper manual. The user will demand:

- information on the system
- knowledge of tasks that can be performed
- clarification of procedures that are undertaken
- the organisational structure of the application
- contents and other navigational aids.

To help the user interact with the system the on-screen system will include:

- an introductory tutorial
- system messages
- system controls
- a complete and accurate manual
- quick reference to specific queries
- embedded levels of technical complexity.

7.7 PROTOYPING AND TESTING

As part of an information system a manual should be prototyped and thoroughly tested before it is 'signed off' and released to the customer, be it as a commercial document or as an item of company reference. Testing is not an activity which is confined to the end of the project but one which begins with its inception. It continues through the life of the project in an iterative manner until the product has been tested as effectively as available time and money allow.

7.7.1 Prototyping

The discussion of testing brings us back to the point made earlier in this chapter, that the design team for an IS product should either contain a specialist writer from the beginning or have clear responsibility assigned to a member or members of the team who will be writing the manual. Software design decisions therefore go hand in hand with decisions about the user documentation. Writing of the manual begins from day one, as the product itself takes shape. Identification of potential users, their needs and limitations, are primary factors in the fulfilment of the whole project, informing both programming and writing decisions. By tying needs to all the outcomes the design team is obviating a range of problems at the marketing end and reducing support costs. These are as important for in-house software as they are for commercial products.

The site for testing is therefore the potential user rather than members of the design team or other professionals. As Brockmann points out:

'Designers have become so proficient with the product that they can no longer perceive or understand the areas that are apt to cause difficulties'.

We can, however, make use of this proficiency in the prototyping process. As the product takes shape, sit down with a couple of potential users and instruct them how to operate the system as it stands at present, perhaps module by module. Record the resultant transactions on a tape recorder.

What you have recorded is a set of teaching procedures probably couched in natural language rather than IS jargon. Where you have slipped into technospeak your tutees will have picked you up and queried the meaning of words and abbreviations. If your instructions are unclear the tutees will have asked questions or found that they have the wrong thing on the screen. In the latter case you need to analyse your instructions in order to find where they are misleading. Remember that the audience is always right. However stupid or perverse you find their responses, those are the appropriate responses for that person, given the stimulation of your instructions.

By the end of the analysis you have a prototype manual for that module or section. At this point you can either repeat the process with two different users or commit the words to paper as the preliminary instruction manual. In the latter case it will, of course, need to be further tested. By the end of the design process a full set of documents should be in existence.

These need to be fully tested before being printed in their final format. Depending on time and finance, exhaustive testing might not be feasible. As a minimum you will need to test representative screens and layouts alongside a representative chapter of the manual which has been mocked up to mimic the expected final format. Where operations are generally similar to one another there is obviously no need to test each one.

The testers will again be taken from your target audience. Emphasise to them that it is the system that is being tested and not them. They need to be reassured that any misunderstandings are the result of poor communications rather than their incompetence. A tape recorder can again be used to advantage at this stage. Try putting two users together on the same machine and recording their conversation. This will identify areas that they find difficult or problematic and allow you to remedy them.

Testing itself should be by simulating the tasks which your system has been designed to undertake. The writer or some other member of the team at the same time simulates the support that will be provided with the system. If you are providing user training, then this will take the form of having the trainer in the room for questioning as the testers work their way through the tasks. On the other hand, if only distance support, such as a help desk or telephone hot line, is to be provided, then the support personnel have to simulate this by putting themselves in a position where they cannot see the testers' screens.

At the end of the testing system it is important to obtain formal feedback from the users. You can do this by a formal questionnaire, by reading the testers' notes and by a structured interview. Identify areas where the users got stuck, places where they felt lost or angry. Were there times when they felt like giving up or smashing the screen in front of them? These are the areas to which you need to pay close attention, since they are the points where unmotivated users will cease to operate your wonderful new system and return to the one they are used to.

Once the areas of difficulty have been corrected you need to return again to the users, preferably ones who did not take part in the first test, and repeat the process. This is akin to the iterative approach of systems analysis, where the analyst checks documentation again and again with the respondent until it is perfect. We may not reach perfection but we should aim to be as close to it as possible.

7.7.2 Field testing

Once user trials have been carried out the whole document has to be field tested. This needs to be done as close to the final conditions of use as possible and with a document that is similarly as close to the format of the final document as is feasible. Make sure that your test document is clearly identified as such and your users are encouraged to annotate it as fully as they wish. Annotations will provide feedback to you on the parts of the document that are unclear or where users have felt that they need to cross-reference information. Users also deserve feedback on their efforts and should be informed, if only in general terms, of where changes have been made in response to their performance.

Field testing also throws up examples of typical user errors. The practise of CCTA in logging errors through their help desk system has already been mentioned. Within the perfect system these errors would never have reached the operational stage. They would have been picked up by observation during field testing or even before, or by the comments of the users themselves. However, it is inevitable that a few will slip through, since all users will not have the same skills or problems. What should not recur, if you have done your testing thoroughly, will be major errors or difficulties that are encountered across the whole spectrum of users.

Finally, you need to test the language that has been used in the manual. This can be done in two ways. First, longer areas of text in particular should be checked using the FOG index outlined earlier. This will indicate that you have used simple words and short declarative sentences. A reading age of fourteen is the absolute maximum, but if you can get it down to single figures, so much the better.

The other test is to use what is known as a CLOZE procedure. For this, simply take an extensive piece of the manual and delete every seventh word, making it clear where deletions have taken place. Give the resulting text to several of the user group and ask them individually to restore the deleted words. The greater their success in this task then the clearer your writing has been. Their insertions do not have to be the exact words that you used in your original, synonyms will do, as long as the meaning is retained. Any synonyms used can be integrated into your index or on-line reference. You should be aiming at a correct response rate of over eighty per cent, whilst a score of under fifty per cent should send you back for an extensive re-write.

Another method of testing involves both writers and programmers in the real use of the system for the purpose for which it was intended. If the system is for use, for example, in recording orders and despatch notes for a mail order company, members of the project team can spend some time in the appropriate department actually logging orders on their new system. The writer, if not a programmer, could do the same, using the manual for reference whenever needed. This way the producers of the system suffer from its shortfalls and become more motivated to correct them!

7.7.3 Editing

Any document needs some form of editing. With a short document like a letter or a memo this can be done almost as part of the composition process. Running the spell checker and a quick read through on screen might suffice. The longer or more complex a document becomes the greater importance is attached to the editing process and the higher the amount of resources devoted to it.

Editing cannot be done efficiently on your own. You are too close to the product, you no longer 'see' it and you can be as blind to its imperfections as parents can be to the imperfections of their own children. Nor can it be done on screen. Besides being slower and more difficult to read, the screen does not give us a proper impression of what the finished product will look like to the user. A paper print-out is both more readable and easier to manipulate in physical terms.

At a basic level you are aiming to produce a manual that is correct in all its content, layout and grammar. Both you and your co-editor should be looking for all the factors that are listed in the section on reviewing that follows. In addition, the editors are looking at basic communication structures. Have you eliminated all unnecessary words? Are your sentences as simple as they could be? Here you are looking both for sentences which go on too long and for ones that are more than simple subject-verb-object. Since dependant clauses, which add to sentence complexity, are conventionally contained within commas, scan your writing for commas and pick out where sentences can be broken in two or where sections can be completely eliminated.

How long are your paragraphs? Looking at the actual pages helps you to pick up blocks of text, which can then be broken up. Can the information be presented as a list, signalled by bullets, rather than buried in text? Are there enough signals of **key words** within the text, denoted by bold type? Is the style mechanical, in the sense that all objects or operations are always referred to by exactly the same term? Are you always concrete in your descriptions with real world analogies; have you eliminated abstract ideas and explanations?

Get your co-editor to skim and scan the manual in the same way that a normal user would do. Are there plenty of cross-references to aid the process? Are abbreviations and acronyms fully explained in a glossary that is easy to find? What jargon is there in the manual; is it unavoidable, and if it is, is it fully explained in a comprehensible manner?

By the end of this process you should have a completely correct manual which is easy to use and which will sail through any subsequent review process. Before you get that far, however, you will need to proof your document. First enter all your corrections and emendations on screen, then subject them to electronic spell checking and grammar checking. Do not assume that is sufficient. Print out two copies of the whole of the document in draft form. Both you and your co-editor should check it for correctness. There should be no need to make changes of content at this stage and you should avoid doing so as far as possible.

If you are using a commercial printer, you will be supplied with galley proofs prior to printing, which you should also check over. Even if you are both using the same electronic system do not assume that everything has come out perfectly. If intermediate copying of some sort has been done you need to be very particular in your reading, even if a professional proof reader has also been employed to check over the text.

7.7.4 Reviewing

Like testing, reviewing is a continuous process, though one whose completion marks the formal end of the project. It involves both experts and users, the experts identifying statements which are untrue or inaccurate and the users identifying areas they do not understand or which do not seem to work in practise. A full review must be carried out immediately before final printing of the manual and upon its receipt from the printers. If the first review has been efficiently performed the second should be little more than a formal validation exercise. However, it still remains an important part of quality control, preventing the publication of documents which may bring the company into disrepute.

The review process embraces three broad areas, all of which demand the participation of reviewers from outside the project team. The Business Review involves the original clients for whom the project was undertaken, the Technical Review takes in IS professionals and the Audience Review involves end users, writing professionals or print layout specialists. Members of the project team naturally take part in all three areas.

The **business review** returns the team's vision to the original terms of reference for the project. Does the product supplied, including the manuals and associated paperwork, meet the business objectives set out when the project began? Can the company now process twice as many documents as before with only half the error rate? We are not talking principles here, we are concerned with actual performance. This is where user documentation proves so important. The software may be capable of meeting the business objectives but if the users do not have sufficient support to be able to perform the task then the performance criteria for the business plan have not been met. Naturally, should this happen, it is important to identify clearly whether the shortfall is in the hardware, software or the support systems in order that revision can take place in the appropriate area.

The **technical review** of the documentation checks for accuracy and consistency. Part of this can be done on a read-through basis, whilst the rest demands an informed outsider working through the procedures as laid out. The sort of questions that need to be answered are:

- Are all the procedures correct?
- Are all the procedures understandable?
- Do the illustrations fully explain the processes to which they relate?
- Are all the technical terms correct?

- Are the same technical terms used consistently?
- Is the sequence of events (where appropriate) correct?
- Is there any necessary information which is missing?

The **audience review** checks that the documentation is acceptable for publication in general, that it gives a good impression of the company, and that it is suitable for the audience for which it was intended. This process is particularly concerned with language and layout and asks questions such as:

- Is the style appropriate to the target audience?
- Is the language easy to understand?
- Are the spelling and grammar correct?
- Is the information well formatted for convenient use?
- Are the formatting and layout consistent throughout?
- Are the illustrations correct?
- Are the illustrations complete?
- Are illustrations numbered and referenced?
- Are there screen shots wherever possible?
- Does the document have efficient reference points in terms of:
    numbering
    section/chapter differentiation
    contents pages
    index
    glossary
    cross-referencing of information?
- Is information presented in an ordered manner?

When the review has finished, the document has been published and the project signed off as complete the final action by the team is to feed back information to the various people and organisations that have been involved. The project sponsors will have their own report, as will the team's own management, where this is different. A brief letter of thanks and explanation should be circulated to the end users who have helped with testing, wherever possible giving details of broad areas where their comments have been incorporated in the finished document. Workers who are consulted and then feel that their responses have been ignored have a right to feel used and resentful.

An in-house document could well have an acknowledgements page which lists the users who have made an input into the finished manual. This engenders a sense of ownership in those people, who feel that they have a personal interest in making the system work. If all has gone well you now have an excellent system, efficient documentation and a well motivated workforce. What could be better?

7.7.5 Warning messages

All manuals need to carry certain basic information, usually in the form of warning messages. How extensive these will be depends upon the nature of your manual and the agreement entered into with the client. Generally, these messages fall into the categories of cautions, which cover safe and sensible use of the product, and warnings, which set out legal liabilities.

Cautions give the user basic information, such as the producers of the product, the date on which it was issued, the version of the software if appropriate and where to apply for further information. With systems that are being constantly updated the cautions may even refer to previous manuals and give information about whether they can be used with the current version. Amstrad's LocoScript 2, for example, contains the following global warning:

> *'The particulars supplied in this manual are given by Locomotive Software in good faith. However, LocoScript 2 is subject to continuous development and improvement and it is acknowledged that there may be errors or omissions in this manual. In particular, the examples, menus and messages shown in this manual may differ from those actually shown on the screen.'*

Despite this catalogue of disclaimers the manual is perfect bound, preventing continuous updates, and contains no indication of the version that the reader has in hand. Still, we at least know not to panic when what is on screen is not exactly what is in the manual. The company's objective is to make it clear that it accepts no liability for anything that may go wrong, causing financial loss to the user, as the result of inaccuracies or omissions in the manual. Whether this will evade the specification in British law that a product must be fit for the purpose for which it is intended is a point yet to be tested in the courts.

Warning messages also inform the user of dangers from using the product. In the past these have been to the effect that misuse of the product may cause loss or corruption of data or even physical damage to the hardware itself. More recently warnings have included references to health and safety procedures, particularly those enshrined in European Union directives. The discovery of repetitive strain injuries (RSI) associated with prolonged keyboard usage has led to claims for compensation by workers. Firms such as Compaq now issue warnings with their products describing proper PC usage and declaring that *'there may be a risk of **serious injuries** from working at your computer workstation.'* Again, what status such disclaimers have in law has yet to be tested but it may be that they will become standard practice over the next few years.

Finally, the user has to be warned about copying the manual or other products. Like any book or piece of intellectual property a computer manual belongs to someone who must give, preferably written, permission before it can be legally copied. IBM is quite unequivocal in its message:

> *'Copyright IBM, 1988. All rights reserved. No part of this publication may be reproduced or distributed in any form or by any means without prior permission in writing from the IBM Corporation.'*

Note that 'in any form', which neatly covers e-mail, bulletin boards or any kind of communication medium which may be developed in the future. You may also wish to set out conditions where the manual may be copied (where the purchaser has a site licence for the software, for example) and this should also appear in an obvious place at the beginning of the manual. Copyright usually resides in the producer of the product except where the individual concerned is producing it as part of a contract of employment. The owner of the copyright should be clearly identified in each copy of the manual.

7.8   A SIMPLE APPLICATION

As his final project, Daniel was requested by one of his tutors to prepare a teaching package which would emulate the actions of a decoder on screen. This was a reasonably straightforward task which Daniel accomplished quite quickly. Once the emulator was written he needed to check that it could be used by his target audience and to prepare a set of user instructions. Quite sensibly he combined the two tasks by giving his test users a set of instructions that he had prepared. These are shown as Fig 7.4.

Initial testing, especially with naive groups did not go well, the software appeared to be too complicated for the testers to use. However, rather than rush ahead and change it, Daniel first analysed his user instructions. Among other things he concluded that they were:

1. Too wordy. Users needed to plough through large amounts of text in order to find what they were supposed to do.
2. Not concise. Sentences themselves were too long and often contained more than one idea or operation.
3. Paragraphs were too long and contained too many sentences. Operations and ideas were therefore hidden away in blocks of text.
4. Poorly presented. As well as the long paragraphs the document was right justified, making it even more unfriendly.
5. Without navigation aids. The only navigation aid in the document was the emboldening of the instruction bar. No other operations or entries were signalled.
6. There were no consistent conventions for operations and consequently no distinctions between processes and operations. Users therefore did not know when they should be entering data, performing operations or observing what was happening on the screen.
7. Confused about whether the instructions were an operational instruction manual or part of the learning system. As a result there were no clear objectives to the user instructions, with observations, learning points and operations jumbled together in one mass

Daniel therefore completely revised his operating instructions before the next set of testing (Fig. 7.5). Although the new version was by no means perfect it was considerably clearer than the original and none of his fifty testers had any problem running the emulator, proving that it was the user documentation that was at fault and not the emulator itself. The emulator is now in use by the project sponsor as a teaching aid within the college.

To use the decoder emulator you should be in possession of the following three files:

decoder.exe

bold.chr

trip.chr

The emulator can be run either from the A:\ drive (which may cause it to run slower) or it can be installed onto your computer's hard drive. At the prompt 'decoder' and press <Enter> the program will run. You will be confronted with an opening screen which will offer two options:

1) Simulation

2) Knowledge test

To run the simulator, press 1 on the keyboard.

Once this has been done the screen should clear and display the decoder. The idea of a decoder is that, by inputting a binary code, one of a number of routes will be chosen which, in this case, is used to access memory locations. At the end of each decoder gate there is a memory location whose contents at the moment are set to zero. These memory locations can hold a three bit binary code which will be stored there to be retrieved by the decoder.

At the bottom of the screen there are eight options that can be selected. These are:

Edit Reset Finish Edit Animate Go Quit Help About

Options that appear in red cannot yet be selected. The first thing that we are concerned with is editing the input codes (top left corner) and the memory locations (middle screen).

Press the 'E' key once (input is not case sensitive) and notice that the yellow box in the top left hand corner has turned to red. This means that the box is ready to receive some input. Type in a 1 and notice that the red box has moved to the next position. Next, type in another 1.

Press the 'E' key four more times. The red box will then be at the first position of the fourth memory location. If you press it too many times, keep pressing it until you arrive back to this location. Now type in 1,0,1. Notice that, once a number has been typed in, the red box will automatically move to the next position. If you type it in incorrectly it will keep circling round the fourth memory location until you press the 'E' key again to move to the next memory location.

Now the decoder should have an input code reading 1,1,0 and in the fourth memory location it should have the value 1,0,1. If this is so, press the 'F' key to finish editing the codes.

There will now be some more options available: 'Animate', 'Go' and 'Reset'. Animate and Go do virtually the same thing, they show the path that the decoder takes. 'Go' shows it immediately and 'Animated' shows it more slowly.

Next press the 'A' key and watch the decoder choose its path. It should choose the fourth gate and take the contents of the memory address to the output.

Once the emulator has finished, press the 'R' key and the screen will reset ready for some more input. Assuming the emulator is not animating at the time the program can be quitted at any time. There is also a help section which is a reminder of what the keys do.

Fig.7.4 Original emulator instructions

You should be in possession of the following three files:
- **decoder.exe**
- **bold.chr**
- **trip.chr**

The emulator can run from
- **floppy disk**
   or
- **hard drive**

At the prompt:
- type **DECODER**
- press **<ENTER>**

You are offered two options
1) Simulation
2) Knowledge test

- **Press '1'**

The decoder will be displayed.

Eight options will appear at the bottom of the screen
Edit Reset Finish Edit Animate Go Quit Help About

Only options in **white** can be selected.

- **Press the 'E' key once**

The yellow box in the top left corner has turned to red;
- **Type in '1'**

The red box has moved to the next position;
- **Type in '1' again**
- Press the **'E'** key **FOUR** more times

The red box will be at the first position of the fourth memory location;
- **Type in '1,0,1'**
- **Press the 'E' key again**

The decoder should have an input code of 1,1,0. The fourth memory location should have the value 1,0,1.
If this is so:
- **Press the 'F' key** to finish editing codes

If NOT, repeat the previous instructions.

- **Press the 'A' key**

Once the emulator has finished:
- **Press the 'R' key**

The screen will reset

When finished:
- **Press 'Q' to quit**

Fig. 7.5 Revised emulator instructions

Daniel's revised version, whilst not being perfect, has addressed most of the problems that he identified in the original. The layout has been totally changed, eliminating paragraphs completely and never having more than two lines of continuous text. As a result it is no longer intimidating and the instructions and key presses are easy to spot. This is emphasised by the use of extensive navigational aids. All actions by the operator are signalled by indented bullets and are emboldened. Information to be keyed in is signalled by inverted commas, with other important information also being signalled either by emboldening or by being printed in capitals. Teaching points have been eliminated, leaving only operational instructions.

Although there are still changes that could be made (the instruction on pressing the 'A' key, for example) Daniel's revised version is clear, easy to follow and well laid out, the sort of quick reference guide that any company would be pleased to use.

7.9 CONCLUSION

Manuals are indispensable aids to the user's understanding and operation of any system. The writer's aim is to make the manual as transparent as possible. Purchasers can be swayed in their purchase by the existence of good documentation which convinces them that they will get full value for money from the product. As Brockmann says: '*products that present themselves with built-in intelligibility are the ones that will survive.*'

An efficient user manual is one that:

- has a range of easy-to-use reference aids
- is easy to understand at all levels
- does not make any assumptions about the user's ability or knowledge
- is complete
- is accurate
- is up to date at all times
- is easy to maintain.

CHAPTER 8
Training users

INTRODUCTION

Despite efforts in schools fuelled by the national curriculum it is still possible for new entrants on the job market to be functionally ignorant of the applications of information systems. This is in addition to the millions who have, by design or accident, never faced a keyboard in their lives. Add on to those categories people whose knowledge of IT systems is limited to a single application or a single supplier's equipment and you will see the great demand that there is for training in the IS area.

In this chapter we will be looking at the methods and approaches that you might use when teaching someone else how to use IT equipment. Because of the demands of the National Council for Vocational Qualifications you may find yourself in a formal training and assessing role within your company or as a trainer teaching others how to use your company's products. You may also find yourself involved with designing and writing programmed learning packages for a range of users.

To aid you in this we take a careful look at how people learn as well as the factors which inhibit that learning and how you can structure your training in order to improve your trainees' performance. Most of the time the assumption has been made that you will have a group of trainees but the points made apply equally well to training individuals on their own.

8.1 THE TRAINING CONTEXT

There are many ways that you may find yourself in a training context. Most obvious is as part of a training section within a large company or as part of a training agency. In this case you will find yourself with groups of people who may be learning generic applications, such as databases or word processing, or updating on the new version of software that the company has purchased. At the other end of the scale you might be a freelance programmer who has to instruct the clients in the operation of the latest program on a one-to-one basis.

Somewhere in between comes the help desk, whose members are employed to sort out operational difficulties that users may encounter. Leaving aside hardware malfunction, most faults are the result of operators being insufficiently aware of the capabilities of their system. Help desk personnel do not just have the job of getting the operator functioning as quickly as possible but also of giving quick instructions on how to avoid the problem in future. In organisations such as the British government's central computing facility CCTA, help desk staff log the nature of calls in order to build up a fault profile. Once calls of a certain type have built up or begin to indicate operational inefficiencies formal training is arranged for staff.

In the early days of user-operated PCs the training function devolved to enthusiastic workers within the organisation. These super-users became enthusiastic about the equipment and explored all its possibilities. Less motivated workers would come to super-users for instruction rather than going through the complicated stages of contacting the DP department or the external suppliers. As Gunton points out, some efficiency savings were made but at the expense of taking the super-users away from the work that they should have been doing elsewhere. Nor were the super-users the most appropriate people in the organisation for this helping function, either in a social or a structural sense.

We still retain super-users and in many ways we always will. There will always be those more at home with the technology than others who are purely needs-driven in their approach to it. What is changing is the determination of companies to co-ordinate the help function and to identify 'nodes of excellence' within the workforce. Thus it will be these people who are sent off on training course and have the responsibility of disseminating what they have learnt. This is known as the 'Cascade' approach, where knowledge and skills are cascaded down through the organisation from a single fountain head. In effect, the role of trainer has been added to that worker's job description.

The list of training situations you might be involved in is vast, from helping a fellow student understand an application to instructing one's children in the elements of word processing. Some local authorities employ trainers to instruct local councillors in how their central information system operates, National Health Trusts are currently re-training large numbers of staff on rationalised hardware and software systems. Somewhere at this very moment a worker is turning to the colleague at the adjoining workstation and saying something like *I can't get this machine to perform this operation. How do you do it?* That colleague has become a trainer.

Formal training in industry is big business. British companies spent £18.6 billion on training in 1986-7, whilst there are as many people in the USA receiving industrial training as there are in the whole of the American higher education system. Even during the recession years of the early nineties nearly half of the British workforce received some training every year, although the actual amount spent on it did decline from the 1987 peak. As might be expected, technical and professional staff received the greatest proportion of that training (23%), with 16% of all training being attributed to 'response to technological change'.

In this chapter we will be looking at the principles of training and giving some examples of what to do and what not to do. Naturally, it is impossible to cover in depth all of the situations mentioned above but it should be possible to adapt the general principles and to use them to improve your training skills in whatever position you might find yourself.

8.2 MOTIVATION

Motivation is a word much bandied about in education and in management. When we ask for somebody's motivation we are asking why people do things. What makes a worker turn up every day? What makes one student work harder than another? What drives some to spend hours working out how a computer package works when others couldn't care less?

To be honest, we do not really know. Or rather, we know too much and have not yet managed to make sense of it. For example, at one time it was assumed that workers worked purely for the money, the more money they were given the harder they worked. Observation and experiments proved this not to be true. Yes, the workers would not work unless they were paid, but extra pay did not seem to increase productivity, especially in repetitive occupations such as car manufacturing. What seemed to motivate the workers was increased interest, tasks that stretched their skills and gave them a pride in the product. Thus companies like Saab and Lotus dispensed with assembly lines and replaced them with assembly circles, where workers could see the whole car gradually taking shape. Social factors also came into force. A strongly bonded team worked well, with members trying not to let the others down.

These findings gave rise to the concept of **maintenance factors** and **motivating factors**. Maintenance factors are necessary to get the worker started but it is motivating factors which lead to higher productivity. Workers will not work unless they are paid (the maintenance factor) but paying them more does not necessarily lead to them working harder. Only a motivator will do that.

Similarly, there is a split between **extrinsic motivation** and **intrinsic motivation**. Extrinsic motivation involves some sort of outside force operating on the individual. '*Do this training course and we will pay you more money*' is a typical example. The worker will drag through the course as well as possible in order to achieve the pay rise. The student finishes the degree course because of desperately wanting a job afterwards, even if by now the subject has been found to be deadly dull.

Intrinsic motivation comes from within. This is what drives you to complete tasks which others perhaps see as beyond you: climbing a mountain, setting up a million pound company. We know that intrinsic motivation is the more powerful, it needs no controlling agent, threats or promises. Intrinsic motivation is what drives great sports people and great artists as well as chess players, top class computer programmers and owners of huge computer companies.

Where is the problem then? All the trainer has to do is to get in touch with the trainee's patterns of motivation and away we go. The school system could end at twelve, degree courses could be cut to one year. It is not that easy. We know what an amazing effect inner motivation can have, what we do not know is what brings it about, why individuals are motivated in one direction rather than another or how to find out what the real motivation of an individual actually is. We can ask, of course, but this rarely produces genuine results, partly because individuals are not always consciously aware of what their true motivations are, either through ignorance or self-deception.

The psychologist Maslow is the best known of many psychologists who have attempted to come to grips with this problem. Rather than delving into the deep subconscious he attempted to rationalise the level of a human being's needs and how they were dependant on one another (Fig. 8.1).

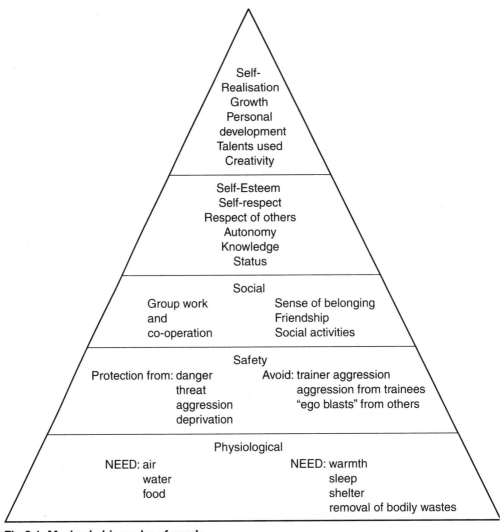

Fig.8.1 Maslow's hierarchy of needs

According to Maslow, each higher level builds on the one below and cannot be satisfied until the lower one is taken care of. Thus there are physiological factors that take priority, the need for food, drink and air. We all know how difficult it is to concentrate when we are desperate to go to the toilet! Once these factors have been taken care of we must then feel ourselves free from danger and aggression. Above a certain level, fear in animals impairs operative competence, a point that we will return to later.

Above the lower level of needs is an ascending hierarchy of higher needs. We wish to work well within the tribe or family grouping and to feel that we belong to it. Thus we wear the uniform of the tribe, be it blue suits or blue jeans. Being part of a coherent high-status group increases productivity even when the maintenance factors are the same, or even less than, similar groups. Once this has been attained we begin to demand the respect of others for our achievements and to be seen as a significant person. We are happy to work independently and to acquire knowledge to enable us to do so. Finally, we may grow into the last stage of self-realisation, where we become truly creative people and our talents are used to the full.

You will notice that Maslow does not try to tell us what specific activities will motivate any individual in any category, just that these are other sorts of areas in which people operate. Nor does he attempt any detailed psychoanalysis of childhood fears and traumas. From our point of view this is a great advantage, since the average trainer has neither the time nor the skills to carry out such an analysis but has, of necessity, to depend on broad ideas.

In practical terms, how can the trainer operate within the concept of motivation? Let us take extrinsic motivators first. These are the least effective, but that does not mean that they have no efficacy at all. Telling a programmer with a young family and a large mortgage that he must go on a course to learn COBOL or he will lose his job is a crude but effective motivator. The programmer will go on the course and will try reasonably hard, despite possible feelings of resentment. Lecturers are continually coming across students who declare that they are not interested in information systems but it seems the area where graduates are assured of jobs. Most of these students manage to finish their course, although rarely are their marks outstanding.

Over the last fifty years behavioural psychologists have built on the application of extrinsic motivators to revolutionise some areas of training. Psychologists such as Skinner found that they could change the behaviour of recalcitrant pupils by giving them suitable motivators. Thus a student who gave three right answers during a thirty minute class might be rewarded with an ice cream cone, satisfying basic physiological needs. Once good behaviour was instilled into the child the motivator could be gradually removed, leaving behind the behaviour.

Teachers and parents still use a crude form of this. Once a child gives a right answer or does something correctly the child is praised, a motivating event within Maslow's category of 'Social', bringing the child closer to the circle of the social group. Sales personnel are given prizes for achievement such as pennants or cups. Whilst not of financial value these prizes act on the self-esteem of the recipient and build up worth in the eyes of others.

A simple smile, a word of praise or physical rewards can all be motivators; *'reinforcers of behaviour'* in Skinner's terminology. For the majority of trainees these can be applied freely and effectively. To be complimented on how one has handled a task, such as learning a new piece of software, makes one feel good, especially if the compliment was heard by one's peers. Degree ceremonies at universities serve a similar function, massaging the graduate's self-esteem before peers and family. They also encourage other students to work towards a similar end. A good trainer therefore:

- encourages trainees at every opportunity
- is positive in attitude to the trainees
- keeps the final end in view at all times
- sets up achievable intermediate goals to act as reinforcers
- provides successful trainees with positive evidence of their achievements.

Despite its obvious successes, behaviourism in training does have its drawbacks. It relies on the trainer being able to find effective motivators. Where trainees do not respond to the common ones it becomes increasingly difficult to control the situation in the absence of any effort on behalf of the trainee. Also, extrinsic motivators do not have the effect of permanently changing behaviour that Skinner and his disciples thought. Over time or as the result of stress at a particular moment the subject will revert to the previously learnt behaviour. Athletes often find that, in the heat of the game, they will revert to their old manner of doing things that their trainer thought had been abandoned long before. It seems that regular reinforcement sessions are the only solution.

At times it can become a major task to find anything to praise some trainees for. The temptation is to ignore these individuals and to get on with the job in hand with the rest of the group. Instead, the trainer needs to break down the task into increasingly simple parts that even the most unwilling or incompetent trainee can manage. Special educational initiatives in the USA and elsewhere have been spectacularly successful in adopting such a methodology.

Intrinsic motivators are far more effective and long-lasting in their effects but much more difficult to apply. In general we are likely to be operating with factors within the top two levels of Maslow's hierarchy: self-esteem and self-realisation. Here the trainee will attain inward satisfaction for a job well done, for becoming a better and more knowledgeable person, for achieving inward goals. What counts as producing all of those things may be hidden even from the conscious knowledge of the trainee, as we saw earlier in the Johari Window. If the trainer can get to grips with these hidden feelings, through counselling interviews, for example, then success for the trainee is highly likely.

In the real world trainers have neither the time nor the expertise to bring out unconscious motivating factors. The best that can be done is to question individual trainees, preferably in private, as to their motivation towards this particular area. If the answers are purely instrumental, along the lines of '*I will get promotion if I get through this course*', the trainer needs to be wary. Once comments along the lines of '*I have always found the use of databases fascinating*' begin to appear, the trainer has much more to work with.

So far nothing has been said about punishment or of negative motivation. This is because they are both to be avoided. Maslow's second category is that of Safety, an area which includes psychological safety as well as physical safety. Human beings try to minimise attacks by building legal and social barriers to aggressive behaviour. The great seventeenth-century political theorist Thomas Hobbes described life in a society without laws as '*nasty, brutish and short*'. He described a society where nobody would grow any food because it would be taken away from them once harvest was complete, where any sort of property laid one open to attack and robbery.

A certain amount of stress is useful in improving the behaviour of all animals. It produces chemical changes in the body which increase physical performance, improving the functioning of flight mechanisms. Above that level it becomes dysfunctional, as does fear. Fear can have the effect of paralysing the system; rational thought and even behaviours which may be considered to be instinctual close down. Laboratory experiments with rats have demonstrated that they will remain rooted with fear to the very site of the attack, when flight would be the rational response. Many people have described times in their educational lives where terror of an overbearing teacher has driven from their heads knowledge which they were certain they had only moments before.

Clinical observations of children show that physical punishment seems to work, but only for very short periods. Desirable behaviour is produced in the short term, then the subject quickly reverts without internalising the lesson that was supposedly learnt. Threats of physical punishment impairs the child's learning ability.

Obviously in the training environment nobody is likely to be inflicting physical punishment on their trainees. There are, however, other more subtle punishments which trainers can, and do, use. Sarcasm and irony, 'showing up' trainees before their peers, are still common. Encouraging, or at least allowing, verbal attacks by trainees on one another is another form of aggression. Remember that these are forms of punishment, they impinge on the subject's need for safety, and as such are ineffective in producing long-term learning, quite apart from questions about their ethical acceptability.

Negative motivation is the bane of all trainers' lives. These are factors from the trainees' backgrounds which militate against them learning the task in hand. One word processing student stubbornly refused to improve, feeling that if she became too competent she would end up typing all her husband's work at home. Another proved to be very slow at learning about databases; it was his way of avoiding transfer to a different section of the company. Technophobic new users sometimes refuse to touch the keyboard out of fear of doing something wrong, for which they will be shamed in front of their peers or exposed to sarcasm. Whether or not these reactions are rational they still have to be dealt with, either by identifying them and overcoming them, or by substituting a stronger and opposite motivator. Unfortunately the trainer often does not discover their existence until well into the course.

Once in the training room the trainer should:

- motivate all of the trainees towards the task
- reward all trainees as frequently as possible
- avoid punishments of any kind
- remove aggression from the training situation
- identify negative motivation and replace it with positive motivation.

Motivation, although important, is not the sole criterion for a successful training programme. As far as the trainees themselves are concerned, they carry a whole collection of 'baggage' which affects their success. Knowledge and attitudes have already been mentioned, but they have also acquired a whole set of work habits. These may be attitudinal, in that they expect to work for a certain amount of hours at a certain pace, or functional, in that they believe that the job is best done in a certain manner. For adult learners a life of employment usually ensures good learning habits linked to the 'nine-to-five' of ordinary work, but can also lead to a certain amount of functional inflexibility.

Employees also have an existing view of the organisational climate of the company. Where this is a positive one, perhaps as a result of perceptions that training is the norm and that it can lead to promotion and increased pay, then performance is increased.

The perception that training is enforced whilst having little benefit to the trainee has the opposite result. Anecdotal evidence suggests that this is a significant factor in the disappointing results from compulsory training schemes for the unemployed.

For trainees new to a company or to industrial training past experience can have similar effects. Where past training or education was enjoyable successful motivation is increased. Poor past experiences reduce performance.

The good news is that a high quality programme of training can override all of these factors, especially if they build upon the trainee's existing knowledge. A good training programme would therefore be one where:

- the learner's interest is aroused
- the content is meaningful and relevant
- the trainee has a positive attitude to the delivery system
- there is an expectation of success by both trainer and trainee
- outcomes are clear and attainable.

8.3   MEMORY

There is no point in teaching somebody something unless they are going to remember it. This applies as much to retaining skilled performance as it does to retaining information. In information systems, where we are looking for intelligent performance and width of application by the trainee, the stronger that learning can be embedded the better. We are seeking not just memory but **long-term memory**.

Our brains are large and complex relational storage systems against which the most sophisticated database is only a poor imitation. When we send a message along to the brain it first has to interrogate the information in order to determine in which file it should be stored. For adults, with their range of experience, this can be a simple and rapid process. There are many files available and the brain has no difficulties about sorting. If there is no file for the information to be stored in it may be stored for a short while in a kind of limbo file and then discarded.

We overcome this problem by labelling information as we take it in. The writer, trainer or instructor says to us 'this information is concerned with X', so that the connection is made. The instructor may add an anecdote or example to illustrate the connection, thus making it easier to remember. Lecturers are not getting as far off the point with their rambling stories as you might think!

Learning a new subject or a new area is a problem. We need to set up a completely new filing system for the new information to be collected into. This is a complicated process and takes some time and repeated efforts to complete successfully. Once set up, the new filing system is as effective a receptacle as all the others. Older learners may not have to go through this process as often as others, although they may experience their own problems associated with the large amount of information they already have 'on file'.

What does this description of the memory process mean for the practical trainer? The overriding problem is to put the new information into a form that is easily assimilated by the learner. As long ago as 1917 it was established that people learn information that they judge to be significant and as having meaning quicker and more efficiently than nonsense words. Try an experiment with the three columns of words in Fig. 8.2.

Spend two minutes studying the first column. Then cover it over and wait for one minute. Write down all the words you can remember. Repeat the process with the other two columns in turn and compare your scores. Except for those with a good knowledge of the Cyrillic alphabet your scores will have deteriorated from column one to column three. If you try again tomorrow to reproduce the words, you will find that your memory of columns two and three will have virtually disappeared. You have no long-term memory of them.

Your memory has failed to function because the information and the signs that carry the information have no meaning for you, there are no existing files to which they can be attached. A trainer always needs to ensure that the trainees thoroughly understand the information that is being presented to them. All new information should be presented in simple elemental chunks which are easy to grasp in themselves and are clearly related to what the trainee already knows. Obviously, the actual content of your presentation will vary depending on your audience. A group of people who have never used a database before will require far more elementary information than a group of senior managers who are being trained in using the new upgrade of the company database after having used the previous version for several years.

LIST 1	LIST 2	LIST 3
chalk	tebeshir	тебешир
teacher	ouchitel	учител
bag	chanta	чанта
tree	durvo	дърво
stork	shturkel	щъркел
key	kliutch	ключ
bear	metchka	мечка
book	kniga	книга
green	zeleno	зелено
window	prosorets	прозорец

Fig. 8.2 Memory columns

Once the information has been broken down to the right level it then has to be passed on to the trainees. Best results are gained if they are interested and well motivated. A company director who is paying for your system which will be used directly every day will be highly motivated, a health visitor who is dubious about the benefits of the new system will be less so. It is up to the trainer to motivate the latter enough for learning to take place, probably by pointing out as the training progresses how each new section will aid the health visitor's work. The greater the trainee's attention, the greater the grasp and length of memory will be.

As well as remembering information that fits well into our existing schema we also remember things that we find particularly striking. Students of British history find it difficult to grasp the basis of Henry VII's financial reforms and the operation of 'Morton's Fork' yet display no problem at all once they have moved on to his son, Henry VIII and the complexities of his six wives! Information systems are not quite so amenable to human interest but it is still the trainer's job to try and find striking illustrations which will impress themselves on the trainees' minds. Horror stories, like the installation of computer systems in the London Ambulance Service and the Wessex Health Authority, are useful as cautionary tales for those likely not to follow proper procedures. Examples of cost savings through the application of IT systems are equally effective as long as they were not followed by staff reductions. At the same time, care must be taken that the illustration does not overwhelm the teaching point. King Henry's marital problems may be very interesting but they only have historical significance as marking the beginnings of the reformation in Britain.

As we pointed out in Chapter 1, information theory's insistence on avoiding redundancy of data does not apply to human beings. The more often we hear, read or do something the more likely we are to be able to remember it, particularly when dealing with new or disconnected information. Readers who have tried to learn a foreign language will be familiar with the technique of repeating new words to themselves over and over again or of writing them down five or ten times; even then many of them do not 'stick'. **Repetition** is vitally important for long-term memory; information that we do not use very often needs to be constantly revised at regular intervals. No doubt you will have found this even on a computer system that you are familiar with, that there will be some functions that you need to look up in the manual on the rare occasions that they are used.

Pure repetition is boring and does not always manage to relate new information to old. Doing things in a variety of different ways is much more interesting and is a better method of inter-relating concepts. Modern teaching methods are attempting to build on this fact by insisting on trainees doing exercises rather than being crammed with information. A simple example should suffice. You are introducing trainees to the concept of databases. After a brief introduction you let them loose on the VDU with a pre-prepared database, such as the list of a company's clients and ask them to produce information from it. This might be on the level of finding one client who lives in Dagenham and one who lives in Zennor. Once they can all do that then they might be asked to carry out more complex searches: all clients who live in Hertfordshire or all clients who have a birthday in January.

Gradually we progress to the students setting up their own databases and generating their own queries. Still quite simple, but progressing on step by step and forcing the students to do the same tasks over and over again, almost without noticing. Thus the student is learning by doing and driving home the lesson by repetition of the newly learnt processes.

To sum up, the trainer can encourage long-term memory in trainees by:

- presenting information in graspable chunks
- relating new information to existing knowledge
- gaining and retaining the trainees' interest
- using relevant and striking illustrations
- repeating new information in a variety of forms
- causing repetition by the trainee of new information
- setting up forms of 'learning by doing'.

8.4 WHAT IS TO BE LEARNED?

Any trainer needs to make decisions about the package to be offered. Shortage of time limits what can be done, as does the receptive capacity of the learners. If the company is prepared to pay for three days training for the users of the new package then three days is all you have got. In-house provision may be more generous and more flexible, but again it is not infinite. Hard choices must be made both by the company and by the individual trainer as to the most beneficial content.

8.4.1 Company level

Some companies begin with what is known as a Training Needs Analysis (TNA). This links business needs with manpower planning to produce a smooth and efficient transition from one year to the next. A TNA should ensure that the company does not suddenly have to advertise, say, for six C++ programmers. Even in times of high unemployment they could be left with having to take employees they are unsure about, whilst their existing COBOL programmers could either be left under-employed or made redundant. Good analysis would have spotted the need well in advance, allowing for in-house retraining of existing staff who are known to be reliable and competent.

Frances and Roland Bee set out the link between training and business needs in what they call the 'Training Wheel'. This shows what needs to be done when planning training for a company and how it should be carried forward. They are rightly cynical about the company which merely sets up a range of training courses which it offers staff year after year. The proper approach, they claim, is to look at problems which exist now and in the future, rather than ones that existed in the past.

Let us look at the example of the tiny Hempnall and Marlingford Building Society. Founded in 1843, the society has failed to grow out of its traditionally agricultural area. Turnover is low and it is feeling the squeeze from the larger building societies, several of which wish to take it over. Proud of its independence, the Hempnall and

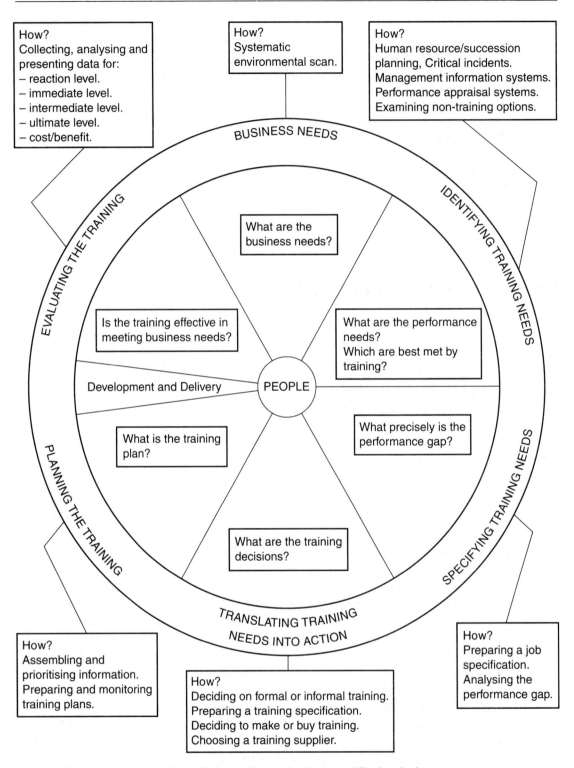

How?
Collecting, analysing and
presenting data for:
– reaction level.
– immediate level.
– intermediate level.
– ultimate level.
– cost/benefit.

How?
Systematic
environmental scan.

How?
Human resource/succession
planning, Critical incidents.
Management information systems.
Performance appraisal systems.
Examining non-training options.

BUSINESS NEEDS

EVALUATING THE TRAINING

IDENTIFYING TRAINING NEEDS

What are the
business needs?

Is the training effective in
meeting business needs?

What are the performance
needs?
Which are best met by
training?

Development and Delivery

PEOPLE

What is the training
plan?

What precisely is the
performance gap?

SPECIFYING TRAINING NEEDS

PLANNING THE TRAINING

What are the training
decisions?

TRANSLATING TRAINING
NEEDS INTO ACTION

How?
Assembling and
prioritising information.
Preparing and monitoring
training plans.

How?
Deciding on formal or informal training.
Preparing a training specification.
Deciding to make or buy training.
Choosing a training supplier.

How?
Preparing a job
specification.
Analysing the
performance gap.

Fig. 8.3 The training wheel (from *Training Needs Analysis and Evaluation*)

Marlingford are resisting. Loans and deposits remain buoyant, mainly due to the loyalty of the local community, who see it as 'their' building society. The managing director knows that this cannot last and has commissioned business consultants to research the society and make recommendations for the future, which have been accepted by the board as a whole, though with some reluctance.

The recommendations are to:

- put the surveying function out to independents
- upgrade the present IT hardware and software
- reduce the number of management
- reduce the number of clerical staff through IT efficiencies
- reduce the number of desk staff through IT efficiencies
- increase amount and range of income by offering financial services.

Forecasts have been produced for manpower needs over the next five years, which are shown in Fig. 8.4.

The net loss of some sixty jobs is not as bad as it might at first appear, since many of them will be accounted for by natural wastage such as retirement and resignations for personal reasons. The bad news is that up to a hundred people may lose their jobs, people who have proved their worth to the society and who it would be sorry to lose. Working from the manpower plan the society can set up a training programme for staff whose current jobs are disappearing but who could easily fit into new posts.

If we look at the newly created DP department we can see that the company needs three people immediately. It is highly unlikely that these could be recruited from existing staff. However, in the following years another twelve people will be required;

TRAINING NEEDS ANALYSIS						
HEMPNALL AND MARLINGFORD BUILDING SOCIETY						
MANPOWER CHANGES OVER NEXT FIVE YEARS						
	Year 1	Year 2	Year 3	Year 4	Year 5	Total
Management	25	22	20	18	15	−10
Data Processing	3	12	15	15	12	9
Clerical	150	140	120	100	80	−70
Desk Staff	40	37	30	25	25	−15
Financial Services	0	5	15	15	20	20
Surveyors	8	4	0	0	0	8
Others	20	20	22	22	22	2

Fig. 8.4 Manpower analysis for Hempnall and Marlingford Building Society

perhaps suitable personnel could be found to re-train. They would have the added advantage of already knowing the society and the sort of data that is required. Some basic training might be offered by the local college with specific training later from the suppliers of the new IT equipment. Government or EEC funds might be sought for the programme.

We should also note that clerical workers will be reduced to 80 and desk staff to 25 *'as a result of efficiencies brought about by IT.'* What this means in practice is that those 105 staff will be required to have a high level of competence in the use of the new equipment and have a greater range of knowledge of the companies services and administrative procedures. They need to be more business literate and more IT literate. The success of the changes in the organisation depend, then, on the training that this group of workers receive and upon its timeliness. Nothing is gained by putting off training until the changes are underway, the workers must be 'ready to run' at the same time as the equipment.

This is one small example of a larger topic, but you can see that the company can use a TNA to forecast what training it will need to undertake, when and to what depth. Not only is training expensive in itself, but the whole future of the company may depend upon its success.

8.4.2 Training room level

Our first question when setting out our training programme is *'what is on the syllabus?'* Standard courses in education such as GCSE, BTEC or RSA will probably have a firm syllabus linked to some sort of assessment process. Where training is in response to an immediate or perceived future need it is up to the trainer, with consultation with concerned parties, to develop a specific syllabus. Even within courses such as BTEC it may not be possible to cover everything in equal depth and choices have to be made.

The process of deciding on syllabus content is easier to explain than it is to do. Write down in the form of headings what there is to be known on the topic, application or program. Now decide what is absolutely essential, what the trainee **must know** in order to be able to progress on to any other topic. Have you any training time left? If you have you progress onto the second area, what the trainee **should know** in order to be said to be competent in the area. Still some time left? Then you can pass onto some of the topics that the student **could know**, those interesting by-paths or the 'bells and whistles' of the system. (See Fig. 8.5.)

Difficult decisions have to be made about what is to be placed in each box and even hardened professionals may disagree. Box edges have to be seen as permeable, depending on the needs and experience of the trainee and the demands of the funding agency. There are also decisions to be made about the balance between:

- Knowledge
- Skills
- Attitudes

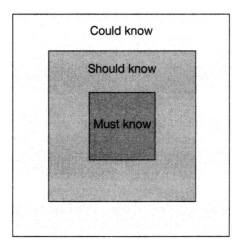

Fig. 8.5 Hierarchy of training content

Knowledge is a difficult word to define, mainly because it operates as a collective noun. That is, it covers a range of processes that have similarities rather than just one simple concept. As far as word processing is concerned, knowledge might cover background information, such as how a computer works, how data is manipulated and the relationship between typewriters and word processors. A certain amount of theory could be involved, such as binary notation or the way that the processor transmits data to the printer. Related applications such as design packages, spreadsheets and DTP might also give a more rounded view of how word processing fits in with other parts of IT.

The idea behind teaching background information and theory is to remove any fear and mystification and to make the learner more independent. If you know how something works you are less likely to be thrown when something goes wrong and you may also have enough knowledge to be able to solve the problem or recover the data. Knowledge also sets the learner on the road to independence, a new file has been opened up in the brain which can be filled up with associated reading or by further courses. In a world where technical advances happen almost daily, particularly in the IS area, workers who can update themselves with the minimum of financial investment by the company are of inestimable benefit.

Skills are what someone can actually do. They can operate the company database, use the invoicing system, program in COBOL. Some skills, usually lower-level ones, can be operated with no knowledge base at all. The clerk who enters information on the sales screen and prints it out may know nothing about the system being used; journalists can quite happily use the company word processing and e-mail system within knowing anything about how they work. Bad training courses concentrate purely on skills to the exclusion of knowledge, failing to empower the trainee towards further development.

We must also be aware that operators can have lesser or greater skills or ones that are developed to a greater level. When setting up syllabuses we need to be particularly careful in specifying what depth of skill level is intended. A simple example is in typing, where trainees are given different certificates for a greater number of consistently error-free operations per minute. Precisely how this is done is set out later.

Attitudes can be taught almost as if by accident. The programming lecturer who always has examples of programs with their associated design structures is telling the students about the way they should proceed; the trainer who treats the trainees politely and courteously is conveying an attitude towards others. In people-based industries such as IS, attitudes to the job, to colleagues and to clients are important. For example, a consultant who consistently alienates his clients does not get repeat business or any word-of-mouth recommendations to new ones. Other attitudes to be encouraged might include the tender handling of hardware and peripherals such as disks or the backing up of work at regular intervals onto alternative storage facilities.

By now you should have sorted out the content of your course, to what depth it will go and have some idea of the relationship within it of knowledge, skills and attitudes. These need to be expressed in a formal manner, partly as a checklist for yourself and partly as a guide for the trainees. Since we are talking about adults who we are trying to get to become autonomous learners we need to be able to clarify for them what they will be able to do by the end of the training period in as much detail as possible.

In order to meet the demands of the National Council for Vocational Qualifications most British vocational education bodies are now expressing their syllabuses in terms of outcomes. That is, in terms of what the student will be able to do once the training has finished. NCVQ specifies that the training that it validates is *'expressed in terms of outcome and will not mention content, modes of delivery or how, where and when competence is developed'*. Thus a trainee could develop skills on a commercial training course, as a result of being instructed by fellow workers or as part of an in-house training scheme, all those areas, in fact, that we mentioned at the beginning of this chapter as being particularly relevant to training in the IS area.

Although most of the training that you are likely to deliver or to undertake yourselves would not fulfil the demands for a full qualification, the NCVQ does allow for a system of Accreditation of Prior Learning. That is, where you can prove that you have already acquired the stated competence you do not have to study it again or be assessed on it. It is useful, therefore, for trainees to be able to produce evidence of precisely what they have learnt to do, and to what level, in order that they can apply at some future date for accreditation.

In order that this can be done more easily it is useful if the training course is presented in the NCVQ manner, a manner which also enables the trainer to lay down clearly those factors which we identified earlier of content, knowledge, skills, attitudes and depth of learning.

Such a syllabus is not immediately understandable if you have not come across one before, so let us unpack it (Fig. 8.6).

Unit of Competence is a standard section heading ('Databases') translated into what the trainees can actually do (*'Uses a database for a range of applications'*). This is rather vague, so it is broken down into its constituent elements (**Elements of Competence**). We now know what a trainee should be able to do, how do we go about

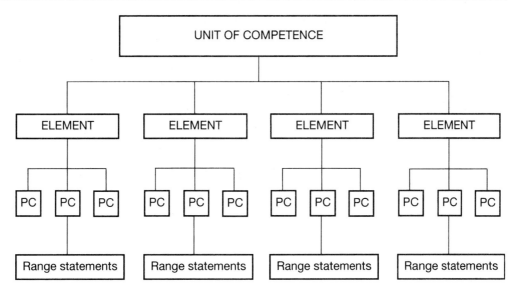

Fig. 8.6 NVQ hierarchy

proving that the trainer can do it? The answer is to lay down carefully the sort of things which count as fulfilling that element. These are known as '**Performance Criteria**', observable actions by the trainee.

This brings us to the problem of level. To illustrate this let us take the example of a hockey player. The player can trap, pass and dribble the ball, thus fulfilling the performance criteria. However, we would not select the player for the national team on this basis. A good club player can do those things but at a certain speed and under a certain amount of pressure. Once the pressure is increased, in a county or district game, for example, the player is no longer in full control. A similar thing happens when a good county player moves into the national squad. There are levels of performance, and these are expressed in NCVQ terms as 'Range Indicators'. Thus we can look at BTEC's range indicators for the same 'core competences' of oral communication and IT (Fig. 8.7).

Within the competence the statement remains the same whatever the level, whilst it is the range statement which indicates that this competence is being fulfilled at an increasingly more difficult stage. The performance indicators and range statements which you specify in your training courses are crucial in establishing the level of the course and the level of any subsequent APL for your trainees. In practice, it is difficult to establish and maintain levels without reference to outside documents such as the syllabuses of the major examining bodies such as the Royal Society of Arts. The example given in Fig. 8.8 of a competency-based course is taken from their Computer Literacy and Information Technology (CLAIT) syllabus.

A useful tool for writing and analysing both performance criteria and range statements is the hierarchy of learning stages commonly known as 'Bloom's Taxonomy' but more properly entitled '*Major Categories in the Cognitive Domain of the Taxonomy of Educational Objectives*'. Bloom's work was utilised extensively in the sev-

LEVEL 2	**LEVEL 3**
Element 2.1 **Take part in discussions with a range of people on routine matters**	**Element 3.1** **Take part in discussions withe a range of people on *a range of matters***

LEVEL 2

Element 2.1
Take part in discussions with a range of people on routine matters

Performance Criteria

1 own contributions are clear and appropriate to the subject matter

2 own contributions are made in a tone and manner suited to the audience

3 contributions from others are listened to attentively

4 own understanding of points made by others is actively checked and confirmed

Range

Subject matters:	routine matters (eg responding to day-to-day enquiries; discussing routine tasks)
Mode:	face to face; using the telephone
Audience:	people familiar with the subject matter as in frequent contact with the individual (eg supervisors, colleagues, peers, tutors);
	people familiar with the subject matter but not in frequent contact with the individual (eg some customer/clients)

LEVEL 3

Element 3.1
Take part in discussions withe a range of people on *a range of matters*

Performance Criteria

1 *own contributions are expressed effectively their purpose and are appropriate to the subject matter*

2 own contributions are made in a tone and manner suited to the audience

3 others are explicitly encouraged to contribute and their contributions listened to attentively

4 *own understanding of points made by others is actively checked and confirmed*

Range

Subject matters:	routine matters (eg responding to day-to-day enquiries; discussing routine tasks);
	complex and non-routine matters (eg solving problems, dealing with sensitive issues)
Mode:	face to face; using the telephone
Audience:	people familiar with the subject matter and in frequent contact with the individual (eg supervisors, colleagues, peers, tutors);
	people familiar with the subject matter but not in frequent contact with the individual (eg some customer/clients);
	people unfamiliar with the subject matter and not in frequent contact with the individual (eg some customer/clients, visitors)

Fig. 8.7 BTEC Levels with performance criteria

Element of certification	Assessment objectives	Performance criteria
2.1 Create database structure and enter data	2.1.1 Initialise database	a System switched on b Program loaded
	2.1.2 Create alphanumeric and numeric fields	a Fields are correctly specified, including at least one which can be sorted alphanumerically b Fields are correctly specified including at least one which can be sorted numerically
	2.1.3 Enter data	a All records are entered, with at least one field encoded as specified b Errors in no more than 3 data items
2.2 Edit data	2.2.1 Edit data	a Specified changes to more than one record are made
	2.2.2 Add a record	a One record is added to the file
	2.2.3 Delete a record	a One record is deleted from the file
2.3 Manipulate data	2.3.1 Sort records alphabetically	a Records are arranged in alphabetical order according to the contents of a specified field
	2.3.2 Sort records numerically	a Records are arranged in numerical order according to the contents of a specified field
	2.3.3 Select records specified by a single criterion	a At least one record is selected according to a specified criterion
	2.3.4 Select records specified by more than one criterion	a At least one record is selected according to at least two specified criteria
	2.3.5 Print specified fields from selected records	a Data from specified fields are printed
2.4 Save database and print contents	2.4.1 Save data	a Database structure and data are stored on disc
	2.4.2 Print data	a All data items are printed in table format
	2.4.3 Exit from system with data secure	a Data is stored on disc b Program is closed down.

Fig. 8.8 RSA computer literacy syllabus

enties as part of a movement which claimed that all outcomes in education must be activities, that is that someone does something that indicates that learning has taken place. You have learned to speak German? Then carry on a conversation with a German shop keeper. You can program in Pascal? Here is an exercise to do, let us have the Pascal program by tomorrow. If you cannot produce any performance then you are not entitled to claim that you know something.

Such a view of learning is easily assimilated to the NCVQ system, especially since Bloom orders his taxonomy in steps of increasing aptitude and complexity. Each step has a collection of verbs associated with it, so that the level of a task can be defined by the sort of verbs used to describe the consequent behaviour. Thus a syllabus might call for a 'Basic knowledge of databases'. Since this is in the domain of knowledge we will describe what the trainee does by using the appropriate verbs: '**states** what is meant by a database; **selects** a database for use; **outlines** uses to which a database may be put.'

An advanced student studying databases might be asked to 'Evaluate a variety of databases for use in various situations'. At this level the student might do things like: '**compare** database X, Y, and Z; **appraise** their usefulness in situations A, B, and C; **judge** their advantages and disadvantages in the various situations; **summarise** the results in a short report.' Students on advanced courses should recognise the sort of verbs that are being used in their own courses and assignments. An abridged version of Bloom's taxonomy appears in Fig. 8.9.

At the very least you should now be in a position to write your course out in such a manner that it will be accepted into an NCVQ framework and will give the trainees a complete idea of what is expected of them by the end of the course. At best you might be able to reassemble your company's training courses in such a way that training levels are established and a pathway becomes clear for full formal accreditation for employees.

8.5   LEARNING METHODS

Now that we know what we are going to teach we need to assess the right way to help the students learn the required knowledge, skills and attitudes. Methods must be found which suit the trainees, the trainers and the material to be learnt. No one teaching method will be right for all occasions and all trainees. Even approaches which have worked for one group will not work with a group which is ostensibly exactly the same. A trainer has to be flexible in approach whilst keeping the objectives of the training firmly in view at all times.

Having said that no one method is right all of the time there is still plenty of research which points the direction in which we might go. Let us take a brief look at what teaching methods we could employ.

8.5.1   Lectures

It has already been noted that lectures are the standard teaching methodology of most western-style universities. They have the advantage of giving large amounts of

Category	Description	Actions
1) Knowledge	Remembering previously learned material e.g. says what a database is for	defines states identifies
2) Comprehension	Grasping the meaning of material Translating material from form to form e.g. producing relevant graph from a choice	explains summarises converts estimates
3) Application	Uses learning in new situations Applying rules, laws and theories e.g. using database after training	computes manipulates modifies solves
4) Analysis	Understanding structures of material Analysis of relationships between parts e.g. database utilisation	relates selects distinguishes
5) Synthesis	Puts parts together to form a new whole Stresses creative behaviour e.g. feasibility study	composes devises summarises creates compiles
6) Evaluation	Judges value of material by criteria Uses relevant value judgements e.g. hardware or software evaluation	appraises justifies compares concludes

Fig. 8.9 Bloom's taxonomy

information to large numbers of students in one place at one time. In particular they are an extremely good way of introducing a new subject or a new area within the subject. When followed by a question-and-answer session this works very well. However, such sessions are less effective the larger the audience.

Lectures have the drawback that they concentrate on teaching rather than learning. Students find it hard to concentrate on them for any length of time (between twenty and fifty-five minutes has been suggested as the optimum) and there is little room for immediate assessment of the students' attention or understanding. On the other hand, older students in particular can regard this as the 'proper' mode of teaching and become restive when faced with other methodologies. Teachers even find that younger students, faced with the demands of imminent examinations demand to be 'taught properly' and given reams of notes.

For the trainer on a tight time schedule the mini-lecture can be used to introduce the topic, to clarify points which trainees have found difficult and to introduce new sections of the course. Twenty minutes at a time for this is quite ample; five or ten minutes will normally be sufficient. In its 1990 survey, *Training* magazine found that 84.1% of all training programmes involved lectures of some sort.

8.5.2 Reading

The correct expression is to 'read for a degree', expressing the emphasis on this mode of learning in traditional universities. Many arts undergraduates have as little as six or seven taught hours each work, the rest of their time supposedly taken up in reading round the subject.

For undergraduates this is an appropriate methodology. They are supposedly mature learners who can be trusted to do the work, make notes on the areas that they do not understand and ask for clarification from lecturers. Books and periodicals are useful in that they can be studied in depth and at leisure, unlike a lecture, and cross-references can be made. For those who have the finances they are also retainable sources of information.

Undergraduates are employed full time in learning, that is their occupation. For trainees or part-time students the task is more difficult. It is unlikely that a trainer will have the time to allow trainees to spend much of it reading through the associated literature. Nor will the trainees, mostly in full time work and with family responsibilities, have much of their own leisure time either to search out the literature or to go through it in detail.

For trainers one solution is to issue short and specific bibliographies in the hope that keen trainees will carry their learning forward. The other is to condense as much information from as many sources as possible and to issue these as course notes either at key points or at the end of the session. These should help in backing up what has been taught and give indications of further areas that could be covered. However, be warned that such detailed preparation is time consuming and may involve difficulties with copyright.

8.5.3 Audio-visual

Much of this area has already been covered in Chapter 4 under 'visual aids'. It is sufficient here to add that good visual aids are an invaluable reinforcer to other methodologies. Their immediacy and impact drive home points far better than mere words. *Training* found videotapes to be the most used methodology, being employed in 88.7% of all courses.

A word of caution on the use of video recordings. Unless specifically made for training purposes, and sometimes even then, video is a slow way of conveying information. Producers of general interest television programmes claim that they can only include up to six main points in one hour of screen time if the audience is going to be able to assimilate it. Six points in one hour does not compare with the information rate available in lectures or in reading. You must consider carefully whether the benefits of using video is worth the time involved, preferring short programmes or excerpts over longer ones.

Like the lecture and reading, videos need to be followed up by the trainer to ensure that the trainees have understood the material and to tease out any difficulties they may have.

8.5.4 Demonstrations

Demonstrations are of the utmost importance in the IS area. They allow trainees to get a preliminary overview of how the system is expected to operate and what they will see on the screen as they go through the various operations. A preliminary demonstration can operate as, or in collaboration with, an introductory lecture. The trainees can see how the whole system is meant to work and what the sub-operations are within it. This provides them with the objectives of this part of the training. Such an overview should not be used on its own, but always as a preparation for breaking learning down into component sub-systems.

Once the students have seen the whole system in operation the trainer can break it down into discrete parts which the trainees can learn to operate. Again, the demonstration is used to illustrate what the outcome of the trainee's own operations should be and what the student will be capable of doing by the end of the session.

A demonstration itself is a carefully structured illustration of what happens in a process. The audience should be able to see clearly what is happening and the demonstrator should 'talk through' events as they happen, adjusting the speed of the demonstration as necessary. A demonstration is *not* the trainer leaning over the shoulder of a trainee, rapidly hitting the keys to cries of 'there, that's how you do it!' The trainee has seen nothing and learnt nothing, except a feeling of being dumber and slower than all the others in the room.

8.5.5 Discussion group

A discussion group might be a formal seminar, a group of people talking over coffee or a formal exercise of some sort. Generally they are used to follow up on information or demonstrations that have been given elsewhere and which have left gaps or puzzlement among the audience. Good trainers know that these are inevitable and use discussions to help identify and eliminate them.

Take as a simple example a company which is demonstrating its new Local Area Network (LAN) system to a group of invited industrialists. The industrialists have seen it working and are quite impressed, though they cannot quite see how it might apply to their own organisation. The company has organised a session where the development manager illustrates how the LAN has been used in a variety of companies and asks the participants on the basis of this how they might use it. New ideas spark off thoughts throughout the group as general ideas are applied to the specific situation.

Such discussions allow new ideas to be aired and objections to be raised about what would and would not work. They have the advantage from a training point of view of forcing the trainees to take on the learned material as their own and to utilise it rather than leaving it lying dormant in their notes. We are at last beginning to get 'hands on' in our training.

The best discussions, such as the one mentioned above, allow the participants to speculate and to solve problems without worrying about loss of status or aggression from the other participants. Bad discussions involve the participants in firing from entrenched positions, the situation that Stephens and Roderick describe as '*an athletic contest of closed mind with closed mind*'. Avoiding such a situation calls for the active intervention of the trainer, not as a participant but as a chairperson and facilitator of the discussion.

A good trainer establishes a relaxed emotional tone to the discussion, probably through a short briefing or introduction. Interventions during its course would consist of the rephrasing of contributions, perhaps in the more formal language of theoretical material that has preceded the discussion, and attempts to involve all participants. Some trainees may need to be prevented from dominating and it is here that the skills of the trainer overlap with the skills of the committee chairperson. Time-keeping is another problem, since this can be a very time-consuming methodology.

Discussions can be allowed to continue for as long as they are fruitful but for no longer. They should be brought to an end before they become boring and counter-productive. Trainers need also to ensure that the participants have enough knowledge and experience in order to be able to take part actively and meaningfully. After all, the main objective is for the pooling of ideas in an active manner, which cannot happen if there are no ideas to pool!

Because of their widespread use in management training for over half a century dis-cussion methodologies are accepted in these circles. Less advanced trainees may be less acquainted with their use and regard them as not 'real learning'. Such problems have to be quickly identified and the advantages of the methodology clearly presented to the trainees. In the IS area resistance may also come from trainees who want to spend all of their time using the computer rather than discussing its applications and limitations.

8.5.6 Practice by doing

The best way to learn and internalise a skill is by doing it. Lectures and book learning are all very well but they do not provide the experience necessary to full application. A good example is that of the Russian revolutionary Lenin, who was exiled to Siberia for his activities. Whilst there he and his wife taught themselves English from a text-book. Later, after their release and arrival in London they found that they could neither understand the language nor be understood. They lacked relevant practice.

Practice by doing is obviously highly important to industrial training, where an operator might be trained in how to use a series of purchase screens, for example. Repetition of the work under controlled conditions ensures that the processes are understood. The user might then be returned to real operations under supervision. The supervisor will be removed once full competence is achieved.

Few operations are simple enough to be undertaken immediately without any form of introduction. Health and safety procedures might be gone over first, as might what to do in an emergency, or backup procedures and frequencies. If using VDUs for your main training it is best to have them switched off for the early introductions to prevent trainees being distracted by them. Remember that the how and the why of systems is as important as the what; interject other forms of learning into your practical sessions in order to reinforce these points.

Another form of practice by doing is what is known as 'programmed learning'. Programmed learning was developed in the fifties by psychologists such as B.F. Skinner (*The Science of Learning and the Art of Teaching*, 1954) on the basis of the theory that learners could be motivated through learning areas by immediate rewards. The idea was to relieve teachers of routine and tedious tasks, such as rote learning, and replace them with individualised work by the learner. Procedures are broken down into the smallest sub-procedures. Once the learner produces the right answer or does the correct action a reward is given ('*Right*', '*Well done*') and the learner goes on to the next one.

In the fifties programmed learning texts tended to be in the form of books, but nowadays the PC provides an excellent vehicle for such methodologies. Trainees can move through computerised programmed learning packages at their own pace, receiving rewards when they get the answers right and automatic references to revision screens when they get them wrong. Computer-based training is examined at greater length later in this chapter.

8.5.7 Immediate application and teaching others

Although there is much to be said for structured exercises and supervised practice nothing beats doing the job for real. This is particularly true of users who are 'needs-driven'; that is they can only motivate themselves to learn a package or application when they have to use it themselves. They have little or no interest in IS for its own sake. Indeed, there are many people who will tell you that they have no knowledge of information technology at all, only then to turn round and operate a complicated washing machine or to book an airline ticket on the on-line booking system. Such users see themselves as assistant chefs or travel agents, not as part of the IS world.

Trainers do not get very far with these trainees with deep explanations of printed circuit boards or neural networks. They have an objective in view and they want it fulfilled quickly and thoroughly. This is not necessarily a bad thing and such an approach also works well on more motivated learners. What it does not do is allow them to proceed further on their own.

Immediate practise allows learners to quickly build up operative skills. For deeper understanding, including the underlying knowledge base, nothing beats having to teach others how to do something. Parents who were useless at mathematics at school suddenly find that they begin to understand it when they have to tutor their own children at home. Workers who have been using a system for some time have their interest aroused by having to teach it to the new recruit and find that they are delving into how the system works rather than merely what it does. Trying to explain how to use a database to your peers highlights both your skills and your deficiencies. Because no-one likes to look stupid in front of others, you quickly rush to rectify your deficiencies before the next session.

The effectiveness of teaching others has been abused in the past, notably by the monitor system of teaching in the nineteenth century, and in our own time by shady training companies. Despite that, it remains the most effective way of getting trainees to remember information and to polish their skills, though its use demands care and professional integrity.

The effectiveness of various methodologies can be summed up as in Fig. 8.10.

No professional trainer would ever use any one of these methodologies in isolation. A typical session might begin with a fifteen minute lecture on the application in question, followed by a demonstration of how it works, a long session of various practice exercises and finishing with a discussion group investigating the various problems encountered during the day. The variety of methodologies are tied to the different sorts of learning involved and take account of the fact that different learners have

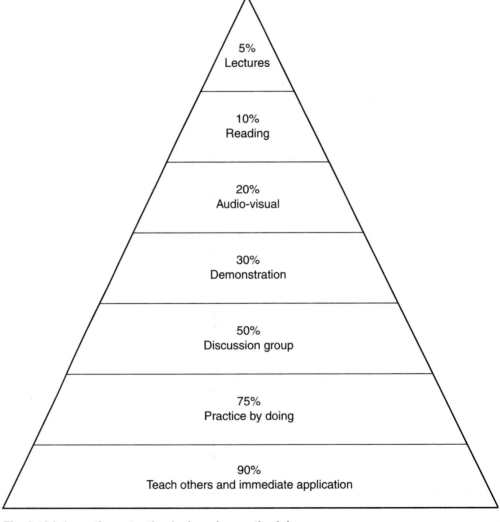

Fig. 8.10 Information retention by learning methodology

preferences for different training methods. No session is allowed to go on beyond the concentration threshold of the trainees.

8.5.8 Computer-based training

Computer Based Training (CBT) is a new and growing field of instruction which builds upon behaviourist psychology and the programmed learning movement of the fifties. In 1980 IBM delivered 5% of its training by use of CBT. In 1990 this had grown to 30% and the company expects it to reach 60% by the year 2000. *Training* magazine's 1990 survey revealed that 38% of all companies with over one hundred employees used CBT. Note, though, that even IBM does not expect classroom teaching to be replaced altogether and that even in the general area of technology training 90% still takes place in classrooms.

As Fig. 8.11 makes clear, there is a plethora of terms used, often interchangeably, to describe the uses of computers in training. We will restrict ourselves in this context to what Phillips refers to as Computer Assisted Instruction (CAI) and Computer Managed Instruction (CMI).

Computer-assisted instruction in its simplest form is used for procedures that demand drills and practise, such as simple language learning. The student is given a prompt and asked for a response. If the response is correct the computer moves on to the next prompt. An incorrect response may bring up an instruction screen which explains why

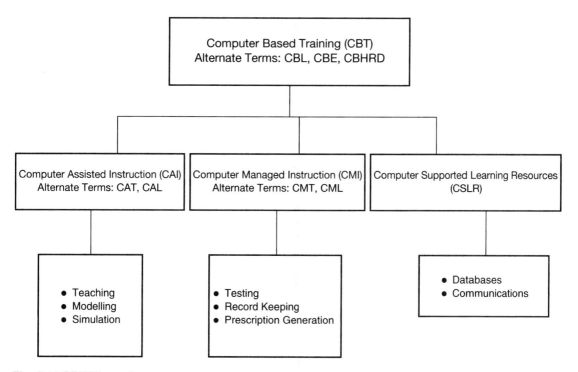

Fig. 8.11 CBT Hierarchy

(from Phillips: *Training Evaluation and Measurement Methods*) the response was incorrect and repeats the rule that is to be applied. Having read this the student can re-enter the main program and attempt the exercise again.

If this sounds similar to your French or Spanish classes at school it is because it mimics what a language teacher does at certain points with the class. Where it differs is in the individualisation of the learning. Each pupil has to respond to each prompt (no chance here of hiding away in the corner in the hope that teacher will not notice!). The response time is also faster. Students will be referred back to revision pages or forward to the next response immediately.

CAI allows for full interaction between the learner and the teaching machine, with continuous input by the learner and at the highest speed possible. Good programs can handle large amounts of material within a sophisticated branching program which can be adjusted for the skill level of the trainee.

More sophisticated uses allow for modelling and simulation of processes which would otherwise be difficult to understand. Demonstrations of what happens with logic gates can be prepared, as can programs which will teach programming itself. Flight simulators and programs which mimic what happens during an emergency at a nuclear power station are highly sophisticated examples of CAI.

These are far more sophisticated than what is thought to have been the first use of a computer in business instruction back in 1956. This was a competitive business simulation where the participants had to make decisions based on known variables and the probable actions of their competitors. An IBM650 was used to work out the results of the decisions made and the success or otherwise of the competing 'companies'.

The introduction of video discs and CD-ROM has widened the scope of CAI even further. With interactive video systems the student is able to get a fuller picture of the situation described. In the case of video whole dramatic case studies can be played out, where such factors as non-verbal communication can be portrayed rather than merely being described or being ignored altogether. In the same way as in simple learning programs, the trainee can be referred back to previous material, but this time it is to a situation or an event which is enacted on the video disc.

Instructors can make use of these systems both for individual and for group instruction, using the disc enactment as a basis for discussion and action by the team. The team's response varies the subsequent response from the computer itself. A final discussion session allows time for reflection and the reinforcement of learning points.

Computer-managed instruction is less exciting but just as important in its application. Analysing trainees' current level of skill and knowledge has always been a difficult and time-consuming process. Good computerised diagnostic programs administer standard tests and mark them almost instantaneously, allowing the trainer instant analysis of groups and individuals. Where regular summative tests are built into CAI programs their results can be obtained far quicker than by human marking.

CMI also covers other areas of learning support, such as computerised learning resources. This might be an educational database, a computerised library catalogue or a newspaper held on CD-ROM.

Advantages of CBT

The proponents of CBT systems point to a whole host of advantages that it has over standard delivery systems. Indeed, there are some situations where any other method would be inconceivable. How would pilots be trained in their responses to emergencies without flight simulators? What else would give the high degree of accuracy that is needed in training within the nuclear power industry? How else can any response at all be elicited from highly disturbed mental patients?

However, most CBT applications are not this pressing or this complex. Their justification is on a more material level of cost and effectiveness.

For large companies spread over a range of sites, perhaps even in different countries, CBT allows them to write and deliver standard training packages untinged by local vagaries. The program can be downloaded centrally to every destination for use by employees. Instead of waiting weeks or months for new updates to arrive they can be entered into the central computer for immediate inclusion into the training programme.

Phillips claims that, once on site, *'Computers, in many applications, are the most cost-effective way to deliver training. There is overwhelming evidence that, under the right circumstances, CBT is considerably more cost-effective than classroom training and has produced learning that is equal to or superior to what classrooms can provide.'*

This cost-effectiveness is achieved in three ways. First, a good CBT program does away with the need for logistical support, such as teaching rooms, ancillary equipment and even trainers themselves. All that has to be supplied is a dedicated machine or perhaps even a series of identifiable programs on a company network.

Second, the users are able to schedule their own time and to pace their own learning. Thus a programmer who is learning a new language will be able to wait until there is a gap in the work-load before signing onto the CAI program instead of having to take time away from work for formal training. The program itself will supply all that is needed in terms of learner interaction, continuous testing and analysis and reinforcement of learning.

Third, computers can save money by compressing time involved in processes. For example, where a chemical reaction may take some hours or even days the computer simulation can reduce this to seconds, allowing the student to move quickly onto the next process rather than having to go away and come back later.

Overall the advantages of CBT are that it:

- allows the delivery of complex and multi-level systems to a varied clientele
- incorporates flexible pacing to fit around the trainee's job demands
- involves trainees in their own career development
- reduces the learning time
- observes participant motivation
- allows exact replication of the target task.

Objections to CBT

The bar to the greater use of programmed learning is the difficulty of writing the packages themselves. Breaking down learning materials to their constituent parts, free of any ambiguity or alternative structures, is of a complexity equivalent to writing an expert system. Once this has been achieved the system may not be commercially viable, given the amount of time that went into its preparation, or have a particularly long shelf life before being superseded by technological innovation in the application to which it refers.

These are valid objections but they do not undermine the use of CBT as such. Instead they point out the importance of undertaking a thorough cost benefit analysis before embarking upon computerisation in the training area. Only then can management make informed decisions on its financial viability.

More problematic is the response of the trainees. Social cohesion is a strong motivating factor in human learning. Certainly entrants to adult education cite contact with other students as being one of the most important factors in their decision. Respondents to the *Training* questionnaire overwhelmingly identified group-based training as their preferred model, irrespective of age, sex, education or occupational area.

Similarly, Richey cites research which indicates widespread anxiety about computers, which again is not predictable by factors such as age, sex and occupation. This seems to imply that CBT could not be used successfully by large numbers of the population. Such a conclusion is, however, far too pessimistic. Experience of the training methodology is only one indicator of success among many, including the trainee's attitude to the job and to training in general, the relationship with the trainer, past experience with the company and the general quality of the training offered.

With any new methodology, be it 'learning by doing', discussion method or role play, the trainees need to be instructed in its use before they become completely happy with it. Thus two parallel activities take place: training in the medium of instruction and training in the intended content. Similarly, trainees need constant feedback on how well they are doing with the computer as well as the training that it supports.

Trainers also need to be aware of what Stephens and Roderick term 'channel fatigue'. That is the overuse of any one particular medium of instruction, leaving the trainee bored and stilted after a while. They suggest that a variety of methodologies are used to prevent this. Certainly there should be plenty of opportunities for discussion offered to new users in particular in order to reduce channel fatigue, to reassure them about their progress and to reassert the social nature of their learning. Even such an enthusiast for CBT as Phillips emphasises that training is not just doing the task that one is training for but also a time of thought, reflection and the acquisition of background knowledge.

Despite these difficulties and the expense involved computerised learning programmes, backed up by information systems on CD-ROM, are beginning to make a significant impact on the educational market. Some companies use them as free-standing entities, quite apart from the training department, for staff to use when they are free to do so. Cost savings which follow from not having to release staff from general duties and the overheads of conventional training courses are certainly attractive. Good on-screen help facilities and manuals are meant to ensure that the trainee is fully autonomous. Sadly such criteria are rarely fulfilled, ensuring the continuing need for human intervention, however slight or fleeting.

8.6 PRESENTING THE TRAINING

8.6.1 Establishing objectives

We are now well on the way towards putting together a relevant, exciting and effective training package. The temptation at this point is to dive straight into the actual delivery, losing sight of the overall objectives At all times the trainer needs to be sure of the reasons for teaching any particular attitude, skill or area of knowledge.

With this in mind, your first job when formally putting your scheme together is to write down its objectives. These should be both practical and attainable within the given constraints. '*To teach all there is to be known about the Access database*' is not an attainable objective for an eight hour training course. Similarly '*To appreciate the applications of information technology in the modern world*' is so woolly as to be meaningless and thus impractical. Moreover, if it means what it says then it is probably a one hundred hour course in itself.

A good check question to use when setting up objectives is to ask '***Can I measure this?***' Is there an outcome that can be objectively assessed? If there is, is the assessment within our capabilities, can we actually administer that assessment? If the answer is '*No*' then we have a meaningless objective, in that we can never be sure whether we have attained it or not. Attitude change and formation are particularly difficult areas in this respect.

Let us return to our Access database and prepare some more meaningful objectives for our eight hour course. Note that the fulfilment of objectives may run parallel to one another rather than be consecutive; we do not have to finish one before embarking on another. Indeed, some objectives may be a portmanteau, containing a clutch of skills demonstrated in reaching other objectives. Some may be obtained quickly, others may be more difficult to reach. Thus we cannot be so simplistic as to say '*I have eight one-hour sessions, therefore I will have eight objectives.*' The objectives must come first, your delivery system flows out of them. Our objectives might look something like this:

1. *Know how the database has been/is/will be used within the company/department.*
2. *Be able to access the database.*
3. *Enter data accurately on prepared screens.*
4. *Prepare and print reports.*
5. *Use existing queries.*
6. *Construct own queries.*

Five of these items are measurable 'doing' objectives for which we can set up easy criteria for assessment. The sixth, '*Know how the database will be used within the department*', might form the introductory session but perhaps will only be fully assessed when trainees begin to construct their own queries and reports. Which ones they produce will indicate to the trainer whether or not the trainee has understood how the database will be operated in practise. This is a case of two or more objectives running parallel to one another.

The example above assumes a one-day course of eight hours duration which only has overall objectives for the full course. Other trainers could find themselves delivering the same course over eight one-hour sessions. In this case, objectives also need to be written for each session, in order that training can be tightly focused. A good principle in such cases is to include as an objective '*Revise material from previous session*' since we have already seen in section 8.3 that revision and reiteration of information is an invaluable aid to memory. Good session objectives should be **practical**, **useful**, **definite** and **limited**.

Our objectives for the second session of our eight might be something like this:

1. *Give a resumé of uses of Access within the department.*
2. *Access the database unaided.*
3. *Locate the 'Sales order' screen.*
4. *Correctly enter data on this screen.*
5. *Locate the 'Cancel sale' screen.*
6. *Correctly enter data on this screen.*

Notice that this session does not just deal with our second main objective but also moves on to cover aspects of the third and revision opportunities for material covered in the first session.

This is a fairly simple example in that we have assumed that the trainees are all from the same company, all have some idea of what a database is and have a degree of IT skills. There are occasions when such assumptions cannot be made. Theoretically the trainer should have all available information about all trainees, their past experience with the system and so on, before the training begins in order to settle in advance what they might be assumed to know. Such is not always the case and the trainer needs to make a quick preliminary assessment before the session begins.

On an extensive course this assessment may take the form of a formal questionnaire delivered to the trainees at the beginning of the first session and which the trainer can scan over the coffee break. For short courses a series of quick general questions along the lines of '*Is there anyone here who does not have a system sign-on? Anyone who is not using our existing company database?*' will establish the base level. This might be turned into an 'icebreaker' where each trainee in turn is asked to give name, department and relevant experience.

8.6.2   Content of training

Section 8.4 has already laid out how we establish the content of our course by '*Must know, should know, could know*'. Any individual session works on precisely the same lines. There is content which is essential and content which is desirable. The two should not be confused. What is to be known and what is to be done should be clearly laid out for each session in their order of importance.

Within the information systems world a large amount of training is based around what might be termed 'operations', processes and applications which the trainee has to learn. Your training content should clearly set out what operations are to be learnt

and why. A trainee who is being taught desk top publishing as part of word processing, for example, needs the 'why' in order to establish motivation for the task.
Sequencing of operations needs to be established in order to increase the effectiveness
of the training. Thus it makes sense to teach both word processing packages and
design packages before progressing to desk top publishing. Similarly, there may be
sub-operations that need to be ordered within a package or operation

Where an operation can be broken down into such sub-sections, each one can be
practised in turn in order to gain familiarity with them before they are put together in
one overall operation. Demonstrations are invaluable at this point, both for the overall operation and for the sub-sections within it. The trainer's presentation could look
something like Fig. 8.12.

During the demonstration it is important to keep up a commentary on what is done
and why, with a particular emphasis on the key points and areas of difficulty. Areas of
inaccuracy in the manual should also be included.

The important factor here is that the instructor should progress in a systematic
manner and that the system should be transparent to the trainees. This increases both
motivation in the students and their confidence in their instructor; they know that
they will achieve valuable results by the end of the session.

8.6.3   Timing

Given that we have established syllabus, objectives and time constraints, timing would
appear to be a simple matter. In fact it is perhaps the most difficult training skill to
master since it combines both advanced planning and *'thinking on your feet'*. Even
experienced trainers can get their timing wrong and have to fill in with extra material
or cut out material that they had planned to cover. Inexperienced trainers can find
that they have covered the whole syllabus in just one short session.

Because we are working with people we should not expect training sessions to be
exactly the same. Examples that hit the mark with one group can seem irrelevant to
the next; where one group struggles for hours with an operation another parallel
group can catch on to it in minutes. Where delivery is purely in the form of a lecture
this is not a problem, but activity-based training, such as most in the information systems area, cannot evade such difficulties.

Trainer	Trainee
1. Demonstrates whole operation	
2. Demonstrates sub-section A	Practises sub-section A
3. Demonstrates sub-section B	Practises sub-section B
4. Demonstrates whole operation	Practises whole operation.

Fig. 8.12 Structuring demonstrations

The inexperienced trainer who delivers the whole syllabus in one hour has often been seduced by the emphasis on teaching rather than learning. Material has been taught, or presented to the trainees, but it has not been learnt. Learning depends on physical and mental activity on the part of the learner, building from their existing knowledge and motivation. With this in mind they will be expected to move from

what is known	**to**	what is unknown		
what is simple	**to**	what is complex		
what is concrete	**to**	what is abstract		
what is particular	**to**	what is general		
observation	**to**	reasoning		
the whole	**to**	constituent parts	**to**	the whole

All of these transformations demand time and practise on behalf of the trainee, perhaps with minimal involvement from the trainer. One of the key questions to be answered when preparing a session is '*What are the trainees going to do?*' Within an operations context it is clear that practice is called for most of the time, with demonstrations and explanations filling out the rest. A rough guide is shown in Fig. 8.13.

The heavy emphasis on activity by the trainees reduces the pressure on the trainer to deliver to a strict schedule and enables individual tuition to be given where necessary. Ideally, the group should progress to the next activity only when everyone has demonstrated their competence in the present one. This entails the trainer having a range of activities or exercises with which to occupy the faster members of the group whilst the others reach the required level. Boredom among the sharper members of the group can be as destructive as failure among the slower learners. Keeping everyone active makes differences less obvious and stops the devil making work for idle hands.

Trainers still have to keep contingency plans to deal with mis-timings that occur. These might include having the material for the next session already prepared or a revision exercise for earlier material. Progression to the next level or topic is depen-

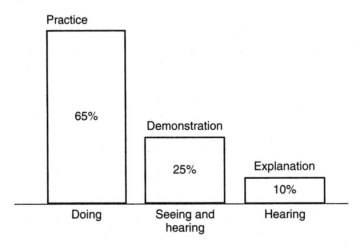

Fig. 8.13 Use of time

dant on achieving competence in the current one, so that some opportunities for assessment need to be built in at each stage of the programme. These will be dealt with later in this chapter.

A variety of learning methods is important to prevent the sessions becoming stale and repetitive, but they do present difficulties when it comes to timing. Discussion groups can be notoriously difficult to forecast in terms of participation and time. As you gain experience you will be able to predict a general time range. Be prepared to cut them short if little of value is coming out of them or allow them to continue when appropriate. Case studies and simulations can be timed by giving the participants strict time limits. Remember to allow a good amount of time for a 'debriefing' session at the end to allow the trainees to discuss the progress of the exercise and its relevance to the objectives of the training.

Visual aids can contain their own timing factors: the length of a video or film is known in advance. Again, discussion or activity should be presumed to flow from them and this should be worked into your timetable.

With experience you will learn how much can be learnt and at what pace, so that your planning becomes looser and less precise. Until that time, remember that it is the trainees who do the learning and their activity should take up the majority of the time available. When in doubt during a session allow extra time for trainee activities rather than for trainer input. Always have a contingency plan and extra material available but do not progress to the next topic, whatever the demands of the trainees, until you are confident that the present one has been mastered by all. Finally, do not be ruled by the clock. If your trainees have achieved their targets and finished ahead of time, to have a session finish early might be a good motivator. If trainees want or need some extra time at the end it is rude and unprofessional to rush off.

8.6.4 Stage management

Armed with objectives and a clear plan of action you now enter the training room for the first time. You probably have little influence over its layout, especially if it is well supplied with workstations. If you can move furniture do so in such a way that all trainees can see both you and one another, in order to maximise interaction and produce a sense of collective purpose. Rows of desks can be counter-productive, inducing a feeling of being back at school, an experience that some of your trainees might not have enjoyed.

Your first task begins before you even open your mouth. That is, to move and act with confidence. This is your show and you are in control, you should act accordingly without being officious. Remember that if anything goes wrong you will be held responsible. At some point you intend to hand over a large amount of control to the trainees but it always remains yours to give out and to demand back if the situation demands it. We are talking here of the sort of control that the skipper of a small boat exercises over the temporary volunteer crew. For the duration of the voyage they have left behind all status and hierarchy and agreed that the skipper is in charge so that they may both enjoy the trip and come safe to land again. Like that skipper you must be firm without being officious, in control without being a martinet.

Begin by introducing yourself and giving some idea of your background. A full c.v. is unnecessary, a couple of sentences along the following lines will do: '*Good morning. My name is Jack Irwin. For many years I was a data processing manager with ICI and I now work for Healthcare Programs Ltd. preparing computer programs for use in the health service.*' Having outlined his professional credentials Mr. Irwin is no doubt now going on to show us how his company's new program works.

One of the reasons for producing objectives before you start is in order to give the trainees an idea of their destination and to help motivate them towards it. Thus they need to be presented to them right at the beginning of the programme. Some trainers prepare a flip chart in advance with the overall objectives and the objectives for each individual phase of the programme written on it. This is an excellent way of keeping everyone firmly 'on track' at all times.

Above all, you must be the one who sticks to the objectives. You should not wander off the path too much or explore all those interesting ('could know') byways. To do so frustrates your audience as well as interfering with your time schedule. On the other hand, you should not be too inflexible. If a real problem arises which you had not considered in your planning then you must deal with it. Some trainees may have questions of procedure that need to be dealt with: '*In my department we have to issue a goods delivered note as well as a sales invoice. How does this new system deal with that?*' Do not be afraid of not covering all the material or all the objectives you had planned to cover. As long as you have proceeded in a professional manner and dealt with their concerns your trainees will be quite happy and time can be made up in later sessions.

Trainees have a right to expect that the trainer is some sort of expert in the subject area, whether it be a particular bespoke program for the company or the whole area of expert systems. Sadly this is sometimes not the case. People go sick and their work has to be taken on by others; a consultant may be desperate for any income at all; the salesman may be sent out on the road with inadequate preparation. Such inadequate background always shows. Delivery is hesitant, demonstrations are halting and erratic, training methods are ill thought out. Wherever possible training should be postponed rather than left to such vagaries.

On the other hand we have the trainer who goes to the opposite extreme, showing off extensive knowledge and stressing superiority over the audience. We may be given a dazzling performance which includes a wealth of technical detail but which leaves the trainees floundering behind. Learning has not taken place.

A similar problem is the talkative veteran who entertains trainees with long stories about how he sorted out the mainframe for British Aerospace or found a new application for digital mapping in the offshore oil industry. All very interesting, but the trainees should be getting on and doing things themselves rather than listening to reminiscences of dubious relevance.

The good trainer is somewhere between these extremes. The knowledge is obviously there, unostentatious in the background. Illustrations of its practical use are given without being aimed at massaging the trainer's ego or belittling the listeners. There is no attempt to fudge an issue. Since no-one can be expected to know everything, '*I don't know the answer to that, I'll look it up and come back to you*' is a perfectly adequate response.

As well as carefully preparing the class, the trainer should take pains to ensure that the trainees are able to follow the flow of ideas. To this end all new technical terms should be explained and all new concepts clearly explained. Questioning is the quickest method of checking that information has been received. As in interviewing, the questions should be of the right type. A closed question such as '*has anybody used this application before*' is a good way of gaining preliminary information. The typical school enquiry of '*do you all understand that?*' is not. The latter assumes that the trainees are reflective enough to know whether they understand it or not and that they are brave enough to publicly admit their ignorance.

Instead, use precise questions such as '*can you give me an example of how this idea might be used in our company?*' or '*what do we do when presented with this error message?*' Wherever possible these should be tied to key teaching points that you have already identified, ones which must be understood as preconditions for continuing to the next topic. Where trainees show misunderstanding or incomprehension then you will need to dispel that before moving on. Do not just ask the quicker or more voluble students, since you need to make sure that everyone understands.

Positive responses should be rewarded verbally: '*well done, that is quite difficult to grasp and you seem to have fully understood it.*' Slower or less enthusiastic students can be brought along by aiming questions at them, not in order to catch them out but to maintain their attention. Allowing them to field the easier questions improves their self-esteem and acts as a reward mechanism even when their achievements are not as great as the rest of the group. Questions must never be used as an opportunity to inflict public humiliation on a trainee; it is demotivating and an abuse of power on behalf of the trainer.

There are times when training resembles a formal oral presentation. Material is prepared well in advance, uses a range of visual aids and is stimulating and interesting. However, there are important differences. The presenter is attempting to sell something, be it a system or a solution. The trainer is attempting to hand over to the trainee at the earliest opportunity, to empower the trainee to take control. Whilst the trainer is using a range of personal skills to motivate and enlighten, the force of personality should not dazzle the audience. There is a temptation for teachers of all sorts to try to become great performers, what the principal of one London college referred to as 'Mr Charisma'. Mr Charisma entertains and excites the audience who have merely to sit back and enjoy themselves. At the end of the session, however, they find that they have learnt little and can do little. This is as bad as the stodgy, dull monotonous type who sends the whole audience to sleep.

As in oral presentations the trainer's manner is important in sending messages to the audience. A good trainer is always enthusiastic in manner, even if going through the material for the hundredth time. Especially in a fast-moving technological area such as information systems it is important to be open to new ideas and developments. On the other hand, information systems are not the end of the world, there are thousands of things that are more important and valuable, especially for users who regard computers as a tool rather than an end in themselves. Present yourself as an expert but not as a fanatic.

One of the most tiring things about training is that you are on show all of the time, often during coffee breaks and meal breaks as well. You cannot just shut the office door or relax in the car on the way to your next appointment; you are constantly available. You need to deal with this with equanimity, keeping your impatience or nervousness under control. Mannerisms can re-surface towards the end of the day and you have to stay alert in order to keep them from being noticed.

At the other end of the spectrum is the danger of assuming too much of a professional persona. We all put on some sort of a show when performing in public. What we do not want is one than appears dishonest and manipulative as this will put off trainees who feel that we cannot be trusted. 'Smooth', 'oily', 'smarmy' and 'slick' are the sort of words used to describe this sort of person.

Finally, the trainer needs to control the situation in a professional and moral manner. This means not playing favourites whilst at the same time realising that people are different. Fast learners need to be excited and encouraged, slow learners need to be helped and supported. Remember that we are aiming for all our trainees to achieve all the objectives, not for a few to achieve excellence. Control comes about through the trainees' immersion in the task rather than the exercise of power by the trainer through dominance and sarcasm, however tempting that may be.

To sum up, a good trainer:

- is purposeful
- knows the subject
- is painstaking
- has a good dramatic sense
- shows enthusiasm
- has a pleasing manner
- can control the training situation.

8.6.5 Assessment

Assessment is a very broad term. Examinations and formal tests are sub-sets of assessment, but so are questions asked in class and informal checks on what is on the VDU. Trainers need to use assessment but it must be appropriate to the topic, the situation and to the trainees. Within a training environment the use of formal pencil and paper tests and examinations are very rare indeed.

For courses that emphasise outcomes rather than content, assessment is an integral part of the training process. It is not something to be bolted on to the course at the end; rather it has to be considered when planning delivery and built in at regular intervals. Even when certification is not an issue we need assessment in order to answer the one burning question: '**has learning taken place?**' We need to assure ourselves that we have achieved our objectives, whatever they might be, and that we can proceed with confidence to the next module of training.

On the other hand we might receive negative confirmation, that learning has not, in fact, taken place. At this point we need to invoke remedial procedures, to identify which are the particular areas of difficulty or deficit and to take steps to remedy the situation. Trainees may have trouble identifying the correct icons to use or the right boxes in which to insert data. In this case the provision of a list of icons or a screen dump with a description of the appropriate data inserted in various boxes would be appropriate. Remember that we are not trying to catch the student out, we are trying to make them able to perform a task by whatever means are available.

Assessment also gives us feedback on how well we have taught. In general, trainees of roughly similar backgrounds should produce roughly similar results. If gross variations occur then variables such as teaching methodologies and trainer competence need to be examined. Good trainers are constantly examining and refining their practise in the light of assessment and feedback from their trainees. Where particular areas of content show consistently poor results these also have to be examined for their appropriateness to the trainees concerned and the delivery method analysed.

For the trainees, assessment confirms that learning has taken place along the lines that the trainer outlined at the beginning of the session. It also identifies areas of weakness or where further study is appropriate. In good training programmes both trainee and trainer work together once an area of difficulty has been identified. This means that major assessments in particular have to be very clear in their outcomes in order to aid the trainee. '*Very good, 65%*' only tells the trainee that the majority of the outcomes have been achieved, but not which outcomes or why the other areas were not up to scratch. In the same way that objectives need to be precise the measurement and reporting on their achievement need to be equally so. We will touch on this again later when we consider the role of feedback in training.

So far we have dealt with the whole range of assessment, from check questions in the training room through to formal tests. We will now deal purely with the more formal end of testing, the sort that might be used at the end of a company induction course or on an adult training scheme.

The Business and Technology Education Council identify three major factors in effective assessment:

- Validity
- Reliability
- Utility

Validity means that an assessment measures those things that it claims to measure. Particularly at lower levels care needs to be exercised that the candidate is being assessed on a task rather than on a knowledge of the language. For example: '*Use the design package to draw a rhombus on the screen*' depends on the candidate knowing what a rhombus is. Lack of this knowledge means that competence cannot be shown in using the design package. Thus we can re-design the question paper to have a drawing of a rhombus with the instruction: '*Use the design package to draw the following figure on the screen.*'

Reliability means that the tests that you use give similar results under similar conditions. In the case of a public examination, a question or assignment would produce the same results in London, Edinburgh or Cardiff. This is the same type of criterion that is applied to scientific experiments, that they are replicable at different times and places.

Utility means that the assessment is **convenient, flexible** and **cost-effective**. We may wish to test our students' ability to write a fully bespoke database that could be used by a major mail order company. In theory the best way to do this would be to get them to actually write the database for the company, complete with proper systems analysis techniques and structured programming methodologies. In practise such an assignment would be near impossible to complete. Quite apart from the accessibility of the requisite number of mail order companies of similar size there is the amount of time that would be required for the students to complete the work. This is time that has to be taken from the course as a whole.

Even if the task were completed the amount of time needed for marking and checking against outcomes would be prohibitive. For the trainer the exercise would not be convenient (it is nearly impossible to set up), is not flexible (it involves the same task in a variety of similar settings) and is not cost-effective either in terms of the time spent by the trainees in doing it or of the assessor's time spent marking it.

In practice the trainer might set up a case study in which the main features of the company are given. The students would use these to produce systems analysis documentation from which they would generate a data structure for their database. Further exercises in structuring and writing the program would follow. This sort of assessment can be constructed simply within the training environment, can be altered at will and is relatively cheap to administer and mark.

Although validity, reliability and utility should be present in all assessments it is obvious that there is a balancing act to be performed between them. The most valid assessments may be too expensive to initiate; the most reliable may not give us an overview of a sufficient number of outcomes; the most cost-effective could be of dubious reliability. Trainers who have built in assessment from the start of their training can obviate most of these problems before they arise.

BTEC lists a series of assessment strategies. This list is by no means exhaustive but provides a useful starting point for an outline assessment plan:

- Case studies
- Role play
- Oral presentations
- Reports
- Short answer and structured questions
- Practical exercises
- Performance at work.

Case studies and role play are familiar methodologies particularly in higher education and management training. The fact that we have already mentioned them in the context of learning methods emphasises the integration of learning and assessment in a properly ordered training programme. They are particularly valuable for judging outcomes at the upper end of Bloom's taxonomy, although the current trend is for them to be used increasingly at all levels.

Both case studies and role play exercises are quite difficult and time-consuming to write. This disadvantage is obviated by the fun factor for both trainer and trainee.

Trainers can get quite excited by the writing of case studies and trainees certainly find them more interesting than formal examinations. Problems arise over the question of validity and care should be taken to match up the tasks which trainees are asked to undertake to the course outcomes.

Oral presentations and reports are often used together for more extensive pieces of work or at the end of a substantial case study. In themselves they can be simulations of commercial practise itself as well as carriers of other skills. They have the advantage of being cheap and easy to administer but great care must be exercised in preparing mark sheets and check lists in order to ensure that results are reliable. Extensive feedback to trainees on their attainment is particularly important in this case, where it is more difficult for individual skills and outcomes to be isolated.

Short answer and structured questions are useful in testing a trainee's grasp of the underlying knowledge base. We know that the trainee can use the package, we also wish to ensure that there is understanding of what is going on beneath the surface, of how and where the data is being held and processed. A series of brief questions will act as a valuable check for both trainer and trainee and can be used either as part of a 'reinforcement' at the end of one session or as revision at the beginning of the next. Quickly running through the answers provides quick and effective feedback.

Practical exercises have the highest validity of all methods in skill-based situations. They test what the trainee can do in the light of the course objectives and outcomes. No simulation is involved and results can be immediate. If the trainee can be involved in self-assessment so much the better. Within information systems practical exercises have decreasing utility as the size of the training group increases. Looking at screen entries with a couple of trainees, for example, is a quick and simple process. Feedback can be quick and progression to the next task immediate. Once the group size rises response time by the trainer declines towards the unacceptable.

In this situation tasks may become larger, filling the available time, and the results printed out for later scrutiny. This increases the time spent on the exercise by the trainer and puts pressure on printing facilities. Despite these drawbacks practical exercises should always be the primary preferred mode of assessment in the training environment since they involve the direct testing of the desired physical outcome.

Performance at work has been left until last as this involves far-reaching changes in the accreditation of workers. The British government set up the NCVQ as a response to a perceived lack of vocational training and the low level of qualified workers in Britain compared to other European countries. Part of NCVQ's analysis was that British workers were not necessarily less skilful nor less well trained but they had not received formal credit for the skills and training that they had.

A system therefore had to be found to identify workers' skills and to give accreditation where appropriate. To this end National Vocational Qualifications (NVQs) were set up using task outcomes as the criteria for judgement. In simple terms, the worker demonstrates to an assessor the ability to perform a given task in the correct manner. Usually this has to be done a minimum of three times in order to show that the original performance was not just a fluke. A profile is built up of the worker's competencies and training schemes initiated to fill in any gaps. A completed profile leads to the award of an appropriate qualification.

Whatever the criticism of such a system in terms of the lack of understanding of the underlying knowledge base there is no doubt of its utility in assessing workers' range of skills. In the information systems area, where many users have had little or no formal training, an NVQ-based system is an important tool in analysing a company's training needs in the sector. Independent trainers will be required by the trainees themselves to issue some sort of accreditation document which will become part of the worker's training portfolio.

Nor will it just be professional trainers who will be required to carry out assessment. Supervisors, training officers and employers can all act as assessors, although their assessment will be moderated by external agencies. The whole of a worker's activity thus becomes susceptible to testing for accreditation purposes, including observed performance at various tasks, reports, drawings, printouts and programs. Assessors will use checklists to record skills and build up a full map of performance. Formerly, where an employee could only receive a qualification by going back to college either full time or part time, now qualifications can actually be gained in part or in their entirety in the workplace.

In the past there have been arguments about the role of assessment in education and training. Educationalists have been worried about the '*assessment tail wagging the teaching dog*', with teaching being geared to the test at the end rather than to the needs of the students. To make a distinction between training and its assessment is to create a false dichotomy since they are two parts of a unitary whole. As long as assessment is built in to training programmes from the beginning and related to the objectives and outcomes of that programme then there is no conflict between the two. Moreover, if the trainer sets up a series of learning methodologies which integrate learning with assessment the result will be a seamless web of teaching, learning and assessment.

8.6.6 Feedback

Feedback is a subset of assessment. Within courses related to the NCVQ feedback is regarded as being an essential part of the assessment process, in that the assessor would be expected to give the trainee a full oral and written report of how the assessment went and to ask the trainees their own views on their performance. These reports can be quite substantial and mark a step forward from the old style '*B+, very good*', or '*67%, should try harder*'. Full feedback identifies precisely where the trainee was weak and what steps need to be taken to rectify them. In other words, the trainee knows where the 23% of the course is located that was missed during the assessment.

Our culture tends to regard criticism as being purely negative, whereas it is positive feedback which increases the trainee's sense of self-worth and achievement and provides motivation for continued learning. When giving feedback, therefore, emphasise the positive, those things that the trainee can do and the growth in attitudes that have been displayed. Negative feedback should only have a minor role.

Most commercial training courses involve comments by the participants on the progress of the course and its efficacy. If you are delivering a training course in industry, for the users of your new database, for example, you will be expected to present your trainees with a properly laid out questionnaire on which they can comment on your performance and on the amount that they have learned. Do not regard this as a chore or as something to be dreaded. Most people are only too happy to be as helpful as possible and to take part in *your* learning. Their responses will help you to improve your practise and by so doing increase the number of satisfied customers who will ask for your services again and again.

8.7 APPLICATIONS: TRAINING IN PROGRESS

To finish off this chapter, here are some training courses which have been run in varying circumstances with a range of trainees. You will see that the trainers used a range of approaches and methodologies adapted to the needs of their trainees. Notice that all of the trainers have carefully mapped out what they are going to teach their trainees, in what order and over what time scale. This is traditionally referred to as a 'lesson plan' and is invaluable for all trainers but especially so for those with little or no experience. There is no agreed method of setting out a lesson plan but Fig. 8.14 gives some idea of what might typically be included.

8.7.1 Some naive users

Julie was asked to conduct an 'Introduction to Computing' course with a group of people who claimed that they *knew absolutely nothing about computers*. She decided that this was an unpromising beginning, suggesting as it did a lack of enthusiasm among her client group as well as probably being an underestimation of their own knowledge and abilities.

In order to increase the group's confidence she devised a small exercise which would also allow the individuals to begin to get to know one another.

Topic:	Introduction to Computers
Number of students	18
Suggested time span	15 minutes (not crucial)
Methodology:	Discussion groups
	Introduction 2 minutes
	what we will be doing
	form five groups
	allocate one question per group
	take questions on methodology (not on the questions)

LESSON PLAN

DATE	TIME	SUBJECT	COURSE
NO. OF STUDENTS	AGE RANGE	TOPIC	

ASSUMED RELEVANT KNOWLEDGE

OBJECTIVES

TIME	JUSTIFICATION	OBJ NOS	LEARNING ACTIVITIES	LINKS WITH RELATED SUBJECTS

EVALUATION TECHNIQUES

EQUIPMENT, MATERIALS, ETC

Fig. 8.14 Example lesson plan format

Questions:
1. What is the difference between computer hardware and software?
2. What is a computer program?
3. Why do companies use computers?
4. What is the essential difference between a computer and a calculator?
5. Would Santa Claus like a computer for Christmas?

Group discussion 5 minutes
Plenary and feedback of ideas 5 minutes

Summary 3 minutes. Connecting ideas to form a coherent whole.

As expected the group discovered that they were not as ignorant of computing as they thought they were. The plenary took longer than anticipated as general discussions developed around such topics as whether Santa Claus would be able to fit all his requests onto a database and what this meant in terms of computer size.

By using this exercise Julie was able to reassure her group and move easily onto the next session, a description of the parts of a PC and the peripherals that are available.

8.7.2 Abandoning the typewriter

Neil was employed on a short-term contract by an NHS Trust to familiarise existing employees with computer applications. Following a survey of users' needs Neil discovered that a large number of people still used manual typewriters and would soon be required to change to the new word processing package. He also realised that his short-term contract meant that he would not have much time in which to carry out the training. Some trainees would have as little as three hours, covering both word processing and spreadsheets. Nor would the new computerised system necessarily be available for their use immediately and follow-up training would be needed when it did become available.

Given these considerations he developed a training course which could be undertaken by users who were familiar with the keyboard but not with word processing. The course had to be suitable for use in the training room with indeterminate numbers of trainees or for use by trainees working on their own.

His solution was to set up an example text which was imported into the trainees' area and then set them a series of simple exercises, with explanatory procedures, that they could work through. See **pages 298–301**.

8.7.3 Introducing databases

The final example is from a straightforward classroom situation. The trainer's task was to introduce students to a database package with which they were not familiar. Four lessons of two hours duration each were allowed for this. Anita is a very organised person who likes to know precisely what she is doing and where she is going and her carefully timed structure reflects this. Notice that she assesses the students at each stage of the learning, either by asking them questions or by asking them to perform the appropriate action. At the end of the course she brought all of the work together in a final assignment where the students had to demonstrate all of the skills that they had learned over the four weeks of the course. See **pages 302–303**.

---

1 MID ANGLIA COMMUNITY HEALTH TRUST
Computer Training

WORD-PROCESSING WITH WORD 6.0

1.1 Enter and load text	**Method**
1.1.1 Load application	Double-click on Word icon
1.1.2 Enter text	Type in the provided text
1.1.3 Save file and close current document	Click on disc icon
	OR Select **S**ave from **F**ile menu Give file appropriate name (max. 8 letters)
	Click on **OK**
	OR Press Enter
	Select **C**lose from **F**ile menu
1.1.4 Retrieve and load file	Click on **O**pen icon 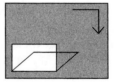
	OR Select **O**pen from **F**ile menu
	Click on selected file
	Click on OK
	OR Press Enter

Fig. 8.15 Neil Scarlett's WORD 6.0 course

2 MID ANGLIA COMMUNITY HEALTH TRUST
Computer Training

WORD-PROCESSING WITH WORD 6.0

1.2 Edit text	**Method**
1.2.1 Insert text	Position cursor at appropriate position using mouse,
Insert the words 'AT THE BRIGHTON METROPOLE HOTEL' after the title	**OR** use cursor keys
1.2.2 Delete text	Position cursor at appropriate position using mouse, **OR** cursor keys. Press and hold left mouse button and drag mouse until the selected text is highlighted.
Harvey Thomas can no longer take part. Please delete this paragraph	Let go of mouse button Select **C**lear from **F**ile menu **OR** use backspace key 
1.2.3 Move text	Position cursor at appropriate position using mouse, **OR** cursor keys. Press and hold left mouse button and drag mouse until the selected text is highlighted.
The order of speakers has changed. Move the paragraph concerning Dr. Ron Berwick to after Professor Sir David Wetherall.	Select Cut icon **OR** select **C**ut from **F**ile menu Place cursor at new position Select Paste icon **OR** select **P**aste from **F**ile menu
1.2.4 Replace words	Select **R**eplace from the **E**dit menu
Replace NHS with the words National Health Service.	Type in selection for **F**ind **W**hat Type in selection for **R**eplace **W**ith Select **S**earch (All, Up or Down) Press Enter

Fig. 8.15 Neil Scarlett's WORD 6.0 course (continued)

3 MID ANGLIA COMMUNITY HEALTH TRUST
Computer Training

1.3 Format text	Method
1.3.1 Change margins	Select **P**age **S**etup from **F**ile menu
Change the side margin to 1" *Change the top margin to 2"*	Change margins as specified Click on OK **OR** Press Enter
1.3.2 Change linespacing	Select **P**aragraph from **F**ormat menu
Select the last paragraph and change to double spacing.	Select **I**ndents and **S**pacing tab Change selection in **L**ine **S**pacing drop down box Click on OK **OR** Press Enter
1.3.3 Justify text	Highlight selected text by holding down left mouse button and dragging. Let go of left mouse button.
Centre the names of the guest speakers.	Click on appropriate Justify icon. e.g. Click left mouse button where cursor is desired
1.3.4 Embolden text	Highlight selected text by holding down left mouse button and dragging. Let go of left mouse button.
Make the title and sub-title bold.	Click on Bold icon **B** Re-position cursor
1.3.5 Change font size	Highlight selected text by holding down left mouse button and dragging. Let go of left mouse button.
Change the font size of the title to 24.	Click on Font size drop down box Select specified font size Re-position cursor

Fig. 8.15 Neil Scarlett's WORD 6.0 course (continued)

4 MID ANGLIA COMMUNITY HEALTH TRUST
Computer Training

WORD-PROCESSING WITH WORD 6.0

1.4 Print text	**Method**
1.4.1 Save file	Repeat 1.1.1
1.4.2 Print file	Click on Printer icon
	OR select **P**rint from **F**ile menu
	Make selections and Click on OK
	OR Press Enter
1.4.3 Close file and exit	Select **C**lose from **F**ile menu
	Select **E**xit from **F**ile menu
	OR double click on Control box (top left corner of screen)

Fig. 8.15 Neil Scarlett's WORD 6.0 course (continued)

8.8 CONCLUSION

The examples of training given in this section by no means cover all the possible situations in which you will find yourself. They do, however, cover different sorts of learners from pure beginners through to more serious and committed users and students. The three examples also suggest ways in which distance and self-directed learning, discussion groups and standard classroom techniques might be used in natural commercial situations. Given the explosion both in IT usage and in industrial training, training skills are vital to anyone entering the world of information systems. This chapter has been aimed at giving you the basic skills that you will need to begin as a trainer but, as in any other major enterprise, success depends upon practise backed up with careful reflection and refining of your approaches.

Lesson Plan – Week Two

Time	Tutor Activity	Student Activity	Assessment	Materials
10.00		Opening Access	Student opens Access	
		Opening Database	Student opens database	
	Explain how to print a table	Listening	Student prints a table	
	Explain queries and their uses	Listening	Gives examples of use	
10.15	Explain how to access query function	Accesses	Student accesses query function	
	Explain how to open a table for query	Opening table	Student opens a table	
	Explain how to select fields to be queried	Selecting fields	Student selects fields	
	Explain how to run a query using 'sort' command	Producing an alphabetical list	Student produces list	
	Explain 'hide' function and its uses	Listening		
	Explain how to use 'hide'	Running a query using hide'	Student runs query	
10.30	Check that the student can run the query types covered so far	Running a number of given queries	Student runs queries	Worksheet
	Explain how to delete and insert query fields	Deleting and inserting query fields	Student runs query	
10.45	Explain criteria and give examples	Listening	Ask student for other examples	
	Explain how to use criteria to run a function	Running a query with a given criteria	Student produces list	
	Explain 'wildcards' and give examples	Listening	Ask student for other examples	
	Explain how to use a 'wildcard' in a query	Using a 'wildcard' in a query	Student produces list	
	Explain 'Total' function and its uses	Listening	Ask student for other examples	
	Explain how to use 'Total' function in a query	Using the 'Total' function	Student uses 'Total' to update records	
11.00	Break			
11.20	Check that the student can run the query types covered so far	Running a number of given queries	Student runs queries	Worksheet
11.30	Explain uses of joining tables in queries and give examples	Listening	Gives example of use	
	Explain how to join two tables	Listening Joins two tables	Student creates a link between two tables	
	Give student list of queries to complete on linked tables	Producing queries as specified on list	Student produces queries as specified	Worksheet

Fig. 8.16 Anita Sutton's database course

Lesson Plan – Week Three

Time	Tutor Activity	Student Activity	Assessment	Materials
10.00		Opening Access	Student opens Access	
		Opening Database	Student opens database	
	Explain 'relationships'	Listening		
	Explain how to create a relationship'	Making a relationship	Student links two tables in a 'relationship'	
	Ask student to run query based on the linked tables	Creating and running query	Student able to run a query on two tables	
	Ask student to save query	Saving query	Student able to save a query	
10.15	Explain 'forms' and their uses	Listening	Student gives examples	
	Explain 'Form Wizards'	Listening	Student creates a 'form' using the wizards	
	Demonstrate how to scroll through the form	Watching	Student scrolls through form	
	Explain how to print form	Listening	Student prints form	
	Explain how to print table contents	Listening	Student prints table contents	
10.30	Explain 'design view'	Listening	Student accesses design view	
	Explain how to edit the form while in 'desgn view'	Listening	Student edts form	
	Ask student to save form	Saving the form	Student able to save form	Worksheet
10.45	Explain 'filter' function	Listening	Gives example of use	
	Explain how to create a filter'	Listening Creating a 'filter'	Student creates a filter	
	Explain how to run a 'filter'	Listening	Student runs a filter	
11.00		Break		
11.20	Explain how to load a saved 'filter'	Listening	Student loads a saved filter	
	Ask student to run the filter'	Running the 'filter'	Student able to run a filter	Worksheet
11.30	Explain purpose of a 'Combo Box'	Listening	Gives example of use	
	Explain how to create a 'Combo Box'	Listening Creating a 'Combo Box'	Student creates 'Combo Box'	
11.45	Ask student to create another 'Combo Box'	Creating a 'Combo Box'	Student able to create Combo Box	Worksheet
		Exiting package	Student exits Access	

Fig. 8.16 Anita Sutton's database course

BIBLIOGRAPHY

Argyle, 1978, *The Psychology of Interpersonal Behaviour*, Penguin
Baddock, 1992, *Professional Writing*, Prentice Hall
Bee and Bee, 1994, *Training Needs Analysis and Evaluation*, IPM
Berne, 1975, *Games People Play*, Penguin
Breakwell, 1990, *Interviewing*, Routledge
Brieger and Comfort, 1992, *Language Reference for Business English*, Prentice Hall
Brockmann, 1990, *Writing Better Computer User Documentation*, Wiley
Burton and Dimbleby, 1988, *Between Ourselves*, Edward Arnold
Buzan, 1982, *Use Your Head*, Ariel/BBC
Corner and Hawthorne, 1980, *Communication Studies*, Arnold
Crystal, 1984, *Who Cares about English Usage?*, Pelican
Davis, Gray and Hallez, 1986, *Manuals that Work*, Kogan Page
Ellis and McClintock, 1992, *If You Take My Meaning*, Arnold
Fast, 1978, *Body Language*, Pan
Fowler, 1986, *Effective Negotiation*, Institute of Personnel Management
Godefroy and Robert, 1993, *The Outstanding Negotiator*, Piatkus
Gunton, 1988, *Business Information Technology, End User Focus*, Prentice Hall
Handy, 1984, *Understanding Organizations*, Penguin
Harry, 1994, *Information Systems in Business*, Pitman
Hide, 1989, *Transferable Personal Skills*, Business Education Publishers
Krebs, 1982, *Readings in Social Psychology*, Harper & Row
Manchester Open Learning, 1993, *Handling Conflict and Negotiation*, Kogan Page
Miles, 1987, *Design for Desktop Publishing*, Gordon Fraser
Miller, 1976, *The Psychology of Communication*, Penguin
NCVQ, 1988, *The NCVQ Criteria and Related Guidance*, NCVQ
Parry, 1970, *The Psychology of Human Communication*, ULP
Phillips, 1991, *Training Evaluation and Measurement Methods*, Kogan Page
Porritt, 1984, *Communication Choices for Nurses*, Churchill Livingstone
Rae, 1988, *The Skills of Interviewing*, Gower
Rae, 1994, *Let's Have a Meeting*, McGraw Hill
Richey, 1992, *Designing Instruction for the Adult Learner*, Kogan Page
Seybold and Dressler, 1987, *Publishing from the Desktop*, Bantam
Shearing and Christian, 1965, *Reports and How to Write Them*, Allen and Unwin
Sillars, 1988, *Success in Communication*, John Murray
Spender, 1985, *Man Made Language*, Routledge
Stanton, 1982, *What do you mean "Communication"?*, Pan
Turk and Kirkman, 1989, *Effective Writing*, Spon
Wheatley, 1988, *Report Writing*, Penguin
White, 1974, *Editing by Design*, Bowker
Yeates, Shields and Helmy, 1994, *Systems Analysis and Design*, Pitman

INDEX

ACAS (Advisory, Conciliation and Arbitration Service) 76, 99
accents, regional 27
accreditation of workers 293–4
  see also National Council for Vocational Qualifications; training principles
acknowledgements within a report 157
action minutes 55–6
action minutes (Fig.) 56
adjournment of meetings 96
Advisory, Conciliation and Arbitration Service (ACAS) 76
agenda 53–5, 92–3
  hidden 95
aggression 62, 104–5
agreement 82–3, 91
  formalising an 100
  mediators 98–9
  reaching 95–7
  see also negotiation; persuasion
aims of interviews 188–9
appendices to a report 159
archives, storage of 22
Argyle, Michael 33
assertiveness 92, 103, 105–8
  aggressive response 104–5
  assertive communication 108–10
  open behaviour 71–2, 92
  passive response 104
assessment & development interviews 211–12
assessment of training 290–4
attitudes, teaching 268
audience
  communicating with 113, 224–5
  and report writing 134–9
  reviews 247
audio-visual training 274–5
author identification in reports 151
authorisation of a report 152
  see also terms of reference

bar chart (Fig.) 168, 169
BCS see British Computer Society
Bee, Frances and Roland (training) 263
behaviour
  aggressive 62, 104–5
  assertive 92, 103, 105–10
  effective, at interviews 200–2
  negative 62–3, 72–3
  non-verbal 200
  passive 104
Berne, Eric 34–5
Bernstein 8
'best guess' solution 7
bibliographies 157–8, 274
binding methods 232–8
  comb binding 234–5
  perfect binding 234
  ring binders 235–7, 238
  saddle stich 234
  side stabbing 233–4
  stapling 233
  see also documentation
Bloom, Coburn and Pearlman 105
Bloom's Taxonomy 269, 272, (Fig.) 273, 292
books
  finding 18–19
  as teaching aids 239
  versus on-line help 239
brainstorming 64–5
Branson, Richard 25
British Airways 25
The British Computer Society (BCS) 3, 4
Brockmann, John 239–40, 243, 252
BTEC see Business and Technology Education Council
Bulgaria 28
Business Monitor 166
business reviews 246
Business and Technology Education Council (BTEC) 3, 269, 270, 291

assessment strategy 291–4
  BTEC levels with performance criteria (Fig.) 270
Buzan, Tony 38, 115, 207
buzz groups 64, 65–6

Cambridge University Press 158
card index storage 21, 221
case studies and role play 292–3
catalogues 18, 19
CBT see computer based training
CD-ROM for data search 20
Central Statistical Office 166
chair/vice-chair persons 57–9, 60–1, 93
'channel fatigue' 282
Channel Tunnel 100
chapter summaries 18
Charles, Prince of Wales 159
charts and diagrams 125–7, 137, 165–70
  chart of Singapore tourism & freight (Fig.) 172
  false zero graph 170, (Fig.) 171
  graph of Singapore tourism & freight (Fig.) 173
  graphs 168–70
  tables 166–7
chronological order 220, 221
circulation of reports 151–2
Clements, Alan 19
clichés and slang 164–5
clip file storage 21
closed questions 195–6
closing an interview session 202
CLOZE procedure 244
Coburn, Bloom and Pearlman 105
codes and jargon 14–17
colour coding 21, 22, 23
comb binding 234–5
committees 44
  see also meetings
communication, definition of 24
communication skills, an example 40–2
communications (Fig.) 17

communication(s) models 5–14, 113
 De Fleur 7
 De Fleur (Fig.) 8
 Gerbner (Fig.) 10
 Maletzke 11, 13
 Maletzke (Figs.) 12, 13
 Schramm, W. 13
 Schramm, W. (Figs.) 14, 15
 Shannon, C. and Weaver, W. 6
 Shannon, C. and Weaver, W. (Fig.) 6
 Stanton 7, 8, 9
 Stanton (Fig.) 9
computer-based training (CBT) 277, 279–82
computer-based storage systems 21–4
computer(s)
 mainframe 4
 programming 4
 in training 279–82
 advantages of 281
 computer assisted instruction (CAI) 279, 279–80
 computer managed instruction (CMI) 280
 objections to 281–2
concessions in negotiation 97, 98
conclusion of a report 156
contents lists 18, 19, 152–3
copyright 248–9
counselling interviews 258
cultures and sub-cultures 138–9

data
 distortion of 169–70
 finding 18–20
 books 18–19
 catalogues 19
 CD-ROM 20
 magazines 19
 microfiche 19
 newspapers 19
 periodicals 19
 organising 18–24
 presentation 169–70
 storing 20–4
 archives 22
 card indexes 21, 221
 clip file 21
 colour coding 21, 22, 23

computer-based systems 21–4
 envelope file 21
 paper storage 20–1
 see also information sources
de Bono, Edward 207
De Fleur's model of communication 7, (Fig.) 8
decision making 63–6
delivery (oral) techniques 113–24
Delphi technique 49
demonstration (teaching) 275, 285
design tasks 222
designers, professional 237
diagrams and charts 125–7, 137, 165–70
discussion groups 66, 94–5, 156, 275–6
documentation
 aims of 252
 binding 232–8
 changing documents 235–7
 packaging 237–8
 paper size 232–3
 permanent documents 233–5
 see also binding methods
 chronological order 220, 221
 contents 223–4
 copyright 248–9
 covers 237
 designers, professional 237
 help, on-line 238–42
 layout 222, 229–32
 graphics 230–2
 on-line manuals 238–42
 order of presentation 220–1
 printing instructions 221
 problems defined 214–16
 prototyping and testing 242–9
 conclusion 252
 editing 245–6
 example 249–52
 field testing 244–5
 CLOZE procedure 244
 FOG index 147, 161, 244
 prototyping 242–4
 reviewing 246–7
 warning messages 247–9
 reference manuals 224
 structure 222–9
 analysis and planning 222–3
 determining contents 223–4
 improving reference 227–9

speaking to the user 224–7
 testing 242–6
 users 216–22
 accidental user 218–19
 beginner 217
 expert 218
 learner 218
 needs 219–22
 novice 218
 as testers 243–6
 see also user documentation
dress and NVC 24–5

Eastern Counties Newspapers 217
editing documents 245–6
effective behaviour 200–2
egocentric communication 33
employment interviews 209–11
envelope file storage 21
examples
 communication skills 40–2
 feasability study 73–5
 prototyping and testing 249–52
 report format 149–59, 174–81
 of training courses 295–301
 written reports 149–59, 174–81
extrinsic motivation 255, 257, 258
eye contact and NVC 28, 29, 30, 122, 185

facial expression and NVC 30
false zero graph 170, (Fig.) 171
feedback, assessment 294–5
Ferlinghetti, Lawrence 185
field testing documents 244–5
 CLOZE procedure 244
 FOG index 147, 161, 244
files see data
filing cards 21, 115, 221
film 130–1
flip charts 125–7
FOG (frequency of gobbledygook) index 147, 161, 244
fonts and typeface 143–4
Ford Motor Company 77
formal meetings 49–53
Fowler (negotiation) 76, 78, 90
Freud, Sigmund 185
'fuzzy logic' 7

galley proofs 246
GANTT charts 137, 165, 169

Gates, Bill 43–4
gaze *see* eye contact
Gerbner's model of commun-
    ication (Fig.) 10
gesture and NVC 28
Giles and Powesland (accents) 27
glossaries 157, 227, 245
Godefroy and Robert 83, 95
Goffman, Erving 183, 184
Good News Press 158
grammar 146–8, 161, 165
    see also language; spelling
graphics 207–8, 230–2, (Fig.) 232
graphs 168–70
Greece 28
group(s)
    horizontal team 46
    meetings *see* meetings
    personal performance 47–9
    and power/aggression 105
    presentation 123
    purpose of 43–5
    standard stages of 48
    vertical team 46
    work-based 45–6
    see also teams
Gunton (information technology)
    3, 254

handouts 132
Handy, Dr Charles B. 43, 44
headings and numbering in reports
    145–6
help desk personnel 253–4
help, on-line 238–42
Henry VII 262
Henry VIII 262
hierarchy of training content (Fig.)
    267
Hobbes, Thomas 258
honesty/dishonesty in negotiation
    90–1
horizontal team groups 46

illocutions 35
index
    card storage 21, 221
    compiling an 227–9
    for data search 18, 19
    FOG (grammar) 147, 161
    for on-line help 240
    for reports 159

information 63–6, 70–1
    brainstorming 64–5
    buzz groups 64, 65–6
    checking 206
    discussion groups 66
    key personnel 186–7
information retention by learning
    methodology (Fig.) 278
information sources
    books 18–19
    catalogues 19
    CD-ROM 20
    Delphi technique 49
    indexes 18, 19
    libraries 18–19
    magazines 19
    microfiche 19
    newspapers 19
    periodicals 19
    see also data
instruction manuals *see* documen-
    tation
interview(s), information system
    controlling 202–3
    counselling 258
    listening skills 194, 198–200
    perception of people 182–5
    preparation 185–9
        aims & objectives 188–9
        key personnel 186–7
    procedures 200–8
        bad interviews 204–6
        effective behaviour 200–2
        graphical representations 207–8
        participant observation 207
        taking control 202–4
        triangulation 206–7
    question techniques 194–8
    resistance to 204–6
    setting up 189–94
        context 190–1
        listening triads 194
        recording & transcription 191–4
        time and place 190
interview(s), management 209–13
    assessment & development
        interviews 211–12
    employment interviews 209–11
intrinsic motivation 255, 258
introductions for data search 18,
    19
introductions in reports 154

jargon and codes 14–17, 113, 225
job interviews 209–11
Johari Window 184, 258
Johari Window (Fig.) 184
judgement, achieving sound 90

Kelly's Directory 166
key personnel 186–7
    information holders 186–7
    system owners 186
    system users 187
keyword prompt sheet (Fig.) 117
King, John Leonard, Lord (Lord
        King of Wartnaby) 25
KISS (Keep It Simple, Stupid) 113
knowledge defined (for training)
    267

language
    computer language 16
    connotation 16
    in reports 159–65
        grammar and punctuation 165
        see also grammar; spelling
        paragraphs 162
        sentences 160–2
        slang, clichés 164–5
        style 162–4
    use of 2–5, 16, 93, 96, 118
layout, documentation 222,
    229–32
leading questions 197
learning *see* training principles
'learning centres' *see* libraries
learning methodology (Fig.) 278
lectures 272–4
Lenin, Vladimir Ilyich 276
lesson plan format (Fig.) 296
libraries 18–19
listening skills 89–90, 194, 198–200
literature surveys 154
lobbying before meetings 69
London Ambulance Service 262
long-term memory 260–3
lose–lose situation 83
'loss of face' 95

McCluhan, Marshall 131
McEnroe, John 33
magazines for data search 19
Maletzke (communications model)
    11, (Figs) 12, 13

management interviews 209–13
managing a training session
    287–90
Manchester Open Learning 79,
    89–90
manpower analysis (Fig.) 265
manuals *see* documentation
Manwatching (Morris) 28
Maslow, A.H. 255–6, 257, 258
Maslow's hierarchy of needs (Fig.)
    256
Mayer, Louis B. 50
mediators 99
meetings
  adjournment of 96
  advantages of 51, 52–3
    collective responsibility 53
    involvement 53
    range of ideas 52, 53
    social bonding 53
    time saving 52
  behaviour at
    negative 62–3, 72–3
    open 71–2
    positive 73
  committees 44
  decision making stages 64
  failure, reasons for 51–3
    action plan 52
    length of meeting 52
    objectives 51
    plan of action 52
    running the meetings 51, 60–8
  formal 49–53
  lobbying 69
  personalities at 52, 61–3, 68–73
  procedures 53–6, 60–1
    action minutes 55–6
    agenda 53–5
    at large meetings 56–7
    minutes 55–6
    motions 56, 57
  project groups 66–8
  roles 69–73
    chairperson 57–9
    minutes secretary 59
    secretary 59–60
    vice-chairperson 59
  running 51, 60–8
  summarising 96
  team briefing 66–8
  see also groups; teams

memoranda (Fig.) 192
memoranda (memos) 170–4
memory columns (Fig.) 261
memory (in training) 260–3
  long-term memory 260–3
  repetition 262–3
methodology, explaining 154
microfiche 19
minutes of meetings 55–6, 174
mnemonics 113
modular group presentation 123
Monthly Digest of Statistics 166
Morris, Desmond 28
motivation
  extrinsic 255, 257–8
  hierarchy of needs 255–7
  intrinsic 255, 258
  maintenance factors 255
  motivation factors 255
  negative 258, 259
multiple choice questions 196–7

Napoleon Bonaparte 44
National Computing Centre
    (NCC) 201, 207
National Council for Vocational
    Qualifications 253, 268, 272,
    293–4
  training course syllabus 268–9
    elements of competence 268–9
    performance criteria 269
    range indicators 269
    unit of competence 268
  see also training principles
National Vocational Qualifications
    (NVQ) *see* National Council
    for Vocational Qualifications
NCC 201, 207
negative behaviour 62–3, 72–3
negative motivation 259
negotiation
  agreement, reaching 95–7
  alternatives to agreement 82–3
  assertive behaviour 92
  beginning 79–80
  closing the deal 99–101
  concessions 97, 98
  defined 76–9
  honesty/dishonesty 90–1
  judgement, achieving sound 90
  knowledge of subject 88
  listening skills 89–90

lose–lose situation 83
non-executive teams 98
other parties 83–4
patience, importance of 91
personal skills 88–92, 103
persuasion strategies 91
post-negotiation review 101
preparation 84–6, 88
presentation, basic procedures of
    89
processes 92–3
rapid response 88–9
reporting back 100
representatives 87–8
structuring objectives 81–2
SWOT analysis 85–6
team structure 86–8
by telephone 102
tender, invitation to 101–2
win–lose situation 83
win–win situation 83
working together 94–5
Neil Scarlett's WORD, 6.0 course
    (Figs.) 298–301
newspapers for data search 19
'noise' 6, 8
non-questions 197
non-executive teams 98
non-verbal communication (NVC)
    200, 210
  dress 24–5
  eye contact 28, 29, 30, 122, 185
  facial expression 30
  gesture 28
  'leakage' 32–3
  non-speech utterances 25–7
    accent 27
    'fillers' 26
    stereotypes 27
    tone 25
  position 28–9
  postural echo 32
  posture 29
  proxemics 27–8
  touch 30–1
note taking 38, 94, 115, 193, 194
NVC *see* non-verbal commun-
    ication
NVQ *see* National Council for
    Vocational Qualifications

objectives
  of interviews 188–9

of negotiations 81–2
of training 283–4
OHP (overhead projectors) 128–30
on-line help 238–42, 240
open behaviour 71–2
open questions 195–6
oral assessment strategy 293
oral communication
  egocentric 33
  expressing emotions and attitudes 35
  informal contact 34–5
  information giving 34
  latent messages 36
  orders and instructions 34
  performative 35–6
  questions 34
  social routines 34
orders and instructions, issuing 34
overhead projectors (OHP) 128–30

page layout, printed 229–30
paper
  sizes 232–3
  storage systems 20–1
  types of 229, 237, 238
paragraphs, writing 162
Parry, J. 17
partial listening 198–9
passive behaviour 104
patience, importance of, in negotiation 91
Pearlman, Bloom and Coburn 105
perfect binding 234
performative utterance 35–6
periodicals for data search 19
perlocutions 36
personal negotiating skills 88–92, 103
personal performance within groups 47–9
persuasion strategies 91
Pitman Publishing 158
Pluto Press 158
Porritt, Lyn 108
portmanteau questions 197
position (spacial) and NVC 28–9
positive behaviour 73, 198
posture and NVC 29, 32
practical assessment strategy 293

practice (learning) 276–7
preparation for interviews 185–9
presentation, oral 132–3
  the audience 113, 122
  basic procedures 89, 119–20
  content 112
  delivery 121–3
    group presentation 123–4
    KISS (Keep It Simple, Stupid) 113
    language 118
    script 114–15
    timing 118–21
    voice 115–18
  eye contact 122
  group presentation 123–4
    modular structure 123
    spinal system 123
  purposes of 111–12
  questions, dealing with 120–1
  rehearsing 121–2, 133
  visual aids 124–32
    choosing 124–5
    film 130–1
    flip charts 125–7
    handouts 132
    overhead projectors (OHP) 128–30
    slides 127–8
    sound tapes 131–2
    video 130
    whiteboards 127
  visual aids (Fig.) 126
primary research 166
printing 148–9, 221, 229–30
printing instructions, documentation 221
process review 101
programmed learning 277
Progress Publishers 158
project groups 66–8
proof-reading documents 245–6
prototype for manuals 242–4
proxemics and NVC 27–8
psychology of interviewing 182–5

question techniques 34, 120–1
  closed 195–6
  demonstrations 198
  leading 197
  multiple choice 196–7
  non-questions 197

open 195–6
portmanteau 197

Rae, Leslie 52, 55
range statements 269
reading (for a degree) 274
recommendations in a report 156–7
recording & transcription of interviews 191–4
reference manual *see* documentation
references in user manuals 227–9
reflective listening 199
rehearsing oral delivery 121–2, 133
reliability of assessment 291
repetition and long term memory 262–3
repetitive strain injury (RSI) 248
report, preparing for oral 113
reports, written
  audience 134–9
  authorisation 152
  charts and diagrams *see* charts and diagrams
  examples 149–59, 174–81
  language *see* language
  memoranda 170–4
  on negotiations 100, 103
  printing 148–9
  terms of reference 135–7, 153
  word processing 139–49
representative negotiators 87–8
research results, reporting 155
'restricted language code' 8
rich picture equivalent (Fig.) 208
Richey (instruction) 282
ring binding 235–7, 238
Robert and Godefroy 83
Rogers and Roethlisberger 158
Routledge Publishing 158
The Royal Air Force 55
Royal Society of Arts 269
RSA computer literacy syllabus (Fig.) 271

saddle stich binding 234
Schramm's model of communications 13, (Figs.) 14, 15, 17
The Science of Learning and the Art of Teaching (Skinner) 277

screen shots, instruction manual 225
screen structure (Fig.) 241
script for oral presentation 114–15
secondary research 166
secretary 59–60
section headings for data search 19
selling *see* presentation
seminars 39
sentences, writing 160–2
setting up for interviews (research) 189–94
Shannon and Weaver's model of communication (Fig.) 6
Shearing and Christian 160
shelf search, library (for data) 18
short answer assessment strategy 293
side stabbing binding 233–4
skills defined (for training) 267–8
Skinner, B.F. 6, 257, 258, 277
slang and clichés 164–5
slides, photographic 127–8
social communications 34–5
sound tapes 131–2, 193
spellcheckers 147
spelling 146–8
  see also grammar; language
Spender, Dale 115
spidergram 115, (Fig.) 116, 207
spinal group presentation 123
SSADM (structured systems analysis and design methodology) 201, 207
standard stages of group development 48
Stanton's communication model 7, 8, (Fig.) 9
stapling as binding 233
Stephens and Roderick (discussion) 276, 282
stereotypes and NVC 27
structured systems analysis and design methodology (SSADM) 201, 207
structuring demonstrations (Fig.) 285
structuring a manual 222–9
student(s) 47–8
  at interviews 210
  exercises 97

group assignments 73–4
performance, improvement of 36–40, 118
study skills 38–40
style checkers (word processing) 146–8
summarising techniques 19, 96, 153, 202
SWOT analysis (strengths, weaknesses, opportunities & threats) 85–6
syllabus, content for training 266–72, 284–5
system descriptions, reporting 154–5
system owners, key personnel 186
system users, key personnel 187
systems analysis 11

tables (graphic) 166–7
tape recorders 131–2, 193
target dates for reports 152
teaching others (as a learning skill) 277–9
team briefing 66–8
team meetings 67–8
team structure 86–8
teams
  and aggressive behaviour 105
  non-executive 98
  see also groups; meetings
technical reviews 246–7
telephone negotiations 102
tender, invitation to 101–2
terms of reference for reports 135–7, 153
  see also authorisation of a report
thesaurus 147–8
time and place for interviews 190
time, use of (Fig.) 286
The Times 3, 230–1
timing of oral presentations 118–21
timing training sessions 285–7
title page of reports 150
TNA (training needs analysis) 263–6
tone of documentation (manuals) 225–7
tone of voice and NVC 25, 96
touch and NVC 30–1
trainers' personal attributes

287–90
training courses, planning 263–72
Training magazine 274, 279
Training Needs Analysis (TNA) 263–6
training principles
  at company level 263–6
  context of 253–4
  examples of courses 295–301
    abandoning the typewriter 297
    introducing databases 297–301
    naive users 295–7
  learning methods 272–82
    audio-visual 274–5
    computer based training (CBT) 277, 279–82
    demonstrations 275, 285
    discussion groups 275–6
    lectures 272–4
    practice 276–7
    reading 274
    teaching others 277–9
  memory 260–3
    repetition 262–3
  motivation 254–60
  presenting the training 283–95
    assessment 290–4
      BTEC strategies 292–4
      reliability 291
      utility 292
      validity 291
    content 266–72, 284–5
    feedback 294–5
    objectives 283–4
    stage management 287–90
    timing 285–7
  training room level 266–72, 284–5
  see also National Council for Vocational Qualifications
training wheel 263, (Fig.) 264
triads, listening 194
tutorials, compiling, for manuals 223–4, 225
typeface and fonts 143–4

undergraduate learning 274
use of time (Fig.) 286
Use Your Head (Buzan) 38, 115
user documentation 216–22
  aims of 252
  testing 242–6